Tax Avoidance and the Law

Tax Avoidance and the Law is a helpful guide for undergraduate and postgraduate students who want a thorough understanding of this dynamic area of law. The book is written in a way which is easy to follow and conveniently summarises complex case law on tax avoidance.

Tax Avoidance and the Law explores the evolution of the UK's General Anti-Abuse Rule. It provides a useful comparison with other Western jurisdictions' anti-avoidance legislation, including the United States of America, Australia, New Zealand, South Africa, Canada and the EU. The underlying theme of the book rests on the notion that the taxpayer's subjective motives, intentions or purposes are irrelevant when assessing tax liability.

The book enables students to gain a good grasp of the fundamental issues in tax avoidance in a clear manner.

Selina Keesoony has lectured law at Brunel University London for over five years. She has also lectured law at SOAS, University of London.

Selina completed her law degree at Brunel University. Following this, she pursued an LLM in international and comparative tax law at BPP Law School. While undertaking her master's, she secured a studentship from Brunel University to undertake a PhD in tax law. Selina was awarded the Vice Chancellor's Prize for Doctoral Research following the completion of her PhD. She has since completed the Legal Practice Course.

Routledge Research in Tax Law Series

Tax Avoidance and the Law
Understanding the UK General Anti-Abuse Rule
Selina Keesoony

Tax Avoidance and the Law

Understanding the UK General Anti-Abuse Rule

Selina Keesoony

Routledge
Taylor & Francis Group
LONDON AND NEW YORK

First published 2022
by Routledge
4 Park Square, Milton Park, Abingdon, Oxon OX14 4RN

and by Routledge
605 Third Avenue, New York, NY 10158

Routledge is an imprint of the Taylor & Francis Group, an informa business

British Library Cataloguing-in-Publication Data
A catalogue record for this book is available from the British Library

Library of Congress Cataloging-in-Publication Data
A catalog record for this book has been requested

ISBN: 978-0-367-47245-0 (hbk)
ISBN: 978-1-032-26488-2 (pbk)
ISBN: 978-1-003-08047-3 (ebk)

DOI: 10.4324/9781003080473

Typeset in Times New Roman
by Apex CoVantage, LLC

In loving memory of my wonderful grandparents
Rampeear Kawol and Radhika Kawol (née Janki)

Contents

Acknowledgements

My sincere thanks to all who helped to make the publication of this book possible.

My mother, Devi Keesoony, helped me to proofread my book. I am forever grateful for her unwavering encouragement throughout my academic journey and beyond.

I am very appreciative of the continued motivation from my uncle, Antritch Kawol.

Many thanks to my PhD supervisor, Professor Abimbola Olowofoyeku. I appreciate his valuable guidance, feedback and genuine interest in my research. I would also like to express my gratitude to Professor Ben Chigara for his moral support.

Professor Barry Rider OBE has been an inspiring and supportive role model. I am thankful for his guidance and advice.

Dr Meryl Dickinson has continually gone above and beyond in supporting me throughout my academic career. She has been a good friend and unofficial mentor. I am eternally grateful to her.

Lucy Urwin's encouragement has been invaluable in helping me to navigate my career journey. I am appreciative of her mentorship.

Thank you to my friends who believed in me and gave me motivation in abundance: Dr Rickin Dattani, Dr Amit Sharma, Koosh Patel, Deven Mehta, Raam Jeganathan and Kewal Patel.

I am grateful for the PhD Studentship I received from Brunel Law School which helped support my research. I am equally thankful to the Chartered Institute of Taxation for awarding me a Research Grant.

Many thanks to my editorial team, particularly Siobhán Poole, for their patience and helpful suggestions.

Thank you to all my readers. I hope this book helps you navigate through the complexities of tax law.

Introduction

This book argues that the UK General Anti-Abuse Rule permits judges to examine taxpayers' motives, intentions and purposes when determining whether the GAAR applies. It will be argued that such an examination is undesirable due to the subjectivity involved in this approach, which can cause uncertainty for taxpayers and tax professionals. As the GAAR permits the consideration of subjective considerations, the argument that the GAAR can be used as a "motive test" will be made.

Where reference is made to the GAAR as being a "motive test" or using the "motive approach", this encapsulates the ability of judges and HMRC to scrutinise the taxpayer's motives, intentions and purposes. The discussion is important as many judges have expressed the view that examining the taxpayer's motive, intention or purpose is undesirable and unnecessary in determining tax liability. Whether or not judges have accepted the consideration of the concepts forming the "motive approach", case law on tax avoidance demonstrates that these concepts are consistently discussed. Therefore, landmark cases in tax avoidance are explored to demonstrate that a subjective style of determining tax liability is ingrained in pre-existing case law. However, the terms "motive", "intention" and "purpose" are frequently conflated, and there has been little research aimed at identifying the differences between these terms. The distinctions between these key terms are important as they have different levels of subjectivity. This book aims to identify clear definitions of these terms which can be applied to cases on tax avoidance and provide an understanding of the level of subjectivity permitted by the GAAR.

The GAAR itself will then be examined to analyse evidence supporting the hypothesis that the GAAR is a motive test and the potential problems associated with this. Although research has been conducted on the general anti-avoidance legislation of other Western jurisdictions, this book examines these pieces of legislation with the aim of uncovering whether allowing subjective considerations is peculiar to the UK GAAR and, if not, how a motive test operates in practice. The five countries analysed are the United States, Australia, New Zealand, South Africa and Canada. These countries have been selected as they are comparable Western jurisdictions with general anti-avoidance rules in place, with the exception of the United States, which has an economic substance doctrine.

DOI: 10.4324/9781003080473-1

This book aims to examine whether the GAAR can truly be considered targeted in light of the motive test and whether this consideration affects the degree of discretion left to the judiciary in deciding tax avoidance cases. Moreover, the GAAR has been criticised for permitting the exploration of subjective considerations; therefore, this issue, as well as general criticisms of the GAAR, will be assessed in order to establish the extent to which subjectivity taints the GAAR. If it is proven that the GAAR puts the motive test on statutory footing, the fundamental question of whether the UK needed a GAAR will be raised to establish whether the GAAR contributes anything new to the pre-existing anti-avoidance measures.

Background

The UK government's concerns surrounding tax avoidance have soared in recent years, and great efforts have been made to draw the public's attention to this alleged harmful phenomenon. It has been suggested that "almost overnight the UK has become a nation apparently obsessed with whether businesses are paying enough tax".[1] Tax avoidance, apparently, according to the Treasury, involves taxpayers lawfully using "tax law to get a tax advantage that Parliament never intended",[2] which results in taxpayers paying less or no tax on their income. The GAAR was drafted "based on the premise that the levying of tax is the principal means by which the state pays for the services and facilities which it provides for its citizens".[3]

Figures explaining the tax gap from a study which HMRC conducted from 2014–2015 demonstrate the rather obvious point that tax avoidance is a source of lost revenue.[4] The amount of revenue lost through tax avoidance during this period was £2.2 billion.[5] However, the figure is not broken down to reveal how much of this tax was lost due to "abusive" tax avoidance. Although £2.2 billion in lost revenue is a big loss, it pales in comparison to the other reasons which HMRC provided for the existence of the tax gap. For example, HMRC's statistics show that the biggest cause of the tax gap is the "hidden economy"[6] "where an entire source of income is not declared".[7] These include "ghosts",[8] which encompass "individuals who receive income from employment or self-employment but are not known to HMRC because they and/or their employers fail to declare their earnings".[9] The figures also show that losses from the "hidden economy"[10] have persistently been rising from a loss of £4.8 billion in 2009–2010 to £6.4 billion in 2013—2014.[11] In 2014–2015, this figure fell to £6.2 billion,[12] although there has been an overall rise in revenue losses from the "hidden economy".

HMRC attributes £5.5 billion in lost tax revenues to a "failure to take reasonable care",[13] which includes "customer's carelessness and/or negligence in adequately recording their transactions and/or in preparing their tax returns".[14] Moreover, the amount of tax lost through taxpayer negligence has steadily risen since 2009 from £3.7 billion in 2009–2010 to £5.5 billion in 2014–2015.[15] In 2009–2010, due to legal interpretation issues, £4.5 billion of taxes were not collected.[16] This figure rose in 2014–2015, and problems regarding the interpretation of the law accounted for £5.2 billion in lost taxes.[17] The tax gap caused by tax evasion has persistently increased over the years from £3.8 billion in 2009–2010 to £5.2 billion in 2014–2015.[18] Therefore, tax evasion accounts for more than double the amount of tax lost through tax avoidance. The costly problem of "criminal attacks"[19] by "organised criminal gangs undertak[ing] co-ordinated and systematic attacks on the tax system"[20] is also a reason the government lost approximately £4.8 billion in taxes from 2014–2015.[21] However, the amount of money lost through these types of criminal activities has reduced by approximately £1 billion between the years 2009 and 2015.[22] The issue of "non-payment"[23] of tax where "tax debts . . . are written off . . . mainly as a result of insolvency"[24] has resulted in a £3.6 billion[25] loss of tax revenue. HMRC's statistics reveal that the amount of tax lost through writing off debts decreased by almost £1 billion from 2009 to 2015.[26] Unlike taxpayer negligence, simple taxpayer "error",[27] "despite the customer taking reasonable care",[28] is the reason £3.2 billion in taxes were lost in 2014–2015.[29]

The tax gap figures from 2008–2009 show that the tax gap reached £42 billion.[30] However, the tax gap significantly lowered between 2011 and 2012, when it was £32 billion.[31] Despite the narrowing of the tax gap during this time, the government sought to tackle tax avoidance by introducing the General Anti-Abuse Rule[32] into the Finance Act 2013.[33] Although the tax gap increased in 2013 to £35 billion,[34] plans had already been made in 2011 to introduce the GAAR.[35] Therefore, the GAAR was not a response to the rise in the tax gap but a general response to abusive tax avoidance in general.

It is also important to emphasise that the GAAR is only one of the government's responses to tackling tax avoidance. There are other anti-avoidance measures already in place, including principles emanating from case law, specific anti-avoidance provisions, the principle deriving from *WT Ramsay Ltd. v IRC*[36] (*Ramsay*) and the Disclosure of Tax Avoidance Schemes regime.[37] However, the GAAR takes precedence over tax legislation covered by the GAAR.[38]

The fact that "legislation is one of the basic building blocks for compliance"[39] means that the GAAR must not promote uncertainty. The GAAR as a motive test is problematic as the subjective factors inherent in this test can decrease the level of certainty for taxpayers in relation to their tax liability. However, the payment of tax must be certain as the very nature of paying taxes represents a selfless act whereby taxpayers are continuously "contributing a part of their own private revenue, in order to make up a public revenue".[40] Certainty of tax liability is also important given that the levying of tax has been stretched further than "its original purpose as a war tax for the defence of the realm".[41] Therefore, it is important that judicial discretion is not stretched too far that it becomes difficult to predict the outcome of tax cases. Furthermore, the Bill of Rights 1688 makes it clear that it is for Parliament to levy taxes; therefore, judges should not be granted the breadth of discretion which could divide the line between acceptable and abusive tax avoidance. The underlying theme of the book focuses on the extent to which judges can exercise their discretion in deciding tax avoidance cases and whether this is incompatible with Parliament's will.

Notes

1 ACCA. *'The UK General Anti-Abuse Rule'*, <www.accaglobal.com/content/dam/acca/global/PDF-technical/tax-publications/tech-tp-ukgaar.pdf>, accessed 02.06.2016, p3.
2 HM Treasury. *'Tackling Tax Avoidance'*, <www.gov.uk/government/uploads/system/uploads/attachment_data/file/197112/Tackling_tax_avoidance.pdf>, accessed 09.07.2014, p5.
3 Aaronson, G. *'A Study to Consider whether a General Anti-Avoidance Rule Should Be Introduced into the UK Tax System'*, [2012], <http://webarchive.nationalarchives.gov.uk/+/http:/www.hm-treasury.gov.uk/d/gaar_final_report_111111.pdf>, accessed 04.06.2016, p15.
4 HMRC. *'UK Tax Gap at a Glance in 2014–2015'*, <www.gov.uk/government/uploads/system/uploads/attachment_data/file/561312/HMRC-measuring-tax-gaps-2016.pdf>, accessed 28.01.2017, p5.
5 *Ibid.*
6 *Ibid.*
7 *Ibid.*
8 *Ibid*, p61.
9 *Ibid.*
10 *Ibid*, p19.
11 *Ibid.*
12 *Ibid.*
13 *Ibid*, p5.
14 *Ibid*, p20.
15 *Ibid*, p19.
16 *Ibid.*
17 *Ibid*, p5.
18 *Ibid*, p19.
19 *Ibid*, p5.
20 *Ibid*, p20.
21 *Ibid*, p19.
22 *Ibid.*
23 *Ibid*, p5.
24 *Ibid*, p20.
25 *Ibid*, p5.
26 *Ibid*, p19.
27 *Ibid*, p5.
28 *Ibid*, p20.
29 *Ibid*, p5.
30 HM Revenue and Customs. *'Measuring Tax Gaps 2010'*, <http://webarchive.nationalarchives.gov.uk/20140206164449/www.hmrc.gov.uk/statistics/tax-gaps/mtg-2010.pdf>, accessed 11.06.2013, p5.
31 HM Revenue and Customs. *'Measuring Tax Gaps 2012'*, <http://webarchive.nationalarchives.gov.uk/20140206164448/www.hmrc.gov.uk/statistics/tax-gaps/mtg-2012.pdf>, accessed 09.07.2014, p2.
32 GAAR.
33 Finance Act 2013, Part 5.
34 The Guardian. *'UK's Tax Gap Rises by £1bn to £35bn'*, reported in <www.theguardian.com/politics/2013/oct/11/uk-tax-gap-rises-hmrc-avoidance-nonpayment>, accessed 10.07.2014.
35 Aaronson, G. *'GAAR Study: A Study to Consider Whether a General Anti-Avoidance Rule Should Be Introduced into the UK Tax System'*, [2011], <http://webarchive.nationalarchives.gov.uk/20130321041222/www.hm-treasury.gov.uk/d/gaar_final_report_111111.pdf>, accessed 10.07.2014.

36 *WT Ramsay Ltd v IRC*; *Eilbeck v Rawling* [1981] 2 W.L.R 449, [1982] A.C. 300.
37 Part 7 Finance Act 2014.
38 s212(1) Finance Act 2013.
39 Braithwaite, V. *'Taxing Democracy'*, [2016], Routledge, London, p1.
40 Smith, A. *'An Inquiry into the Nature and Causes of Wealth of Nations'*, [2005], "An Electronic Classics Series Publication" <https://eet.pixel-online.org/files/etranslation/original/The%20Wealth%20of%20Nations.pdf>, accessed 01.02.2022, p675.
41 Sabine, B.E.V. *'A History of Income Tax: The Development of Income Tax from Its Beginning in 1799 to the Present Day Related to the Social, Economic and Political History of the Period'*, [2010], Routledge, London, p11.

1 Defining motive, purpose and intention

The jurisprudence on tax avoidance widely uses the terms "motive", "intention" and "purpose", often interchangeably. However, there has been no real attempt at providing definitions for these terms. The lack of clear definitions is problematic given that the terms have important connotations in tax avoidance, particularly when ascertaining whether a transaction was not executed merely for tax avoidance reasons. Consequently, it is imperative to provide clear definitions for these terms to provide greater precision in the use of language and to ensure that they are applied in the correct manner.

The terms "motive", "intention" and "purpose" have also been used widely in an array of other disciplines and are often used in different contexts to denote different meanings. Therefore, an exploration into how these terms are used in criminal law, psychology and philosophy will be made. These areas have been chosen as they regularly examine motives, intentions and purposes. Consequently, analysing how these selected areas have used the terms "motive", "intention" and "purpose" will provide a deeper understanding of how these terms should be defined. Moreover, the way in which motive, intention and purpose are used in trading, expenditure, accountancy and dividend stripping will be examined in order to identify possible convergences in the usages of the terms. Definitions of these terms will then be created in order to provide clarity as to what is precisely meant by "motive", "intention" and "purpose" in tax avoidance and what is not. These definitions will be provided at the conclusion of this chapter. Emphasis on these terms accordingly rejects actions explained by the general "doctrine of instincts"[1] as this unscientific approach "ends our search and drives us into the unknown".[2]

1.1 Criminal law perspective

Criminal law places significant weight on the mind of the defendant to determine criminal liability; therefore, it is surprising that the terms "motive", "intention" and "purpose" have not been defined or differentiated in this field. The subjective perception of a defendant is central as defendants are usually "held criminally liable only for events or consequences which they intended or knowingly risked".[3] The defendant's intention and motive are significant when the defendant's *mens rea* is sought in order to establish fault.

DOI: 10.4324/9781003080473-2

There are some areas of criminal law which place much weight on the subjective intentions of defendants and others which do not: for example, driving offences, which are strict liability offences. Consequently, motives are irrelevant in these cases, and the person charged with the offence can thenceforth be "convicted without proof of intention, knowledge, recklessness or negligence".[4] Although strict liability offences eliminate the risk of a motive being attributed to the defendant, they diminish the defendant's "ability to explain, excuse or justify the conduct".[5] This can be distinguished from a more objective form of *mens rea*, as discussed later in this chapter.

Constructive liability specifically examines the defendant's intention. "Constructive crimes"[6] are a category of crimes in which the defendant sought to commit a less serious crime but is convicted of a crime with a heavier penalty. By analogy, in the tax avoidance field, in which the avoidance of tax is not the aim but, nevertheless, the result, a tax avoidance intention may be attributed to the taxpayer, as demonstrated in *Five Oaks Properties Ltd. v HMRC*.[7] In criminal law, the argument which defends imposing constructive liability rests upon an assumption that people should be liable "for what they intended or foresaw and for what lay within their control".[8] Intention, therefore, includes what the defendant foresaw in terms of the consequences of the defendant's actions to indicate a realistic possibility of the prohibited act materialising and excludes remote possibilities. Foreseeability is highly subjective, although the control requirement contributes an objective dimension to the concept of intention to curtail liability according to what lay within the defendant's control, irrespective of what the defendant desired.[9] Moreover, foresight is an important element of intention as "consequences intended are necessarily foreseen, but not all consequences foreseen are necessarily intended".[10] Therefore, if the defendant foresaw a result, he or she is taken to have intended that result. Foreseeability is thus a less certain measure of future events occurring than intentions. This is because what is foreseen may not materialise or may materialise differently to a person's original intention.

The subjectivity of the *mens rea* requirement is reinforced in "the belief principle",[11] which relates to "what defendants believed they were doing or risking, not on actual facts which were not known to them at the time".[12] The belief principle strongly values the subjective beliefs of the defendant and disregards what he or she ought to have known, thereby discounting the need for an ascribed secondary intention. Implicit in the *mens rea* requirement is the need for an element of choice on the part of the defendant.[13] Therefore, choice can help form the definition of "intention". Requiring that the defendant made a conscious choice also implies that the defendant is aware of the consequences of his or her actions but has nevertheless knowingly chosen to embark on a particular course of action. Proving that the defendant has made a conscious choice is essential in valuing the defendant's autonomy.[14]

Whilst an intention can relate to what the defendant believed and the likelihood of it occurring according to what lay within the defendant's control, a motive can be relevant when examining "rationale-based defences, such as self-defence and duress".[15] Where a defendant seeks to rely on "rationale-based defences",[16] the defendant both does the prohibited act and intends to commit the act. However, the motive behind committing such offences is what diminishes liability as there are ulterior reasons for carrying out the prohibited act. Therefore, examining motive scrutinises the defendant's mind further than an intention by examining the reasons for embarking on the chosen act.

Although discussing tax law, Millet sought to discuss the meanings of the terms "motive", "intention" and "purpose". The discussion is relevant under criminal law due to the nature of the example he gives to illustrate how the various definitions work in practice. Millet has asserted that "'motive' is the reason why; 'purpose' is the aim, or object, or end in view".[17] The aforementioned terms are all considerations which are deliberated upon before the execution of an act. The term "aim" can be interpreted as meaning the same as "object".[18] "Purpose" denotes "object [or] thing intended".[19] Therefore, Millet argues, an intention can correspond with the eventual purpose. Motive relates to "that which induces a person to act"[20] and can also connote "the purpose behind a course of action".[21] Therefore, motive and purpose can have the same meaning. To reinforce the connection between the two terms, "intention" is the "thing intended [or] purpose".[22] Therefore, Millet's example demonstrates how the terms "motive", "purpose" and "intention" can be conflated.

Millet's example shows a clear distinction between motives and purposes. He gives the example of a murderer's intent to kill to illustrate his argument. Millet claims that in carrying out the attack, the murderer's "*motive* may be greed, or jealousy, or revenge; his *purpose* is to kill".[23] The example excellently illustrates how motives are elusive and can be numerous. In Millet's murder example, as well as the many different possible motives, the murderer's purpose may not be to kill but to injure or to frighten. Moreover, the effect – or, in Millet's example, the death of the victim – may not be the true intended effect, which is why intentions are an unreliable measure. In addition to this, Millet's murder example illustrates how a person's motive reveals nothing about his or her purpose.

It is clear that motive and intention have distinct connotations in the criminal law sphere. Whilst "intention" refers to what the defendant foresaw as the probable consequences of his or her actions, "motive" refers to the defendant's innate "emotion leading to action",[24] such as envy, hatred or both. Moreover, in *R v Mohan*,[25] it was held that intention includes the desire to act. Therefore, a defendant's intentions do not require any emotional involvement in acting.[26] It is also material to assess the process by which to establish the particular intention which gave rise to criminal liability since people generally "do things with more than one intention in mind".[27] In criminal law, the material issue is "whether one particular intention was present when the act was committed"[28] and not "with what intentions D committed the act" in general.[29] The latter question would involve digressing from ascertaining whether the defendant had the precise intention for the particular crime as prescribed by legislation. Tax law tends to ask the latter question as demonstrated in *Ramsay*, in which the judge examined "why the taxpayer had purchased the scheme".[30] If tax avoidance aligns with criminal law in examining intentions, it will bring tax avoidance into the sphere of deciding cases based on constructive liability.

The terms "motive" and "intention" are therefore treated as distinct in criminal law, although there are some definitional and practical overlaps. For example, occasionally, the finding of a justifiable motive can mitigate the original intention. As both influences guide behaviour, motives and intentions may sometimes be blurred because the two mind-frames will have the same effect by producing the same act. Motives and intentions can co-exist, but it must be recognised that they are different categories of influence which guide behaviour.

From this analysis, there are certain keywords which together can form the definition of "intention" in the context of criminal law. Therefore, a person has the necessary intention where he or she knowingly and consciously chooses to commit the prohibited act which the person believed was a foreseeable consequence of his or her actions by wilful means which lay within his or her control. However, defining "intention" does not overcome practical difficulties in pinpointing the relevant intention because "a man may do an act with a number of intentions"[31] and can also have multiple motives. In contrast, motive examines the defendant's reasons or emotional justification in committing the crime and not merely whether they wanted to or were practically able to commit the prohibited act. Consequently, it can be said that a motive lacks objectivity. An assessment of how the criminal law has informed the discussion on tax avoidance will be evaluated in this chapter's conclusion.

1.2 Psychological perspective

Dissecting "the consciousness of a motive"[32] implies that there exists a distinction between "conscious"[33] and "unconscious"[34] motives. These types of motives relate to whether a person is aware of what he or she is doing or whether the person's actions merely form part of the person's character.[35] It is the conscious motive which is more relevant as the unconscious motive "cannot as such be a factor in deliberation"[36] due to its invariable intrinsic quality.

Psychological views on the concepts of motive and intention provide an understanding of how these concepts relate to the individual. For example, motive has been described as "that characteristic tendency or disposition of a man in virtue of which a given act possesses an attraction for him".[37] Therefore, an individual's motive is typically discussed in terms of why he or she performs an act, rather than why the person refrains from acting. Thus, the psychological definition of "motive" closely corresponds to the equivalent definition in criminal law, which involves emotions that actively guide behaviour. In addition to this, a motive exists only where a degree of "reflection or deliberation"[38] has taken place before a person acted. The requirement of a calculated and "carefully pondered design"[39] excludes "instinctive or impulsive action".[40] Consequently, a person's motive is formed after a fairly lengthy amount of deliberation.

Motive and intention have also been differentiated according to the degree of dominance each influence has in a person's mind. In psychology, an intention has been described as existing in the present tense as the more conscious form of intellectual guidance as it is said to be "actually present to the mind of the agent at the moment of action".[41] Conversely, a motive is described obscurely as the unconscious guidance and is "something . . . at the back of a man's mind which influences his decision".[42] This idea of motive as a subconscious influence links with the problematic notion that a person's motive can be "hidden not only from the spectator but even from the agent himself".[43] Therefore, the psychological view of motive appears to portray this guidance as vague and incapable of accurate ascertainment, which illustrates why it is unsuitable for judicial determination. However, in some circumstances, a person may be aware of his or her motive, particularly when the motives are positive, such as love or admiration. Conversely, motives such as jealousy and greed may be less obvious to a person.

Despite the subjectivity of a motive, psychology has recognised an objective dimension akin to the criminal law control requirement. It has been rationalised that "that which influences the mind must be something in that which is before the mind".[44] Therefore, the chosen form of conduct must also be realistic and capable of accomplishment. However, this objective component does not assist in establishing one's motive where several avenues of action are present, all of which may be achievable. Establishing what can be achieved only narrows down the range of possible motives.

The psychological perspective of a motive accentuates the individuality of the concept. Snow places emphasis on the individual environmental and historical factors which shape a person's motives.[45] Although motives cannot be quantified, generally, "a motive is said to be selfish".[46] Consequently, a motive is the reason for acting whereby the individual hopes to achieve an advantage or personal gain, which can be difficult for anyone other than the individual to ascertain. Snow elucidates the problem of establishing motive by theorising that motives can differ in "case[s] of like activity of different individuals".[47] To complicate matters further, differences in motives can also exist during "the same activity at different times for the same person".[48] Therefore, the elusive nature of motive makes it difficult for anyone, including the judiciary, to decipher the motive of another. Stocks, however, reinforces that a motive is highly subjective as it can be coloured by one's personal character.[49] One's character can shape their decision-making "since it is from his character that his projects of action draw their attractiveness or repulsiveness".[50]

Although character drives action, it has also been recognised that people are judged by their actions, not by their character, as the latter is not always known, particularly by those not known to the individual.[51] Furthermore, a motive can be attached to blame where "the man does not employ his attained experience and intellectual capacity".[52] Experience and intellect are highly subjective traits which further reinforces the multifarious nature of motives as they differ greatly between different people according to what is expected of them. Moreover, people tend to "infer in the first instance from the act to the character and not from the character to the act".[53] Consequently, the act itself should be examined first, which renders an exploration of his or her motive unnecessary.

Despite psychology being concerned with the minds of individuals, Stocks has rightly asserted that "evidence of character or motive is action".[54] Therefore, the only way to ascertain one's motive is to observe their actions. It is consequently futile to examine the actions of the individual in conjunction with his or her motives. Moreover, the scientific approach is to ask, "[W]hat have you done?"[55] rather than to question why it has been done.

Purpose has been entangled with motive in psychology, which suggests that perhaps the concepts cannot be disentangled. There are similarities between "the idea in mind, the purpose [and] desire".[56] Desire or the reason a person is acting is also associated with motive as demonstrated earlier.

The emphasis in psychological literature seems to be on motive as evidenced in action rather than being an emotion which drives action, although it is capable of both interpretations. It is more scientific to focus on motive as evidenced by action, although it could be argued that if motive is evidenced in action, one only has to scrutinise the evidence, unless establishing the relevant emotion is explicitly required in addition to the traceable action. Moreover, there is a logical preference to judge action based on what is conscious as even "the will, [although] not conscious of itself, is yet conscious of all that it enacts".[57]

From the analysis of the psychological views of motive, the definition of "motive" is clearer. A motive is a conscious or unconscious influence, which is coloured by a person's character and formed after deliberation. It is the reason why the person performed the achievable act, which is typically selfish and can be an emotion. In contrast to this, an intention is a conscious form of intellectual guidance which is associated with the present tense and is followed through to the time of action.

1.3 Philosophical perspective

Philosophical views follow the consensus that a motive relates to why a person acts. Similarly, Scott defines a motive as "that on account of which a person acts".[58] As will be seen, motives, intentions and purposes can differ according to what time frame each is referring to.

Scott claims that a motive is different from a justification,[59] which suggests that "a person can have a desire to do something without thinking that she ought . . . to do it".[60] Therefore, motives can lack justification. Interestingly, Anscombe suggests that intentions can also legitimately lack justification, as when "people . . . give accounts of future events . . . they do not justify these accounts by producing reasons why they should be believed".[61] However, Anscombe draws a similarity between an intention and a command[62] as they both suggest "what . . . would be good to make happen with a view to an objective",[63] but it is not the objective. Moreover, whilst a motive can describe why a person acts, intentions are recognised by their descriptive nature.[64] It is important to recognise that both motives and intentions can exist without any subsequent action. Anscombe recognises that "a man can form an intention which he then does nothing to carry out . . . but the intention itself can be complete, although it remains a purely interior thing".[65]

Similarly, a person can, for example, have a motive for murder and be questioned as one of the potential suspects but still be innocent. Nevertheless, Scheer believes that motive precedes action and that, without action, there can be no motive.[66]

The terms "motive", "intention" and purpose have been generally described as "what we and others are doing or will do".[67] Although vague, this definition is useful as it indicates a distinction between what a person is presently doing and what he or she will do in the future. An intention can be described as a state of mind in the future tense which refers to "a course of action that a person has adopted as well as an objective, end or goal".[68] However, Anscombe believes that "intention . . . only occurs in present action".[69] The notion of an intention being a present influence derives from the fact that intentions are formed in the present and may not materialise even though the person had the intention for his or her actions to be realised at that time. Anscombe's view is more verifiable as she asserts that there cannot be a "further intention *with* which a man does what he does; and no such thing as intention for the future".[70] In contrast, a motive is "pointing to something past as a reason"[71] and is also associated with guiding behaviour in the present. Therefore, motive and intention are used to indicate different time frames.

Motives and intentions also differ according to the levels of persuasion they have on a person. For example, "a motive may prove compelling",[72] although the same cannot be said about intentions.[73] Intentions can be described as both "goals and courses of action",[74] and it is for this reason that the judiciary switches between examining the intention of the end result and intentions within the process of executing a course of action. When a person has an intention, the desire to act is implied; however, motives reveal "what produces the desire".[75]

Interestingly, motives are related to acts which are "slightly or egregiously shady",[76] although one can be described as having "honourable intentions".[77] Consequently, there is an element of deceit with motives. Moreover, analogous to the psychological view of motives being selfish, Scott believes that "self-interest is the only motive to which a reasonable person can give such absolute weight in planning her life".[78] However, the negative connotations associated with one's motive cannot be applied to all types of motives as both "revenge and gratitude are motives".[79] Therefore, motives are not always selfish or suspicious.

The Utilitarian view of motive emphasises the subjective nature of the concept. The Utilitarian viewpoint also contributes to the distinction between motive and intention and differs from the psychological perspective of the importance of motive as an innate feeling. The Utilitarian definition of motive is "the personal frame of mind which indicates *why* he means to do"[80] the act. Anscombe further explains the distinction between a motive and an intention by rationalising that "a man's intention is *what* he aims at or chooses, his motive is what determines the aim or choice".[81] Anscombe uses the example of when someone wants to make a gain and states that the "gain must be the *intention*, and *desire of gain* the motive".[82] An intention is "descriptive of the end"[83] that an actor wishes to bring about. Therefore, an intention elucidates what the choice of the actor is. In contrast, a motive precedes an intention as it is "what produces or brings about a choice".[84]

To the Utilitarians, it is far more significant to judge behaviour based on "the external outcome [and] the objective change which is made in the common world".[85] A motive is therefore considered to be the manifestations of one's actions. Thus, it is "irrelevant and misleading to bother with the private emotional state of the doer's mind".[86] Consequently, "acts, not feelings count"[87] as the former are more verifiable. The Utilitarian approach also coincides with the criminal law descriptions of motive as involving emotions.

The Utilitarians place emphasis on the concept of motive as involving pluralistic reasons for acting as the concept has been described as "certain states of consciousness which happen to be uppermost in a man's mind as he acts".[88] This view differs greatly from the psychological description of motive, which refers to a motive as being a subconscious influence.

There are proponents of the view that these influences cannot be distinguished. To distinguish these influences would indicate that "there are three or four different entities 'within me' – a reason, an intention, a motive or purpose – each of which explain why I did what I did".[89] However, when these terms are dissected, it is clear that different meanings are attributed to them. Wilkins divides the term "motive" into three different meanings: "to mark the presence of a reason for acting",[90] "a reason for acting *and* to indicate that this is in fact an agent's reason for acting"[91] and lastly, "to mark the presence of a disposition in an agent for acting in a certain way under certain kinds of circumstances".[92] Wilkins emphasises that merely having a reason for acting does not mean someone has, in fact, acted.[93] The first meaning of "motive" therefore lacks coercive force and supports the aforementioned notion that motive can exist without action.

The second connotation of motive provides a more active dimension by including "prepositions such as 'in order to'".[94] Wilkins refers to the second meaning as "the occurrent sense of motive"[95] and claims this form of motive most closely relates to the meaning of intention.[96] He elucidates how motive and intention can only be interchangeable where motive is used in this context.[97] Wilkins describes an intention as being "a decision or choice to bring about a certain, rather specific state of affairs".[98] Wilkin's definition of intention and motive, in the "occurrent sense",[99] are both used in the present tense and relate to a specified future goal.[100] However, he is careful to highlight that the similarities between these terms are limited where "means to that goal or end"[101] are discussed. In this situation, "'intention'" is marking the means and "motive" the end.[102] It is impossible to combine motive with intention in this sense as intention is used to denote the method used, and a motive can never mean a method.

Anscombe also differentiates between the first two meanings of motive as described by Wilkins but does not recognise the connection between motive and intention in the second sense of the interpretation. Anscombe identifies an intention similar to Wilkin's first interpretation of motive, which lacks coercive force and refers to "a man's intention *of* doing what he does".[103] This form of intention can be largely descriptive and merely elucidates "what a proposed action is".[104] The second understanding of intention is similar to a motive as it examines "his intention *in* doing it"[105] or the "intention *with* which a man does what he does".[106]

When scrutinising the latter meaning, Anscombe asserts that this can "often not be seen from seeing what he does".[107] A person's intention in carrying out an act seems to question what benefit he or she plans to derive from acting; therefore, this limb of intention closely accords to a motive. Wilkins's third sense of motive utilises "a preposition such as 'from'"[108] and uses emotions to describe where the motives derived from.[109] When used in this sense, motive and intention differ greatly as an intention cannot be an emotion, but one's motive can be an emotion.

Anscombe further categorises an intention as including a "reason for acting",[110] which is differentiated from a cause.[111] She makes this distinction in order to highlight that an intention should be voluntary as "it is a reason, as opposed to a cause, when the movement is voluntary and intentional".[112] A reason is "a response to something as *having a significance* that is dwelt on by the agent . . . surrounded with thoughts and questions".[113] In contrast to this, a cause is more of a trigger external to the actor which causes the actor to act involuntarily without aforethought. Anscombe also likens intentions to predictions by referring to "expressions of intention . . . [as] predictions justified . . . by a reason for acting as opposed to a reason for thinking them true".[114]

The notion of an intention being a reason for acting rather than being a cause is an important distinction as reasons and causes can be unclear in practice. Anscombe asserts that a motive "is what *moves* . . . glossed as 'what *causes*' a man's actions".[115] However, it must be borne in mind that intentional actions cannot be recognised by "any extra feature which exists when it is performed".[116] As Dworkin recognised, an intention is "a conscious mental state".[117] Moreover, there are also common actions that people want to and do perform without any deep thought, which Anscombe terms "preintentional"[118] actions.

Motives and intentions have also been differentiated according to the tense in which these terms are used. Anscombe divides the concept of motive according to whether it is a motive relating to the past, present or future. She distinguishes "backward-looking motives"[119] from those which are "forward-looking".[120] Anscombe explains that "backward-looking motives"[121] relate to the past[122] and include motives such as "revenge . . . gratitude . . . remorse and pity".[123] These motives in the past tense are also differentiated from "motives-in-general",[124] which Anscombe generally describes as an influence which is specifically thought of prior to acting.[125] Significantly, Anscombe blurs motives and intentions by stating that "a motive [is] forward-looking if it is an intention".[126] This analogy reinforces that an intention is an influence associated with the future tense.

Whilst intentions and motives broadly explain what a person will do or why the person is performing an act, Krikorian claims that "the purpose of an act . . . is observable in the results of that act".[127] Purpose as an end result is clearly observable through the example "the purpose of a saw is to cut"[128] as "the result [is] the fulfilment of [the] purpose".[129] However, Krikorian warns that one should not simply look for the results of an act, which may be merely consequential,[130] but the "purposive result".[131] The rationale derived from the example of the purpose of the inanimate, saw however, cannot be applied to people in the same way. This is because, with inanimate objects, "there is a common result which is usually . . .

accomplished".[132] It is more difficult to establish the purpose of a tax avoidance scheme unless similar schemes have been carried out in a similar way and correspond with the common result of the type of scheme.

Due to the inherent problems in examining the common result to ascertain a purpose, Krikorian advises assessing the "expected result of that class of act".[133] The "expected result"[134] is one of two "levels of action"[135] and is described as the "anticipation of the *observer* who interprets the activity because of prior acquaintance with certain routine[s]".[136] Consequently, a person's purpose may be established by a spectator who has experience of dealing with the same practices. Whatever the spectator predicts as the likely result is the purpose of the act. However, the predicted result is not always the correct purpose.[137] Even if the predicted purpose is the correct purpose, it may not be fulfilled.[138] The second level of the act is the "subordinate acts which are the means for the attainment of the end".[139] The means-end relationship is important to establish whether an accurate prediction of purpose can be made because "as ends become definite the means become definite".[140]

A purpose is aligned with a specific goal and the person usually "persist[s] until they reach the goal or are defeated".[141] Therefore, a person's purpose is generally to achieve his or her ultimate goal. Motives can be what causes the desire, though; a purpose is the "foresight or desire".[142] However, purposes are as changeable as intentions as there can be a "growing purpose of which we become aware at a comparatively advanced stage of our action".[143] Similarly, it cannot be assumed that all purposes are clear and achieved through a seamless relationship of steps. With "complex, confusing purposes . . . these relations become tentative, experimental and delayed".[144]

Despite the variable nature of a purpose, it is described as a conscious influence which the actor is aware of and works towards achieving. Unlike an unconscious motive, a purpose is "what is most dominant in our attention at that moment".[145] However, if a person discovers "new suggestions and possibilities . . . the final result can hardly be described as the realisation of a preconceived plan".[146] Therefore, a predetermined plan is intrinsic to the concept of a predictable purpose. However, if new ideas are considered and implemented, they may lead to a new purpose being sought. Moreover, the requirement of a plan connects with the idea that a purpose is usually discussed in the future tense as "prospective expressions"[147] because "the expected result has not been accomplished".[148] Consequently, a purpose can be described "as a future cause which determines the present action",[149] such as the means to attain the end.

Anscombe, Wilkins and Scheer all appear to agree that intention is discussed in the present tense regarding future action. Moreover, if a person has a motive, intention or purpose, it insinuates that he or she also has a reason for acting. Therefore, the presence of a reason is a wide concept which is not helpful on its own in differentiating between motive, intention and purpose. Both motive and intention can exist without subsequent action.

Anscombe and Finnis appear to disagree with regard to the limits of what a person can intend. Anscombe believes that "agents can intend performances that are actually possible (what is possible falling as it does within the constraints of the actual) not performances that are merely conceivably possible".[150] In contrast, Finnis argues that "it is assumed that one's actual choice of means can be defined in terms of what is conceivably possible".[151] However, Anscombe's argument has greater merit as "she is said to identify intention by reference to the cause-effect sequence that might be transparent to an observer rather than by reference to the practical reasoning of the agent".[152] Moreover, Anscombe argues that "practical thinking about means has to count as determinative of one's means, what one has to aim to do in the circumstances in which one is obliged to act".[153] Furthermore, Anscombe distinguished between an intention and a side effect,[154] which led her to conclude that "the inseparability of the effect is not a ground for regarding it as intended".[155]

Laurence theorised "an Anscombian approach to collective action",[156] which is relevant given that many tax avoidance schemes, which will be discussed in chapter 2, are carried out by companies. He raised the problem of uncovering the intention of a group as "there is no one mind shared by a collective agent that might serve as the subject of psychological states".[157] Laurence sought to ascertain the "shared intention"[158] of a collective. He argues that the collective intention is not where "each has an individual intention with the same content as the individual intentions of the other agents acting. But we're interested in a thicker sense of sharing an intention".[159] The latter type of intention is where the individuals within the collective "share in one and the same intention".[160] Laurence states that "people are acting together intentionally *if and only if their actions can all be straightforwardly instrumentally rationalised by the same action*".[161]

There are limits to Laurence's argument, which Laurence himself recognises. He admits that

> sometimes the people performing a particular action may not know why they're performing it, and sometimes the people who know the end that ultimately explains what everyone is doing may not know what particular actions are serving that end.[162]

However, despite the confusion that may arise from collective activities, Laurence maintains that "everyone will know something"[163] due to their "non-observational knowledge".[164] Therefore, "just as a collective agent can only act through the actions of its individual members, it can only know through their knowing, and reason through their reasoning".[165] Consequently, Laurence's theory is "mysterious [as to] what it is to share an intention".[166] His theory explains that a group can share a purpose, but their collective intentions can be difficult to ascertain, even for members of the collective. Therefore, whilst a collective purpose may be ascertainable by the judiciary, a collective intention is less clear.

From this analysis, a motive can be said to be a compelling guidance which produces the desire to act. It explains why a person wants to embark on a particular course of action and can be pluralistic in nature. Motives also encapsulate emotions as a person may choose to act based on their emotions, which are driving them unconsciously towards performing the eventual act.

An intention has been portrayed as being descriptive of the steps which lead to the person's objective. Intentions also reveal what the person wants to do as well as what his or her choice or decision is. They are used in the present tense regarding actions in the future. A person's intentions are usually specific and explain what means or method will be used to accomplish the eventual goal. This sense of intention referring to which methods will be used is the most suitable for the purposes of tax law. Intentions have also been described as what the person hopes to benefit, and intentions in this sense can inadvertently be blurred by motive.

A person's purpose is a conscious guidance which relates to what his or her specific end goal is. It is predetermined, although, like intentions, purposes are changeable. Purposes must be differentiated from what Krikorian terms "subordinate acts",[167] which are the steps executed in the plan rather than the predetermined eventual result.

1.4 Tax law perspective

The taxpayer's motives, intentions and purposes are discussed at length in the area of trading within tax law. The clearest way to assess the context in which the judiciary use these terms is to examine case law. Scrutinising how motive, intention and purpose are used by the judiciary may help further refine the definitions of these terms. Where the judiciary have used these terms interchangeably or inconsistently, the consequences of doing so will be highlighted. Also, the difference in outcomes where the judiciary examined subjective factors over objective considerations will be examined.

1.4 (a) Trading

Trades are not defined effectively under the Income Tax Act 2007 as the Act merely states that a trade "includes any venture in the nature of trade".[168] The definitional problem has been aided, but not resolved, by the common law due to the fact that a "'trade' is more indefinite than most words used in Acts of Parliament".[169] The badges of trade developed by the Royal Commission on the Taxation of Profits and Income and subsequently refined and supplemented by the common law are used to help in establishing whether a person is trading. Interestingly, one of the badges allows the judiciary to examine the taxpayer's motives where the transaction is deemed to be equivocal.[170] In addition to the badges of trade, it has been held that judges should also seek to establish the existence of a commercial purpose to establish that a taxpayer is trading.[171] As seen earlier, the term "purpose" has been described in philosophy as pertaining to the end result and will be applied to this context.

The taxpayer's motives and purposes were considered in *Iswera v Commissioner of Inland Revenue*[172] (*Iswera*). In this case, Lord Reid emphasised that as the taxpayer's activities satisfied all the badges of trade, there was no need to examine the taxpayer's purpose.[173] Nevertheless, it was held that the taxpayer was trading, and a relevant consideration was the subjective assumption that "the appellant's dominant motive was to make a profit".[174] However, making a profit could be both the taxpayer's motive and purpose, and it is questionable why an examination of purpose was excluded. Moreover, the finding that the desire to make a profit was a dominant motive suggests that there exists some other motive or motives. Lord Reid accepted that the taxpayer had "obtained what she had been seeking – an opportunity to reside near her daughters' school".[175] Consequently, she did not have a commercial purpose, and even if it was submitted that she did, it was admitted that being near her daughter's school was her main purpose. Therefore, she would have two purposes. However, if it was truly believed that there existed two purposes, their Lordships would have submitted that she obtained part of what she sought by residing close to her daughters' school. Nevertheless, when the issue of purposes and motives became too complex, the court bluntly concluded that the taxpayer's "purpose or object alone cannot prevail over what he in fact [did]".[176]

Iswera clearly illustrates the problems of dividing the taxpayer's purpose into dominant and ancillary purposes, and it has been suggested that perhaps this complex issue should not be brought under scrutiny at all.[177] As established by the philosophical interpretation of purpose, purposes are changeable, although a person usually has one distinct purpose. Any acts in between are merely "subordinate acts"[178] which are a means to achieve that primary purpose.

The earlier case of *Religious Tract and Book Society of Scotland v R.S. Forbes*[179] (*Forbes*) took a different approach to that in *Iswera*. The court in *Iswera* reasoned that the taxpayer's actions were decisive and that her purpose could not be material in light of the activities executed.[180] Had this reasoning been applied in *Forbes*, the court would have concluded that the taxpayer was trading. However, in *Forbes*, the taxpayer's purpose of "administering religious advice"[181] was paramount in deciding whether their colportage activities constituted trading. A finding of trading would have allowed the taxpayer to offset their losses against the profits made from their bookshop business. The court seemed to focus on the fact that the colportage activities did not make a profit,[182] although making a profit is not one of the badges of trade and should therefore not be relevant. However, the colporteurs had books for sale. Thus, it can be argued that the colportage activities were not solely charitable as the books could have been distributed for free. Moreover, it is uncertain whether a preference for considering the taxpayer's purpose over their motive altered the outcome of the case.

In *Iswera*, had the court acknowledged that the plots of land were bought in order to achieve the taxpayer's purpose of being near her daughter's school, the trading conclusion would not have been reached. Similarly, in *Forbes*, had the court focused on the taxpayer's purpose of selling religious materials which were available for sale by the colporteurs, it is likely that the taxpayer would have been found to be trading. The judiciary in *Forbes* decided that the taxpayer's primary purpose was purely religious despite the fact that the colportage activities comprised "a combination of the sale of books with a missionary enterprise".[183]

The facts of *Iswera* are similar to those in *Kirkham v Williams*[184] (*Kirkham*); however, the taxpayer's intentions in the latter case were decisive. The taxpayer bought property for use as office space and storage. Permission and work to build a dwelling-house on the land was obtained and carried out after the purchase. Once sold, the issue of whether the taxpayer was trading was raised, but the court took into account that he did not intend to reside there with his family.[185] When making the initial purchase, the intention of the taxpayer, or the steps taken in order to achieve his purpose, had not "moved out of the zone of contemplation – out of the sphere of the tentative, the provisional and the exploratory – into the valley of decision".[186] The taxpayer was deemed not to be trading. The court therefore emphasised the speculative and changeable nature of one's intention and, in turn, conveyed the stability of a decided purpose. Moreover, in order to examine the taxpayer's intentions, the court effectively implied that the facts in *Kirkham* were more equivocal than those in *Iswera*. This is because in *Kirkham*, the taxpayer's actions pointed in a number of different directions, some of which pointed to trade and some of which pointed to the acquisition of a capital asset for the business. The taxpayer's tentative intentions were decisive in *Kirkham*, whereas in *Iswera*, the court examined what the taxpayer actually did. The discrepancies between *Iswera* and *Kirkham* illustrate how examining intentions can drastically alter a decision.

Interestingly, although the taxpayer's purpose was considered paramount in *Forbes*, in *Grove v YMCA*[187] (*Grove*), motive was not considered paramount despite the fact that the case appeared to be equivocal. The YMCA's undisputed purpose was said to be the "improvement of the spiritual, mental, social and physical condition of young men".[188] However, this charitable purpose was said to apply to all departments within the YMCA, excluding the restaurant, which was found to be a trade.[189] There were no issues raised of ambiguity as it was held that the restaurant was operated on "usual commercial principles".[190] Due to the charitable intentions of the YMCA, *Grove* implies that a profit motive is irrelevant in determining whether an activity amounts to a trade as it was recognised that the restaurant would continue to operate irrespective of a profit.[191]

The irrelevance of a profit motive was also supported in *Commissioners of Inland Revenue v Reinhold*[192] (*Reinhold*), despite the fact that the taxpayer "admitted that he had bought the property not as a residence for himself but for sale",[193] unlike in *Iswera*, where the court placed emphasis on the isolated nature of the purchase and sale of the four properties.[194] Lord Carmont warned that conclusions of trading should not be drawn automatically based on "a man's intention not to hold an investment".[195] Similarly, Lord Russell advised against viewing the taxpayer's purpose as conclusive[196] as it disregards other important factors.[197] Despite the self-confessed intention to sell the property, the court held that the taxpayer was not trading and that an intention to make a profit on the sale of property is insufficient to amount to trading.[198] The purchase of the property was instead viewed as an investment. *Reinhold* reinforces the fact that the taxpayer's motive is irrelevant where a transaction is deemed to be unequivocal, and the question of what amounts to an equivocal transaction is for the judiciary to decide.

Similarly, in *Taylor v Good*[199] (*Taylor*), the taxpayer was held not to be trading despite the fact that a profit was made. The point of contention in the case was the controversy surrounding whether the taxpayer engaged in "supervening trading"[200] after acquiring the property, which relied heavily on his intentions to resolve. The taxpayer purchased property and adjoining land with the intention of residing in it. Approximately three years later, the taxpayer's intentions had changed, and he sought planning permission in order to develop it before resale by building 90 houses. The difficulty arose from the fact that "an adventure in the nature of trade had started at some time after the purchase".[201] When the case was heard in the High Court prior to appeal, the judge placed emphasis on the prerequisite of an intention to trade. Subjective considerations were given emphasis where Megarry J. stated that "a man cannot trade before he begins to trade, nor embark upon an adventure before he has thought of it".[202] In *Taylor*, the court analysed the taxpayer's intentions in conjunction with the timing of the events. However, the isolated nature of the transaction also facilitated a conclusion of not trading as buying and selling properties were not in line with the taxpayer's ordinary business activities.[203] However, this point was not given weight in *Iswera*.

Although the taxpayer's motives are examined in trading, they are meant to be considered as a last resort where the judge has exhausted applying the other objective badges of trade. It is arguable that, in tax avoidance, examining subjective factors should equally only be used as a last resort. The concept of what constitutes an equivocal activity is a source of the confusion in trading as it determines whether the court can consider the taxpayer's purpose or motives. Furthermore, there is no guidance to suggest what constitutes an equivocal transaction, which ultimately leaves the concepts of motive, intention and purpose to the discretion of the judiciary. Nevertheless, the common trend appears to deem a transaction equivocal where it conflicts with "the way the individual makes his living".[204] Although examining the taxpayer's current occupation does not aid in defining a trade, it has been held that "it is inevitable that the boundary line should not be precisely drawn".[205] However, the task of establishing whether a taxpayer is trading or merely seeks to obtain a fiscal advantage is assisted by the fact that there is usually a tax avoidance motive where large losses are generated or where tax relief is sought.[206]

Consistency could be achieved through the decision as to whether there should be an "abandonment of motive, or, acceptance of motive . . . in *all* cases".[207] Although the case law on trading demonstrates that there are problems as to when motive should be examined, the case law in this area also illustrates the inconsistencies in scrutinising motive. An assessment of the area of trading reveals that the conclusions as to tax liability should be decided "by a detailed analysis of the terms and circumstances of the transaction itself without inquiry into the motives and subjective aspirations of those who affected it".[208] However, as motive is one of the badges of trade, it is unlikely that motive will be disregarded as a consideration. Although, as demonstrated, where judges are seeking the motives of the taxpayer, they are in fact seeking what the taxpayer's purpose is in embarking on the transaction. Therefore, purpose would be a more fitting badge of trade.

1.4 (b) Expenditure

In the majority of the aforementioned trading cases, it was fiscally advantageous to the taxpayer not to be seen as trading. However, there are circumstances in which taxpayers desire to be classified as trading: for example, to deduct losses incurred in trade from the computation of their profits,[209] which was the position in *Ensign Tankers (Leasing) Ltd. Stokes*[210] (*Ensign Tankers*). The taxpayers sought to deduct a $14 million spend on the production of a film, although no more than $3.25 million was spent in reality. In this case, it was held in the High Court that the motives of the taxpayer were irrelevant, and the focus should be on the purpose of the transaction.[211] The House of Lords found that the arrangement was carried out "with the object of avoiding tax and not with the object of trading".[212] Moreover, motives and intentions were criticised by the Court of Appeal as being subjective,[213] which implies that purpose is more objective. Examining the "purpose or object of the transaction"[214] allows for more objective scrutiny to be made by questioning what end the transaction appeared to be aiming for. However, the judge accepted that previous cases had shown that "evidence of the subjective intention of the parties is admissible and relevant".[215] Therefore, it is important that any conclusions based on subjective assessments must be supported by evidence. Furthermore, despite the inherent difficulties in seeking to establish the subjective mind of a company,[216] the intentions of the five partners of the taxpayer, Victory Partnership, were discussed in *Ensign Tankers*.[217]

Interestingly, in *Ensign Tankers*, there was a union of the terms "object" and "purpose". It was held that "the sole object of the transaction was fiscal advantage";[218] therefore, there was "no place for there being any commercial purpose".[219] This presupposes that a person cannot have an object that conflicts with his or her purpose as they are the same. However, the terms "purpose" and "intention" were equated and blurred in *Ensign Tankers*, in which it was assumed that as the "*paramount* intention was a fiscal advantage . . . it postulates the existence of some other purpose".[220]

In contrast to the decision in *Taylor*, the court did not find it relevant that the taxpayer in *Arndale Properties Ltd. v Coates*[221] (*Arndale*) was a dealer in property. In *Arndale*, the taxpayer companies wanted the assignment of a lease of land to another subsidiary to be regarded as trading in order to claim loss relief among the subsidiary group. The lease was acquired for £2.2 million more than its market value. The lease was assigned by the property developer company, SPI, to the property dealer company, Arndale. The point of dispute was whether the subsequent assignment from Arndale to the subsidiary investment company, APTL, could be regarded as trading and therefore an allowable trading loss. The court held that although Arndale was a dealer in property, "the object of the assignment was to enable Arndale to convert the potential capital loss . . . into a trading loss".[222] Moreover, the lease was not viewed as part of Arndale's trading stock.[223] Therefore, the taxpayer companies were not trading, nor did the taxpayers have "any intention of trading with the lease".[224]

1.4 (c) Dividend stripping

As demonstrated earlier, a profit is not indicative of trading. Dividend stripping cases also demonstrate how a profit or a lack of profit is not conclusive as to trading. In dividend stripping cases, there are generally no obvious profits made, but the taxpayer can nevertheless be trading, although the more recent cases have departed from this view. A typical dividend stripping case involves a taxpayer who buys a company with forthcoming dividend disbursements and removes the profits from the business. The taxpayer then sells the shares in the business at a loss due to the extracted profits and claims that he or she has made an overall loss in order to offset the gain and avoid paying tax. In reality, no gain or loss is sustained through buying then selling the shares as the profits are extracted without paying tax on the profits. However, courts have acknowledged that the transactions entered into are genuine and cannot rightly be labelled sham transactions,[225] which has led to mixed responses among the judiciary.

The matter of whether one could seek a fiscal advantage and still be categorised as trading was settled in *Griffiths v J.P. Harrison Ltd.*[226] (*Harrison*). The case concerned a typical dividend stripping scenario whereby shares of the company Claiborne Ltd. were bought and sold with the aim of avoiding tax. Despite the court acknowledging that the object of the transactions was clearly to offset the losses against the dividend the taxpayer gained in Claiborne Ltd, the court held by a majority that the taxpayer was trading.[227] The decision was arrived at using objective methods as, despite the taxpayer's motives for dealing in shares, Viscount Simonds for the majority asserted that there is "nothing that enables me to say that it is not a trading transaction".[228] Moreover, the irrelevancy of a profit motive was applied to its fullest in order to support the trading finding.[229] Interestingly, Lord Denning in his dissenting speech asserted that a profit motive would indicate trading.[230] Lord Guest, for the majority, implied that the issue is not whether there is a profit motive at the beginning or during the arrangement as "the Revenue is not concerned with the particular method of trading: they are only concerned with the results of the business".[231] This suggests that the existence of a profit is given more weight than a profit motive when deciding whether a taxpayer is trading, although neither factor is a legal requirement. Moreover, the dissenting views expressed that the intentions of the taxpayer should be taken into account in order to arrive at the conclusion that a fiscal advantage was sought beneath the cloak of trading.[232] However, Lord Guest concluded that the intention of obtaining a fiscal advantage and generating a loss was irrelevant.[233]

The objective criterion formulated in *CIR v Livingston*[234] was applied in *Harrison* to conclude that the taxpayer was trading. This asked

> whether the operations involved in it are of the same kind, and carried on in the same way, as those which are characteristic of ordinary trading in the line of business in which the venture was made.[235]

In *Harrison*, although the taxpayer's motive was to obtain a fiscal advantage, the transactions indicated trading when viewed objectively. Conversely, in *Finsbury*

Securities Ltd. v IRC[236] (*Finsbury*), when viewed objectively, the arrangement indicated that the taxpayers sought a fiscal advantage and were not trading. Furthermore, little weight was attributed to the taxpayers' motives in arriving at the conclusion against trading. In contrast to *Harrison*, in *Finsbury*, the taxpayers owned preferred shares in Warshaw & Sons Ltd. which guaranteed that the taxpayers would receive regular dividends for the successive five years in order to gradually reclaim the company's profits.[237] The company wanted the court to hold that it was trading in order to claim loss relief on the diminution of the shares. However, the court held that the scheme was constructed so that the taxpayers "did not stand to lose and that the company did not stand to gain"[238] when the shares were later sold at a loss. The court affirmed the decision in *Harrison* by stating that even if motive was examined in that case, it made little difference, and "it was not capable of being made better or worse"[239] by doing so. *Finsbury* also involved an unusual condition in the arrangement as there was an agreement to hold the shares for five years, which was held to be remote from ordinary share-dealing transactions in which shares could be freely bought and sold.[240] This rationale led the court to conclude that "it was a wholly artificial device remote from trade to secure a tax advantage".[241]

The issue of whether the taxpayer's motives are relevant in deciding whether a taxpayer is trading was discussed at length in *F.A. & A.B. Ltd. v Lupton*[242] (*Lupton*). The taxpayer company, a dealer in shares, sought to claim relief for losses sustained during the course of its trade. The court acknowledged that the general view is that one cannot be trading where the motive for entering into the transaction was to obtain a fiscal benefit, although it cited *Harrison* as breaking away from this trend.[243] Furthermore, it was recognised that a finding of trading could be drastically changed "once the motive which inspired it is known".[244] Accordingly, in *Lupton*, greater weight was placed on the taxpayer's motives for embarking on the transaction; thus, the court departed from the approach in *Harrison*. Consequently, the court concluded that the taxpayer was not trading. *Lupton* is a landmark case which clearly illustrated how the judges reasoned that the "the fiscal motive had so infected the transactions themselves that they had ceased to be trading transactions".[245] The dividend stripping cases are an important illustration of how the subjective intentions of the taxpayer can determine whether a person is trading. As demonstrated here, the more recent cases have placed greater emphasis on the subjective motives of the taxpayer in buying and selling shares in order to deny the taxpayers loss relief. The growing trend of examining the taxpayer's motive and condemning dividend stripping operations is due to the taxpayer being seen as "a wolf in sheep's clothing with the revenue as the prey".[246]

1.4 (d) Targeted anti-avoidance rules

The research into defining the motive approach can be further strengthened by examining the use of the term "purpose" in targeted anti-avoidance rules.[247] The Aaronson Report "estimated that there are now more than 300 targeted anti-avoidance rules".[248] Therefore, it is useful to examine a selection of the TAARs which make reference to the taxpayer's purpose in order to gain a deeper understanding of how this term is used in practice.

Many of the TAARs in tax legislation use the term "purpose" without attempting to provide a definition for it. For example, the TAAR introduced by the Finance Act 2016 in relation to peer-to-peer lending uses the term "purpose". The TAAR was inserted into s412I of the Income Tax Act 2007. The provision states that income tax relief would be permitted where the "loan . . . is not part of a scheme or arrangement the main purpose or one of the main purposes of which is to obtain a tax advantage".[249] Similarly, section 353 of the Income Tax Act 2007 includes a TAAR with respect to community investment relief. This relates to the "entitlement to tax reductions in respect of amounts invested by individuals in community development finance institutions".[250] The TAAR states that "the investment must not be made as part of a scheme or arrangement the main purpose or one of the main purposes of which is the avoidance of tax".[251] Again, there is no attempt to define the term "purpose".

A TAAR was introduced in 2016 to prevent the treatment of a distribution from a company winding up as being capital in nature. Therefore, the distribution would be treated as income for tax purposes. This change was made under s35 of the Finance Act 2016 and amends chapter 1 of the Income Tax Act 2007. Various conditions are examined to ascertain whether this TAAR should apply. These conditions include whether "the individual carries on a trade or activity which is the same as, or similar to, that carried on by the company or an effective 51% subsidiary of the company".[252] More importantly, one of the conditions is that "the winding up forms part of arrangements the main purpose or one of the main purposes of which is the avoidance or reduction of a charge to income tax".[253] As will be demonstrated in chapter 3, this is similar to the language used in the main purpose test within the GAAR. Cullen remarked that the amendment to the Income Tax Act 2007 has made

> the main purpose test objective (rather than subjective) by requiring consideration of the purpose of the transaction in securities or any of the transactions in securities rather than the purpose of a party to such a transaction or transactions.[254]

However, Cullen recognises that the provision is "very broadly framed".[255] Moreover, as *Ensign Tankers* demonstrated, the arrangement's purpose can become conflated with the taxpayer's intentions.[256]

The TAAR within section 123(4) of the Capital Allowances Act 2001 has also been the subject of debate in relation to the taxpayer's purpose. The provision specifies when a ship would be deemed to be "used for a qualifying purpose at any time when it is let on charter in the course of a trade".[257] In order to be deemed a "qualifying purpose" to qualify for capital allowances, the person operating the ship must be "resident in the United Kingdom or [carry] on the trade there".[258] Secondly, that person must be "responsible for navigating and managing the ship",[259] particularly in relation to the expenses.[260] However, these rules do not apply where, in letting the ship,

> the main object, or one of the main objects . . . was to obtain a writing-down allowance determined without regard to section 109 (writing-down allowances at 10%) in respect of expenditure incurred by any person on the provision of the ship or aircraft".[261]

Therefore, the TAAR is drafted in the form of a main object test.

The main object test within section 123(4) was the subject of debate in *Lloyds Bank Leasing (No 1) Limited v The Commissioners for Her Majesty's Revenue and Customs*[262] (*Lloyds*). The case concerned whether Lloyds Bank Leasing (No 1) was entitled to make use of the writing-down allowance provided for under the Capital Allowances Act 2001. The claim was made in relation to two ships which the bank had purchased. The bank then leased the ships for commercial purposes to a Norwegian company. The ships were paid for over a period of four years. Allowances were claimed for each payment. A company called K-Euro took over "possession and use of the vessels over the 20-year bareboat charter period".[263] K-Euro's business was later reorganised with the effect that the ships were to be managed by K LNG.[264] The tribunal stated that the reorganisation took place

> because it was expected that . . . K-Euro would make a substantial loss in operating the vessels and because certain of the security arrangements with respect to the lease structure through which K-Euro held its interest in the vessels were proving to be a commercial restraint upon the management and development of K-Euro's other business interests.[265]

The main object test was discussed where the tribunal accepted that

> the paramount purpose of the transactions, at least taken as a whole, was commercial, namely the operation of the vessels by K-Euro with the objective of earning a profit and expanding its Atlantic basin business.[266]

However, problems arose where the tribunal considered whether "obtaining of capital allowances was not also a main object, even if not the paramount object, of the transactions".[267] The tribunal was critical of the main object test under section 123(4) of the Capital Allowances Act 2001. The judge explained that the TAAR was unclear as "it also does not . . . offer any guide to the boundary between an object which is a main object and one which, though necessarily still an object, is not a main object".[268] Nevertheless, it was held that it was "quite impossible to reconcile with the proposition that the availability of the allowances was of mere incidental interest to the various participants".[269] The tribunal acknowledged that "even if commercial considerations were paramount, the aim of securing the allowances had become a material factor".[270] Ultimately, "the obtaining of writing-down allowances at 25% was a main object, or one of the main objects, of the transactions into which the various parties entered".[271] In the *Lloyds* case, Parliament's intentions were clear due to the inclusion of a TAAR. The TAAR made it clear that "the legislative aim is to exclude from the benefit of writing-down allowances those who take steps to obtain them when otherwise they would not be available".[272]

The decision in *Lloyds* has been criticised for its interpretation of the main object test. McGowan has argued that the tribunal's "approach illustrates how elusive the distinction is now between a taxpayer's main object/purpose and a more incidental objective".[273] The decision was also criticised on the basis that it "provide[d] little or no guidance on how to prove that tax is not a main purpose/object".[274] The subjectivity of the main object test was also condemned as "this elusive dividing line is never satisfactorily drawn by the FTT and is very much in the subjective eye of the beholder".[275] The *Lloyds* decision was also criticised for having wider-reaching consequences. McGowan argued that

> it will be increasingly difficult for commercial actors to know whether tax considerations will be considered to be one of the main objects of a transaction, simply because (as in most sophisticated commercial transactions) a structure has been put together with tax in mind, and with the benefit of detailed tax advice, not least to avoid the many "elephant traps" in the UK's tax legislation.[276]

The ease of satisfying the main object test was also highlighted by McGowan. He remarked that

> the courts have now made it difficult for taxpayers to show that tax is not "a main object/purpose" in any situation where they have taken tax advice, and elected to adopt a more rather than less tax-efficient structure for a commercial transaction.[277]

The resulting problem is that the Capital Allowances Act 2001 can be "read so broadly that it is disapplied only where the taxpayer did not know it would be able to receive such allowances or found itself by happy coincidence in the position".[278] Moreover, *Lloyds* demonstrated that a main object test can still be satisfied where there exists a genuine commercial purpose. The problem is not trying to distinguish between a main object or one of the main objects of the arrangement as both fall within the remit of the main object test. The difficulty is in attempting to distinguish between a main purpose and a secondary purpose, which McGowan rightly argued is a subjective test.[279]

1.5 Conclusions

The semantic composition of the terms "motive", "intention" and "purpose" have been differentiated to some extent. However, "some degree of polysemy is unavoidable".[280] As illustrated, there are several ways in which the terms can become blurred, depending on the context in which they are used. Nevertheless, from the analysis in this chapter, it is possible to provide demarcated definitions of these terms for tax law purposes.

A motive is a conscious or unconscious guiding influence which produces the desire to act. This influence is the reason a person feels compelled to act. A person may have multiple motives which are usually coloured by his or her character, developed after deliberation. Motives are formed in relation to achievable acts, which are formed through self-interested reasons. However, analysing motive does not reveal whether the person was objectively able to carry out the act. A motive in the emotional sense should not be a relevant consideration in tax law as it is a highly subjective interpretation of motive.

The intricacies of one's intentions are explicated intelligibly by Dworkin, who asserts that an "intention is always a more complex and problematic matter"[281] than simply examining a person "when he said or wrote or did what he did".[282] A person has an intention to perform an act where they consciously make a decision as to what they specifically want to achieve and plan the methods or means to lead them to their object. The intention is knowingly formed in the present tense, which is usually followed through to the time of action and is within their control. Intentions are descriptive and can be equated to and materialised in what Krikorian terms the "subordinate acts"[283] taken in order to fulfil a goal.

A purpose or object is a conscious and predetermined goal which is usually specific. However, purposes can change according to how the steps taken to fulfil the eventual purpose unfold. A purpose is the more objective measure compared to intentions and motives. Furthermore, Dworkin linked a purpose to interpreting the acts of a community,[284] which suggests that it is better to examine a purpose when interpreting a collective. Therefore, when examining corporate taxpayers, it may be intelligible to ascertain its purpose.

The problem in tax law is that all three stages of thought are considered in adjudication, and different judges will have their preferences as to which stage to examine. The inevitable inconsistency generated from this multifarious approach invariably results in different outcomes. This inconsistency can best be illustrated by the conflicting trading cases of *Iswera*, *Forbes* and *Kirkham*. In *Iswera*, the court focused on the taxpayer's motive, whilst in *Forbes*, the emphasis was on the taxpayer's purpose. Moreover, in *Kirkham*, the judiciary examined the taxpayer's intentions. The three trading cases illustrate that although motive is a badge of trade, this badge has been blurred with the terms "purpose" and "intention". Furthermore, cases like *Grove* and *Reinhold*, in which the taxpayer's motives are not examined, can cause confusion as it is difficult to see why these are not considered equivocal in comparison to other ambiguous cases. Interestingly, although motive is a badge of trade, in *Ensign*, this was highly criticised, and a preference for purpose was advocated.[285]

Consistency could be generated by examining objective factors as elucidated in *Livingston*.[286] Furthermore, the dividend stripping case of *Finsbury* illustrates that objective means of deciding a case do not always favour the taxpayer but can nevertheless produce a reasonable outcome. There is no clear statutory definition of what constitutes a trade because there are many different varieties of trades, and producing an exhaustive list of them would be impossible. However, *Taylor* assisted with deciding whether a person is trading by asking whether the activities were in line with the taxpayer's ordinary business.[287] However, *Arndale* illustrated how this criterion was abused unsuccessfully and was resolved by examining the taxpayer's purpose.

The discussion on TAARs usefully demonstrates that examining whether tax issues are a main purpose involves examining many purposes. An arrangement which has a commercial end but has achieved that end through a tax-saving route is likely to come under the remit of a TAAR, due to the breadth of the main object test. Furthermore, cases such as *Lloyds* demonstrate that the existence of a commercial purpose does not negate a tax purpose.

Whilst the subjective thoughts of the taxpayer can help settle equivocal cases, the judiciary should apply objective criteria before resorting to subjective considerations. As demonstrated, the terms "motive", "intention" and "purpose" have been used interchangeably by the judiciary, although their meanings are different. For the purposes of this book, motive is what drives behaviour before action is carried out. In contrast, an intention is the intermediate planning whilst undertaking the course of action and is changeable according to what is achievable. A person's purpose is what they aim to be the end result of their action. Therefore, purposes are fundamental as these are what materialise and are observable. However, examining the taxpayer's motive, intention or purpose is not specifically permitted by legislation in tax avoidance. Consequently, it is helpful to ascertain whether the taxpayer's motive, intention or purpose was examined before the implementation of the GAAR.

Notes

1 Snow, A.J. *'An Approach to the Psychology of Motives'*, [1926], Vol. 37, No. 1, The American Journal of Psychology, p129.
2 *Ibid.*
3 Ashworth, A. and Horder, J. *'Principles of Criminal Law'*, [2013], 7th edn, Oxford University Press, Oxford, p74.
4 *Ibid*, p160.
5 *Ibid*, p162.
6 *Ibid*, p75.
7 *Five Oaks Properties Ltd v HMRC* [2006] STC (SCD) 769.
8 Ashworth, A. and Horder, J. *'Principles of Criminal Law'*, [2013], 7th edn, Oxford University Press, Oxford, p156.
9 *R v Mohan* [1975] 2 W.L.R. 859, [1976] Q.B. 1, 11 (James L.J.).
10 *Hyam v DPP* [1974] 2 W.L.R. 607, [1975] A.C. 55, 58 (Lord Hailsham of St. Marylebone L.C.).
11 Ashworth, A. and Horder, J. *'Principles of Criminal Law'*, [2013], 7th edn, Oxford University Press, Oxford, p156.
12 *Ibid.*
13 *Ibid.*
14 *Ibid*, p162.
15 Simester, A.P. and Chan, W. *'Four Functions of Mens Rea'*, [2011], Cambridge Law Journal, pp381, 382.

16 *Ibid.*
17 Millet, P. *'Artificial Tax Avoidance: The English and American Approach'*, [1986], British Tax Review, pp327, 330.
18 Coulson, J., et al. *'The Oxford Illustrated Dictionary'*, [1981], 2nd edn, Oxford University Press, Wiltshire, p15.
19 *Ibid*, p686.
20 *Ibid*, p551.
21 Law, J. and Martin, E.A. *'Oxford Dictionary of Law'*, [2009], Oxford University Press, Oxford, p359.
22 Coulson, J., et al. *'The Oxford Illustrated Dictionary'*, [1981], 2nd edn, Oxford University Press, Wiltshire, p436.
23 Millet, P. *'Artificial Tax Avoidance: The English and American Approach'*, [1986], British Tax Review, pp327, 330.
24 *R v Mohan* [1975] 2 W.L.R. 859, [1976] Q.B. 1, 8 (James L.J.).
25 *Ibid.*
26 *Ibid*, p11.
27 Ashworth, A. and Horder, J. *'Principles of Criminal Law'*, [2013], 7th edn, Oxford University Press, Oxford, p169.
28 *Ibid.*
29 *Ibid.*
30 *WT Ramsay Ltd v IRC* [1982] AC 300, 338 (Lord Fraser of Tullybelton).
31 *Hyam v DPP* [1974] 2 W.L.R. 607, [1975] A.C. 55, 82 (Viscount Dilhorne).
32 Stocks, J.L. *'Motive'*, [1911], Vol. 20, No. 77, Mind Association, p64.
33 *Ibid.*
34 *Ibid.*
35 *Ibid.*
36 *Ibid.*
37 *Ibid*, p56.
38 *Ibid.*
39 *Ibid*, p57.
40 *Ibid.*
41 *Ibid*, p59.
42 *Ibid.*
43 *Ibid*, p54.
44 *Ibid*, p63.
45 Snow, A.J. *'An Approach to the Psychology of Motives'*, [1926], Vol. 37, No. 1, The American Journal of Psychology, p130.
46 Stocks, J.L. *'Motive'*, [1911], Vol. 20, No. 77, Mind Association, p56.
47 Snow, A.J. *'An Approach to the Psychology of Motives'*, [1926], Vol. 37, No. 1, The American Journal of Psychology, p130.
48 *Ibid*, pp130–131.
49 Stocks, J.L. *'Motive'*, [1911], Vol. 20, No. 77, Mind Association, p63.
50 *Ibid.*
51 *Ibid.*
52 Dewey, J. and Tufts, J.H. *'Ethics'*, [1908], Henry Holt and Company, New York, HathiTrust Digital Library, <http://babel.hathitrust.org/cgi/pt?id=mdp.39015002747221;view=1up;seq=266>, accessed 02.04.2015, p246.
53 Stocks, J.L. *'Motive'*, [1911], Vol. 20, No. 77, Mind Association, p63.
54 *Ibid*, p64.
55 *Ibid.*
56 Snow, A.J. *'An Approach to the Psychology of Motives'*, [1926], Vol. 37, No. 1, The American Journal of Psychology, p130.
57 Stocks, J.L. *'Motive'*, [1911], Vol. 20, No. 77, Mind Association, p65.
58 Scott, S. *'Motive and Justification'*, [1988], Vol. 85, No. 9, Journal of Philosophy Inc., p479.

59 *Ibid*, p480.
60 *Ibid.*
61 Anscombe, G.E.M. *'Intention'*, [1963], 2nd edn, Basil Blackwell, Oxford, p7.
62 *Ibid*, p4.
63 *Ibid.*
64 *Ibid*, p3.
65 *Ibid*, p9.
66 Scheer, R.K. *'Intentions, Motives and Causation'*, [2001], Vol 76, No. 297, Philosophy, p400.
67 *Ibid*, p397.
68 *Ibid*, p398.
69 Anscombe, G.E.M. *'Intention'*, [1963], 2nd edn, Basil Blackwell, Oxford, p31.
70 *Ibid.*
71 Scheer, R.K. *'Intentions, Motives and Causation'*, [2001], Vol 76, No. 297, Philosophy, p399.
72 *Ibid*, p400.
73 *Ibid.*
74 *Ibid*, p399.
75 *Ibid*, p400.
76 *Ibid*, p399.
77 *Ibid.*
78 Scott, S. *'Motive and Justification'*, [1988], Vol. 85, No. 9, Journal of Philosophy Inc., p479.
79 Anscombe, G.E.M. *'Intention'*, [1963], 2nd edn, Basil Blackwell, Oxford, p20.
80 Dewey, J. and Tufts, J.H. *'Ethics'*, [1908], Henry Holt and Company, New York, HathiTrust Digital Library, <http://babel.hathitrust.org/cgi/pt?id=mdp.39015002747221;view=1up;seq=266>, accessed 02.04.2015, p247.
81 Anscombe, G.E.M. *'Intention'*, [1963], 2nd edn, Basil Blackwell, Oxford, p18.
82 *Ibid.*
83 *Ibid.*
84 *Ibid*, p19.
85 Dewey, J. and Tufts, J.H. *'Ethics'*, [1908], Henry Holt and Company, New York, HathiTrust Digital Library, <http://babel.hathitrust.org/cgi/pt?id=mdp.39015002747221;view=1up;seq=266>, accessed 02.04.2015, pp246–247.
86 *Ibid*, p247.
87 *Ibid.*
88 *Ibid*, p246.
89 Scheer, R.K. *'Intentions, Motives and Causation'*, [2001], Vol 76, No. 297, Philosophy, p398.
90 Wilkins, B.T. *'Concerning "Motive" and "Intention"'* [1971], Vol. 31, No. 4, p140.
91 *Ibid.*
92 *Ibid.*
93 *Ibid.*
94 *Ibid.*
95 *Ibid.*
96 *Ibid.*
97 *Ibid*, p139.
98 *Ibid*, p141.
99 *Ibid*, p140.
100 *Ibid*, p141.
101 *Ibid.*
102 *Ibid*, p142.
103 Anscombe, G.E.M. *'Intention'*, [1963], 2nd edn, Basil Blackwell, Oxford, p9.
104 *Ibid*, p22.

105 *Ibid*, p9.
106 *Ibid*, p31.
107 *Ibid*, p9.
108 Wilkins, B.T. *'Concerning "Motive" and "Intention"'*, [1971], Vol. 31, No. 4, p141.
109 *Ibid.*
110 Anscombe, G.E.M. *'Intention'*, [1963], 2nd edn, Basil Blackwell, Oxford, p9.
111 *Ibid*, p10.
112 *Ibid.*
113 *Ibid*, p23.
114 *Ibid*, p15.
115 *Ibid*, p18.
116 *Ibid*, p28.
117 Dworkin, R. *'Law's Empire'*, [1998], Hart Publishing, Oxford, p55.
118 Anscombe, G.E.M. *'Intention'*, [1963], 2nd edn, Basil Blackwell, Oxford, p28.
119 *Ibid*, p20.
120 *Ibid*, p21.
121 *Ibid*, p20.
122 *Ibid*, p21.
123 *Ibid*, p20.
124 *Ibid.*
125 *Ibid.*
126 *Ibid*, p21.
127 Krikorian, Y.H. *'The Meaning of Purpose'*, [1930], Vol. 27, No. 4, The Journal of Philosophy, p96.
128 *Ibid.*
129 *Ibid*, p97.
130 *Ibid.*
131 *Ibid.*
132 *Ibid*, p98.
133 *Ibid*, p99.
134 *Ibid.*
135 *Ibid*, p101.
136 *Ibid*, p99.
137 *Ibid*, p103.
138 *Ibid*, p104.
139 *Ibid*, p101.
140 *Ibid.*
141 *Ibid*, p100.
142 *Ibid*, p97.
143 *Ibid.*
144 *Ibid*, p103.
145 *Ibid*, p102.
146 *Ibid*, p98.
147 *Ibid*, p102.
148 *Ibid.*
149 *Ibid.*
150 Gormally, L. *'Intention and Side Effects: John Finnis and Elizabeth Anscombe'* cited in Keown, J. and George, R. *'Reason, Morality and Law: The Philosophy of John Finnis'* [2013], Oxford University Press, Oxford, p95.
151 *Ibid.*
152 *Ibid*, p93.
153 *Ibid*, p103.
154 *Ibid*, p104.
155 *Ibid*, p106.

156 Laurence, B. *'An Anscombian Approach to Collective Action'* in Ford, A., Hornsby, J. and Stoutland, F. (ed.), *'Essays on Anscombe's Intention'*, Harvard University Press, United States of America, p272.
157 *Ibid*, p271.
158 *Ibid*, p273.
159 *Ibid*, p274.
160 *Ibid.*
161 *Ibid*, p282.
162 *Ibid*, p290.
163 *Ibid.*
164 *Ibid.*
165 *Ibid*, pp293–294.
166 *Ibid*, p291.
167 Krikorian, Y.H. *'The Meaning of Purpose'*, [1930], Vol. 27, No. 4, The Journal of Philosophy, p101.
168 s989 Income Tax Act 2007.
169 *Griffiths v J.P. Harrison Ltd.* [1962] 2 W.L.R. 909, [1963] A.C. 1, 16 (Lord Reid).
170 *Iswera v Commissioner of Inland Revenue* [1965] 1 W.L.R. 663, 668 (Lord Reid).
171 *Ensign Tankers (Leasing) Ltd. v Stokes* [1992] 2 W.L.R 469, [1992] A.C. 655, 687 (Lord Jauncey of Tullichettle).
172 *Iswera v Commissioner of Inland Revenue* [1965] 1 W.L.R. 663.
173 *Ibid*, p668 (Lord Reid).
174 *Ibid.*
175 *Ibid*, p666.
176 *Ibid*, p668.
177 Olowofoyeku, A. *'The Taxation of Income'*, [2013], 2nd edn, Cambridge Academic, United Kingdom, p126.
178 Krikorian, Y.H. *'The Meaning of Purpose'*, [1930], Vol. 27, No. 4, The Journal of Philosophy, p101.
179 *Religious Tract and Book Society of Scotland v R.S. Forbes* [1896] 23 R. 390.
180 *Iswera v Commissioner of Inland Revenue* [1965] 1 W.L.R. 663, 668 (Lord Reid).
181 *Religious Tract and Book Society of Scotland v R.S. Forbes* [1896] 23 R. 390, 393 (Lord President).
182 *Ibid.*
183 *Ibid.*
184 *Kirkham v Williams* [1991] W.L.R. 863.
185 *Ibid*, p868 (Nourse L.J.).
186 *Cunliffe v Goodman* [1950] 2 K.B. 237, 254 (Asquith L.J.).
187 *Grove v Young Men's Christian Association* [1903] 4 TC 613 K.B.
188 *Ibid*, p616 (Ridley, J.).
189 *Ibid.*
190 *Ibid*, p617.
191 *Ibid.*
192 *Commissioners of Inland Revenue v Reinhold* [1953] 34 TC 389.
193 *Ibid*, p391 (Lord Carmont).
194 *Ibid*, p392.
195 *Ibid*, p393.
196 *Ibid*, p394 (Lord Russell).
197 *Ibid*, p395.
198 *Ibid*, p397 (Lord Keith).
199 *Taylor v Good* [1974] 1 W.L.R. 556.
200 *Taylor v Good* [1973] 1 W.L.R. 1249, 1258 (Megarry J.).
201 *Taylor v Good* [1974] 1 W.L.R. 556, 558 (Russell L.J.).
202 *Taylor v Good* [1973] 1 W.L.R. 1249, 1260 (Megarry J.).

203 *Taylor v Good* [1974] 1 W.L.R. 556, 559 (Russell L.J.).
204 *Commissioners of Inland Revenue v Reinhold* [1953] 34 TC 389, 393 (Lord Carmont).
205 *Edwards v Bairstow* [1955] 3 W.L.R. 410, [1956] A.C. 14, 30 (Viscount Simonds).
206 Lee, N. *'Revenue Law: Principles and Practice'*, [2012], 13th edn, Bloomsbury Professional Ltd., Croydon, p281.
207 Olowofoyeku, A. *'The Taxation of Income'*, [2013], 2nd edn, Cambridge Academic, United Kingdom, p137.
208 *Ensign Tankers (Leasing) Ltd. v Stokes* [1989] 1 W.L.R. 1222, 1233 (Millett J.).
209 s64 Income Tax Act 2007.
210 *Ensign Tankers (Leasing) Ltd. v Stokes* [1992] 2 W.L.R 469, [1992] A.C. 655.
211 *Ensign Tankers (Leasing) Ltd. v Stokes* [1989] 1 W.L.R. 1222, 1232 (Millett J.).
212 *Ensign Tankers (Leasing) Ltd. v Stokes* [1992] 2 W.L.R 469, [1992] A.C. 655, 668 (Lord Templeman).
213 *Ensign Tankers (Leasing) Ltd. v Stokes* [1991] 1 W.L.R. 341, 352 (Sir Nicolas Browne-Wilkinson V.C.).
214 *Ibid.*
215 *Ibid.*
216 Olowofoyeku, A. *'The Taxation of Income'*, [2013], 2nd edn, Cambridge Academic, United Kingdom, p127.
217 *Ensign Tankers (Leasing) Ltd. v Stokes* [1991] 1 W.L.R. 341, 354 (Sir Nicolas Browne-Wilkinson V.C.).
218 *Ibid*, p355.
219 *Ibid.*
220 *Ibid.*
221 *Arndale Properties Ltd. v Coates* [1984] 1 W.L.R. 1328.
222 *Ibid*, p1330 (Lord Templeman).
223 *Ibid*, p1331.
224 *Ibid*, p1333.
225 *Griffiths v J.P. Harrison Ltd.* [1962] 2 W.L.R. 909, [1963] A.C. 1, 23 (Lord Morris of Borth-Y-Gest).
226 *Griffiths v J.P. Harrison Ltd.* [1963] A.C. 1.
227 *Ibid*, p11 (Viscount Simonds).
228 *Ibid.*
229 *Ibid*, pp11–12.
230 *Ibid*, pp20–21 (Lord Denning).
231 *Ibid*, p26 (Lord Guest).
232 *Ibid*, p13 (Lord Reid).
233 *Ibid*, p27 (Lord Guest).
234 *CIR v Livingston* [1927] 11 TC 538.
235 *Ibid*, p542 (Lord President Clyde).
236 *Finsbury Securities Ltd. v IRC* [1966] 1 W.L.R. 1402.
237 *Ibid*, p1412 (Lord Morris of Borth-Y-Gest).
238 *Ibid*, p1413.
239 *Ibid*, p1417.
240 *Ibid.*
241 *Ibid*, p1418.
242 *F.A. & A.B. Ltd. v Lupton* [1971] 3 W.L.R 670, [1972] A.C. 634.
243 *Ibid*, p646 (Lord Morris of Borth-Y-Gest).
244 *Ibid.*
245 Peakcock, J. *'When, If Ever, Can an Activity Motivated by Tax Constitute a Trade?'*, [2014], British Tax Review, pp509, 512.
246 *F.A. & A.B. Ltd. v Lupton* [1971] 3 W.L.R 670, [1972] A.C. 634, 645 (Lord Morris of Borth-Y-Gest).
247 TAARs.

248 Aaronson, G. *'A Study to Consider whether a General Anti-Avoidance Rule Should Be Introduced into the UK Tax System'*, [2011], <http://webarchive.nationalarchives.gov.uk/+/http:/www.hm-treasury.gov.uk/d/gaar_final_report_111111.pdf>, accessed 25.08.2014, p18.
249 s412I Income Tax Act 2007.
250 s353 Income Tax Act 2007.
251 *Ibid.*
252 s35(4)(a) Finance Act 2016.
253 s35(5)(b) Finance Act 2016.
254 Cullen, F. *'Finance Act 2016 Notes: Section 33: Transactions in Securities: Company Distributions; Section 34: Transactions in Securities: Procedure for Counteraction of Advantage; Section 35: Distributions in a Winding Up'*, [2016], British Tax Review, pp537, 538.
255 *Ibid*, p542.
256 *Ensign Tankers (Leasing) Ltd. v Stokes* [1991] 1 W.L.R. 341, 355 (Sir Nicolas Browne-Wilkinson V.C.).
257 s123(1) Capital Allowances Act 2001.
258 s123(1)(a) Capital Allowances Act 2001.
259 s123(1)(b) Capital Allowances Act 2001.
260 *Ibid.*
261 s123(4) Capital Allowances Act 2001.
262 *Lloyds Bank Leasing (No 1) Limited v The Commissioners for Her Majesty's Revenue and Customs* [2015] UKFTT 0401 (TC).
263 *Ibid*, [13] (Judge Colin Bishopp).
264 *Ibid*, [16].
265 *Ibid.*
266 *Ibid*, [24].
267 *Ibid.*
268 *Ibid*, [29].
269 *Ibid*, [88].
270 *Ibid*, [87].
271 *Ibid*, [91].
272 *Ibid*, [90].
273 McGowan, M. *'HMRC v Lloyds Bank Leasing (No 1) Ltd.: The Troublesome Increase in the Scope of the "Sole or Main Object" Test'*, [2015], British Tax Review, pp649, 653.
274 *Ibid.*
275 *Ibid.*
276 *Ibid.*
277 *Ibid*, p654.
278 *Ibid*, p652.
279 *Ibid*, p653.
280 Mazzone, M. *'Intentions as Complex Entities'*, [2011], Vol. 2, No. 4, Review of Philosophy and Psychology, p769.
281 Dworkin, R. *'Law's Empire'*, [1998], Hart Publishing, Oxford, p55.
282 *Ibid.*
283 Krikorian, Y.H. *'The Meaning of Purpose'*, [1930], The Journal of Philosophy, Vol. 27, No. 4, p101.
284 Dworkin, R. *'Law's Empire'*, [1998], Hart Publishing, Oxford, p63.
285 *Ensign Tankers (Leasing) Ltd. v Stokes* [1991] 1 W.L.R. 341, 352 (Sir Nicolas Browne-Wilkinson V.C.).
286 *CIR v Livingston* [1927] 11 TC 538, 542 (Lord President Clyde).
287 *Taylor v Good* [1974] 1 W.L.R. 556, 559 (Russell L.J.).

2 A move towards motive, intention and purpose

Introduction

The purpose of this chapter is to ascertain whether the practice of analysing the taxpayer's motive, intention and purpose was implanted within the UK's tax system before the GAAR was introduced. In establishing whether there has been a move towards considering the taxpayer's cognitive influences, it is necessary to examine the common law, where opinions as to acceptable and unacceptable tax avoidance have divided the judiciary. This chapter demonstrates how the divide was caused by the different approaches to statutory interpretation and the judges' respective views on the "substance over form" doctrine. These differences in adjudication effectively created a gulf between the supporters of *Westminster* and those of *Ramsay*. However, the *Ramsay* approach was placed on a pedestal and marked the move towards examining motive, intention and purpose. The discussion seeks to juxtapose the difference in approaches to tax avoidance.

2.1 Tackling tax avoidance

Until *Ramsay*, the applicable form of statutory interpretation was decided according to the clarity of the corresponding legislation. Judges could apply the literal approach without being accused of not also observing what the taxpayers intended by their actions through studying disproportionate profit and losses. *Ramsay* began the trend of carefully analysing the taxpayer's intentions by examining their actions and the substance of the arrangement. This inevitably involved a degree of discretion. The conflicting approaches taken in *Ramsay* and *Westminster* forced subsequent cases to choose one of these approaches to follow until one of them eventually emerged victorious.

In the *Westminster* case, the House of Lords' views on tax avoidance was made unmistakably clear. Lord Tomlin famously proclaimed that "every man is entitled if he can to order his affairs so as that the tax attaching under the appropriate Acts is less than it otherwise would be".[1] An objective approach to deciding tax liability was adopted in *Westminster*. The respondent Duke chose to pay a selection of his workers, including his gardener, in the form of an annuity by way of deed of covenant for a period of seven years. The covenantees were expected not

DOI: 10.4324/9781003080473-3

to demand their wages as the annuity effectively paid them an amount equal to their wages, irrespective of whether they rendered their services. To ensure that the annuity adopted a different character to wages, the workers were still entitled, in theory, to request their wages under the deed. However, their theoretical right to claim their wages was curtailed by the terms of the accompanying letters to the employees, which required their signed consent. The legal effect of executing the deed resulted in the Duke being able to deduct the annuity payments from his total income for tax purposes. Therefore, the same procedure of paying the employees could be executed directly or indirectly, although the indirect method involved the avoidance of tax. Despite the fact that the accompanying letters created the impression of wages, his arrangement was successful, and it was held that simply because of his "ingenuity, he cannot be compelled to pay an increased tax".[2]

There was a desire by the court in *Westminster* to understand the reasoning behind the arrangement and to tackle the suitability of the concept of substance over form in general. The court took the taxpayer's intention into consideration by concluding that the "document was intended to be contractual".[3] An investigation into the substance of the arrangement was also made, and it was acknowledged that, in substance, the annuities were wages.[4] However, despite the acknowledgement of the substance of the arrangement, Lord Tomlin bluntly asserted that the substance over form doctrine should be "given its quietus".[5] He criticised the doctrine for basing "its support upon a misunderstanding of language".[6] Furthermore, the notion that examining the substance of an arrangement involves exercising discretion was confirmed by Lord Tomlin as he stated that the substance over form doctrine effectively prefers "the incertain and crooked cord of discretion [over] the golden and streight metwand of the law".[7] The substance over form doctrine was also attacked for compelling a taxpayer to "pay notwithstanding that he has so ordered his affairs that the amount of tax sought from him is not legally claimable".[8] Therefore, whilst the court accepted that the surrounding circumstances of a case should be ascertained,[9] it is clear that this must not be to the detriment of taxpayers who are within the confines of the law.

The substance over form doctrine was therefore dismissed due to the level of discretion involved and the inequitable results this approach would deliver. Furthermore, the substance over form doctrine led to the judiciary examining the taxpayer's intentions. Examining the substance of the deed and letter would essentially involve applying a purposive approach whereby the judge would ascertain what Parliament intended by the taxing provision and whether the taxpayer's case, in substance, fell within that provision. Consequently, the court adopted a literal approach to the facts as the annuity was evidenced in the deed of covenant despite the letter which spread doubt as to the nature of the payments. The court found no need to examine any surrounding substance as the covenant was clear. Therefore, it was unnecessary to "go beyond the legal effect of the agreements".[10] Instead, the court believed it was "necessary to treat the legal relations . . . as governed by the deed alone".[11]

Lord Atkin recognised the possible moral outrage that could arise from the decision as the wealthy Duke was able to reduce his tax liability. However, Lord

Atkin maintained that tax avoidance can be practised by anyone "whether poor and humble or wealthy and noble",[12] which indicates that it is a morally acceptable act and that the sum involved does not affect the acceptability of tax avoidance. Therefore, although the court in *Westminster* agreed that tax liability could potentially be decided through exercising discretion to ascertain the taxpayer's intentions, this method was considered neither desirable nor equitable. Importantly, the court warned against allowing sham transactions to be "used as cloak to conceal a different transaction"[13] where the "documents are not . . . intended to be acted upon".[14] This form of intention accords with Anscombe's analysis of an intention as she states that an intention can exist without action.[15] However, Lord Tomlin did not provide any guidance as to how to determine a taxpayer's intentions. This left the concept of intention vulnerable to manipulation. The issue as to what amounted to acceptable and unacceptable tax avoidance was also left open, although later cases suggested that the *Westminster* approach should be limited to those cases which involve a "single document".[16]

The desire to distinguish between cases involving one and many documents began as *Ramsay* involved a complex scheme with many documents, which was admittedly beyond the creative ambit of the average taxpayer. The scheme was designed to enable the taxpayer company, W.T Ramsay Ltd., to offset a chargeable gain against artificial capital losses on share transactions. The taxpayer's company banker, Slater Walker Ltd., gave the value of two loans[17] to the taxpayer to enable it to lend the money to Caithmeade Ltd. as an investment. A profit was made upon selling the debt as the loan was sold at market value. Therefore, the difference between the loan amount and the purchase price generated a gain. The taxpayer was also a shareholder in Caithmeade Ltd. Each loan was worth £218,750. However, the L2 loan was capable of being varied, which meant that the capital gain or loss could also be varied. The interest on L2 was duly increased to 22%, which decreased its value. The taxpayer then sold the value of Caithmeade's L2 debt, which had decreased substantially in value, to Masterdene Finance Ltd. Consequently, the original creditor essentially made a profit using a circular scheme, and the gain was taxable. The decision of whether the profit was a chargeable gain rested upon whether the L2 debt could be classified as a debt on security as its disposal would amount to a chargeable gain.[18]

There were strong arguments in favour of not taxing the taxpayer. Fundamentally, the legitimacy of the individual transactions could not be questioned as they were genuine and not shams. Therefore, in order to bring the genuine transactions into the realm of taxation, the substance of the arrangement was examined. However, the "cardinal principle"[19] exemplified in *Westminster* and echoed in *Ramsay* was that where a "document or transaction is genuine, the court cannot go behind it to some supposed underlying substance".[20] The court in *Ramsay* therefore warned that examining the substance of an arrangement is undesirable, although it then went on to do this. The legitimacy of the individual transactions faded in significance when the transactions were contrasted against the entirety of the scheme, which was labelled "artificial and fiscally ineffective".[21] The court decided to "consider the scheme as a whole".[22] This involved examining both the factual and legal reality of the arrangement through a different lens. Significantly, the *Ramsay* approach encouraged an assessment of the taxpayer's intention to discern whether the arrangement formed "the result which the parties actually intended".[23] However, as Anscombe stated, intentional actions cannot be recognised by "any extra feature which exists when it is performed".[24] Therefore, in many cases, it is difficult for the judiciary to discern what the taxpayers intended. Consequently, judges may impute a constructive intention on the taxpayer based on an objective analysis of what the person actually did.

The court in *Ramsay* believed that the reason for the scheme was to cancel out a gain made from the selling of the taxpayer's farm, which amounted to £187,977.[25] The whole aim of the "self-cancelling"[26] scheme was said to generate artificially a capital loss,[27] a conclusion based on mathematical findings. However, it is undesirable to allow mathematical evaluations to take precedence and create a principle whereby "the fiscal element has so invaded the transaction itself that it is moulded and shaped by the fiscal elements".[28] The court was contradictory in its approach by asserting that taxpayers are "only to be taxed upon clear words, not upon 'intendment'".[29] However, the court held that the nature of the "self-cancelling" transactions meant that they "were from the outset designed to produce neither gain nor loss".[30] Therefore, the court adopted Krikorian's definition of a purpose as he stated that "the purpose of an act . . . is observable in the results of that act".[31] The court went on to construe the facts in a holistic manner in order to fit the facts within the letter of the law. The undesirable practice of "reconstituting the facts"[32] into a "composite transaction"[33] was shielded behind the generally accepted purposive approach which the courts adopted. However, *Ramsay* clearly went further than utilising the purposive approach as the purposive approach does not involve examining the facts of the case holistically. The purposive approach involves examining the purpose of the applicable taxing provision.

The taxpayer's intentions were discussed where Lord Wilberforce asserted that the "gain is intended not to be taxable",[34] despite the fact that the taxpayer's presumed intention is an "expectation without contractual force".[35] Furthermore, although the court affirmed that intentions should not be examined, Lord Fraser held that the L2 loan "was intended to be exempt from corporation tax [and] . . . that intention has been successfully realised".[36] Therefore, Lord Wilberforce and Lord Fraser accord with Scheer's view on an intention "as an objective, end or goal".[37] The issue of motive was also raised, although it was stressed that "the fact that the motive for a transaction may be to avoid tax does not invalidate it".[38] Motive was therefore viewed as an unnecessary consideration. The court also had regard to what the taxpayers had "in mind when they devised the scheme"[39] and questioned "why the taxpayer had purchased the scheme",[40] although it was previously mentioned that tax avoidance motives are irrelevant. The use of motive in this sense accords with Millet's definition in which "'motive' is the reason why".[41]

Once the court thoroughly examined the taxpayer's motives and intentions in carrying out the scheme, the objective term "effect" was used frequently throughout the judgement, possibly to mask any subjective considerations. However, as

Anscombe argued, the fact that an action has a particular effect does not necessarily mean that it was intended.[42] Nevertheless, if the outcome was planned, it can be said that it was intended. Even the terms "aim" and "effect"[43] were blurred. The term "aim" reiterates the desire to examine the intention of the taxpayer, whereas "effect" is the more objective consideration which analyses the end result. The effect of the scheme, as a whole, was said to be that the taxpayer was relatively in the same position at the beginning and end of the scheme as no loss or gain was sustained. Lord Russell, Lord Roskill and Lord Bridge were all in agreement with Lord Wilberforce and Lord Fraser in regards to the points raised in this case.

Ramsay marked a significant change in how tax avoidance was subsequently perceived. The court commented that "the taxpayer does not have to put his hand in his pocket"[44] in tax avoidance schemes. However, it does raise the question of why tax avoidance is viewed negatively despite the fact that the taxpayer is typically "never in a position to make a profit".[45] Despite the court reaffirming that tax principles are for Parliament to devise,[46] the practice of rearranging schemes is "an indiscriminate adoration of substance",[47] and adopting a wide approach to interpreting legislation became known as the *Ramsay* approach. Since its creation, it has operated like a "doctrine to counter tax avoidance".[48] However, as later cases found, "it is much easier to state such a doctrine than to define its limits".[49]

2.2 The divide between supporters of *Ramsay* and *Westminster*

2.2 (a) Supporters of Ramsay

The conflicting cases of *Westminster* and *Ramsay* unsurprisingly created a notable division in subsequent case law, which generated supporters of either the *Westminster* approach or the *Ramsay* approach. For example, in *IRC v Burmah Oil Co Ltd.*[50] (*Burmah Oil*), the court extracted elements of the *Ramsay* approach by stating that the court can "ignore the intermediate circular book entries and look at the end result".[51] Therefore, whilst examining the end result and viewing the arrangement holistically were highlighted in *Ramsay*, *Burmah Oil* explicitly held that it was permissible to ignore some steps in an arrangement.

Burmah Oil concerned whether the parent company, Burmah, was entitled to deduct both the cost of shares and the sum of the acquisition of new shares in computing its tax liability. Burmah underwent a series of circular transactions involving the transfer of stock which Burmah owned in British Petroleum Company[52] to its subsidiary, OMDR (Holdings) Ltd.[53] The stock was later sold at a lower price and transferred back to Burmah, which resulted in a debt remaining from Holdings to Burmah, although this was not classified as an allowable loss by the court. The court contended that neither loss nor gain was made as the companies were in the same group. Another subsidiary of Burmah, Manchester Oil Refinery Holdings Ltd,[54] then borrowed from Burmah the same amount of debt owed by Holdings to Burmah. MORH then lent the loan to Holdings, which repaid the money it owed to Burmah on the same day. Holdings subsequently made a rights issue of shares, leading to Burmah applying for 700,000 shares in Burmah Oil Trading

Ltd.[55] Holdings then repaid its loan to MORH, which then repaid this to Burmah. Holdings was dissolved shortly after, and its only monetary asset was distributed to its shareholders, of which Burmah represented the majority.

The court preferred to examine the end result in *Burmah Oil* to reach the conclusion that there was no real loss sustained in the first circular scheme concerning the BP shares. The second circular scheme was also dismissed on the grounds that, although a loss was sustained by Burmah for its acquisition of shares in Holdings, the money was returned on liquidation and also when the debt owed by MORH was returned. The court also considered the value of the BP shares which could later be realised[56] and, as a result of this, stated that the taxpayers suffered "little or no hardship".[57]

As well as examining the end result, the court also examined the "clear and stated intention[s]"[58] of the taxpayers by asserting that the scheme was planned and executed "according to a timetable prepared in advance".[59] However, as Krikorian recognised, there can be a "growing purpose of which we become aware at a comparatively advanced stage of our action".[60] Moreover, Lord Fraser held that rather than purchasing the shares in Holdings,

> no doubt the directors could have chosen, even at that stage, to abandon the scheme but the reality was that the decision had already been taken to carry it through to completion, and that was unquestionably the intention of the directors in this case, just as it was the intention of all parties concerned in Ramsay.[61]

Therefore, the judges in *Burmah Oil* recognised that in determining whether a scheme was planned in advanced, the judges will evaluate the taxpayer's intentions. However, Lord Fraser criticised *Ramsay* for examining the taxpayer's purpose[62] and stated that "the fact that the purpose of the scheme was tax avoidance does not carry any implication that it was in any way reprehensible".[63] Nevertheless, *Burmah Oil* also extended the holistic approach in *Ramsay*. Lord Diplock stated that *Ramsay* heralded

> a significant change in the approach adopted by this House in its judicial role to a pre-ordained series of transactions . . . into which there are inserted steps that have no commercial purpose apart from the avoidance of a liability to tax which in the absence of those particular steps would have been payable.[64]

The key term in Lord Diplock's speech is "commercial purpose",[65] which requires schemes to be examined holistically with a view to ascertaining whether they have a commercial purpose. The judge also considered "whether certain transactions, which on the face of them and according to the taxpayer's submission, resulted in an allowable capital loss, should be disregarded as artificial".[66] Therefore, the concept of what is real and what is artificial also forms part of the *Ramsay* approach.

Interestingly, *Burmah Oil* demonstrated a distinct preference for the *Ramsay* approach by attacking the decision in *Westminster* for failing to define the limits of permissible tax avoidance,[67] despite the fact that *Ramsay* equally fails to define the parameters of unacceptable tax avoidance. Therefore, it can be argued that *Burmah Oil*'s apparent allegiance to the *Ramsay* approach is unjustified. However, Lord Scarman confirmed that "Ramsay's case marks a significant change in the approach 'adopted by this House in its judicial role' towards tax avoidance schemes".[68] Lord Roskill and Lord Brandon were also in agreement with both Lord Fraser and Lord Diplock on the issues raised in this case.

The *Ramsay* approach was also endorsed in *Furniss v Dawson*[69] (*Furniss*). The judges in *Furniss* extended the *Ramsay* approach by including that a planned or "preordained series of transactions"[70] is also indicative of an unacceptable tax avoidance scheme. The additional "preordained" element requires that the taxpayer has carefully planned the scheme and intends to follow it through to the end. The test assumes that there is "little or no likelihood that [they] would do otherwise".[71] However, Krikorian has recognised that if a person discovers "new suggestions and possibilities . . . the final result can hardly be described as the realisation of a preconceived plan".[72] In *Furniss*, the taxpayers and the wife of Mr Dawson were shareholders in two companies which they sought to sell to Wood Bastow Holdings Ltd. Mr Dawson consulted with solicitors to ascertain how stamp duty could be avoided when making the transaction. The solicitor advised the taxpayers to reorganise the share capital of the companies to be sold and establish a new investment company in the Isle of Man, which they named Greenjacket Investments Ltd. The new company, Greenjacket, then acquired the reorganised share capital in order for it to then sell the shares to Wood Bastow Holdings Ltd., the original buyers, for the original price. *Furniss* followed the decision in *Ramsay* by examining the end result and discarded the additional step of setting up the Manx company. The court therefore treated the transaction as the original sellers making the disposition directly to the original purchaser.[73] The method of examining the end result of a transaction was defended as "not . . . to remould the transactions but to re-analyse them".[74] This assertion suggests that the courts recognise it is undesirable to modify the facts of the case, although the court effectively remoulded the scheme by examining it holistically.

Furniss discussed the taxpayers' intentions at length due to the fact that "there was nothing sham about"[75] the transactions; therefore, the court took a different route to secure tax liability. The preordained arrangement of the selling of the shares to Wood Bastow Holdings Ltd. to take place at the end of the scheme was said to have "intended to operate as such".[76] Therefore, the intentions of the taxpayers were a material consideration in the eventual decision. Although the cases supporting *Ramsay* affirm that examining the facts holistically is objective, Kerr L.J. refined the holistic approach by scrutinising the "overall assessment of what the taxpayer intended to achieve".[77] Kerr L.J.'s approach admits an inextricable connection between the holistic approach and the taxpayer's intentions. Nevertheless, Kerr L.J. asserted that the motive of taxpayers is irrelevant.[78] The taxpayers' intentions were a focal point in *Furniss* and were referred to at numerous points within the judgement. The court found that "what happened was what had all along been intended to happen".[79] *Furniss* also refined the parameters of the *Ramsay* approach. With regard to the "preordained"[80] requirement, the court held that *Ramsay*

> established that where one finds a series of preconceived transactions which are entered on solely for fiscal purposes and are clearly interconnected and mutually dependent on one another one should look at the overall transaction to ascertain what has been and what was intended to be achieved.[81]

Therefore, *Furniss* established that both the intention of the parties and the purpose of the arrangement form part of the *Ramsay* approach. The reference to the interconnection of the steps in the arrangement also signifies that there is usually no flexibility in these types of transactions.

Lord Bridge rationalised *Furniss* using the substance over form doctrine as he stated that this was appropriate given that the case involved a series of transactions.[82] Lord Bridge explained that there were "two features of the pre-ordained scheme [which] were purely formal and had no effect on the substance of the composite transaction".[83] The first preordained element in the case was "to avoid a direct disposal of the shares to Wood Bastow".[84] The second preordained element was designed "to ensure that . . . the beneficial interest in the shares was held by Greenjacket".[85]

Lord Brightman also sought to further define the parameters of the *Ramsay* approach in *Furniss*. In regards to a "preordained series of transactions",[86] Lord Brightman held that "Ramsay says that this fiscal result cannot be avoided because the preordained series of steps are to be found in an informal arrangement instead of in a binding contract".[87] Therefore, Lord Brightman widened the *Ramsay* approach by explaining that "the day is not saved for the taxpayer because the arrangement is unsigned or contains the words 'this is not a binding contract'".[88] Lord Brightman also refined the *Ramsay* approach into a two-stage test. He stated that "first, there must be a pre-ordained series of transactions; or, if one likes, one single composite transaction".[89] However, Lord Brightman elucidated that "this composite transaction may or may not include the achievement of a legitimate commercial (i.e. business) end".[90] He was careful to include that a set of facts can fall under the *Ramsay* approach even where there was a genuine business result as "the composite transaction does, in the instant case; it achieved a sale of the shares in the operating companies by the Dawsons to Wood Bastow. It did not in Ramsay".[91] However, in the second stage of the test, Lord Brightman stated that "there must be steps inserted which have no commercial (business) *purpose* apart from the avoidance of a liability to tax – not "no business *effect*".[92] Therefore, Lord Brightman emphasised the difference between a business purpose and a business effect. Under the *Ramsay* approach, it is the existence of a business purpose, not a business effect, which will make the approach applicable. *Ramsay* was applicable in *Furniss* because "the inserted step was the introduction of Greenjacket"[93] and "that inserted step had no business purpose apart from the deferment of tax, although it had a business effect".[94]

Lord Roskill exemplified his disapproval of the *Westminster* approach in *Furniss*. He claimed that

> Westminster . . . has haunted the administration of this branch of the law for too long. I confess that I had hoped that that ghost might have found quietude with the decisions in Ramsay and in Burmah. Unhappily it has not. Perhaps the decision of this House in these appeals will now suffice as exorcism.[95]

Lord Roskill also criticised judicial opinions which sought to rely on the *Westminster* approach.[96] This criticism was evident where he held that "the error, if I may venture to use that word, into which the courts below have fallen is that they have looked back to 1936 and not forward from 1982".[97] Therefore, Lord Roskill expressed his preference for the *Ramsay* approach as opposed to the *Westminster* approach as the former was heard in 1982, and the latter was heard in 1936. Nevertheless, *Westminster* was decided in the House of Lords, and its importance should not be undermined.

Lord Scarman emphasised the role of the judiciary in deciding tax avoidance cases.[98] He held that it would be too "ambitious . . . to determine finally the limit beyond which the safe channel of acceptable tax avoidance shelves into the dangerous shallows of unacceptable tax evasion".[99] As mentioned earlier in *Burmah Oil*, Lord Scarman in *Furniss* also discussed the *Westminster* approach as to "the limits within which this principle is to operate remain to be probed and determined judicially".[100] Defining the limits of the *Westminster* approach was said to be "beyond the power of the blunt instrument of legislation".[101] Lord Scarman concluded that ultimately, judges mould the field of tax avoidance as

> whatever a statute may provide, it has to be interpreted and applied by the courts: and ultimately it will prove to be in this area of judge-made law that our elusive journey's end will be found.[102]

In *Ensign Tankers (Leasing) Ltd. v Stokes*[103] (*Ensign Tankers*), the court also favoured the *Ramsay* approach over the *Westminster* approach and focused on the taxpayer's purpose for executing the arrangement. The taxpayer in *Ensign Tankers* sought to claim a first-year allowances for capital expenditure amounting to $14 million, which was expended on the production of a film. In reality, the appellants, which consisted of a partnership of four companies, expended $3.25 million and were not liable to pay any more than this. The transactions, which were evidenced in 17 documents, were classified as a "single composite transaction",[104] which is a concept taken from *Ramsay*.[105] The scheme was classified as a tax avoidance scheme as the first-year allowance which the appellant was claiming was equal to the film's total cost.

The court examined the effect of the transaction, which was essentially viewing the scheme holistically as in *Ramsay*.[106] Furthermore, the court allowed the purpose of the taxpayers to be decisive of the fiscal consequences by asserting that the taxpayers "entered into a scheme with the object of avoiding tax".[107] The court did not choose to focus only on those transactions with a commercial purpose but rather "ignore[d] all the fiscal consequences which [were] beneficial to the taxpayer".[108] *Ensign Tankers* is an example of how the legislation permits the court to assess the taxpayer's purpose as section 41(1) of the Finance Act 1971 states that the expenditure must be made "for the purposes of the trade".[109] Therefore, *Ensign Tankers* is an exception to the general rule established in *Burmah Oil* that tax avoidance purposes are irrelevant.

Lord Templeman reasoned the decision on the basis that "the tax advantage claimed by the taxpayer . . . [was] inconsistent with the true effect in law of the transaction".[110] Therefore, he held that "in the present case the fiscal consequences claimed by the appellant do not correspond to the legal consequences of the scheme documents read and construed as a whole".[111] However, Lord Templeman also stated that "a taxpayer who chooses a form of transaction which reduces his burden of tax is not to be criticised or punished or deprived of that reduction in tax which his ingenuity has achieved".[112] Moreover, Lord Templeman acknowledged that

> Victory Partnership expended capital in the making and exploitation of a film. That was a trading transaction which was not a sham and could have resulted in either a profit or a loss.[113]

Nevertheless, he held that the case involved "the planning and execution of a raid on the Treasury using the technicalities of revenue law and company law as the necessary weapons".[114]

Lord Templeman also raised the moral issue of the fact that

> if successful, the scheme would have been operated at the expense of the British public and, whether successful or unsuccessful, involved the exploitation of British capital allowances for the making of a foreign film.[115]

Nevertheless, Lord Templeman recognised that tax law and morality should remain separate as "there is no morality in a tax and no illegality or immorality in a tax avoidance scheme".[116] Lord Brandon[117] and Lord Keith[118] both concurred with Lord Templeman on the issues he raised. Questions of the appropriateness of moral considerations in tax law will be examined in chapter 5.

Lord Goff defined unacceptable tax avoidance to convey that the facts in *Ensign Tankers* fit within his definition.[119] He stated that

> unacceptable tax avoidance typically involves the creation of complex artificial structures by which, as though by the wave of a magic wand, the taxpayer conjures out of the air a loss, or a gain, or expenditure, or whatever it may be, which otherwise would never have existed. These structures are designed to achieve an adventitious tax benefit for the taxpayer, and in truth are no more than raids on the public funds at the expense of the general body of taxpayers, and as such are unacceptable.[120]

Lord Goff emphasised the importance of examining the transactions in the case as a "composite transaction".[121] He explained that

> it is that composite transaction which we have to analyse, as a whole, in order to ascertain its true nature and effect, and to decide whether the transaction so analysed results, on a true construction of the relevant statutory provision, in the taxation consequences for which the taxpayer contends"[122]

Lord Goff also expressed that "self-cancelling payments . . . are typical examples of artificial transactions, the sole purpose of which is the avoidance of tax".[123]

Lord Jauncey acknowledged the acceptability of tax avoidance where he held that

> when Parliament has provided that a taxpayer shall be entitled to certain allowances in certain circumstances I can see no reason in principle why when those circumstances exist he should be deprived of those allowances simply because he has sought and failed to engineer a situation in which he obtained allowances greater than those to which the circumstances entitled him.[124]

However, he qualified this tolerance of tax avoidance by stating that

> where, as here, there is . . . an end result which has both financial and fiscal consequences, the proper approach is to disregard the steps in this scheme which have no commercial purpose rather than to treat those steps as somehow affecting or denaturing other steps in the scheme having such a purpose.[125]

IRC v McGuckian[126] (*McGuckian*) also praised "the new *Ramsay* principle"[127] for liberating tax law from being "left behind as some island of literal interpretation"[128] by promoting the purposive approach as a means through which tax avoidance schemes could be prevented rather than for legislation to be better understood. In *McGuckian*, the taxpayers sought to avoid tax payable on dividends despite the fact that there is a charge to income tax where someone overseas makes a gain which is enjoyed by a person domiciled in the UK under s478 of the Income and Corporation Taxes Act 1970. The taxpayers had an equal share in the company Ballinamore. The shares in Ballinamore were transferred to a trustee of a Guernsey settlement named Shurltrust Ltd., with the taxpayers as the beneficiaries. When a dividend of £400,055 became due, the trustee assigned to another company, Mallardchoice Ltd., the right to any dividend ordinarily payable to Ballinamore. Mallardchoice Ltd. paid £396,054 as consideration for the assignment. Ballinamore declared the dividend on shares held by Shurltrust and gave a cheque to their solicitor for Mallardchoice Ltd. The solicitor gave 99% of the sum to Shurltrust Ltd. and gave 1% to Mallardchoice Ltd. The assessment to income tax was on the £396,054 received by Shurltrust Ltd. The court asserted that the assignment between Mallardchoice Ltd. and Shurltrust Ltd. should be disregarded for fiscal purposes. Therefore, the holistic approach in *Ramsay* was again followed by "stripping out the artificial steps and applying the provisions of Taxes Acts to the real transaction".[129]

McGuckian undoubtedly went further than merely echoing the purposive approach in *Ramsay*. The court overtly enquired into the thought process of those involved in the scheme. Although *Ensign Tankers* established that the arrangement's purpose can be deciphered objectively, in *McGuckian*, the court held that

> given the genesis of the composite transaction in the mind of the tax consultant, Mr Taylor, the only possible inference is that the assignment was inserted for the sole purpose of gaining a tax advantage.[130]

Therefore, it is apparent how the purpose of an arrangement can be decided through subjective considerations. However, when discussing tax avoidance purposes, Lord Clyde made it clear that

> it is not required that the transaction should itself be carried out with that purpose. The statute is simply expressing the purpose of the section, not of the substance of the transaction.[131]

Section 478 of the Income and Corporation Taxes Act 1970 was drafted "for the purpose of preventing the avoiding by individuals ordinarily resident in the United Kingdom of liability to income tax".[132] Even though the applicable legislation had an anti-avoidance provision, Lord Clyde stated that tax avoidance purposes are still irrelevant. However, Lord Browne-Wilkinson gave more importance to the purpose of the transactions than their effect. He claimed that

> the question is not what was the effect of the insertion of the artificial steps but what was its purpose. Having identified the artificial steps inserted with that purpose and disregarded them, then what is left is to apply the statutory language of the taxing Act to the transaction carried through stripped of its artificial steps.[133]

Therefore, *McGuckian* reinforced the notion that the purpose of the individual transactions should be sought rather than the entire arrangement. Consequently, it can be said that the judges examined the "purposive result"[134] as exemplified by Krikorian.

The cases supporting *Ramsay* generally focused on examining either the purpose of the taxpayer or the purpose of the arrangement. The court in *McGuckian* also tried to make it clear that it "refer[red] not to the intention of the transferor of the assets or the effect of such transfer but to the intention of Parliament in enacting the section".[135] This is because Lord Steyn believed that *Ramsay* was

> founded on a broad purposive interpretation, giving effect to the intention of Parliament. The principle enunciated in *Ramsay* was therefore based on an orthodox form of statutory interpretation.[136]

Interestingly, Lord Clyde perceptively distinguished between the purpose of the relevant taxing provision and the taxpayer's purpose.[137] He emphasised that it is unnecessary to prove that the taxpayer had a tax avoidance purpose.[138] Nonetheless, the court placed great importance on the *Ramsay* approach by emphasising that it "is an approach to construction"[139] which was viewed as an "intellectual breakthrough".[140]

Lord Cooke also placed great emphasis on the *Ramsay* approach as he stated that "the matter is clinched by the authority of *W T Ramsay Ltd.* . . . and the subsequent cases in the same line".[141] In addition to this, he stated that "the principle of looking on a planned series of steps as a whole transaction appears to be, as one would expect, perfectly natural and orthodox".[142] Moreover, Lord Cooke expressed his disapproval of *Westminster* as he stated that *Ramsay* is "decidedly more natural and less extreme than the decision which in 1935 a majority of their Lordships felt forced to reach in the *Duke of Westminster's case*".[143] Lord Lloyd concurred with the decision of the other judges.[144]

2.2 (b) Supporters of Westminster

Despite the overwhelming support for the *Ramsay* approach, the more recent cases have tended to uphold the *Westminster* approach. *Westmoreland Investments Ltd.* v *MacNiven*[145] (*Westmoreland*) viewed the *Ramsay* approach negatively and as operating like "a broad spectrum antibiotic which killed off all tax avoidance schemes".[146] *Westmoreland* rightly challenged the propriety of using *Ramsay* as a principle of construction as "there is . . . only one principle of construction, namely to ascertain what Parliament meant by using the language of the statute".[147] The *Ramsay* approach instead focuses on "arithmetical differences"[148] under the guise of statutory interpretation, which effectively became "judicial legislation".[149]

The scheme in *Westmoreland* was circular; therefore, it could be said to fall within the ambit of the *Ramsay* approach as the borrower paid interest received from the lender. Westmoreland Investments Ltd.[150] was owned by the Electricity Supply Pension Scheme,[151] which was a superannuation and exempt from tax.[152] WIL had financial difficulties and borrowed £20 million from the scheme. On the same day, WIL paid the scheme back £14,760,00 and accounted to the Revenue for £5,459,400 which the scheme was able to reclaim. The scheme was repeated the following year and again in 1990 until the scheme had £2 million worth of assets and found a purchaser of WIL. However, the court in *Westmoreland* did not view the transactions as an impermissible tax avoidance scheme. Examining the motive of the taxpayer was considered wholly irrelevant as "one cannot disregard a transaction which comes within the statutory language . . . simply on the ground that it was entered into solely for tax reasons".[153] Furthermore, the court rationally expressed a dislike for common law tests and held that it is "the statute itself which applies the tests of ordinary business".[154] Therefore, the decision in *Westmoreland* is the antithesis of *Ramsay*.

Barclays Mercantile Business Finance v Mawson[155] (*Barclays*) also refused to consider the intention of the taxpayers and classed the incidences which made up the scheme as "happenstances"[156] rather than pre-planned. In *Barclays*, the taxpayer ran a business of providing capital to purchase an asset which was paid for by periodic payments wherein the asset was the security enabling the selling of the asset in the event of defaulting on the payments. The taxpayer bought capital equipment comprising a gas pipeline from a seller who leased it at below market value. The difference in price was the seller's fee, although the seller returned the money to the taxpayer's company as a security. The taxpayer, in arithmetical terms, did not make a loss as it reclaimed the money spent. However, the taxpayer claimed depreciation deductions. It was held that the deduction was within the statute as a capital investment.

Barclays criticised supporters of the *Ramsay* approach for essentially "reconstituting the facts"[157] in order to entrap the taxpayer within the purview of the taxing statute. The mere presence of allowable deductions could not have "infected the whole scheme".[158] Therefore, the scheme could not be viewed as a sham. The fact that the scheme "was not an entirely risk free transaction"[159] also served to reinforce the notion of a genuine transaction. Therefore, the more risk involved in an arrangement, the more likely it will be regarded as genuine. *Barclays* marked a significant step in tax avoidance due to claims that it "killed off the *Ramsay* doctrine".[160]

The conjoined appeals within *Craven v White*[161] (*Craven*) can be said to have created an additional test of remoteness which examines the preordained requirement in reverse. The remoteness test essentially asks how remote the end result is at the time of the intermediate transactions rather than seeking to establish whether the whole arrangement was preordained, the latter being broader and having greater scope for judicial discretion. The facts of the case were similar to those in *Furniss*. The taxpayers in *Craven* owned all the shares in the company Queensferry and were advised by their financier to either merge the business with another or sell it. Both options presented themselves as equally feasible. Whilst negotiations took place to decide whether a merger or sale could be executed, the taxpayers acquired another company in the Isle of Man named Millor. As part of the scheme, Millor acquired the share capital of Queensferry in exchange for shares in Millor. Millor then found a buyer for Queensferry and sold it to the company J Ltd. for over £2 million. From 1977 to 1981, Millor began to make interest-free loans to the taxpayers until eventually, all the proceeds from the sale were transferred. The taxpayers were then assessed to capital gains tax on the disposal of the shares by Millor to J Ltd. Had the court applied the *Ramsay* approach, the conclusion would have been that the exchange of shares between Millor and Queensferry "had no business purpose apart from the avoidance of tax".[162] There were also arguments that the "dominant, if not the sole, motive"[163] was to secure a tax advantage.[164] However, the court maintained the approach heralded in *Westminster*: that a taxpayer can select the most tax-advantageous route in arranging their transactions.[165] Moreover, regarding the final sale of Queensferry, it was "wholly uncertain whether that disposal [would] take place".[166] This element of remoteness therefore served to uphold the scheme's legitimacy.

Furniss and *Craven* were similar on the facts of the cases, although the significant feature which distinguished them was the likelihood of the final sale. In *Craven*, it was "wholly uncertain whether that disposal [would] take place".[167] The certainty of the arrangement was further weakened as, prior to the sale, "neither the identity of the purchaser nor the price to be paid nor any of the other terms of the contract [were] known".[168] Therefore, the final sale was too remote to be classified as preordained. However, this extra-statutory caveat is inadequate to distinguish two very similar cases which both otherwise came within the letter of the law and could be viewed as acceptable tax avoidance.

In *Tower MCashback LLP 1 and another v Revenue and Customs Commissioners*[169] (*Tower MCashback*), the Supreme Court also adopted the *Ramsay* approach which was referred to as "the fountain-head".[170] The taxpayers wanted to claim capital allowances on expenditures on software rights. MCashback was the company which created the software, which manufacturers could use to advertise their products to customers.[171] In return for promoting their products, manufacturers agreed to pay MCashback a "clearing fee".[172] In order to raise money to promote the software, MCashback was advised by a financial services company, Tower Group plc, to sell the rights to part of its software to newly formed LLPs.[173] The newly formed LLPs were also entitled to part of the clearing fees. LLP2 "claimed an allowable loss of just under £30 million, £27.5 million of which was for capital allowances".[174] Lord Hope explained the matter succinctly when he stated that the matter was

> whether the whole of the £27.5m paid by LLP2 to MCashback under the terms of the software licence agreement was expenditure incurred by LLP2 on the provision of software within the meaning of the Capital Allowances Act 2001.[175]

He elucidated how parts of the arrangement were not artificial as the "transfer of ownership was itself enough to show that real expenditure was incurred".[176] However, Lord Hope held that

> much of the consideration paid by the LLPs for the software was derived from funds borrowed by members of the LLPs on non-recourse terms which was immediately passed back by way of a chain of banks to the lender.[177]

These series of events were regarded as "pre-ordained"[178] and amounted to a "composite transaction".[179] Much of the funds "did not go to MCashback as payment for the rights in the software, even temporarily".[180] Contrary to the Capital Allowances Act 2001, it could not be proven that "the whole of the claimed expenditure of £27.5 million was *actually incurred* on acquiring rights in the software".[181] However, Lord Walker stated that the LLPs "themselves put up only 25% of the consideration",[182] and "the remaining 75% was provided by interest-free loans".[183] Therefore, Lord Walker concluded that the taxpayers would be entitled to an allowance of 25% of the expenditure claimed.[184]

Lord Walker emphasised that following *Barclays*, "it is not enough for the revenue, in attacking a scheme of this sort, to point to the money going round in a circle".[185] However, he held that

> there was not, in any meaningful sense, an incurring of expenditure of the borrowed money in the acquisition of software rights. It went into a loop in order to enable the LLPs to indulge in a tax avoidance scheme.[186]

Ascertaining the purpose of the arrangement was central to the case as

> the transfer of ownership (or at least of rights) indicated the reality of some expenditure on acquiring those rights, but was not conclusive as to the whole of the expenditure having been for that purpose.[187]

Therefore, the court did not allow the taxpayers to claim more than the amount that was actually expended on the acquisition of the software rights.

The effect of having a divide between the *Ramsay* approach and the *Westminster* approach is that some judges will examine the motive, intention or purpose of the taxpayer while others will focus on whether the facts fall within the ambit of the law and, therefore, the intention of Parliament. The danger with the former approach is that it can eclipse what Parliament intended simply because a tax advantage existed or the degree of certainty in an arrangement was too great. However, the battle between the *Ramsay* approach and *Westminster* approach was finally put to rest when the GAAR was introduced. The GAAR guidance specifically states that it provides an "overriding statutory limit".[188] The guidance also accuses a line of cases which support acceptable tax avoidance, including *Westminster*, as "providing legitimacy to even the most abusive tax avoidance schemes".[189]

2.3 Motive, intention and purpose considered across other areas of tax law

To support the hypothesis that judges hearing tax avoidance cases examine the taxpayer's motive, intention or purpose, it is helpful to scrutinise case law from other areas of tax law to establish whether assessing motive, intention and purpose is a common theme. If these considerations are proven to be a common theme across other areas of tax law, it will strengthen the argument that the GAAR may also encourage these factors to be examined in tax avoidance. Case law which decided whether trade profits should be taxed has shown a tendency to explore the taxpayer's motive in determining tax liability. Similarly, in classifying the income and capital distinction, the subjective thoughts of the taxpayer in making the expenditure are often taken into account. To a lesser extent, accountancy has shown evidence of examining the taxpayer's subjective state of mind in determining tax liability to their detriment.

2.3 (a) Trades, professions and vocations

The charge to income tax on trade profits is laid down under s5 of the Income Tax (Trading and Other Income) Act 2005,[190] which details that tax is payable "on the profits of a trade, profession or vocation".[191] The legislation does not expressly state how courts should decide whether a taxpayer is trading but merely states that a "'trade' includes any venture in the nature of trade".[192] The Royal Commission on Taxation of Income and Profits[193] developed badges of trade to assist with determining whether a person is trading. Motive is openly one of the badges of trade. In this area of tax law, courts are permitted to explore a taxpayer's motive where a transaction is considered equivocal in order to ascertain why the taxpayer embarked on a course of action. Specifically, courts usually assess whether there exists a "profit motive".[194] However, due to the highly unscientific results which considering a taxpayer's motive would cause, motive is only relied on where the facts are ambiguous. The motive badge is also optional, indicating that not all cases are required to consider it. In addition to the motive badge, case law has established that "trading requires an intention to trade".[195]

Earlier case law which sought to ascertain the existence of a business placed greater emphasis on the internal workings of the business rather than profits. For example, in *Bramwell v Lacy*[196] (*Bramwell*), the court did not find it relevant that a hospital which treated limited illnesses accepted voluntary payments rather than regular remuneration by those who could afford it. The mere fact that the hospital was "in the nature" of a business"[197] was sufficient to hold that there was a breach of covenant which forbade the establishment of a business. Despite this strict interpretation of what constitutes a business, the court also held that "whether it is a business carried on for the purposes of profit or not, is not . . . material".[198] Although the term "purpose" is used, Jessel M.R. is essentially referring to the irrelevancy of a profit motive. Therefore, the case illustrates that a profit motive is not always relevant. However, in subsequent case law, the existence of a profit motive was found to be of great importance.

Resembling *Bramwell*, profit motives were equally unimportant in *Religious Tract and Book Society of Scotland v R.S. Forbes*[199] (*Forbes*). The case involved a religious book society. The society owned two bookshops which were undoubtedly taxable entities. However, the society also had colporteurs who visited people's homes selling books and "administering religious advice and counsel".[200] Their colportage activities were funded by the money acquired from subscriptions; however, it was running at a loss, and it was questioned whether it could amount to a trade despite the lack of a profit and a profit motive.[201] Unlike in *Bramwell*, the voluntary nature of the payments was not given weight. The lack of a profit motive was described as "an intentional loss".[202] Therefore, rather than a profit motive, the court found the existence of a loss motive, indicating that motive remained significant.[203] However, the tax realities of the colportage activities were decisive in concluding that it was distinct from the profit-making businesses and, therefore, not a trade. The tax realities were that the losses arising from the colportage undertakings were not set off against the profits made from the businesses for tax purposes.[204] It is doubtful whether the court would arrive at the same conclusion if the facts had indicated a profit rather than loss, which may have led to the conferral of a profit motive. *Forbes* therefore established that an intention to make a profit is important in order for an activity to be classified as a trade.

As demonstrated by case law in this area, where the courts affix a constructive motive on the taxpayer, it can create inequitable results. For example, in *Wisdom v Chamberlain*[205] (*Wisdom*), the taxpayer bought £200,000 worth of silver bullion to safeguard against the possible devaluation of the British pound. The taxpayer argued that rather than to produce a gain, the aim of the purchase was to safeguard against a possible loss in the event the pound devalued.[206] However, the pound did not devalue, and the value of silver increased unexpectedly, leading to the taxpayer making a profit when he later sold his silver bullion. Rather than examine whether the taxpayer was motivated by making a profit, the court held that making a profit was not the taxpayer's purpose, stating that "the fact that it was not an expected profit is really quite irrelevant".[207] Contradictorily, Harman L.J. later stated that the taxpayer's purpose was to make a profit and that this was relevant, asserting that "the whole object of the transaction was to make a profit".[208] A profit-making purpose was therefore imputed by the courts in concluding that the taxpayer was trading. *Wisdom* illustrates how courts can consider or disregard the taxpayer's purpose at will. The case also demonstrates how purposes can be imputed by the courts even where it is not entirely clear what the taxpayer's purpose was. Moreover, as Krikorian argued, a person can have "complex [and] confusing purposes".[209]

As in *Wisdom*, the court in *Iswera v Commissioner of Inland Revenue*[210] (*Iswera*) overlooked the taxpayer's explanation for purchasing acres of land as her true motive would have negated trading. The taxpayer purchased a site of over two acres for the purpose of residing there to be closer to her daughters' school. A large amount of land was bought as the seller refused to sell her the modest plot of land she wanted in isolation. Therefore, the taxpayer later sold the surplus land. She was taxed on the difference between the market value of the land and the remaining balance owed after the sale of the surplus land. The court could not escape the appellant's primary purpose of her wanting to be nearer to her daughters' school. Consequently, the court sought to neutralise the issue of subjective influences by adding that "too much emphasis has been put on motivation",[211] and a taxpayer's "purpose or object alone cannot prevail over what he in fact does".[212] Nevertheless, the court paradoxically, and contrary to the decision in *Bramwell*, concluded by stating that the appellant's "dominant motive was to make a profit".[213] However, the taxpayer's purpose was arguably to be nearer her daughter's school; therefore, it is "difficult to see how motive can . . . be relevant in cases of such clarity".[214] By ensuring the motive test remains optional, courts can consider motive where it indicates trading or omit a motive assessment even where the taxpayer's motive is clearly unrelated to trading.

Despite the court in *Ramsay* emphasising the importance of the context of transactions,[215] in *Iswera*, the court ignored the wider context of why the land was purchased. The purpose of buying the land to reside closer to her daughters' school was viewed as immaterial and not given weight. Furthermore, the fact that she was essentially "forced to purchase a quantity of land which she neither wanted nor needed"[216] was also deemed unimportant, despite the fact that this reflected her motives and revealed that there was a lack of a profit motive. *Iswera* is a good example of Ashworth and Horder's point that people generally "do things with more than one intention in mind".[217]

Conversely, the court in *Kirkham v Williams*[218] (*Kirkham*) held that the taxpayer was not trading despite the profit which the taxpayer made upon reselling his property. The taxpayer was a demolition contractor who had differences of opinion with his local authority over storing his materials at his mother's home address. After demolishing buildings for a client, he bought the remaining land at Havannah Mills to store his materials and establish an office. From 1977 to 1982, the taxpayer used the land for limited farming activities such as growing crops and rearing calves for future reselling. Soon after purchasing the land, the taxpayer sought planning permission for the construction of a dwelling-house, which was granted in 1980. The Havannah Mills property was sold two years later to buy Sandy Lane farm. He was assessed to income tax for the profit made on the sale of Havannah Mills, under the assumption that the property was trading stock. An in-depth exploration into the taxpayer's intentions was made in conjunction with the timing of the transactions in order to ascertain whether he was trading. The court concluded that "it was never the taxpayer's intention . . . to purchase Havannah Mills as a residence for himself",[219] as he acquired planning permission for the dwelling-house subsequent to the purchase of Havannah Mills. The need for office space made the taxpayer's alleged "subsidiary purpose"[220] of profiting from the sale of the property implausible as this could not be "implemented concurrently with his principal purpose"[221] of finding a storage place.

The fundamental difference between *Iswera* and *Kirkham* was how the taxpayers' respective intentions and purposes were construed. Significantly, both courts distinguished between primary and secondary purposes. In *Iswera*, the court held that her primary purpose was to trade, and living nearer her daughters' school was her secondary purpose. Conversely, in *Kirkham*, the taxpayer's primary purpose was to obtain storage space, and his secondary purpose was the prospect of trading. The contrast between the two cases illustrates how the courts finely construe and categorise a taxpayer's purpose and the drastic impact of such categorisation, unconnected to fiscal realities. The taxpayer's purpose was determinative in these cases, and it is questionable whether the same decisions would be reached without considering the taxpayers' primary and secondary purposes. The court in *Kirkham* defended its decision by stating that the intention of the taxpayer and whether they plan to dispose of the property when they acquire it is conclusive.[222] However, the court's focus in *Iswera* was on what she planned to do with the building rather than why she bought the building, which unfairly disregards the fact that the taxpayer did not want to purchase the entire plot of land. From Krikorian's perspective, it can be said that, in *Iswera*, acquiring the plot of land was a "subordinate act",[223] which was a step executed in the overall plan rather than the predetermined eventual result. Furthermore, as in *Kirkham*, it cannot reasonably be argued that the taxpayer in *Iswera* was "driven by a desire to make a profit".[224] Both taxpayers bought properties for reasons other than profit, although both made a profit, which indicates that the same decision should have been reached in both cases. The decision in *Iswera* therefore illustrates how judges can consider parts of taxpayers' purpose to produce an inequitable result.

As discussed earlier, *Ensign Tankers* was concerned not only with the issue of tax avoidance but also with whether the taxpayer was trading. The express overlap between the two areas of tax law signifies that the courts can apply trading principles to tax avoidance: namely, the motive badge of trade. In *Ensign Tankers*, the Revenue sought to prove that the appellant companies were not trading to prevent them claiming first-year allowances of $14 million for capital expenditure on the production of the film. The taxpayer's purpose was very narrowly construed as Lord Templeman claimed that the arrangement was designed "with the object of avoiding tax and not with the object of trading".[225] It is interesting that the court found it pertinent to add that the taxpayer planned to avoid tax as simply stating that they were not trading would have been sufficient. The court instead concluded that the taxpayer could not be trading as they planned to avoid tax, as if to say both could not be their objective. However, Lord Templeman added that the solitary act of the partnership giving money for the film "would admittedly constitute trading".[226] Only $3.24 million of the $14 million claimed was considered to be the amount involved in the trade as the remaining sum was part of a tax avoidance scheme that operated "as a corporate cancer which infect[ed] and destroy[ed] any fiscal effect advantageous to the taxpayer".[227] However, it is inequitable that the tax avoidance element could ruin an otherwise legitimate scheme.

Despite earlier case law, the taxpayer's motive, intention and purpose are becoming increasingly more important. The case law on trading reveals great inconsistencies which derive from assessing the taxpayer's thoughts and the lack of attempting to establish broad general principles. *Bramwell* and *Forbes* demonstrate the greatest inconsistencies in relation to the relevance of a profit motive where voluntary payments are made. However, the existence of a profit or a profit motive is not one of the badges of trade which were devised in order to introduce uniformity to this area of law. The decisions in *Kirkham* and *Iswera* only serve to reinforce the inconsistencies which can arise from assessing the taxpayer's thoughts. Moreover, commentators have argued that "where . . . [motive] is used it seems to be an *ex post facto* justification for arriving at the result the court wanted to reach in any event".[228]

2.3 (b) Expenditure

In deciding whether expenditure may be deductible from a taxpayer's annual profit, the courts may examine the purpose behind making the payment as demonstrated by case law in this area. The ITTOIA 2005 sets out the conditions for deductible expenditure, including that the expense must be both income in nature and not capital[229] and "incurred wholly and exclusively for the purposes of the trade".[230]

Examining the taxpayer company's purpose based on the aims of the company and the detrimental consequences of not acting were objectively considered in *Lawson v Johnson Matthey Plc*[231] (*Lawson*). The parent company, Johnson Matthey (JM), sought to help its subsidiary bank (J.M.B) after it became insolvent due to financial difficulties. The financial hardship suffered by the subsidiary directly affected its parent company as it would attract negative publicity, and their creditors would also lose faith in the company and demand repayment of money.[232] The Bank of England agreed to buy the share capital of J.M.B for £1 on the condition that JM contributed £50 million into J.M.B. The scheme successfully enabled J.M.B to continue its business. The court concluded that the £50 million was a revenue payment as it "did not bring an asset into existence and did not procure an advantage for the enduring benefit of the trade".[233] Lord Goff was careful to convey that the decision was not reached on the basis of the taxpayer's motive or purpose.[234] However, he then went on to state that the £50 million provided was not for disposal of the shares but to salvage J.M.B and, therefore, examined the taxpayer's purpose.[235]

The ITTOIA 2005 specifically allows courts to consider the taxpayer's purpose by providing that there can be no deduction where the expenditure was disbursed for more than one purpose, even if one purpose is wholly and exclusively connected to the taxpayer's trade.[236] In contrast to the decision in *Lawson*, in *Mallalieu v Drummond*[237] (*Mallalieu*), the taxpayer's purpose was assessed to her detriment. A barrister sought to deduct the cost and upkeep of unobtrusive work wear which she was required to wear by the Bar Council. The court examined her purpose at the time of purchase and held, akin to *Iswera* and *Kirkham*, that she had "two objects in making the expenditure",[238] the second being the "preservation of warmth and decency".[239] However, the distinction between the taxpayer's primary and secondary purposes was seen to be less important than in *Iswera* and *Kirkham*. In *Mallalieu*, the court held that "it is immaterial . . . that the business purposes are the predominant purposes intended to be served"[240] as the unconscious motive was inextricably linked to her predominant purpose. The duality of influences, due to the courts imposing an unconscious motive, disallowed the deduction. Therefore, the decision in *Mallalieu* concurs with Stocks's notion that a person's motive can be "hidden not only from the spectator but even from the agent himself".[241] The judgement, however, does not accord well with those cases which "consistently maintained that . . . motive *by itself* is not relevant".[242]

An objective analysis was used in *Vodafone Cellular Ltd. v Shaw*[243] (*Vodafone*). The case concerned the lump sum of $30 million, which was sought to be deducted from the computation of profits after the taxpayer expended this sum to terminate a fee agreement. The taxpayer company was formed by a joint venture of the companies Millicom and Racal. Millicom agreed to grant the taxpayer company five licences to manufacture its products and incorporate them into equipment on the condition that it obtain an operating licence from the Department of

Trade and Industry (DTI). However, in order for the licence to be granted, the DTI insisted that the company should form two separate subsidiary companies for the network and sale of the business. The company subsequently entered into share and fee agreements with Millicom. The fee agreement included the manufacturing licences and the supplying of know-how as and when needed. The taxpayer agreed to pay a percentage of its profits for 15 years to Millicom in return for this. However, when Millicom's know-how became unnecessary, the fee agreement sought to be terminated, and the taxpayer company agreed to pay $30 million to extinguish their contractual liabilities to make recurring revenue payments. Rather than examine unsubstantiated motives, the court examined the agreement itself, concluding that it "was an ordinary commercial contract and not a capital asset".[244] The court characterised know-how as a service rather than an asset.[245] Furthermore, objectively, the agreement could not be classified as a capital asset as it did not represent "the whole or virtually the whole of the taxpayer company's business".[246]

The court agreed that the payment was revenue in nature, although questions regarding the taxpayer's intentions were raised in determining whether the payment was made wholly and exclusively for the purposes of the trade. If there was a dual purpose – namely, to benefit their subsidiary in terminating the agreement – it could not have been made wholly and exclusively for the taxpayer's trade. The court rightly refused to construe the taxpayer's intentions narrowly and held that it "did not consciously set out to benefit any particular one of them".[247] Moreover, the court asserted that questions of intention should be avoided as the "case does not involve an inquiry whether the directors . . . consciously intended to obtain a benefit".[248] The court also clearly made a distinction between subjective and objective considerations by examining the object which the taxpayer pursued in terminating the agreement rather than inquiring about the intended effects of the object materialising.[249] It was held that the object of the parent company was to benefit itself, and any other effect was incidental and remote. This approach supports Anscombe's view that "the inseparability of the effect is not a ground for regarding it as intended".[250] If this reasoning was used in *Mallalieu*, the case may have had a very different outcome to that which was decided.

Indian law in the area of expenditure follows UK law closely. India's Income Tax Act 1961 states that in order for an expense to be deductible, it must not be a capital expenditure nor a personal expense,[251] and it must be "expended wholly and exclusively for the purposes of business".[252] The Indian courts have approached the issue of compensation received from the termination of an agency contract with a UK company in a more straightforward manner. In *Commissioner of Income Tax v Shaw Wallace*,[253] the court held that the compensation was a revenue payment as taxpayers should only be taxed on profits earned through their business or for continuance of their business.[254] Therefore, no questions arose as to the taxpayer's motive.

American federal law governing deductible expenditure is akin to Indian law in this area. The Internal Revenue Code 1986 states that deductible expenses include "all the ordinary and necessary expenses . . . incurred . . . in carrying on any trade" and details examples of such expenditure.[255] The US case of *Pevsner v Commissioner of Internal Revenue*[256] (*Pevsner*) was similar to *Mallalieu*. The case involved the manager of a Yves St Laurent (YSL) boutique who was required to wear YSL clothing at work, commuting to and from work, at fashion shows and at business luncheons.[257] As in *Mallalieu*, the taxpayer claimed that she did not wear YSL clothing when she was off duty. Although the court reached the same decision as in *Mallalieu* in holding that the cost of the clothes could not be deducted, they did not consider the taxpayer's motives in reaching their decision. The court followed guidance from the decision reached in *Donnelly v Commissioner of Internal Revenue*[258] that clothing could be deductible where it is an occupational requirement, it cannot be worn in daily life, and the taxpayer does not use it as such.[259] The decision in *Pevsner* illustrates that the taxpayer's motive or unconscious motive does not need to be considered in reaching a fair decision. The court reiterated the importance of "an objective test [as it] . . . promote[s] substantial fairness among the greatest number of taxpayers".[260]

It is clear how the motive test can be manipulated to consider primary and secondary motives, impose constructive unconscious motives and disallow tax benefits due to the imposition of a constructive motive. From the *Vodafone* case, it is clear that the courts should not concern themselves with what the taxpayer intends or hopes are the effects of the transaction after it is made. An objective analysis of the taxpayer's purpose would therefore examine the taxpayer's object of the transaction and would be preferable.

2.3 (c) Accountancy standards

The taxpayer's intentions have also been considered in accountancy cases, particularly where a trader appropriates his or her own stocks and inconsistencies arise when profits and losses are brought into account. For example, in *Sharkey v Wernher*[261] (*Sharkey*), the taxpayer appropriated her stock for her own use in a non-arm's length transaction. She owned two enterprises: namely, a stud farm and racing stables. The stud farm engaged in profitable activities such as the selling of produce from the stud farm and the servicing of mares by the taxpayer's stallions, in exchange for fees. Therefore, the farm was undoubtedly classified as a taxable entity under s31(1)(a) of the Finance Act 1948. However, her private racing stables were not classified as a taxable entity as they were regarded as "recreational activities"[262] and, therefore, did not generate profits. In 1948, the taxpayer transferred five horses from her stud farm to her racing stables. The question in dispute was whether the taxpayer should be liable for income tax on the cost or market value of the horses, the latter being substantially higher. However, as the taxpayer entered the cost value of the transfer into her accounts, the court stated that she acquiesced that some value should be brought into account.[263] The court held that she should be taxed on the market value of the horses. The taxpayer's intentions were persuasive rather than decisive, although it is interesting that the court extracted the taxpayer's agreement to be taxed by her actions. However, as Anscombe argues, an intention can "often not be seen from seeing what he does".[264]

In *Sharkey*, it is clear that the taxpayer's intentions were used to extract the higher amount of tax. However, some may argue that *Sharkey* merely followed the principle previously established in *Watson Brothers v Hornby (HM Inspector of Taxes)*[265] (*Watson*). In *Watson*, day-old chicks were transferred from the appellant's hatchery business to the appellant's farm. It was held that a sum must be brought into account when computing the profits of the hatchery to reflect that the transfer was a taxable activity. Therefore, *Watson* established that a taxpayer must pay tax where they appropriate their trading stock under this principle. Unlike in *Sharkey*, the taxpayer sought to establish market value as the correct computation to demonstrate a loss as the market value was lower than the cost value. The Revenue argued that cost value was the correct computation. However, no reference to the taxpayer's motives was made, indicating that motive is an unnecessary consideration when ascertaining what value should be brought into account. However, in *Sharkey*, by following the decision in *Watson*, the court effectively departed from the decision in *Briton Ferry Steel Co Ltd. v Barry*,[266] which found cost value to be the correct value.

If the Revenue argues that cost or market value should be imputed into the taxpayer's accounts based on whichever sum is higher, it can generate precedential inconsistencies where the Revenue's will is adhered to. Indian courts have found fault with accepting market value as the correct computation. This is because market value assumes that the taxpayer intends to make a profit, and Indian courts have therefore held that "a man cannot be compelled to make a profit out of any particular transaction".[267] Furthermore, while the court in *Sharkey* took into account the market value of the transactions, Indian courts found it "unreal and . . . artificial to separate the business from its owner".[268] The uncertainty inherent in the adjudication allows judges to use their discretion to place greater weight on particular facts in order to arrive at certain decisions.[269]

It is apparent that the motive approach is considered widely across various areas of tax law. Therefore, it is unsurprising that the approach has leaked into the realms of tax avoidance. However, as demonstrated, the motive approach can cause considerable inconsistency and inequitable results, even in areas in which it is specifically permitted. Therefore, it is necessary to ascertain why the motive approach is utilised in tax avoidance.

2.4 Why the "motive approach" is considered

The concept of examining intentions is not intrinsically damaging, although when the intention of the taxpayer is considered, rather than Parliament's intention as evidenced in legislation, it can create broad approaches to deciding tax avoidance cases, such as the *Ramsay* approach. However, as demonstrated by the cases supporting *Ramsay*, the taxpayer's motive, intention or purpose is assessed by the courts. Therefore, it is helpful to examine why and when the taxpayer's motive, intention or purpose is taken into account in order to rationalise later whether applying the motive approach is necessary in calculating tax liability. As the taxpayer's intentions are usually evidenced in the documents used in tax avoidance schemes, it is important to understand the methods judges can use to import a constructive motive on the taxpayer. The move from objective considerations to subjective interpretations of tax cases will be observed further to reinforce the main hypothesis that the motive, intention or purpose of the taxpayer is frequently assessed in tax avoidance cases.

As previously mentioned, a long line of cases has arguably implemented the motive approach in deciding tax liability, although it is questionable as to why the motive approach may have been introduced in the area of tax avoidance. The motive approach also places much power in the hands of the judiciary. Therefore, it is necessary to examine the reasons behind such a conferral of power. Furthermore, assessing the relationship between the motive approach and the desire to secure tax liability can demonstrate why the motive approach is an effective anti-avoidance tool, particularly where an arrangement is complex or where large sums of money are involved.

In the cases which tended to consider the taxpayer's motives, intentions or purposes – namely, the cases supporting *Ramsay* – there was a general disapproval of tax avoidance schemes. Therefore, courts tended to defend their use of extra-statutory principles and extended them as demonstrated in *Furniss*, where there was a tax avoidance scheme which the court wished to obstruct. Consequently, the motive approach may be applied as a means to stifle tax avoidance schemes, which is plausible, given the government's graduating dislike of tax avoiders. Fundamentally, tax avoidance is permissible, which is why it is unclear as to why a "pre-planned tax-saving scheme"[270] should give rise to condemnation.

Importantly, where the court assesses the taxpayer's' motive, intention or purpose, it involves judicial discretion. Consequently, the motive approach in cases may have been upheld due to the fact that "discretion is also associated with a lower amenability to legal challenge as compared with rule-based decision making".[271]

As the motive approach is a product of judicial discretion, it enjoys a considerable degree of immunity from being abandoned in subsequent cases. On the other hand, Parliament's explicit intention is unlikely to be challenged, whereas judicial "decisions are [generally] more difficult to defend".[272] Despite the difficulty in defending the motive approach, many cases have acceded to it. Lord Wilberforce defended the permissibility of the discretionary manner in which tax avoidance cases are decided by emphasising that an otherwise "step by step dissecting approach . . . would be a denial . . . of the true judicial process".[273] However, judges must firstly construe the facts in accordance with the law before resorting to using their discretion as they are subordinate to Parliament.

The motive approach may also be utilised as a device to secure tax liability where the court cannot claim that the arrangement is a sham. For example, in *Furniss*, the court admitted that the scheme could not be considered a sham. Therefore, the court inserted an element of subjectivity by stating that the taxpayer's intention remained the same throughout the scheme and that the thought of selling the companies to the original buyers ceaselessly resided in the taxpayer's mind.[274] The court therefore relied on the continuity of intention. Similarly, in *Mallelieu*, the expenditure on work wear could not be prevented from being deducted unless the court explored the taxpayer's unconscious purpose. Therefore, the taxpayer's purpose was assessed in order to secure the payment of tax. However, in *Kirkham*, the taxpayer's intentions were scrutinised in order to secure tax relief for the taxpayer.[275]

The pre-planned nature of tax schemes has attracted condemnation by the courts, which may also be a reason the motives, intentions or purposes of taxpayers are assessed. Taxpayers may be criticised for entering a realm of unreality in their schemes, and courts disallow this by asserting that an "artificial tax avoidance scheme does not alter the incidence of tax".[276] However, an artificial motive imputed on the taxpayer cannot categorically result in a chargeable gain.

As demonstrated in *Ramsay* and *Burmah Oil*, judges will examine what the intention of the taxpayer was in embarking on the scheme where the scheme is complex or involves a variety of documents. Rather than untangling the web of transactions, it is far simpler for the courts to speculate what the taxpayer may have been thinking at the time of embarking upon the arrangement and ascertain whether this motive, intention or purpose accords with the end result which bypasses the intermediate transactions. In order to avoid the intricacies of the transactions involved, the court viewed them as "a composite transaction or a number of interdependent transactions".[277] The motive of the taxpayer in relation to the entire scheme is then examined. However, scrutinising the taxpayer's motive in each individual scheme would not necessarily result in an unacceptable tax avoidance motive. Furthermore, this approach ignores the will of Parliament, is immeasurable and can generate unfair results. In addition to this, the ability to choose the relevant facts and the possible multiplicity of parties in an arrangement also allows the court to decide whose motive to uphold.

Even judges have recognised that a transaction may be challenged simply due to the enormous amount of capital involved.[278] There is some truth to this observation as those cases which support the *Ramsay* approach, including *Ramsay* itself, *Burmah Oil*, *Furniss*, *Craven*, *Ensign Tankers* and *McGuckian* all involved taxable sums in excess of £100,000 and substantially higher in some. For example, in *Burmah Oil*, the assessment to income tax was on £3 million. Therefore, the motive approach may be used to ensure these sums are taxed to increase government funds. Moreover, as *Ramsay* illustrated, there is a general judicial aversion to arrangements in which "the taxpayer does not have to put his hand in his pocket"[279] due to the existence of a "self-cancelling"[280] transaction. Therefore, when there is no profit or loss, the motive approach is likely to be applied.

The motive approach, therefore, appears to be employed to make the role of adjudication simpler rather than the outcome for the taxpayer fairer. It is a means through which the judiciary can secure tax liability in the absence of a sham arrangement, although it is arguable that an arrangement should not be labelled unacceptable where there is no sham. As motive was not a statutory requirement when the *Ramsay* line of cases were decided, it is important to analyse how the courts developed the motive approach without being seen to act unconstitutionally.

2.5 How motive, intention and purpose are considered

It is important to understand the circumstances in which the courts would resort to considering the motive approach. This will help determine the degree to which motive is relied upon and whether it is necessary. Judges have commonly used seemingly objective measures when applying the motive approach, such as the substance over form doctrine, examining the purpose of the transaction, whether there exists a business purpose and the step transaction doctrine. However, in some cases, judges do not attempt to conceal subjective considerations and discuss the issue of motive openly. The problem with the *Ramsay* approach's wide requirements is that it left it "open to later courts to interpret them in 'inventive' ways",[281] which allowed the motive approach to born.

2.5 (a) The "substance over form" doctrine

The motive approach is commonly examined where judges explore the substance of the scheme rather than its form. However, it is important to note that the courts may not necessarily admit to favouring form over substance. For example, in *Ramsay*, Lord Wilberforce criticised the use of substance where there is "a document or transaction [which] is genuine".[282] Nevertheless, he stated that it is permissible to consider the context of a transaction[283] where it "was intended to have effect . . . as an ingredient of a wider transaction intended as a whole".[284] Therefore, although Lord Wilberforce discouraged examining the substance of an arrangement, he then contradictorily advocated assessing the effect of the transaction and, importantly, the taxpayer's intention. The decision in *Ramsay* also demonstrated that the courts prefer to impose a constructive intention rather than to give effect to the parties' true motives as it "cannot be . . . desirable to . . . arrive at a conclusion which corresponds with the parties' own intentions".[285] Consequently, Lord Wilberforce encouraged the assignment of a constructive intention which is established after examining the scheme holistically. However, in order to assign a constructive intention, judges consider the substance of the arrangement. Furthermore, it can broadly be said that any consideration which deviates from the form of the arrangement reviews the substance of it.

As previously mentioned, Lord Tomlin thoroughly criticised the substance over form doctrine which has since been utilised in cases supporting the *Ramsay* approach. The substance over form doctrine was also criticised for promoting discretion, which generates uncertainty.[286] In practice, an otherwise legitimate arrangement can be branded an unacceptable tax avoidance scheme and the substance over form doctrine employed in order to block any relief the taxpayer would otherwise be entitled to.

The court did not utilise the substance over form doctrine in the American case of *Zenz v Quinlivan*[287] (*Zenz*) in deciding whether retrieval of stock on liquidation was equal to a dividend under the income tax code or whether the sum received could attract capital gains tax. Through transiently considering the substance of the arrangement, the court acknowledged that "redemption of said stock is essentially equivalent to the distribution of a taxable dividend".[288] However, the court ultimately held that the sum was not equal to a dividend as the court found both motive and examining substance to be irrelevant.[289]

The substance over form doctrine is thoroughly ingrained in UK tax law. *Ramsay*'s supporting line of cases and the approval of *Ramsay* in the GAAR guidance illustrate the "adoption of an indiscriminate adoration of substance".[290] Moreover, in *McGuckian*, the court held that the *Ramsay* approach involved applying the taxing provisions to the substance of the transactions.[291] Therefore, the court in *McGuckian* admits an undeniable link between the *Ramsay* approach and the substance over form doctrine.

Significantly, Tiley made a direct correlation between examining the taxpayer's intention and the substance over form doctrine.[292] He observed that not only does ascertaining the end result of a transaction involve assessing the taxpayer's intentions,[293] but the "end result test"[294] is also "indistinguishable from the doctrine that the tax law must be applied to the substance of a transaction".[295] This is an important observation as examining the end results includes scrutinising intentions, and the substance over form doctrine is similar to the scrutinising of the end result. The notion that there is a connection between the end result and the taxpayer's intentions coincides with Scheer's definition of intentions as both "goals and courses of action".[296] Consequently, considering the substance of an arrangement involves assessing the taxpayer's intentions.

Similarly, in *Westminster*, examining substance was viewed as having subjective connotations as Lord Russell expressed that he disagreed with taxing an individual based on the "court's view of what it considers the substance of the transaction"[297] to be. Although *Westminster* has been seen as an exception due to the fact that only one document was involved, it does not follow why tax avoidance cases supporting *Westminster* and *Ramsay* are not in agreement regarding legal doctrines.

As well as assessing the substance of arrangements rather than the form, courts also assess whether the "case falls within the contemplation or spirit of the statute".[298] "Spirit" is an elusive term, capable of wide interpretation by the judiciary and developed in *Ramsay* as "an approach to construction".[299] Therefore, by scrutinising the taxpayer's motive, intention and purpose, the spirit of legislation and assessing the facts holistically, the outcome can present a truly distorted image of the arrangement: imposing a tax where none may have been due.

Substance therefore gives the courts a greater measure of flexibility to interpret legislation and the facts of each case as widely as they wish. For example, in *Ramsay*, Lord Wilberforce displayed a significant willingness to determine the legitimacy of an arrangement without documentary evidence as he proclaimed that "the existence of a document may be an indicative factor, but absence of one is not fatal".[300] The disposition of the judges in *Ramsay* is in stark contrast to that of those in *Westminster*, who regarded the covenant in that case as decisive. By examining substance, Lord Bridge in *Furniss* has held that it has "free[d] the courts from the shackles which . . . [were] imposed upon them by the Westminster case".[301] Therefore, the substance over form doctrine is a practice markedly different from the purposive approach; otherwise, the court would not have welcomed it as if it were new. Moreover, Edmond argues that

> the reference to "substance of the scheme" is another concept which is sufficiently "slippery" to provide fertile ground for disputation. It implies that a scheme will always have a form different from its substance when, in fact, in many cases, the form and substance of a transaction assailed as a scheme will be coterminous.[302]

2.5 (b) Purpose

Among the various subjective influences encompassing the motive approach, "purpose" is the least deplorable. This general acceptability is due to the fact that it is usually conflated with the arrangement's purpose and can therefore be accepted as a more objective measure in theory. *Ramsay* popularised the use of the term "purpose" but also extended the reach of this term by discussing the taxpayer's motive and intentions, as discussed earlier. Consequently, discussing "purpose" is a technique by which judges may scrutinise all the subjective factors under the motive approach.

Examining the motives, intentions and purposes of the taxpayer is a circular mission, as exemplified in *Craven*. In *Craven*, Lord Templeman held that a typical tax avoider

> plans and carries out an artificial tax avoidance scheme to avoid . . . an assessment to tax by combining a taxable transaction with a tax avoidance transaction whose purpose is the avoidance of the assessment.[303]

However, this statement presupposes that even an acceptable tax avoidance transaction would fail, due to the fact that a tax advantage was sought and where this was also the motive behind embarking on the scheme. The taxpayer's motive alone is insufficient to differentiate acceptable and unacceptable tax avoidance transactions.

Lord Wilberforce in *Ramsay* also placed emphasis on the assumption that "the whole and only purpose of each scheme was the avoidance of tax".[304] Therefore, Lord Wilberforce examined the taxpayer's subjective thoughts rather than viewing the transactions objectively, although the latter would have been more appropriate. The blurring of objective and subjective terms does little to rectify the confusion and "conflict between purpose and motive"[305] as the term "purpose" has been seen to have subjective connotations. As demonstrated in chapter 1, a motive can also connote "the purpose behind a course of action".[306] However, the two terms cannot easily be separated as "one necessarily colours the other".[307]

In *McGuckian*, the court also considered the taxpayer's purpose. Lord Browne-Wilkinson made an important distinction between the terms "purpose" and "effect" by stating that judges should not be concerned with the "effect of the insertion of the artificial steps but what was its purpose".[308] This reasoning is in contrast with Anscombe's argument that "the inseparability of the effect is not a ground for regarding it as intended".[309] Lord Browne-Wilkinson's approach signifies that the term "purpose", which can have subjective connotations, should be given priority over the objective term "effect", which also indicates that the courts are less concerned with fiscal realities than they are about subjective factors. Similarly, in *Furniss*, "purpose" was reinforced as a subjective term when the court reiterated that the commercial purpose must be examined and not the existence of a "business effect",[310] although the latter would have been a more objective measure. Consequently, it is difficult to defend the view that *Ramsay* did no more than encourage the finding of the "relevant transaction".[311]

There were different approaches in applying the term "effect" in *Furniss* and *Westminster*. In *Westminster*, the term was applied to the facts to conclude that "the legal effect of this deed was to give Allman . . . the right to a weekly payment".[312] However, in *Furniss*, the judges narrowed the scope of "effect", placing emphasis on whether there was a "business effect".[313]

2.5 (c) Commercial or business purpose

The court in *McGuckian* then tried to conceal its subjectivity beneath commercial considerations by stating that the assignment of the dividend to Mallardchoice Ltd. had no business purpose; therefore, this artificial step should be disregarded.[314] The term "business purpose" confines purpose to a business purpose rather than examining the taxpayer's purposes in general or whether tax avoidance was a purpose by examining business purposes or the aims of the taxpayer for the benefit of the business. *Furniss* also used the term "commercial purpose"[315] to judge whether the taxpayer had engaged in an acceptable or unacceptable tax avoidance scheme. According to Oliver L.J., unacceptable tax avoidance is given an objective definition where a scheme is "without any objective economic reality and therefore incapable of having fiscal consequences".[316]

The holistic approach as extended in *Furniss* requires there to be a "preordained series of transactions into which are inserted steps that have no commercial purpose apart from the avoidance of a liability to tax".[317] Therefore, the purpose of avoiding tax must exist, as well as a lack of commercial purpose, which renders the latter less important and still involves grappling with a subjective element.

The business purpose test derives its roots from American law and is known for its application in *Gregory v Helvering*[318] (*Gregory*), which repeatedly affirmed that the taxpayer's motive is of no significance. Despite the apparently objective term "business" imputed into the test to suggest it has no connections with motive, judges have succeeded in interpreting this test subjectively. For example, in *Rice's Toyota World Inc. v CIR*[319] (*Rice*), the court flagrantly studied the taxpayer's motives by subjectively interpreting the business purpose test. The taxpayer in *Rice* purchased a computer using recourse and non-recourse notes. He subsequently leased the computer back to the seller for eight years. The taxpayer claimed depreciation deductions for the computer and interest deductions paid on the non-recourse notes. The original seller then subleased the computer, which generated an income. The arrangement was found to be a sham in applying the business purpose test, which the court held "concerns the motives of the taxpayer in entering the transaction".[320] The business purpose test was therefore applied subjectively, although economic substance was held to be an objective test.[321] The twofold test resulted in the court taking into account both objective and subjective considerations by holding that the taxpayer "subjectively lacked a business purpose and the transaction objectively lacked economic substance".[322] The court, however, allowed the interest deductions as "a sham transaction may contain elements whose form reflects economic substance".[323]

The requirement of a business or commercial purpose does little to resolve cases where there exists a business purpose, as in *Furniss*, although the court inferred that there was a lack of a subjective business purpose by stating that the transactions were preordained with the intention of avoiding tax. Therefore, it is clear how examining whether there is a commercial or business purpose can involve assessments of motive, particularly where a twofold test is applied which examines whether there is a business purpose in reality and whether the taxpayer's motives involved tax avoidance.

2.5 (d) The step transaction doctrine

The step transaction doctrine has also facilitated the taxpayer's intentions being assessed. As Tiley observed, there are three variations to the step transaction doctrine.[324] The first is the "binding commitment test",[325] which encourages a holistic assessment of the facts as "once the first step has been taken there is a binding commitment to take the later ones".[326] The "mutual interdependence test"[327] also facilitates a holistic approach where the transactions "are so interdependent that the legal relations created by one transaction would have been fruitless without a completion of the series".[328]

Judges have proclaimed to be either ignoring the intermediary steps in an arrangement or grouping the individual transactions together. Both approaches involve examining the arrangement holistically and "cutting the knot rather than unravelling it".[329] The final test examines the "end result"[330] of an arrangement. This test is most susceptible to manipulation as it involves "separate transactions [being] amalgamated . . . when it appears that they were really component parts of a single transaction".[331]

Tiley overtly states that the final test involves examining the taxpayer's intentions[332] as it seeks to uncover what "the parties sought when they began their transaction".[333] Tiley's approach therefore accords with Anscombe's definition of an intention as being what a person "aims at or chooses".[334] Consequently, the step transaction doctrine does facilitate the motive approach. Along with the problems inherent in determining subjective intentions, Tiley also warns that the "end result"[335] test can encourage more judicial discretion and, disturbingly, allows the courts to decide who the relevant parties to the arrangement are.[336]

All the terms used by the courts have the effect of "piercing the external manifestations of the taxpayer's transactions".[337] Along with the common doctrines that are employed, judges will also have regard to other factors in determining whether an arrangement is an unacceptable tax avoidance arrangement. For example, the court will evaluate the difference between "independent [and] interdependent steps"[338] in order to form a holistic view of the events. The court will also examine "the timing between the steps"[339] to determine whether they are preordained – where, for example, the transactions are made in close succession or on the same day, as occurred in *Burmah Oil* and *Ensign Tankers*. Both cases were based on the fallible premise "that quick-step transactions are less likely to fall apart than slow ones".[340] However, issues of timing inevitably raise the difficult question of "how much patience did the taxpayer need to exercise for his tax-avoidance to be acceptable to the courts?"[341]

In *Furniss*, the court asserted that an arrangement would be dubious if "it was all over in time for lunch".[342] Therefore, a taxpayer would need to insert a delay of at least a day into an arrangement to avoid suspicion. However, it is unlikely that the question regarding timing will be definitively answered, and timing measurements are likely to turn on the particular facts of the case. Despite the uncertainty regarding timing, in *IRC v Bowater Property Developments Ltd.*[343] (*Bowater*), timing was a measurable and material factor. Among other factors, the court also held that the duration of 19 months between the first and the second transactions was sufficient to regard the latter as an "independent transaction",[344] which fell short of the arrangement being regarded as a "composite transaction"[345] as required by the *Ramsay* approach. Therefore, the *Ramsay* approach did not apply.[346] The court discussed the taxpayer's intentions, although the Revenue found the lack of a specific buyer irrelevant.[347] The court also stated that where the purchase of land was withdrawn, there was a "break . . . in the continuity of the intention . . . of Bowater".[348] Therefore, not only can judges infer primary and secondary motives, intentions and purposes, but they can also decide when these influences cease during an arrangement. The break in intention meant that the arrangement could not be seen as preordained.[349] However, transactions taking place in quick succession have been deemed to be "the normal sort of *Ramsay* situation".[350]

Timing is therefore of crucial importance to form a nexus with the succeeding transactions and secure tax liability. Examining the timing between the transactions therefore operates to neutralise a tax avoidance motive. However, as Tiley pointed out, the intentions of the taxpayer can still be examined under the step transaction doctrine.

2.5 (e) Motive or intention

There are instances when the court overtly examined the taxpayer's motive or intention without acknowledging that there might be some impropriety in doing so. Peculiarly, in *Bowater*, the court displayed a general dislike towards the *Ramsay* approach, although it discussed the taxpayer's intentions. The case concerned the taxpayer, the Bowater Group, wishing to sell some land to another company named Milton Pipes Ltd. Prior to the agreed sale to Milton Pipes Ltd., the taxpayer company sold the land to five companies within the Bowater Group in order to utilise the companies' land tax development exemption. However, a couple of months later, the sale failed to go through due to the buyer's lack of capital. Nonetheless, a year later, the buyer secured the necessary capital for the purchase of the original land, and the sale was completed several months later. The Revenue contended that the *Ramsay* approach should operate to nullify the first sale within the Bowater Group.[351] However, the extension of the *Ramsay* approach operated to the Revenue's detriment. Ironically, where the court interpreted the taxpayer's intentions in favour of the taxpayer company, the Revenue asserted that it was irrelevant that the taxpayer "had had no specific purchaser in mind at the time of the first transaction".[352] This was argued despite the fact that the lack of a specific buyer weakened the requirement for acceptable tax avoidance arrangements to be considered, preordained in *Furniss*.

Significantly, in *Bowater*, the initial withdrawal of the purchase of the land by Milton Pipes Ltd. was seen as a "break . . . in the continuity of the intention . . . of Bowater".[353] In this case, the extension of the *Ramsay* approach in *Furniss* was used as a doubled-edged sword as the court held that "in no sense was the second transaction . . . preordained at the time when the first transaction was carried out".[354] Therefore, the argument was that there was a lack of intention rather than deciphering the existence of the taxpayer's intention. However, in utilising this *Ramsay*-style argument in reverse, the court based their conclusions on "fact[s] of which the events of May and July 1980 are but evidence".[355]

The motive approach has seldom been applied in the taxpayer's favour, although the *Bowater* case illustrates how proving the lack of intention can provide equitable results. The application of the motive approach in this manner is, however, rare, and it is unlikely that Lord Brightman envisaged that his preordained requirement would be employed to uphold the taxpayer's position. By using the chameleon terms "purpose", "business purpose" and "substance", it camouflages the subjective nature of the motive approach. Each objective expression utilised "gives the courts another term to inject with legal meaning and anti-avoidance venom".[356] Even if motives, intentions or purposes could be quantified, it is unfathomable why the existence of "a conscious plan"[357] should attract liability. Therefore, the suitability of the motive approach must be examined to determine whether *Ramsay* has facilitated "an injustice caused by . . . judicial legislation".[358]

2.6 Suitability of the motive approach in tax law

From examining the cases supporting the *Ramsay* approach, including how the term "purpose" can be subjectively construed in other areas of tax law, it is evident that the taxpayer's motive is widely considered across the field of tax law. Due to the acceptance of the motive approach as a persuasive and sometimes a central factor in determining tax liability, it is important to establish whether assessing the taxpayer's motive is suitable and whether it generates equitable results. Fundamentally, where the taxpayer's claims do not accord with the assigned motive, intention or purpose this "must involve an assumption that the seller is lying".[359] Therefore, there must be sufficient justification for this assumption.

2.6 (a) Is the motive approach necessary?

In light of the cases invoking the motive approach, the test appears unnecessary in determining tax liability, and fundamentally, it is not "intellectually sustainable"[360] to apply it uniformly. To support this view, many judges have echoed that motive is an unnecessary measurement,[361] including the cases which support the *Ramsay* approach. Whilst many cases have conceded that motive is irrelevant, it is necessary to ascertain whether the motive approach is purposeless or whether it serves to help apportion tax liability justly.

It is helpful to consider why some judges believe that motive is an irrelevant concern. In *F.A. & A.B. Ltd. v Lupton*[362] (*Lupton*), Lord Morris exemplified why motive was not necessary in tax cases whilst simultaneously giving his opinion on the substance over form doctrine. He stressed that it is irrelevant because "motive does not and cannot alter or transform the essential and factual nature of a transaction".[363] Consequently, Lord Morris emphasised that the motive of the taxpayer has no bearing on deciphering the legitimacy of an arrangement. Therefore, Lord Morris's view coincides with the Utilitarian notion that "acts, not feelings count".[364] However, where motive is predicted in an artificial manner, it does modify the results of cases, usually in favour of the Revenue. Therefore, judges should look to the legitimacy of the transactions to determine tax liability rather than what was sought in embarking on the scheme. Lord Morris emphasised that "it is the transaction itself and its form and content which are to be examined".[365] Accordingly, he reinforced that examining the form of the agreement does not involve assessing motive, which correspondingly suggests that scrutinising the substance of the arrangement involves the motive approach. Lord Oliver in *Craven* also stressed that "the fact that the motive for a transaction may be to avoid tax does not invalidate it".[366] Those members of the judiciary who have struck down the relevance of motive have done so vehemently.

Lupton was a case regarding trading, an area of law which specifically allows motive to be considered. Thus, if judges presiding over cases where trading is permitted reject the motive approach, motive should not be considered in tax avoidance cases where no such authorisation exists. Therefore, the motive approach is not necessary in tax avoidance, and "reliance on motive must disappear".[367] This view accords with Stocks's idea that "evidence of character or motive is action".[368]

The court in *Zenz* clearly established that motive was irrelevant. Despite the "circuitous approach"[369] employed in *Ramsay*, the judge in *Zenz* also disregarded the use of the motive approach as he perceptively stated that "the taxpayer's motive to avoid taxation will not establish liability if the transaction does not do so without it".[370] Therefore, the court encourages examining the transaction rather than the taxpayer's motives as motive alone is insufficient and unreliable. This approach coincides with Lord Guest's argument in *Harrison*, as outlined in chapter 1, that judges should "only [be] concerned with the results of the business".[371]

As demonstrated in many cases involving companies – for example, *Burmah Oil* – it is difficult to comprehend "how one would attribute motive to an artificial person".[372] Cases involving companies could include many different people who represent the mind of the company, and it is unreasonable to assume that they all had the same joint intention. Laurence's "Anscombian approach to collective action"[373] further reinforces the view that "sometimes the people who know the end that ultimately explains what everyone is doing may not know what particular actions are serving that end".[374]

The motive approach appears to be thoroughly ingrained in tax avoidance precedent. Judges apply the motive approach as a matter of custom, although it is not imperative to adopt the motive approach. However, where the motive approach is discussed, *Bowater* illustrates how it can operate in reverse to establish the lack of an avoidance motive where there is the real possibility of "inchoate tax planning".[375] Nevertheless, the motive approach should not be regarded as having any importance in tax avoidance cases, and it is wholly unnecessary. The approach detracts from tax legislation and diverts judges into examining a variety of intangible possibilities.

2.6 (b) Restructuring transactions

As mentioned earlier, in order to ascertain the taxpayer's intentions, the court restructures the facts of the case, which is an extra-statutory practice. Due to the fact that many disposals are typically made, the court will "reconstruct [these] into a single direct disposal from the taxpayer".[376] However, this disregards the legitimacy of the intermediate transactions and the costs involved in executing them. Moreover, this approach only considers a selective motive which has been artificially constructed by the courts through restructuring the scheme. This is ironic, given the judicial criticisms aimed at taxpayers for constructing artificial arrangements.

The practice of restructuring transactions and ignoring the intermediate transactions was also put under scrutiny in *Craven*, indicating that judges are mindful that this practice could be regarded as unconstitutional. It was asserted that restructuring cannot take place in every tax avoidance case.[377] The artificial custom of restructuring would "prevent a taxpayer from availing himself of the fiscal immunities, privileges, allowances and other mitigating factors provided or permitted by Parliament".[378] As the judiciary are subordinate to Parliament, they must allow a transaction to benefit from the immunities laid down by Parliament.

Lord Oliver in *Craven* warned against restructuring the facts of any given arrangement. He noted that where restructuring was utilised in *Furniss*, this took a "considerable step further"[379] than the original holistic formulation of the *Ramsay* approach. Lord Oliver asserted that the judges in *Furniss* were "reconstituting the actual constituent transactions into something that they were not in fact, attributing to the parties an intended result which they did not in fact intend".[380] Therefore, it illustrates that judges can and have attributed an intention to the taxpayer which is far from the realities of their motives. Additionally, Lord Oliver emphasised how in order to arrive at the artificial intention, judges will distort the reality of the arrangement. The contrived manner of ascertaining tax liability is not reasonable or permitted by Parliament. Moreover, Lord Oliver stated that by restructuring the transactions in *Furniss*, the judges "disapplied the specific statutory consequences"[381] and, therefore, ignored the will of Parliament. Furthermore, in restructuring the schemes, it does not seek to determine what Parliament intended and instead focuses on what the taxpayer intended. It is therefore difficult to see how the *Ramsay* approach was developed as an aid to construction. Lord Oliver went further in his critical opinion of restructuring tax arrangements by stating that even if *Ramsay* were simply an aid to construction, it should only be utilised where "that which has taken place is not, within the meaning of the statute".[382]

Notwithstanding Lord Oliver's criticisms of *Furniss* and *Ramsay*, he nevertheless approved of the holistic approach taken in both cases by expressing that a transaction is to be viewed as a composite transaction where the "successive transactions are so indissolubly linked together, both in fact and in intention".[383] Therefore, he acknowledges that the holistic approach involves examining the taxpayer's intentions. However, Lord Oliver went further than this to reinforce the importance of viewing transactions as a composite whole by asserting that "the court is both bound and entitled so to regard them".[384] Declaring that the courts are bound to follow the *Ramsay* approach reinforces the importance of *Ramsay*.

Restructuring schemes can therefore create a misleading perception of the facts of the case. Despite all the arguments opposing the practice of restructuring transactions, *Ramsay* has permitted "so radical a reconstruction of the actual events",[385] which is, alarmingly, regarded as "rationally and logically possible"[386] by judges. However, the practice of restructuring arrangements heralded by *Ramsay* "is to legislate, not to construe".[387]

2.6 (c) Inconsistencies

The motive approach has many complications and problems, one of which is the inevitable inconsistencies which arise from the test. This is because the motive approach involves looking into the mind of the taxpayer, although "the subjective nature of this test detracts from the certainty".[388] Therefore, it creates uncertainty for taxpayers as to their potential tax liability, depending on how their motives will be interpreted. The lack of certainty also defies Adam Smith's tenet of creating a better tax system: namely, the need for taxes to be "certain and not arbitrary".[389] Furthermore, as the taxpayer's motives, intentions or purposes cannot be measured or definitively determined, and case law supporting the motive approach "says nothing about the weight to be accorded to motive",[390] it is difficult to apply the approach consistently.

The precedential inconsistencies created by the motive approach can be demonstrated by the conflicting trading cases of *Iswera* and *Kirkham*, which permitted motive to be considered. Although the transaction in *Iswera* was not viewed as equivocal, the court nevertheless examined the taxpayer's motives. Trading was held to be the primary motive in *Iswera* and the secondary motive in *Kirkham*. The inconsistencies could therefore have been avoided had motive not been assessed, then narrowly construed and subsequently ascribed.

Besides the inconsistencies deriving from trading cases, tax avoidance has also suffered from inconsistencies due to the formulation of judicial doctrines. For example, in *Craven*, the court did not apply the test Lord Brightman developed in *Furniss* despite the similarity of the facts. This fuels uncertainty as to the efficacy of the judicial tests as well as when they should be applied. Lord Oliver found differences between the two cases, including that the events in *Craven*

> were not contemporaneous. Nor were they pre-ordained or composite in the sense that it could be predicated with any certainty at the date of the intermediate transfer what the ultimate destination of the property would be . . . or even whether an ultimate transfer would take place at all.[391]

The uncertainty of who would be the ultimate owner of the shares in the company Millor, coupled with the doubt as to whether the shares would be disposed to J Ltd., serve to strengthen the unreliability of predicting the motive of the taxpayer. Moreover, the many varying outcomes signify that it is difficult to isolate a particular motive with any degree of certainty.

The uncertainty in deciding tax avoidance cases can be said to have derived from distinguishing between a *Westminster*-style arrangement and a *Ramsay*-style arrangement. *Ramsay* was differentiated on the basis that the arrangement was more complex than the arrangement in *Westminster*, which is why the court insisted on a holistic approach, and questions of the taxpayer's motive, intention and purpose arose. However, the legal "issue in *Ramsay* was in fact a very simple one".[392] Therefore, on this basis, the *Ramsay* approach was unnecessary and created avoidable inconsistencies. In addition to the common law rules emanating from *Ramsay*, the purposive approach was no longer viewed as an aid to construction where the legislation was ambiguous but a customary mechanism. In order to allow the purposive approach to gain further importance, "judges . . . over-emphasise[d] a narrow version of the literal rule".[393]

Even with the cases supporting *Ramsay*, there is some uncertainty as to what the *Ramsay* approach includes due to the absence of a definition.[394] What has come to be known as the *Ramsay* approach is a list of anti-avoidance tactics which are capable of being extended, as demonstrated by *Furniss* supplementing the pre-ordained requirement. It is likely that the *Ramsay* formulation purposely created a "broad-brush approach"[395] to inhibit more tax avoidance attempts, although the broadness of the principle has caused inconsistencies in application.

2.6 (d) Constitutional legitimacy of the motive approach

Prior to the GAAR, the motive approach was not expressly permitted by Parliament, and one could argue that "to look beyond what Parliament actually intended raises constitutional issues".[396] Moreover, it is undesirable to allow the development of judicial legislation – namely, *Ramsay* – in "an area in which Parliament is demonstrably capable of legislating effectively but has not sought to do so".[397]

Many of the supporters of the *Ramsay* approach ironically oppose assessing motive, and the judges have openly advocated how irrelevant this consideration is. For example, despite the taxpayer's purpose being at the fore of judicial reasoning in *Ensign Tankers*, Lord Templeman contradictorily stated that judges are not "competent or obliged to decide whether there was a sole object or paramount intention".[398] Despite this contention, in the earlier cases of *Iswera* and *Kirkham*, the judiciary clearly distinguished between primary and secondary intentions. Lord Templeman's assertion that the motive approach should not be considered is evidence that the judges themselves believe that the motive approach is an unsuitable step in concluding tax liability. Judges expressing their disapproval of the motive approach further conceals their discussion of motives, intentions and purposes when coupled with a tactic of concealing the motive approach, as previously mentioned.

By ascribing motives, intentions and purposes, judges are currently sitting at the fringes of constitutional legitimacy due to the

> role of the courts as an agency for preventing taxpayers from taking advantage of the statutory consequences which the legislature has seen fit to attach to certain actions for the purpose of avoiding, minimising or postponing . . . tax.[399]

The judges referring to the extension of the *Ramsay* approach in *Furniss* as having "crossed the Rubicon"[400] leave no doubt that the anti-avoidance rules were not merely additional aids to construction. *Furniss* reinforced *Ramsay* as "the legal basis for *Dawson* is the case of *Ramsay*"[401] and not the purposive approach.

Judges have cautioned against treating *Ramsay* as some form of "judge-made anti-tax-avoidance rule".[402] The case of *Bowater* warned that to honour the rule as such "would be nothing short of unconstitutional".[403] Warner J. warned that *Ramsay* has been "open to the courts to mould and develop",[404] indicating that the *Ramsay* approach was capable of effortless expansion in a palpable act of defiance against Parliament. Warner J. felt so strongly about the issue of *Ramsay* being treated as an indispensable rule that he found it necessary to restate basic principles of levying taxation as if to indicate that they had been long forgotten on the advent of *Ramsay*. He emphasised that "under our constitution the imposition of taxation is a matter for Parliament"[405] and specified that this referred to the House of Commons.[406] The true role of the courts is to do no more than "interpret and apply the legislation enacted by Parliament in accordance with relevant legal principles".[407] However, in the Court of Appeal, Warner J. declined to suggest that *Ramsay* is any more than a principle of examining the substance of the arrangement. Nonetheless, he omitted elucidating what he would encompass as the substance of an arrangement which left *Ramsay* condemned but not limited.[408]

2.7 Conclusion

It was not only those cases supporting the *Ramsay* approach which considered the taxpayer's cognitive influences. Lord Atkin examined both the taxpayer's intentions and the substance of the arrangement.[409] Motives were held to be irrelevant in *Ramsay*,[410] although the taxpayer's intentions were given significant weight at various times in the judgement in concluding that the taxpayer intended to generate an artificial loss to offset a chargeable gain.[411] The court referred to the taxpayer's motive, intention and purpose in *Ramsay*; however, these were not always discussed in the correct context. *Ramsay* is undeniably a case involving a tax avoidance scheme since there were many factors, other than the taxpayer's intentions, to suggest that it was. For example, there were unusual and profitable conditions attached to the L2 loan.[412] Therefore, examining the taxpayer's motive, intention and purpose was not necessary or appropriate in dismissing the appellant taxpayer's claim.

Although *Burmah* upheld *Ramsay*, the judges nevertheless criticised *Ramsay* for enquiring about the taxpayer's purpose and added that tax avoidance purposes are irrelevant.[413] *Furniss* focused on the arrangement's purpose; however, in *Ensign Tankers*, the court focused on the taxpayer's purpose. Although Lord Clyde in *McGuckian* stated that it is unnecessary to examine whether a tax avoidance purpose exists,[414] the relevant legislation in *McGuckian* had an anti-avoidance provision.[415] However, the relevant legislation in *Ramsay*[416] made no reference to the purpose of the arrangement or that it must not be for tax avoidance purposes. Therefore, examining the taxpayer's purpose was an extra-statutory consideration.

Supporters of the *Westminster* approach tended not to examine the taxpayer's motive, intention or purpose, although *Craven* was an exception to this and discussed how the taxpayer's motive was tax avoidance.[417] However, the timing of the arrangement was the focal point in *Craven*. Without explicitly stating so, the court formulated a remoteness test, which examined how remote the end result was at the time of the intermediate transactions.[418] This remoteness test was also applied in *Barclays*, where the court held that the events were not pre-planned and that there was some risk involved which made the arrangement genuine.[419] *Westmoreland* gave importance to Parliament's intentions rather than developing another test to add to the *Ramsay* approach.

The *Ramsay* approach was clearly left intentionally undefined to create a broad principle capable of wide interpretation with scope to extend it. However, whilst helping to formulate the principle, Lord Wilberforce held that "general principles against tax avoidance are . . . for Parliament to lay down".[420] Furthermore, the House of Lords in *Ramsay* arguably provoked the creation of the GAAR by signalling to Parliament that "if the taxpayer escapes the charge, it is for Parliament, if it disapproves of the result, to close the gap",[421] although *Ramsay* provided a means through which successive cases could close the gap. The subtle plea by the House of Lords indicates that the judges were insinuating that, rather than a GAAR, Parliament should implement a wider general anti-avoidance principle.

The decision in *Westmoreland* also demonstrated that "the courts have been reluctant to adopt the role of tax policeman".[422]

The decision in *Wisdom* demonstrates how courts can ascribe a particular motive to a taxpayer. Although the court conceded that the taxpayer did not expect a profit,[423] it held that the purpose of buying the silver bullion was to obtain a profit.[424] *Wisdom* is similar to *Iswera*, in which the court discussed how motive was irrelevant but nevertheless held that the taxpayer had a profit motive which was ascribed to her. In contrast, the taxpayer in *Kirkham* made a real profit although they were held not to be trading. Therefore, even in trading where there has been a long-established practice of examining taxpayer motives, there is still unpredictability, inconsistency and "nothing about the weight to be accorded to motive".[425]

Even though the ITTOIA 2005, in the field of expenditure, permits the consideration of purpose,[426] in *Lawson*, the judiciary emphasised that whether a payment was capital or revenue in nature "does not depend upon the motive or purpose of the taxpayer".[427] Moreover, *Mallalieu* demonstrated how the courts can hold that the taxpayer had a particular purpose when the taxpayer herself is unaware.

As established, there are various reasons why motives, intentions and purposes are examined. Firstly, it can be argued that examining cognitive influences and ascribing a particular motive, intention or purpose can help secure tax liability. As discussions about cognitive influences require discretion, there is greater flexibility in deciding cases. Where a scheme is complex or involves many documents, it is also easier to ignore the intricacies of the scheme and determine what the taxpayer sought to achieve overall.

Examining taxpayers' motives, intentions or purpose in tax avoidance is carried out in a number of ways under the guise of a variety of well-known anti-avoidance principles. For example, it has been demonstrated in the cases supporting *Ramsay* how the substance over form doctrine can lead to examining the taxpayer's motives, intentions or purposes. Tiley also stated how the step transaction doctrine involves examining the taxpayer's motives.[428] Finally, judges have examined the taxpayer's motive, intention or purpose overtly without resorting to concealing the considerations behind an established principle or approach.

Ramsay preferred examining the substance of transactions over their form. However, the substance over form approach led to an assessment of the motive approach, which is undesirable. Therefore, a more appropriate method for assessing substance "involves classification rather than recharacterisation of the facts".[429] Consequently, the court in *Ramsay* should have classified each transaction as legally permissible or not, rather than change its character. Motive is neither necessary nor expressly permitted by statute which is recognised by most judges presiding over tax avoidance cases. The motive approach not only seems to cause precedential inconsistencies but can also be regarded as unconstitutional. Therefore, it is necessary to explore the provisions of the GAAR to establish whether the motive approach has been given approval by Parliament.

Notes

1 *IRC v Duke of Westminster* [1936] A.C. 1, 19 (Lord Tomlin).
2 *Ibid.*
3 *Ibid*, p13 (Lord Atkin).
4 *Ibid*, p15.
5 *Ibid*, p19 (Lord Tomlin).
6 *Ibid.*
7 *Ibid.*
8 *Ibid*, p20.
9 *Ibid.*
10 *Ibid*, p15 (Lord Atkin).
11 *Ibid*, p16.
12 *Ibid*, p8.
13 *Ibid*, p21 (Lord Tomlin).
14 *Ibid.*
15 Anscombe, G.E.M. *'Intention'*, [1963], 2nd edn, Basil Blackwell, Oxford, p9.
16 *Furniss v Dawson* [1983] 3 W.L.R. 635, 642 (Oliver L.J.).
17 L1 and L2.
18 *WT Ramsay Ltd v IRC*; *Eilbeck v Rawling* [1981] 2 W.L.R 449, [1982] A.C. 300, 330 (Lord Wilberforce).
19 *Ibid*, p323.
20 *Ibid.*
21 *Ibid*, p321.
22 *Ibid*, p325.
23 *Craven v White*; *IRC v Bowater*; *Property Developments Ltd. v Gregory* [1988] 3 W.L.R. 423, [1989] A.C. 398, 497 (Lord Oliver).
24 Anscombe, G.E.M. *'Intention'*, [1963], 2nd edn, Basil Blackwell, Oxford, p28.
25 *WT Ramsay Ltd v IRC*; *Eilbeck v Rawling* [1981] 2 W.L.R 449, [1982] A.C. 300, 333 (Lord Fraser of Tullybelton).
26 *Ibid*, p328 (Lord Wilberforce).
27 *Ibid*, p333 (Lord Fraser of Tullybelton).
28 *F.A. & A.B. Ltd. v Lupton* [1971] 3 W.L.R 670, [1972] A.C. 634, 648 (Lord Morris of Borth-y-Gest).
29 *WT Ramsay Ltd v IRC*; *Eilbeck v Rawling* [1981] 2 W.L.R 449, [1982] A.C. 300, 323 (Lord Wilberforce).
30 *Ibid*, p328 (Lord Wilberforce).
31 Krikorian, Y.H. *'The Meaning of Purpose'*, [1930], The Journal of Philosophy, Vol. 27, No. 4, p96.
32 *Barclays Mercantile Business Finance Ltd v Mawson* [2002] EWCA Civ 1853, [2002] WL 31676325, [65] (Lord Justice Carnwath).
33 *WT Ramsay Ltd v IRC*; *Eilbeck v Rawling* [1981] 2 W.L.R 449, [1982] A.C. 300, 324 (Lord Wilberforce).
34 *Ibid*, p322.
35 *Ibid.*
36 *Ibid*, p333 (Lord Fraser of Tullybelton).
37 Scheer, R.K. *'Intentions, Motives and Causation'*, [2001], Vol. 76, No. 297, Philosophy, p398.
38 *WT Ramsay Ltd v IRC*; *Eilbeck v Rawling* [1981] 2 W.L.R 449, [1982] A.C. 300, 323 (Lord Wilberforce).
39 *Ibid*, p334 (Lord Fraser of Tullybelton).
40 *Ibid*, p338.
41 Millet, P. *'Artificial Tax Avoidance: The English and American Approach'*, [1986], British Tax Review, pp327, 330.

42 Gormally, L. *'Intention and Side Effects: John Finnis and Elizabeth Anscombe'* cited in Keown, J. and George, R. *'Reason, Morality and Law: The Philosophy of John Finnis'* [2013], Oxford University Press, Oxford, p106.
43 *WT Ramsay Ltd v IRC*; *Eilbeck v Rawling* [1981] 2 W.L.R 449, [1982] A.C. 300, 338 (Lord Fraser of Tullybelton).
44 *Ibid*, p322 (Lord Wilberforce).
45 *WT Ramsay Ltd. v IRC* [1979] 1 W.L.R 974, 979 (Templeman L.J.).
46 *WT Ramsay Ltd. v IRC*; *Eilbeck v Rawling* [1981] 2 W.L.R 449, [1982] A.C. 300, 325 (Lord Wilberforce).
47 Tiley, J. *'Judicial Anti-Avoidance Doctrines: The US Alternatives- Part 2'*, [1987], British Tax Review, pp220, 234.
48 Tiley, J. *'Judicial Anti-Avoidance Doctrines: The US Alternatives- Part 1'*, [1987], British Tax Review, pp180, 185.
49 *Ibid*, p194.
50 *IRC v Burmah Oil Co Ltd.* [1982] S.C. (H.L.) 114.
51 *Ibid*, p125 (Lord Diplock).
52 (BP).
53 (Holdings).
54 (MORH).
55 (BOTL).
56 *IRC v Burmah Oil Co Ltd.* [1982] S.C. (H.L.) 114, 132 (Lord Fraser of Tullybelton).
57 *Ibid*, p131.
58 *Ibid*, p130.
59 *Ibid.*
60 Krikorian, Y.H. *'The Meaning of Purpose'*, [1930], Vol. 27, No. 4, The Journal of Philosophy, p97.
61 *IRC v Burmah Oil Co Ltd.* [1982] S.C. (H.L.) 114, 130 (Lord Fraser of Tullybelton).
62 *Ibid.*
63 *Ibid.*
64 *Ibid*, p124 (Lord Diplock).
65 *Ibid.*
66 *Ibid*, p126 (Lord Fraser of Tullybelton).
67 *Ibid*, p124 (Lord Diplock).
68 *Ibid*, p132 (Lord Scarman).
69 *Furniss v Dawson* [1984] 2 W.L.R. 226, [1984] A.C. 474.
70 *Ibid*, p512 (Lord Fraser of Tullybelton).
71 *Furniss v Dawson* [1983] 3 W.L.R. 635, 640 (Oliver L.J.).
72 Krikorian, Y.H. *'The Meaning of Purpose'*, [1930], The Journal of Philosophy, Vol. 27, No. 4, p98.
73 *Furniss v Dawson* [1984] 2 W.L.R. 226, [1984] A.C. 474, 513 (Lord Fraser of Tullybelton).
74 *Furniss v Dawson* [1983] 3 W.L.R. 635, 641 (Oliver L.J.).
75 *Furniss v Dawson* [1984] 2 W.L.R. 226, [1984] A.C. 474, 522 (Lord Brightman).
76 *Ibid*, p512 (Lord Fraser of Tullybelton).
77 *Furniss v Dawson* [1983] 3 W.L.R. 635, 656 (Kerr L.J.).
78 *Ibid*, p655.
79 *Furniss v Dawson* [1983] 3 W.L.R. 635, 640 (Oliver L.J.).
80 *Furniss v Dawson* [1984] 2 W.L.R. 226, [1984] A.C. 474, 512 (Lord Fraser of Tullybelton).
81 *Furniss v Dawson* [1983] 3 W.L.R. 635, 651 (Oliver L.J.).
82 *Furniss v Dawson* [1984] 2 W.L.R. 226, [1984] A.C. 474, 517 (Lord Bridge).
83 *Ibid*, p518.
84 *Ibid.*
85 *Ibid.*

86 *Furniss v Dawson* [1984] 2 W.L.R. 226, [1984] A.C. 474, 527 (Lord Brightman).
87 *Ibid.*
88 *Ibid.*
89 *Ibid.*
90 *Ibid.*
91 *Ibid.*
92 *Ibid.*
93 *Ibid.*
94 *Ibid.*
95 *Ibid*, p515 (Lord Roskill).
96 *Ibid*, p514.
97 *Ibid.*
98 *Ibid*, p513 (Lord Scarman).
99 *Ibid.*
100 *Ibid*, p514.
101 *Ibid.*
102 *Ibid.*
103 *Ensign Tankers (Leasing) Ltd. v Stokes* [1992] 2 W.L.R 469, [1992] A.C. 655.
104 *Ibid*, p662 (Lord Templeman).
105 *WT Ramsay Ltd v IRC*; *Eilbeck v Rawling* [1981] 2 W.L.R 449, [1982] A.C. 300, 325 (Lord Wilberforce).
106 *Ensign Tankers (Leasing) Ltd. v Stokes* [1992] 2 W.L.R 469, [1992] A.C. 655, 661 (Lord Templeman).
107 *Ibid*, p668.
108 *Ibid*, pp676–677.
109 s41(1) Finance Act 1971.
110 *Ensign Tankers (Leasing) Ltd. v Stokes* [1992] 2 W.L.R 469, [1992] A.C. 655, 661 (Lord Templeman).
111 *Ibid*, p670.
112 *Ibid*, p666.
113 *Ibid*, p680.
114 *Ibid.*
115 *Ibid*, p667.
116 *Ibid*, p668.
117 *Ibid*, p661 (Lord Brandon).
118 *Ibid* (Lord Keith).
119 *Ibid*, p681 (Lord Templeman).
120 *Ibid.*
121 *Ibid*, p681.
122 *Ibid.*
123 *Ibid*, p684.
124 *Ibid*, p685.
125 *Ibid.*
126 *IRC v McGuckian* [1997] 1 W.L.R. 991.
127 *Ibid*, p1000 (Lord Steyn).
128 *Ibid*, p999.
129 *Ibid*, p996 (Lord Browne-Wilkinson).
130 *Ibid.*
131 *Ibid*, p1006 (Lord Clyde).
132 *Ibid*, p1002 (Lord Steyn).
133 *Ibid*, p998 (Lord Browne-Wilkinson).
134 Krikorian, Y.H. *'The Meaning of Purpose'*, [1930], Vol. 27, No. 4, The Journal of Philosophy, p97.
135 *IRC v McGuckian* [1997] 1 W.L.R. 991, 997–998 (Lord Browne-Wilkinson).

136 *Ibid*, p1000 (Lord Steyn).
137 *Ibid*, p1006 (Lord Clyde).
138 *Ibid.*
139 *Ibid*, p998 (Lord Browne-Wilkinson).
140 *Ibid*, p999 (Lord Steyn).
141 *Ibid*, p1004 (Lord Cooke).
142 *Ibid.*
143 *Ibid.*
144 *Ibid*, p998 (Lord Lloyd).
145 *Westmoreland Investments Ltd. v MacNiven* [2001] UKHL 6, [2003] 1 A.C. 311.
146 *Ibid*, [49] (Lord Hoffmann).
147 *Ibid*, [29].
148 *Ibid*, [32].
149 *Ibid*, [42].
150 (WIL).
151 (The scheme).
152 *Westmoreland Investments Ltd. v MacNiven* [2001] UKHL 6, [2003] 1 A.C. 311, [22] (Lord Hoffmann).
153 *Ibid*, [59].
154 *Ibid*, [34].
155 *Barclays Mercantile Business Finance v Mawson* [2004] UKHL 51, [2005] 1 A.C. 684.
156 *Ibid*, [42] (Lord Nicholls of Birkenhead).
157 *Barclays Mercantile Business Finance v Mawson* [2002] EWCA Civ 1853, [2002] WL 31676325, [65] (Lord Justice Carnwath).
158 *Ibid*, [52].
159 *Ibid*, [36] (Peter Gibson L.J.).
160 Hoffmann, L. *'Tax Avoidance'*, [2005], British Tax Review, pp197, 203.
161 *Craven v White*; *IRC v Bowater*; *Property Developments Ltd. v Gregory* [1988] 3 W.L.R. 423, [1989] A.C. 398.
162 *Ibid*, p414 (Lord Templeman).
163 *Ibid*, p496 (Lord Oliver).
164 *Ibid.*
165 *Ibid*, p480 (Lord Keith).
166 *Ibid*, p481.
167 *Ibid.*
168 *Ibid.*
169 *Tower MCashback LLP and another v Revenue and Customs Commissioners* [2011] UKSC 19, [2011] 2 A.C. 457.
170 *Ibid*, [42] (Lord Walker).
171 *Ibid*, [27].
172 *Ibid*, [29].
173 *Ibid.*
174 *Ibid*, [30].
175 *Ibid*, [86] (Lord Hope).
176 *Ibid*, [87].
177 *Ibid.*
178 *Ibid*, [88].
179 *Ibid*, [33] (Lord Walker).
180 *Ibid*, [89] (Lord Hope).
181 *Ibid*, [88].
182 *Ibid*, [25] (Lord Walker).
183 *Ibid.*
184 *Ibid*, [79].

185 *Ibid*, [77].
186 *Ibid*, [75].
187 *Ibid*, [76].
188 *'HMRC GAAR Guidance with Effect from 11 September 2020: Parts A, B and C'*, <https://assets.publishing.service.gov.uk/government/uploads/system/uploads/attachment_data/file/916667/gaar_parts_a_b_c_2020.pdf>, accessed 29.04.2021, p6.
189 *Ibid.*
190 ITTOIA 2005.
191 s5 ITTOIA 2005.
192 s989 Income Tax Act 2007.
193 The Radcliffe Commission.
194 Peacock, J. *'When, if Ever, Can an Activity Motivated by Tax Constitute a Trade?'*, [2014], British Tax Review, pp509, 510.
195 *Simmons v IRC* [1980] 2 All ER 798, 800 (Lord Wilberforce).
196 *Bramwell v Lacy* [1878] B. 634 [1879] 10 Ch. D. 691.
197 *Ibid*, p695 (Jessel M.R.).
198 *Ibid.*
199 *Religious Tract and Book Society of Scotland v R.S. Forbes* [1896] 23 R. 390.
200 *Ibid*, p393 (Lord President).
201 *Ibid*, p394 (Lord Adam).
202 *Ibid*, p394 (Lord M'Laren).
203 *Ibid.*
204 *Ibid.*
205 *Wisdom v Chamberlain* [1969] 1 W.L.R. 275.
206 *Ibid*, p280 (Harman L.J.).
207 *Ibid*, p281.
208 *Ibid*, p282.
209 Krikorian, Y.H. *'The Meaning of Purpose'*, [1930], Vol. 27, No. 4, The Journal of Philosophy, p103.
210 *Iswera v Commissioner of Inland Revenue* [1965] 1 W.L.R. 663.
211 *Ibid*, p668 (Lord Reid).
212 *Ibid.*
213 *Ibid.*
214 Olowofoyeku, A. *'The Taxation of Income'*, [2011], Cambridge Academic, United Kingdom, Cambridge, p121.
215 *WT Ramsay Ltd. v IRC*; *Eilbeck v Rawling* [1981] 2 W.L.R 449, [1982] A.C. 300, 323 (Lord Wilberforce).
216 Olowofoyeku, A. *'The Taxation of Income'*, [2011], Cambridge Academic, United Kingdom, Cambridge, p126.
217 Ashworth, A. and Horder, J. *'Principles of Criminal Law'*, [2013], 7th edn, Oxford University Press, Oxford, p169.
218 *Kirkham v Williams* [1991] W.L.R. 863.
219 *Ibid*, p868 (Nourse L.J.).
220 *Ibid*, p872.
221 *Ibid.*
222 *Ibid*, p868.
223 Krikorian, Y.H. *'The Meaning of Purpose'*, [1930], The Journal of Philosophy, Vol. 27, No. 4, p101.
224 Peacock, J. *'When, if Ever, Can an Activity Motivated by Tax Constitute a Trade?'*, [2014], British Tax Review, pp509, 510.
225 *Ensign Tankers (Leasing) Ltd. v Stokes* [1992] 2 W.L.R 469, [1992] A.C. 655, 668 (Lord Templeman).
226 *Ibid.*
227 *Ibid.*

228 Kerridge, R. *'Clarke (Inspector of Taxes) v BT Pension Scheme Trustees [2000] S.T.C., 222 (CA (Civ Div))'*, [2000], British Tax Review, pp397, 400.
229 s33 ITTOIA 2005.
230 s34(1)(a) ITTOIA 2005.
231 *Lawson v Johnson Matthey Plc.* [1992] 2 W.L.R. 826, [1992] 2 A.C. 324.
232 *Ibid*, p332 (Lord Templeman).
233 *Ibid*, p334.
234 *Ibid*, p341 (Lord Goff).
235 *Ibid.*
236 s32(2) ITTOIA 2005.
237 *Mallalieu v Drummond* [1983] 3 W.L.R. 409, [1983] 2 A.C. 861.
238 *Ibid*, p872 (Lord Brightman).
239 *Ibid*, p867 (Lord Elwyn-Jones).
240 *Ibid*, p870 (Lord Brightman).
241 Stocks, J.L. *'Motive'*, [1911], Vol. 20, No. 77, Mind Association, p54.
242 Olowofoyeku, A. *'The Taxation of Income'*, [2011], Cambridge Academic, United Kingdom, Cambridge, p121.
243 *Vodafone Cellular Ltd v Shaw* [1997] (ChD), STC 734.
244 *Ibid*, p741 (Millett L.J.).
245 *Ibid.*
246 *Ibid*, p740.
247 *Ibid*, p744.
248 *Ibid*, p743.
249 *Ibid*, p744.
250 Gormally, L. *'Intention and Side Effects: John Finnis and Elizabeth Anscombe'* cited in Keown, J. and George, R. *'Reason, Morality and Law: The Philosophy of John Finnis'* [2013], Oxford University Press, Oxford, p106.
251 s37(1) Income Tax Act 1961.
252 *Ibid.*
253 *Commissioner of Income Tax v Shaw Wallace* [1931] No. 108 (Cal.).
254 *Ibid*, p4 (per curiam).
255 s162(a) Internal Revenue code 1986.
256 *Pevsner v Commissioner of Internal Revenue* 628 F.2d, 467 (5th Cir. 1980).
257 *Ibid*, per Judge Johnson, p469.
258 *Donnelly v Commissioner*, 262 F.2d 411, 412 (2d Cir. 1959).
259 *Ibid*, p412 (Judge Waterman).
260 *Pevsner v Commissioner of Internal Revenue* [1980] 628 F.2d 467, 471 (Judge Johnson).
261 *Sharkey v Wernher* [1955] 3 W.L.R. 671, [1956] A.C. 58.
262 *Ibid*, p67 (Viscount Simonds).
263 *Ibid*, p66.
264 Anscombe, G.E.M. *'Intention'*, [1963], 2nd edn, Basil Blackwell, Oxford, p9.
265 *Watson Brothers v Hornby (HM Inspector of Taxes)* [1942] 2 All ER 506 K.B.
266 *Briton Ferry Steel Co Ltd. v Barry* [1940] K.B. 463.
267 *Sir Kikabhai Premchand v Commissioner of Income Tax* [1953] A.I.R. 509 (Bom.) 214, 222 (per curiam).
268 *Ibid*, p223.
269 Freeman, M.D.A. *'Lloyd's Introduction to Jurisprudence'*, [2008], 8th edn, Sweet and Maxwell Limited, London, p717.
270 *Furniss v Dawson* [1984] 2 W.L.R. 226, [1984] A.C. 474, 526 (Lord Brightman).
271 Harris, N. *'Law in a Complex State: Complexity in the Law and Structure of Welfare'*, [2013], Hart Publishing, Oxford, p6.
272 *Ibid.*

273 *WT Ramsay Ltd. v IRC*; *Eilbeck v Rawling* [1981] 2 W.L.R 449, [1982] A.C. 300, (Lord Wilberforce), p326.
274 *Furniss v Dawson* [1983] 3 W.L.R. 635, 640 (Oliver L.J.).
275 *Kirkham v Williams* [1991] W.L.R. 863, 868 (Nourse L.J.).
276 *Craven v White*; *IRC v Bowater*; *Property Developments Ltd. v Gregory* [1988] 3 W.L.R. 423, [1989] A.C. 398, 483 (Lord Templeman).
277 *WT Ramsay Ltd. v IRC*; *Eilbeck v Rawling* [1981] 2 W.L.R 449, [1982] A.C. 300, 324 (Lord Wilberforce).
278 *Anglo-Persian Oil Company Ltd. v Dale* [1932] 1 K.B. 124, 139 (Lawrence L.J.).
279 *WT Ramsay Ltd v IRC*; *Eilbeck v Rawling* [1981] 2 W.L.R 449, [1982] A.C. 300, 322 (Lord Wilberforce).
280 *Ibid*, p328.
281 Lee, N. *'Revenue Law: Principles and Practice'*, [2012], 13th edn, Bloomsbury Professional Ltd., Croydon, p23.
282 *WT Ramsay Ltd. v IRC*; *Eilbeck v Rawling* [1981] 2 W.L.R 449, [1982] A.C. 300, 323 (Lord Wilberforce).
283 *Ibid.*
284 *Ibid.*
285 *Ibid*, p326.
286 *IRC v Duke of Westminster* [1936] A.C. 1, 19 (Lord Tomlin).
287 *Zenz v Quinlivan* 213 F.2d 914 (6th Cir. 1954).
288 *Ibid*, [25] (Judge Gourley).
289 *Ibid*, [17].
290 Tiley, J. *'Judicial Anti-Avoidance Doctrines: The US Alternatives – Part 2'*, [1987], British Tax Review, pp220, 234.
291 *IRC v McGuckian* [1997] 1 W.L.R. 991, 998 (Lord Browne-Wilkinson).
292 Tiley, J. *'Judicial Anti-Avoidance Doctrines: The US Alternatives – Part 2'*, [1987], British Tax Review, pp220, 236.
293 *Ibid.*
294 *Ibid*, p235.
295 *Ibid*, p236.
296 Scheer, R.K. *'Intentions, Motives and Causation'*, [2001], Vol 76, No. 297, Philosophy, p399.
297 *IRC v Duke of Westminster* [1936] A.C. 1, 24 (Lord Russell of Killowen).
298 *Ibid.*
299 *IRC v McGuckian* [1997] 1 W.L.R. 991, 998 (Lord Browne-Wilkinson).
300 *WT Ramsay Ltd v IRC*; *Eilbeck v Rawling* [1981] 2 W.L.R 449, [1982] A.C. 300, 329 (Lord Wilberforce).
301 *Furniss v Dawson* [1984] 2 W.L.R. 226, [1984] A.C. 474, 517 (Lord Bridge).
302 Justice Edmonds, R. *'Judicial Construction of Part IVA: What to Expect from the Application of Existing Principles Going Forward'*, [2013], Vol. 42, Australian Tax Review, pp213, 220.
303 *Craven v White*; *IRC v Bowater*; *Property Developments Ltd. v Gregory* [1988] 3 W.L.R. 423, [1989] A.C. 398, 486 (Lord Templeman).
304 *WT Ramsay Ltd. v IRC*; *Eilbeck v Rawling* [1981] 2 W.L.R 449, [1982] A.C. 300, 323 (Lord Wilberforce).
305 Olowofoyeku, A. *'The Taxation of Income'*, [2011], Cambridge Academic, United Kingdom, Cambridge, p129.
306 Law, J. and Martin, E.A. *'Oxford Dictionary of Law'*, [2009], Oxford University Press, Oxford, p359.
307 Olowofoyeku, A. *'The Taxation of Income'*, [2011], Cambridge Academic, United Kingdom, Cambridge, p132.
308 *IRC v McGuckian* [1997] 1 W.L.R. 991, 998 (Lord Browne-Wilkinson).

309 Gormally, L. *'Intention and Side Effects: John Finnis and Elizabeth Anscombe'* cited in Keown, J. and George, R. '*Reason, Morality and Law: The Philosophy of John Finnis'* [2013], Oxford University Press, Oxford, p106.
310 *Furniss v Dawson* [1984] 2 W.L.R. 226, [1984] A.C. 474, 527 (Lord Brightman).
311 *Craven v White*; *IRC v Bowater*; *Property Developments Ltd. v Gregory* [1988] 3 W.L.R. 423, [1989] A.C. 398, 499 (Lord Oliver).
312 *IRC v Duke of Westminster* [1936] A.C. 1, 26 (Lord MacMillan).
313 *Furniss v Dawson* [1984] 2 W.L.R. 226, [1984] A.C. 474, 527 (Lord Brightman).
314 *IRC v McGuckian* [1997] 1 W.L.R. 991, 996 (Lord Browne-Wilkinson).
315 *Furniss v Dawson* [1983] 3 W.L.R. 226, [1984] A.C. 474, 492 (Oliver L.J.).
316 *Ibid*, p646 (Oliver L.J.).
317 *Ibid*, p492.
318 *Gregory v Helvering* 293 U.S. 465 (2nd Cir.1935).
319 *Rice's Toyota World Inc. v CIR* 752 F.2.d 89 (4th Cir. 1985).
320 *Ibid*, p92 (Judge Phillips).
321 *Ibid*, p95.
322 *Ibid.*
323 *Ibid*, p96.
324 Tiley, J. *'Judicial Anti-Avoidance Doctrines: The US Alternatives – Part 2'*, [1987], British Tax Review, pp220, 235.
325 *Ibid.*
326 *Ibid.*
327 *Ibid.*
328 *Ibid.*
329 *Ibid*, p239.
330 *Ibid*, p235.
331 *Ibid.*
332 *Ibid*, p236.
333 *Ibid.*
334 Anscombe, G.E.M. *'Intention'*, [1963], 2nd edn, Basil Blackwell, Oxford, p18.
335 Tiley, J. *'Judicial Anti-Avoidance Doctrines: The US Alternatives – Part 2'*, [1987], British Tax Review, p235.
336 *Ibid*, p236.
337 *Zenz v Quinlivan* 213 F.2d 914 (6th Cir. 1954), [16] (Judge Gourley).
338 Mansfield, G. *'The New Approach to Tax Avoidance: First Circular, Then Linear, Now Narrower'*, [1989], British Tax Review, pp5, 6.
339 *Ibid.*
340 *Ibid*, p12.
341 *Ibid*, p7.
342 *Furniss v Dawson* [1984] 2 W.L.R. 226, [1984] A.C. 474, 520 (Lord Brightman).
343 *IRC v Bowater Property Developments Ltd* [1985] STC 783 (Ch.).
344 *Ibid*, p799 (Warner J.).
345 *WT Ramsay Ltd v IRC*; *Eilbeck v Rawling* [1981] 2 W.L.R 449, [1982] A.C. 300, 324 (Lord Wilberforce).
346 *IRC v Bowater Property Developments Ltd* [1985] STC 783 (Ch.), 796 (Warner J.).
347 *Ibid*, p795.
348 *Ibid*, p794.
349 *Ibid*, p797.
350 *Ibid*, p798.
351 *Ibid*, p794.
352 *Ibid*, p795.
353 *Ibid*, p794.
354 *Ibid*, p797.
355 *Ibid*, p799.

356 Tiley, J. *'Judicial Anti-Avoidance Doctrines: Some Problem Areas: Part 2'*, [1988], British Tax Review, pp63, 69.
357 *Craven v White*; *IRC v Bowater*; *Property Developments Ltd. v Gregory* [1988] 3 W.L.R. 423, [1989] A.C. 398, 498 (Lord Oliver).
358 *IRC v Bowater Property Developments Ltd.* [1985] STC 783 (Ch.), 798 (Warner J.).
359 Olowofoyeku, A. *'The Taxation of Income'*, [2011], Cambridge Academic, United Kingdom, Cambridge, p121.
360 Tiley, J. *'Judicial Anti-Avoidance Doctrines: The US Alternatives – Part 2'*, [1987], British Tax Review, p220.
361 *F.A. & A.B. Ltd. v Lupton* [1971] 3 W.L.R 670, [1972] A.C. 634, 646 (Lord Morris of Borth-y-Gest).
362 *Ibid.*
363 *Ibid.*
364 Dewey, J. and Tufts, J.H. *'Ethics'*, [1908], Henry Holt and Company, New York, HathiTrust Digital Library, <http://babel.hathitrust.org/cgi/pt?id=mdp.39015002747221;view=1up;seq=266>, accessed 02.04.2015, p247.
365 *F.A. & A.B. Ltd. v Lupton* [1971] 3 W.L.R 670, [1972] A.C. 634, 646 (Lord Morris of Borth-y-Gest).
366 *Craven v White*; *IRC v Bowater*; *Property Developments Ltd. v Gregory* [1988] 3 W.L.R. 423, [1989] A.C. 398, 498 (Lord Oliver).
367 *F.A. & A.B. Ltd. v Lupton* [1971] 3 W.L.R 670, [1972] A.C. 634, 647 (Lord Morris of Borth-y-Gest).
368 Stocks, J.L. *'Motive'*, [1911], Mind Association, Vol. 20, No. 77, p64.
369 *Zenz v Quinlivan* 213 F.2d 914 (6th Cir. 1954), [15] (Judge Gourley).
370 *Ibid*, [17].
371 *Griffiths v J.P. Harrison Ltd.* [1963] A.C. 1, 26 (Lord Guest).
372 Olowofoyeku, A. *'The Taxation of Income'*, [2011], Cambridge Academic, United Kingdom, Cambridge, p131.
373 Laurence, B. *'An Anscombian Approach to Collective Action'* in Ford, A., Hornsby, J. and Stoutland, F. (ed.), *'Essays on Anscombe's Intention'*, Harvard University Press, United States of America, p272.
374 *Ibid*, p290.
375 Mansfield, G. *'The New Approach to Tax Avoidance: First Circular, Then Linear, Now Narrower'*, [1989], British Tax Review, pp5, 8.
376 *Craven v White*; *IRC v Bowater*; *Property Developments Ltd. v Gregory* [1988] 3 W.L.R. 423, [1989] A.C. 398, 494 (Lord Oliver).
377 *Ibid*, p487 (Lord Templeman).
378 *Ibid.*
379 *Ibid*, p497 (Lord Oliver).
380 *Ibid.*
381 *Ibid.*
382 *Ibid.*
383 *Ibid*, p504.
384 *Ibid.*
385 *Ibid*, p497.
386 *Ibid.*
387 *Ibid*, p504.
388 Williams, D.F. *'Avoidance through the Creation and Use of Capital Losses By Companies'*, [2006], British Tax Review, pp23, 24.
389 Smith, A. *'An Inquiry into the Nature and Causes of the Wealth of Nations'*, [2005], "An Electronic Classics Series Publication" <https://eet.pixel-online.org/files/etranslation/original/The%20Wealth%20of%20Nations.pdf>, accessed 01.02.2022, p676.
390 Olowofoyeku, A. *'The Taxation of Income'*, [2011], Cambridge Academic, United Kingdom, Cambridge, p121.

391 *Craven v White*; *IRC v Bowater*; *Property Developments Ltd. v Gregory* [1988] 3 W.L.R. 423, [1989] A.C. 398, 498 (Lord Oliver).
392 *Ibid*, p499.
393 Freedman, J. *'Improving (Not Perfecting) Tax Legislation: Rules and Principles Revisited'*, [2010], British Tax Review, pp717, 722.
394 Stockton, F. and Bretten, G.R. *'The Ramsay Doctrine: An Interim Review'*, [1987], British Tax Review, pp280, 281.
395 *Ibid.*
396 Freedman, J. *'Defining Taxpayer Responsibility: In Support of a General Anti-Avoidance Principle'*, [2004], British Tax Review, pp332, 356.
397 *Craven v White*; *IRC v Bowater*; *Property Developments Ltd. v Gregory* [1988] 3 W.L.R. 423, [1989] A.C. 398, 496 (Lord Oliver).
398 *Ensign Tankers (Leasing) Ltd. v Stokes* [1992] 2 W.L.R 469, [1992] A.C. 655, 677 (Lord Templeman).
399 *Craven v White*; *IRC v Bowater*; *Property Developments Ltd. v Gregory* [1988] 3 W.L.R. 423, [1989] A.C. 398, 496 (Lord Oliver).
400 *Ibid*, p497.
401 *Ibid*, p498.
402 *IRC v Bowater Property Developments Ltd.* [1985] STC 783 (Ch.), 797 (Warner J.).
403 *Ibid.*
404 *Ibid.*
405 *Ibid.*
406 *Ibid.*
407 *Ibid.*
408 *Ibid.*
409 *IRC v Duke of Westminster* [1936] A.C. 1, 13 and 15 (Lord Atkin).
410 *WT Ramsay Ltd. v IRC*; *Eilbeck v Rawling* [1981] 2 W.L.R 449, [1982] A.C. 300, 323 (Lord Wilberforce).
411 *Ibid*, p333 (Lord Fraser of Tullybelton).
412 *Ibid*, p335.
413 *IRC v Burmah Oil Co Ltd.* [1982] S.C. (H.L.) 114, 130 (Lord Fraser of Tullybelton).
414 *IRC v McGuckian* [1997] 1 W.L.R. 991, 1006 (Lord Clyde).
415 s478 Income and Corporation Taxes Act 1970.
416 Sch.7, para 11, Finance Act 1965.
417 *Craven v White*; *IRC v Bowater*; *Property Developments Ltd. v Gregory* [1988] 3 W.L.R. 423, [1989] A.C. 398, 496 (Lord Oliver).
418 *Ibid*, p481 (Lord Keith).
419 *Barclays Mercantile Business Finance Ltd. v Mawson* [2002] EWCA Civ 1853, [2002] WL 31676325, [36] (Peter Gibson L.J.).
420 *WT Ramsay Ltd. v IRC*; *Eilbeck v Rawling* [1981] 2 W.L.R 449, [1982] A.C. 300, 325 (Lord Wilberforce).
421 *Ibid.*
422 Slater, A.H. *'Part IVA: An International Perspective'*, [2013], Vol. 42, No. 3, Australian Tax Review, pp149, 152.
423 *Wisdom v Chamberlain* [1969] 1 W.L.R. 275, 281 (Harman L.J.).
424 *Ibid*, p282.
425 Olowofoyeku, A. *'The Taxation of Income'*, [2011], Cambridge Academic, United Kingdom, Cambridge, p121.
426 s34(1)(a) ITTOIA 2005.
427 *Lawson v Johnson Matthey Plc.* [1992] 2 W.L.R. 826, [1992] 2 A.C. 324, 341 (Lord Goff).
428 Tiley, J. *'Judicial Anti-Avoidance Doctrines: The US Alternatives – Part 2'*, [1987], British Tax Review, pp220, 236.
429 Tiley, J. *'Judicial Anti-Avoidance Doctrines: Part 3 – Corporations and Conclusions'*, [1988], British Tax Review, pp108, 109.

3 The GAAR provisions analysed

Introduction

The GAAR states that it is aimed at "counteracting tax advantages arising from tax arrangements that are abusive".[1] The GAAR has various stages to determine whether an arrangement is abusive. This chapter provides an outline of the central provisions of the UK GAAR in order to ascertain the extent to which a taxpayer's motive, intention or purpose can be subjectively examined by the judiciary. An evaluation of the meaning of the central provisions of the GAAR will be given. These central provisions include a tax advantage,[2] a tax arrangement,[3] the main purpose test[4] and the double reasonableness test.[5] Scrutinising the GAAR's provisions will strengthen the argument that the GAAR allows for a significant amount of discretion to be exercised by the judiciary in determining whether an arrangement amounts to acceptable tax avoidance. In order to reinforce the view that the level of discretion afforded to the judiciary is undesirable, the usefulness of the guidance on what amounts to abuse, according to the GAAR and the GAAR guidance, will be assessed, including what does not qualify as abusive. The requirements within the GAAR guidance will also be examined as the GAAR legislation states that the courts must take it into consideration.[6] Consequently, when discussing the scope of the GAAR, it will be suggested that the targeted GAAR can be interpreted widely and has the potential to apply to a broad range of arrangements due to its inherent ambiguity. Lastly, the proposed penalties of the GAAR will provide an insight into how the government plans to tackle the perceived problem of tax avoidance.

3.1 The GAAR: An overview

The GAAR states that it applies to various taxes, including income tax,[7] corporation tax,[8] capital gains tax,[9] petroleum revenue tax,[10] inheritance tax,[11] stamp duty land tax[12] and annual tax on enveloped dwellings.[13] Despite the various judicial views on what amounts to acceptable and unacceptable tax avoidance, the GAAR "has imposed an overriding statutory limit on the extent to which taxpayers can go in trying to reduce their tax bill".[14]

The GAAR has two main objectives and was introduced to operate primarily as a deterrence aimed at taxpayers and prospective promoters of tax avoidance

DOI: 10.4324/9781003080473-4

schemes.[15] The second objective of the GAAR is to "counteract the abusive tax advantage"[16] by requiring a tax adjustment to be made.[17] The GAAR was introduced by the Coalition Government in 2013 in order to tackle abusive tax arrangements.[18] The requirements of an abusive arrangement will be analysed to ascertain what factors the judiciary may take into account when establishing whether a tax scheme is abusive.

3.2 The GAAR provisions

The GAAR's provisions are laid down in Part 5 of the Finance Act 2013. The GAAR is separated into three key stages. Firstly, there must be a tax advantage.[19] Secondly, there must be a tax arrangement which is also the point at which the main purpose test is utilised.[20] Lastly, the double reasonableness test is applied in order to establish whether an arrangement is abusive.[21] The GAAR does not apply unless the double reasonableness test is satisfied. Therefore, the first two stages of the test can be seen as the preliminary stages which filter the permissible arrangements.

3.2 (a) Tax advantage

Significantly, the HMRC GAAR guidance admits that the scope of the term "tax advantage" is broad.[22] Such broadness "sets a low threshold".[23] Moreover, the guidance asserts that "it is likely that many transactions that would achieve some tax advantage will come within this definition".[24] The GAAR has also provided a list of examples of what can constitute a tax advantage.[25] The broadest example is where a tax advantage is equated to the "avoidance or reduction of a charge to tax or an assessment to tax".[26]

Other benefits which would constitute a tax advantage include a "relief or increased relief from tax",[27] a "repayment or increased repayment of tax",[28] an "avoidance of a possible assessment to tax",[29] a "deferral of a payment of tax or advancement of a repayment of tax"[30] and lastly, "avoidance of an obligation to deduct or account for tax".[31] The way in which a tax advantage has been described ensures that a diverse range of transactions will attract the GAAR. The definition of a tax advantage should rightly encompass reliefs, repayment and the avoidance of tax. However, it is questionable as to whether a deferral should amount to avoidance since tax is not being avoided completely.

3.2 (b) Tax arrangement

The GAAR dissected the term "abusive arrangement"[32] and provided definitions for both words for tax purposes. A tax arrangement is described as "obtaining of a tax advantage was the main purpose, or one of the main purposes, of the arrangements".[33] The test can be criticised for the difficulty in determining whether tax avoidance was one of the main purposes as it would involve an exploration of all the possible purposes. Furthermore, as Krikorian explains, if a person discovers "new suggestions and possibilities . . . the final result can hardly be described as the realisation of a preconceived plan".[34] This test can also lead to examining the taxpayer's or their advisor's purpose and result in a purpose being imputed.

The GAAR does not explain in great detail the meaning of an arrangement. The legislation broadly states that an arrangement includes an "agreement, understanding, scheme, transaction or series of transactions".[35] The GAAR guidance acknowledges that the definition of a tax arrangement undeniably "set[s] a low threshold"[36] for arrangements falling under the supposed targeted GAAR. Gammie has also remarked that the definition of a tax arrangement "encompass[es] most ordinary tax planning".[37] Moreover, others have also recognised that "any arrangements which have been structured in such a way as to give effect to tax advice, are likely to be caught".[38]

Other tax legislation has sought to delve deeper into the meaning of an arrangement. For example, the Corporation Tax Act 2010 states what constitutes an arrangement for transferring reliefs according to what effect the arrangement has.[39] These effects are based on the different possible people who could receive payment and encompass a company,[40] a person connected with the company,[41] a partner[42] and "a person connected with another partner".[43] Therefore, the definition of an arrangement in the GAAR could also outline what effect each type of arrangement would have, such as a circular scheme or a series of transactions carried out in quick succession.

The GAAR guidance also elucidates the flexibility of the term "arrangement". Interestingly, "the GAAR can be applied to an arrangement that is part of a wider arrangement or to the wider arrangement as a whole".[44] Therefore, the judiciary can select which part of the arrangement the GAAR will be applied to. This provision is also reminiscent of how Lord Oliver in *Craven* described the underlying principle of *Ramsay*. He asserted that *Ramsay* promoted the use of establishing the "relevant transaction".[45] However, Lethaby justifiably argues that

> the fact that elements of a commercially driven transaction can be isolated and treated as discrete tax arrangements for the purposes of applying the rules is particularly concerning.[46]

3.2 (c) ***The main purpose test***

The main purpose test gives the judiciary the opportunity to examine the arrangement's purpose.[47] Interestingly, Aaronson first envisaged the main purpose test to be subjective in his supplementary report, although it was acknowledged in the report that this would be inappropriate.[48] The apparent safeguard was entitled "arrangements without tax intent",[49] and initially, Aaronson believed that "there would be no need to give any thought to the GAAR in the context of transactions without any tax motivation".[50] Therefore, this shows that the initial conceptions of the main purpose test essentially used motive to distinguish between acceptable and abusive tax avoidance. However, it was recognised that the "safeguard operated on the basis of subjective intent".[51] Although this appears to be a minor revelation, it is significant as it demonstrates that those who were involved in designing the GAAR believe that the term "intention" has subjective connotations. The subjective affiliations with intention are particularly important when examining its use in the double reasonableness test. The revelation is interesting as it provides an indication as to the mindset of those who formulated the GAAR. Moreover, it has been recognised by some practitioners that explicitly examining the absence of a tax motive would be unfeasible as it is "unlikely to be satisfied in any scenario where a taxpayer had sought professional advice".[52] However, in practice, schemes may truly fail due to the inclusion of fiscal advice.

Judges are at liberty creatively to interpret the facts to ascribe a purpose to the arrangements. However, this could also extend to scrutinising the taxpayer's purpose in embarking on the transactions, although Lord Clyde in *McGuckian* proclaimed that the taxpayer's purpose is irrelevant.[53] Similarly, the GAAR guidance echoes that "it is neither necessary nor appropriate to enquire whether any particular person . . . actually had that intention".[54] However, this can be interpreted as meaning that the relevant intention can be imputed without investigating whether the taxpayer actually had the intention. Despite the assurance that the taxpayer's intention is both an irrelevant and an inappropriate consideration, the GAAR guidance acknowledges that an assessment of the objective purpose of the arrangement can coincide with the taxpayer's subjective intentions in practice.[55] This notion corresponds with the view that a purpose can also denote the "object [or] thing intended".[56] Therefore, although tax law exudes objectivity through emphasising the separateness of the taxpayer's intentions and the arrangement's purpose, the two influences are generally regarded as potentially similar in practice and can overlap. The GAAR guidance then discusses the taxpayer's purpose in the same context, which suggests that the guidance views these terms as interchangeable.[57] Undoubtedly, there can be situations in which a taxpayer intends to avoid tax, and the main purpose of the arrangement is also to avoid tax. However, there may also be instances when there was no tax avoidance intention but, due to a tax advantage gained, the courts infer a tax avoidance purpose.

The taxpayer's purpose is inextricably linked to the arrangement's purpose as the guidance explains:

> [I]t would be very rare to find a situation where objectively the obtaining of a tax advantage appeared to be one of the main purposes of an arrangement although, subjectively, the participators did not in fact have any such aim.[58]

Therefore, it is evident that HMRC views the arrangement's purpose as being virtually inextricably linked to the taxpayer's subjective purpose. This may suggest that the former formulation was devised in order to give the appearance of objectivity, when this was not the real intention. Consequently, the taxpayer's purpose may be sought under the guise of examining the arrangement's purpose.

Deciding whether the tax advantage was the main purpose of the arrangement is deemed a seemingly simple task in the HMRC GAAR guidance. It states that a tax advantage would be considered the main purpose of an arrangement where it

> would not have been carried out at all were it not for the opportunity to obtain the tax advantage; or where any non-tax objective was secondary to the benefit of obtaining the tax advantage.[59]

However, the guidance acknowledges that it would be a harder task to prove that a tax advantage was only one of the main purposes,[60] which is perhaps why this part of the test should be excluded from the GAAR. It is important to acknowledge that if a tax advantage is only "one of the main purposes of the arrangement",[61] it presupposes the existence of another or other main purposes, as stated in *Ensign*.[62] Therefore, the task in uncovering whether the tax advantage was a main purpose is complicated by untangling the competing purposes. Consequently, the GAAR seeks to ascertain the "purposive result"[63] as advocated by Krikorian. The HMRC GAAR guidance advises that in order to establish whether the tax advantage was a main purpose, regard must be taken of a twofold test. The test seeks to uncover

> whether a transaction which would otherwise have occurred has been reshaped, or has been entered into under different terms and conditions, in order to change significantly the tax result that would otherwise have arisen, and where the desired tax result is itself a substantial objective.[64]

Therefore, the two key elements in the tests question whether the arrangement has been reshaped or whether the terms and conditions have been constructed so as to bring about a different tax result than had these methods not been utilised. There is much to consider in this test, and it is unclear how the judiciary should apply the GAAR alongside the additional tests within the guidance. The test does not seem particularly helpful as it still involves a degree of judicial discretion and restructuring of the facts.

DAC6, an EU directive imposing mandatory disclosure rules, has similar wording to the GAAR and has implemented a main benefit test. This test is more objective than the UK GAAR's main purpose test as the latter objectively considers whether a tax advantage may be expected to arise from an arrangement. In contrast, the main purpose test can give rise to subjective considerations.

3.2 (d) The double reasonableness test

The GAAR does not imply that a tax arrangement alone is sufficient to amount to an abusive tax arrangement. Similarly, the main purpose test is also not conclusive of an abusive arrangement. This indicates that a tax advantage can be the main purpose of a genuine, non-abusive transaction. The key term in the GAAR is "abusive" as this is what separates the GAAR from the pre-existing targeted anti-avoidance provisions,[65] as discussed in chapter 1. What amounts to an abusive arrangement has been defined in the "crux of the GAAR",[66] which is the double reasonableness test. According to the GAAR, an arrangement is abusive where it "cannot reasonably be regarded as a reasonable course of action in relation to the relevant tax provisions".[67] The test is essentially twofold. It requires both the view of the judge making the decision and the arrangement to be reasonable. Therefore, "the two instances of reasonableness operate independently of each other".[68] The double reasonableness test is vague, which is concerning given that it is regarded as "the most important of the protections . . . for responsible tax planning".[69] The test is pivotal as it determines whether the GAAR applies. Therefore, the double reasonableness test effectively decides the demarcation between abusive and non-abusive tax avoidance.

The issue of what is reasonable has been described as involving the "type of question that if you have to think about it for too long, you probably have a problem and should consider alternative transactions or steps".[70] However, many taxpayers and advisors are likely to consider carefully whether their arrangement can be viewed as reasonable, particularly as the untested GAAR is vague. It is difficult to know what is reasonable or, more importantly, what amounts to unreasonable and where the demarcation between reasonable or unreasonable tax avoidance is. There are various ways in which the term "reasonable" can be interpreted. Tax advisors, corporations and HMRC are all likely to have different interpretations of whether an arrangement is reasonable. Therefore, the double reasonableness test is unhelpful to taxpayers and the judiciary. The Aaronson Report attempts to provide an objective dimension to the double reasonableness test by stating that an arrangement would be reasonable

> not only if the judge himself regards the arrangement as a reasonable exercise of choices of conduct but also, where he does not himself take that view, he nonetheless considers that such a view may reasonably be held.[71]

Reasonableness is an important concept in the GAAR. Gammie has asserted that

> the United Kingdom has now decreed that taxpayers are not necessarily to be taxed according to the purpose of the Act and the reality of the arrangements but by reference to whether their tax arrangements can or cannot be characterised as reasonable.[72]

However, it would be more objective to consider whether the taxpayer should be taxed according to the specific words of the Act or the purpose of a particular provision. As the concept of reasonableness is of importance in deciding abusive tax avoidance cases, it will be explored further.

3.2(d)(i) Reasonableness in tort and contract law

The concepts of reasonableness and the reasonable person are commonly used in tort law. Therefore, it is helpful to analyse the meanings given to them to clarify how the double reasonableness test might operate. In tort law, what is reasonable has been described as "a rough approximation to exactness"[73] because "complete exactness is neither attainable nor desirable".[74] However, as McKie stated, it has been recognised that

> the judge has to decide what "reasonable" means, and it is inevitable that different judges may take variant views on the same question with respect to such an elastic term.[75]

Therefore, even with a subject like tort law which habitually refers to reasonableness and the reasonable person, it has been acknowledged that the term "reasonable" is open to interpretation. Consequently, standards of reasonableness are likely to vary, which is why the double reasonableness test is not an accurate measurement for deciding whether tax avoidance cases are acceptable.

The term "reasonableness" has also been used in deciding cases of negligence. Legislation in this area has also sought to define what "reasonableness" entails. Section 11(1) of the Unfair Contract Terms Act 1977 outlines what encompasses the "reasonableness test".[76] In relation to excluding negligence liability from contractual terms, the legislation states that

> the requirement of reasonableness for the purposes of this Part of this Act . . . is that the term shall have been a fair and reasonable one to be included having regard to the circumstances which were, or ought reasonably to have been, known to or in the contemplation of the parties when the contract was made.[77]

Reasonableness is judged from the litigant's perspective. However, even in the sphere of negligence where the concept of reasonableness is commonly used, James believes that the "reasonableness test"[78] "leaves a great deal of discretion in the hands of the courts".[79] James also asserts that an excessive amount of discretion will reduce certainty for those affected.[80] Therefore, the double reasonableness test in the GAAR is likely to fuel judicial discretion.

Others argue that what can be deemed reasonable is decided on a case-by-case basis[81] and that "reasonableness is assessed according to the special features of a case".[82] Tully also believes that reasonableness is difficult to define as "it is not a benchmark capable of precise definition or mechanical application".[83] However, the double reasonableness test may have been included as "it provides flexibility for a court, the concept is vague and offers little clear or practical guidance to decision makers".[84]

3.2(d)(ii) "Reasonableness" in public law

The concept of reasonableness has also been used in public law where "reasonableness [is used] as a test for judicial review of discretionary determinations".[85] Craig supports the notion that examining the reasonableness of a decision limits discretion.[86] Although Craig's interpretation of reasonableness largely revolves around its meaning in judicial review proceedings, the interpretations are useful as he considers what reasonableness entails in practice. Craig believes that "reasonableness is concerned with review of the weight and balance accorded by the primary decision-maker".[87] Therefore, in deciding whether a transaction was a "reasonable course of action",[88] as prescribed by the GAAR, judges will undergo a balancing exercise, and reasonableness will be judged on the balance of probabilities.[89] The balancing approach involves distinguishing between "reasoning errors that rob the decision of its logical integrity, or a common-sense decision reached in the light of all the material".[90]

Craig provides the case of *R (on the application of Bancoult) v Secretary of State for Foreign and Commonwealth Affairs*[91] (*Bancoult*) as an example of balancing competing interests in order to reach a decision which was deemed reasonable.[92] The judges had to decide whether it was reasonable to allow the Chagos Islanders to return to their homeland of Diego Garcia and fund the resettlement. The court was tasked with balancing the interests of the Chagos Islanders with equally pressing issues such as national security and the scale of the expenditure involved in the resettlement. Although the appeal was ultimately rejected, Craig believes that the rejection was due to the weight placed on the competing interests.[93] For example,

> Lord Hoffmann placed less weight on the islanders' interest because he found that they did not really wish to re-settle the islands, and were primarily seeking to improve their bargaining position in relation to compensation. He placed more weight on the governmental interest on the ground that issues of security and expenditure from the public purse were matters peculiarly in the competence of the government.[94]

The landmark judicial review case of *Associated Provincial Picture Houses, Limited v Wednesbury Corporation*[95] (*Wednesbury*) also discussed the concept of reasonableness. The plaintiffs owned a cinema theatre and sought to challenge conditions imposed on their operating licence by the defendant local authority. The condition was that "no children under the age of fifteen years shall be admitted to any entertainment, whether accompanied by an adult or not".[96] The legislation which the local authority relied on was the Sunday Entertainments Act 1932 which "legalised the opening of cinemas on Sundays, subject to certain specified conditions and subject to such conditions as the licensing authority think fit to impose".[97]

The concept of reasonableness came to the fore where Lord Greene M.R. discussed how "discretion must be exercised reasonably".[98] He made it clear that

> the task of the court is not to decide what it thinks is reasonable, but to decide whether what is prima facie within the power of the local authority is a condition which no reasonable authority, acting within the four corners of their jurisdiction, could have decided to impose.[99]

In deciding whether the local authority has kept within their jurisdiction,

> the court is entitled to investigate the action of the local authority with a view to seeing whether they have taken into account matters which they ought

> not to take into account, or, conversely, have refused to take into account or neglected to take into account matters which they ought to take into account.[100]

However, Lord Greene M.R. stated that even where the local authority has kept within their jurisdiction, the court may still hold "that they have nevertheless come to a conclusion so unreasonable that no reasonable authority could ever have come to it".[101]

The concept of reasonableness can be differentiated from the concept of proportionality. The concept of proportionality "applies when human rights are engaged to ensure that any limitation on a human right is proportionate to the social and political considerations that justify that limitation".[102] Therefore, "administrative measures must not be more drastic than is necessary for attaining the desired result".[103] Applying the test of proportionality "requires the making of a judgement by the primary decision-maker".[104] Therefore, the test "requires the court to judge whether the action taken was really needed as well as whether it was within the range of courses of action that could reasonably be followed".[105]

While the concept of reasonableness remains elusive, the judgement in *Wednesbury* affirms that judges should not determine whether the parties acted reasonably according to their own standards of what is reasonable. In relation to reasonableness, he acknowledged that "all over the country I have no doubt on a thing of that sort honest and sincere people hold different views".[106] The task is to decide whether another local authority would have acted in a similar way.[107] *Wednesbury* provides an example of how the concept of reasonableness is applied in practice. However, *Wednesbury* focused more on identifying what is unreasonable. As will be discussed, the GAAR guidance specifies that judges should not examine whether an arrangement would be regarded as unreasonable.[108] The fact that regard has to be given as to whether an arrangement can be regarded as reasonable places pressure on the courts to grapple with the concept of reasonableness. Whether or not reasonableness will be applied in the same manner as in *Wednesbury* is yet to be seen.

3.2(d)(iii) Reasonable man

The HMRC GAAR guidance states that it may be necessary to test whether the view as to the reasonableness of an arrangement is in itself reasonable.[109] Therefore, it may be necessary to consider the requirements of a reasonable person in making that decision. In tort law, the reasonable person has been described as "not [having] the courage of Achilles, the wisdom of Ulysses nor the strength of Hercules".[110] The law "does not expect the reasonable person to be all-seeing and all-knowing, and he can therefore make reasonable mistakes",[111] although the reasonable person is not deemed to be an "average person".[112] Similarly, "the law requires him to show such skill as any ordinary member of the profession or calling to which he belongs, or claims to belong, would display".[113]

The standard of reasonableness required to make the decision is not high and allows for a margin of error. Consequently, the reasonableness requirement is laced with subjectivity and is likely to generate inconsistency in practice. In relation to testing the reasonableness of the decision is reasonable, Craig asserts that

> in making the determination as to whether the contested decision was within the range of reasonable decisions the court is assessing the balance struck by the decision-maker.[114]

However, Craig commented on testing the reasonableness of a decision in relation to judicial review. In regards to tax law, it may not be necessary for judges to decide whether the arrangement was reasonable, then re-examine whether their own view was reasonable. Therefore, Mishcon de Reya's view of a "single reasonableness test"[115] appears adequate for the purposes of tax law.

3.2 (e) Abuse according to the GAAR

Due to the vagueness of the double reasonableness test alone, the Finance Act 2013 goes on to detail three factors which the court should be mindful of when deciphering whether an arrangement is abusive. Firstly, the court is permitted to examine "the substantive results of the arrangements"[116] and whether these are "consistent with any principles on which those provisions are based (whether express or implied) and the policy objectives of those provisions".[117] The aforementioned provision is wide because it permits judges to develop general broad principles and also examine policy considerations. Canadian courts have rightly viewed the formulation of policy by judges as undesirable as

> to send the courts on the search for some overarching policy and then to use such a policy to override the wording of the provisions of the *Income Tax Act* would inappropriately place the formulation of taxation policy in the hands of the judiciary, requiring judges to perform a task to which they are unaccustomed and for which they are not equipped.[118]

The provision regarding policy considerations has received criticism for being "a radical and untested departure from the established principles of statutory interpretation that [is] . . . unique to English law".[119] This is because "*Ramsay* did not alter the principle that the court must look to the words of an Act of Parliament to ascertain Parliament's intentions".[120] However, the

> GAAR departs from this principle by requiring the taxpayer (and, ultimately, the court) to consider the "principles" underlying a given legislative provision and, even worse, their policy objectives. Gone is the rule that Parliament's words are the guide to its intentions.[121]

Moreover, Gothard and Austen argue that

> how a taxpayer is supposed to divine with any certainty the "principles" purportedly underlying a given statutory provision or the relevant policy objectives – particularly in such unchartered legal territory – is not explained.[122]

The GAAR also allows an investigation into the method of executing the transactions in order to determine "whether the means of achieving those results involves one or more contrived or abnormal steps".[123] There is no guidance on what would amount to an abnormal step, which indicates that the judiciary can use their discretion in relation to how an abnormal step is defined. This provision is also reminiscent of the approach taken in *McGuckian* where Lord Browne-Wilkinson held that the abnormal transactions should be ignored, and the legislation should be applied to the resulting arrangement in a holistic manner.[124] However, the GAAR does not suggest that any abnormal steps should be ignored. Instead, the abnormal step will be regarded as abusive, which relieves the courts of the task of imagining what the arrangement would have looked like had the abnormal step not been inserted. The existence of an abnormal step would point to abuse. As *McGuckian* favoured and built on the *Ramsay* approach, it can be said that the GAAR has been influenced by *Ramsay* and its supporting cases. Therefore, the advent of the GAAR has generated a shift from "a judicial GAAR to a legislative GAAR".[125]

Lastly, in determining whether an arrangement is abusive, the courts can also deliberate on "whether the arrangements are intended to exploit any shortcomings in those provisions".[126] This provision is important as it indicates that the judiciary can examine the taxpayer's intentions to determine whether the design of the arrangement was constructed so as to take advantage of loopholes in the tax system. However, as Anscombe recognised, a person's intention can "often not be seen from seeing what he does".[127] As previously mentioned, even HMRC acknowledges that there is an overlap between the arrangement's purpose and the taxpayer's intentions. The judiciary are therefore permitted to examine the arrangement's purpose in the main purpose test as well as the taxpayer's intentions. This clearly indicates that they are two distinct considerations. In this instance, the Finance Act 2013 has sought to include the more subjective term "intention", which can more easily be equated to the taxpayer's intentions. The provision also serves to cloud the demarcations between abusive and non-abusive tax avoidance. Associating a tax avoidance intention with unacceptable tax avoidance implies that those engaging in legitimate tax avoidance schemes must do so without the corresponding intention. However, Anscombe argued that intentional actions cannot be recognised by "any extra feature which exists when it is performed".[128] Moreover, there is an

> inherently objective nature of tax avoidance; intention on the part of the taxpayer, which constitutes an essential element of evasion, is not required as a condition for the existence of avoidance.[129]

The aforementioned provision regarding exploiting Parliament's shortcomings has attracted strong criticism for facilitating the "transferred fault of the citizen and not the responsibility of the Executive who perpetrated it".[130] Greenberg has largely based his criticisms on the addition of the term "shortcoming" in the provision.[131] The worrying implication is that

> if the drafter and the Executive get a particular piece of fiscal legislation "wrong", in the sense that they fail to achieve what they might have wished to achieve, they can absolve themselves of any responsibility, and transfer responsibility to the citizen.[132]

Greenberg therefore insinuates that the taxpayer is used as a scapegoat for lawfully taking advantage of inadequacies in tax legislation. Others have also remarked "that HMRC and parliamentary draftsmen may use [the] GAAR as a cover for inadequate draftsmanship".[133]

The burden is on the taxpayer to uncover what the legislation ought to tackle and, if not, "penalise him or her for not working out what it was intended to achieve and how Parliament and the Executive meant to achieve it".[134] Moreover, Gammie also argues that

> the UK GAAR is based on the wrong premise and does little to improve the tax system and address its manifest "shortcomings". An objection to the GAAR is that it tolerates such shortcomings rather than addresses them.[135]

An apparent safeguard is that the burden is on HMRC to establish whether an arrangement is abusive.[136] The GAAR guidance had anticipated views such as Greenberg's and has asserted that these views in particular are "inconsistent with one of the basic purposes of the GAAR, namely to deter or counteract the deliberate exploitation of shortcomings in legislation".[137] By the inclusion of the term "deliberate",[138] the GAAR guidance indicates that tax avoidance must be intentional. Nevertheless, it does raise the argument of why the shortcomings were not blocked in the first place rather than placing a blanket ban on avoidance with the onus on the taxpayer to respect Parliament's shortcomings.

Due to the ambiguous nature of the double reasonableness test, the GAAR has also sought to elucidate on what amounts to an abusive arrangement by outlining three key points which are indicative of abuse. Firstly, the GAAR warns that an arrangement resulting in profit which is "significantly less than the amount for economic purposes"[139] would be regarded as abusive. The provision is very unclear as the term "economic purposes" has not been defined in the GAAR; therefore, it is difficult to ascertain what that amount is and, consequently, how low a profit must be in order to constitute abuse. Gammie has also argued that

> an economist would not think it especially helpful to refer to "the amount for economic purposes" and a reference to the financial outcome or result of the arrangements might have been better.[140]

If it is presumed that the term "economic purposes" refers to a tax advantage, the requirement means that the arrangement must obtain a higher profit than the tax advantage gained. However, this is a speculative interpretation of this provision; therefore, it can be interpreted in other ways. For example, "economic purposes" could also refer to the amount of profit which one would have in a similar arrangement under slightly different terms. In this case, the aforementioned provision indicates that if the profit is significantly less than profit resulting from a similar arrangement, it would indicate abuse. As it is unclear what "economic purposes" means, it not only causes confusion and inconsistency in adjudication, but it also does little to provide guidance as to what will be considered abusive.

Secondly, if the arrangement "result[s] in deductions or losses of an amount for tax purposes that is significantly greater than the amount for economic purposes",[141] the arrangement may be held to be abusive. The provision may simply be indicating that large losses or unusually generous deductions are indicative of abuse. However, due to the inclusion of the elusive term "economic purposes", it is difficult to attribute concrete meaning to this provision. The deductions and losses must be much less than the "amount for economic purposes",[142] which may mean that the deductions and losses must be less than the overall tax advantage gained. However, without explicit confirmation by Parliament, it is difficult to interpret this provision accurately.

Lastly, wherever an arrangement leads to a "repayment or crediting of tax [that] . . . is unlikely to be paid",[143] it may be conclusive of an abusive arrangement. Despite these calculation-based and objective tests which are indicative of abuse, the GAAR has a significant caveat which colours the objective provisions with an important requirement which is subject to judicial discretion. Although the three aforementioned examples would point to an abusive arrangement, the GAAR specifies that these situations would only amount to abuse if "such a result was not the anticipated result when the relevant tax provisions were enacted".[144] Therefore, the GAAR leaves open scope for considerable judicial discretion to ascertain whether Parliament had foreseen such results, and if it is decided that Parliament had not foreseen the result, it amounts to an abusive arrangement. This provision is important as it suggests that ultimately, the GAAR will apply in all circumstances in which the judiciary believe that Parliament had not anticipated the result of the arrangement. While it is generally accepted that the courts can seek to ascertain Parliament's intentions, there is less justification for judges to have the task of barring arrangements which Parliament had not even contemplated. Moreover, "there is often fierce debate, at least in Australia, about what was or was not within the contemplation of Parliament when enacting a specific provision".[145] However, courts may decide what Parliament did not intend by examining whether the arrangement falls within the wording of the statute when read literally or purposively.

The breadth of the GAAR is therefore wide and unclear. Although the GAAR is seemingly targeted through specifying that it should only apply to abusive arrangements, the definition of an abusive arrangement branches out in order to define an abusive arrangement, an arrangement and what is abusive. The assortment of tests which these definitions contain are wide and leave the judiciary with little limitation or guidance in adjudication. Therefore, "the concept of 'abusiveness', which seems so clear to politicians, activists and columnists, is near-impossible to define satisfactorily in the context of the UK tax code".[146]

3.3 Abuse according to the GAAR guidance

The HMRC GAAR guidance describes the double reasonableness test as not being as simple as it appears in an attempt at ensuring objectivity and minimising judicial discretion. The guidance states that judges should not base their decisions on whether they believe the arrangement is unreasonable or not.[147] However, if an arrangement cannot be regarded as reasonable, it is analogous to regarding the arrangement as unreasonable. The GAAR would be made clearer if principles were laid down to explain what would be deemed unreasonable rather that than what is reasonable. A single unreasonableness test would work better as it is far simpler to explain what is not permitted rather than what is permitted.

In an attempt to avoid subjectivity, the guidance states that judges must study "the range of reasonable views that could be held in relation to the arrangements".[148] However, this guidance is unhelpful as it does little to remedy the problem of subjectivity inherent in the double reasonableness test. The application of the test is further obscured by the possibility of a multitude of views arising as to the reasonability of the arrangement. The guidance states that where there exists a view which regards the arrangement as being reasonable, "it is necessary to test that view to see whether that view itself can be regarded as reasonable".[149] The requirements of tediously evaluating the reasonable views, then testing the reasonability of the view in favour of the arrangement arguably create a stratified GAAR, layered by the obligation to investigate and then test the views. The complexity of the double reasonableness test may instead lead to judges analysing whether, in their view, based on common law principles, the arrangement can be considered unreasonable. An investigation as to how judges have examined "reasonableness", based on common law principles, will be explored in chapter 6. Furthermore, although the test is presumably designed to appear as if it is setting a higher threshold for tax avoidance, judges are still at liberty to define what is reasonable.

The vagueness of the double reasonableness test fuels uncertainty and inevitable judicial discretion, although the GAAR guidance states that a targeted GAAR "would help reduce the risk of stretched interpretation and the uncertainty which this entails".[150] Significantly, HMRC acknowledges that discretion leading to wide interpretation leads to uncertainty, which is undesirable.

The GAAR Advisory Panel is important as the GAAR states that the judiciary "must take into account . . . any opinion of the GAAR Advisory Panel about the arrangements".[151] Moreover, the guidance provides a safeguard to taxpayers in relation to the double reasonableness test which requires HMRC to consult with the independent advisory panel as to whether the taxpayer's actions were reasonable before the GAAR is applied.[152] However, the extent to which this safeguard will protect taxpayers is uncertain as the advisory panel will merely be consulted. Consequently, if the taxpayer's actions are deemed an unreasonable course of action by the advisory panel, the ultimate decision lies with the judiciary to apply the wide GAAR provisions using their discretion, although the GAAR guidance also reiterates that the views of the advisory panel can be considered by the court.[153]

3.4 What is not abusive

Another form of defence to the taxpayer is contained in s207(5) Finance Act 2013, which lays down in what circumstance an arrangement would not be viewed as abusive. The defence is a twofold test that requires an arrangement to firstly "accord with established practice",[154] which the GAAR guidance states is "published material".[155] Secondly, in relation to the evidenced practice, HMRC must have also "indicated its acceptance of that practice".[156] The guidance also infers that the location the acceptance is published is key to determining whether HMRC accepts the practice.[157] Acceptance of the practice may be published "from HMRC, or textbooks or articles in journals",[158] which includes a vast array of material. However, the guidance widens this selection of materials by adding that acceptance can also be indicated "by other evidence of what had become a common practice by the relevant time".[159] This is less specific as it can encompass many sources. It would have been useful if the guidance was more specific by citing a particular source, such as case law. The reason that vague sources are unhelpful is that, in practice, HMRC may exclude particular sources for not coming within the scope of their preferred source list to the detriment of the taxpayer.

The published information alone cannot provide a defence to taxpayers, unless HMRC also clearly indicates that it supports the practice. Therefore, this particular defence is extremely narrow and, inevitably, subject to change. The two-stage test makes it difficult for taxpayers to satisfy both stages, which renders the safeguard minimally protective.

The disclosure of tax avoidance schemes[160] regime may also be relevant in determining what is not abusive. The regime requires that "certain people must provide information to HMRC about avoidance schemes within 5 days of the schemes being made available or implemented".[161] Therefore, if HMRC has advance notice of a scheme from the taxpayer and HMRC has indicated that it is content with it, the taxpayer's scheme is less likely to attract the scrutiny of the GAAR. This is because HMRC has not objected to the scheme. Consequently, schemes which pass the scrutiny of the DOTAS regime can be deemed not abusive.

3.5 The scope of the GAAR

The GAAR's intended scope is "targeted at abusive arrangements".[162] The alleged targeted nature of the GAAR has been designed by the GAAR study group in order to avoid "a broad spectrum general anti-avoidance rule [which] would *not* be beneficial for the UK tax system".[163] The GAAR "began life as a general anti-avoidance rule but was re-designated a general anti-abuse rule".[164] The GAAR study group has acknowledged that creating a broader rule may result in "undermining the ability of business[es] and individuals to carry out sensible and responsible tax planning".[165] Therefore, it is essential that the scope of the GAAR has clearly identifiable limitations for the sake of economic growth, if not for the ease of compliance for the taxpayer.

The scope of the GAAR is particularly important as its legislative rules take precedence over common law rules. As previously mentioned, the GAAR is aimed at "counteracting tax advantages arising from tax arrangements that are abusive".[166] The GAAR guidance itself attributes a wide definition to a tax arrangement which it admits will encompass many arrangements.[167] It is uncertain why a targeted GAAR would have supplementary guidance indicating that a vast number of arrangements can fall within the legislation. The GAAR guidance is influential as it can be used as an aid to interpretation of the GAAR.[168] Gammie has also stated that, under the GAAR, "anything is an arrangement and everything is a tax advantage",[169] which also reinforces the argument that the GAAR is wide.

The GAAR was "intended to apply only to egregious, or very aggressive, tax avoidance schemes".[170] However, Lethaby has perceptively recognised that what amounts to egregious tax planning "necessarily [implies] value judgements",[171] which insinuates scope for subjectivity. Abusive tax avoidance schemes which are deemed "GAAR-able"[172] are therefore placed in this category using discretion. Lethaby recognises that the GAAR embodies Parliament's will.[173] However, she stated

> that is not to say that I necessarily agree that the GAAR is appropriately narrowly framed so as to catch only the most 'egregious' transactions at which it was allegedly targeted. I don't agree.[174]

Furthermore, the case law on tax avoidance has illustrated that the judiciary have been probing the taxpayer's intentions. Therefore, the GAAR can be said to "simply serve to legitimise a discretion that the courts are already exercising".[175] Consequently, whilst the GAAR "should not affect the large centre ground of responsible tax planning",[176] there is no guarantee that it will not do so in practice. However, Freedman makes the very compelling argument that "even if legitimisation were the only outcome, then this would be a worthwhile one".[177] Constitutional legitimisation is invariably important, although the design of the GAAR must have identifiable boundaries for taxpayer certainty.

In addition to the provisions being broad, the GAAR guidance also widens normal rules of evidence in relation to abusive arrangements.[178] The court can examine "all relevant material, whether or not such material would be admissible in court proceedings under the normal rules of evidence".[179] The GAAR also takes precedence over tax legislation to which it applies.[180]

The requirement of whether Parliament had anticipated the resulting arrangement is crucial in determining abuse. However, this provision is broad as

> the GAAR moves away from a focus on what Parliament intended to a focus on what Parliament anticipated, and allows the courts to have regard to a wider range of material as evidence of what was anticipated.[181]

The analysis of the GAAR's scope demonstrates that there is an "unspecified boundary set by the GAAR beyond which taxpayers stray at their peril".[182] The GAAR guidance has provided specific definitions for key terms in the GAAR, and these are left purposely broad. Therefore, if there was any uncertainty over whether specific terms of the GAAR should be interpreted widely, the guidance confirms that this is the correct approach. Consequently, the scope of the targeted GAAR is obscured by ambiguity and the further "uncertainty as to what even the architects of the draft GAAR intend to be caught by it".[183] There is also the general parallel concern of "whether such schemes can be accurately targeted",[184] which suggests that a targeted GAAR is understandably challenging to design due to the inherent complexity of tax avoidance schemes.

3.6 The Aaronson Report

It is useful to analyse the recommendations and draft GAAR laid down in the Aaronson Report in order to establish what it recommended, why these recommendations were made and the extent to which the final legislation bears resemblance to the report's recommendations. It will be helpful to examine whether the problems which the Aaronson Report sought to avoid can be avoided by the way the final draft of the GAAR was written.

The scope of the GAAR was not intended to be wide as the Aaronson Report acknowledged that "a broad spectrum general anti-avoidance rule would *not* be beneficial for the UK tax system".[185] Similarly, Aaronson recognised that, prior to the implementation of the GAAR, "judges inevitably . . . [were] faced with the temptation to stretch the interpretation"[186] of taxing statutes and that this caused uncertainty.[187] However, as mentioned previously, the scope of the GAAR is potentially wide and relies heavily on judicial discretion. Consequently, the GAAR is capable of being applied to more than "the most egregious tax avoidance schemes".[188]

The enacted GAAR is targeted at a wider range of taxes than laid down in the Aaronson Report. The report only envisaged "income tax, capital gains tax, corporation tax and petroleum revenue tax"[189] being covered by the GAAR. However, the enacted GAAR extended the recommendations made by Aaronson to cover inheritance tax,[190] stamp duty land tax[191] and annual tax on enveloped dwellings.[192] Therefore, the enacted GAAR is undoubtedly wider than the scope envisaged by the Aaronson Report. It was also recommended that stamp duty land tax should only be included within the GAAR's remit once the GAAR was "seen to operate fairly and effectively".[193] However, this recommendation went unheeded.

As well as differences in the intended scope of the GAAR, the Aaronson Report also made it clear that "where there can be reasonable doubt as to which side of the line any particular arrangement falls on, then that doubt is to be resolved in favour of the taxpayer".[194] This reasoning was adopted from the words of Salmon L.J. in *Fleming v Associated Newspapers*,[195] wherein he stated that "if in a taxing statute words are reasonably capable of two alternative meanings, the courts will prefer the meaning more favourable to the subject".[196] However, no such assurances were made in the GAAR. Instead, the GAAR guidance states that where an arrangement could be regarded as reasonable, that view must then be tested as to its reasonableness.[197]

The Aaronson Report states that, in applying the GAAR,

> the starting point should be to see whether the arrangement is abnormal, in the sense of having abnormal features specifically designed to achieve a tax advantageous result.[198]

The effect of examining abnormalities in the early stages of the GAAR means that "if there is no such feature then it is immediately dismissed from consideration".[199] However, the GAAR only examines the existence of abnormal steps at the final stage when considering whether an arrangement is abusive. The approach taken by Aaronson would have ensured that arrangements which were not abusive were dismissed at an earlier stage.

Despite the differences between the Aaronson Report and the final GAAR, there are some similarities. For example, the double reasonableness test is similar to the Aaronson Report's equivalent that "the arrangement *cannot* reasonably be regarded as a reasonable exercise of choice".[200] Similarly, the main purpose test in the draft GAAR also closely resembles the main purpose test in the Aaronson Report.[201]

As previously mentioned, the GAAR does examine the taxpayer's intentions.[202] The draft GAAR in the Aaronson Report also examines the taxpayer's intentions.[203] Nevertheless, the report states that it is "unlikely that arrangements which have no tax intent at all would in fact give rise to a tax advantage. However, that is nonetheless possible".[204] Aaronson gives the case of *Five Oaks Properties Ltd v HMRC*[205] as an example in which there was no intention to gain a tax advantage despite the possibility of a tax advantage being made. The case concerned five appellant companies which were all part of the Tribeca Group and previously members of the Delancey Group. The issue was whether the losses incurred by these companies prior to the merging with the Tribeca Group could be used to offset gains made by another company within the Tribeca Group.[206] Although HMRC conceded that the "transactions were not pre-planned as part of a tax avoidance scheme",[207] the Special Commissioners held that the pre-entry loss rules prevented the companies from offsetting their losses against the gain made by a company in the same group. It was recognised that

> the pre-entry loss legislation fails to deal with the present factual situation, which it is common ground, results from commercial transactions not intended to avoid the effect of the legislation.[208]

Therefore, the case illustrates how examining intentions is an unreliable consideration.

The Aaronson Report also states that "it is not necessary to demonstrate that the promoter of the arrangement or the parties to it subjectively intended the abnormal feature to have such purpose".[209] Moreover, the Aaronson Report states that "the absence of intent must be shown to extend to every person involved in the planning and execution of the arrangement".[210] This formulation of examining the taxpayer's intentions is wider than required by the GAAR. However, the Aaronson Report illustrates that there is scope to examine the intentions of all involved in the scheme, which could mean imputing the intention of a tax advisor on the taxpayer. The requirement that no participant in the scheme may have an intention to gain a tax advantage also sets a low bar for unacceptable tax planning, which could widen the scope of the GAAR.

Where the GAAR mentions the term "economic purposes"[211] in relation to whether an arrangement can be regarded as abusive, this term is not defined in the GAAR. However, the Aaronson Report provides a better understanding of what this term means. Consequently, Aaronson states that an arrangement would be regarded as abusive where that

> arrangement would, apart from the operation of this Part, result in receipts being taken into account for tax purposes which are significantly less than the true economic income profit or gain.[212]

Similarly, an arrangement would also be regarded as abusive where that

> arrangement would, apart from the operation of this Part, result in deductions being taken into account for tax purposes which are significantly greater than the true economic cost or loss.[213]

Therefore, it is clear that the "economic purposes" requirement refers to profit and losses. However, this is not made clear in the GAAR. Hence, this term can still be open to interpretation.

The Aaronson Report also includes hallmarks of abuse which were not included in the GAAR. For example, an indication of abuse is where "the arrangement includes a transaction at a value significantly different from market value, or otherwise on non-commercial terms".[214] The report also states that an arrangement could be regarded as abusive where "the arrangement, or any element of it, is inconsistent with the legal duties of the parties to it".[215] Moreover, the report outlines how an arrangement is likely to be abusive where "a person, a transaction, a document or significant terms in a document, which would not be included if the arrangement were not designed to achieve an abusive tax result".[216] In addition to these factors, other indications of abuse include where an

> arrangement omits a person, a transaction, a document or significant terms in a document which would not be omitted if the arrangement were not designed to achieve an abusive tax result.[217]

Furthermore, an arrangement could be abusive where it

> includes the location of an asset or a transaction, or of the place of residence of a person, which would not be so located if the arrangement were not designed to achieve an abusive tax result.[218]

These factors are all objective considerations which would limit the amount of discretion exercised by the judiciary when deciding whether an arrangement is abusive.

The report lists material which can be considered when deciding whether an arrangement is abusive. The list in the Aaronson Report resembles the list in the GAAR. However, the Aaronson Report states that the courts may take into account "evidence of practice commonly adopted at the time of the arrangement".[219] However, the GAAR states that HMRC must have "indicated its acceptance of that practice"[220] in order for an arrangement to be considered unabusive.

3.7 Penalties

HMRC issued a consultation document in January 2015 detailing penalties which a tax avoider could be subject to. The document contains key guidance which can help clarify the types of avoidance deemed unacceptable.

Tax avoidance schemes are perpetrated by what the government terms "serial avoiders".[221] This term has underlying criminal connotations as it resembles the term given to "serial killers". The term ascribed to tax avoiders brings tax avoidance closer to tax evasion as the latter is a criminal offence. However, the new term "serial avoiders", coined for tax avoiders, denotes those who regularly avoid paying their taxes and suggests that the GAAR's scope encompasses a seemingly small minority of avoiders. However, despite the narrower scope of the consultation document, judges will follow the GAAR in practice, which undoubtedly encompasses a larger category of taxpayers. The term "serial avoider" has been placed on statutory footing.[222]

Along with the abusive arrangements described in the GAAR legislation, the government's consultation document on penalties outlines the types of schemes which will be targeted. Worryingly, the consultation states that a characteristic of a "serial avoider" is carrying out many schemes annually "that were intended to offset their tax liability several times over in the hope that at least one will work".[223] A person's hopes are equated with motives as previously established. The intention described is irrefutably that of the taxpayer, which indicates that the government encourages the taxpayer's intentions to be scrutinised when refining the lines between acceptable and unacceptable tax avoidance. Moreover, examining what taxpayers hope not only involves examining their intentions but also allows for their motives to be brought into question as the term "hope" can be blurred with "motive", as established earlier. The recommendation is therefore laced with subjective connotations.

Another indicator of an improper tax avoider is where a taxpayer "repeatedly use[s] tax avoidance schemes to shelter the same type of income".[224] Therefore, a key factor in identifying an unacceptable tax avoidance scheme is the issue of regularity and consistency. This view is also reflected in the subsequent characteristic described in the consultation document in which a taxpayer "repeatedly use[s] avoidance schemes to cover the majority of income or gains as they arise".[225] By looking at the amount of income, HMRC indicates it is more concerned where larger sums of money are the subject of a tax avoidance scheme. The requirement of regularity is maintained through to the last provision, where it states that it would be unacceptable if a taxpayer "often use[s] tax avoidance schemes to cover major life or commercial events".[226]

Due to the concern for tackling persistent tax avoiders, the government has recommended that a surcharge penalty should be used as a deterrent where several schemes have failed to be brought to fruition.[227] Other measures aimed at "shift[ing] their behaviour"[228] have been recommended, providing that the taxpayer triggers the threshold conditions outlined in the government's report.[229] The conditions seek to establish whether a taxpayer has a history of unsuccessfully utilising tax schemes for avoidance purposes, used a scheme outlined in the Promoters of Tax Avoidance Schemes Regulations 2015[230] or has failed "to comply with information notices or DOTAS requirements".[231]

Where a tax arrangement is found to be abusive, the GAAR specifies that counteraction of that advantage will be made in a manner which is "just and reasonable".[232] In order to quantify counteraction, judges are advised to examine

> what transaction would have been carried out in order to achieve the same commercial purpose, but without including the steps or features which make the arrangement abusive.[233]

Therefore, the guidance also echoes Lord Browne-Wilkinson's words in *McGuckian* about ignoring certain steps and re-evaluating the arrangement in a different light.[234] The connection between *McGuckian* and the GAAR guidance also reinforces a preference for supporters of the *Ramsay* approach. In order to discover what other arrangement might have been executed with the aim of attaining the same commercial purpose, another test must be applied. The guidance asserts that this objective test questions

> what in all the circumstances would have been the most likely transaction to have been carried out by *a taxpayer* who wished to achieve the commercial objective without seeking to achieve the abusive tax advantage.[235]

Consequently, at the root of counteraction is ascertaining whether there is a commercial purpose and if not, re-arranging the transactions by ignoring the artificial steps to ascertain the "real transaction".[236] Where there is a circular arrangement, as in *Ramsay*, the judges must quantify counteraction based on radically "ignoring the entire arrangement".[237]

In 2020, amendments were made to the UK GAAR. These are contained in Schedule 14 of the Finance Act 2020. A new s209AA was introduced, allowing an officer of HMRC to issue a protective GAAR notice. This involves informing the relevant person that their tax arrangement is considered abusive and should be counteracted.[238]

A number of amendments to the GAAR were made under the Finance Act 2016, which included a penalty of 60% of the counteracted tax advantage.[239]

3.8 An EU-wide GAAR

Examining EU law on tax avoidance is useful to make comparisons and establish whether the UK may have been inspired by EU tax law as the EU also focuses on abuse. Furthermore, although the UK GAAR failed to define abuse, in the case of *Emsland-Stärke GmbH v Hauptzollamt Hamburg-Jonas*[240] (*Emsland*), the ECJ defined abuse in the context of tax avoidance. The court held that abuse involves a two-stage test, including

> first, a combination of objective circumstances in which, despite formal observance of the conditions laid down by the Community rules, the purpose of those rules has not been achieved.[241]

The court then added that examining abuse

> requires, second, a subjective element consisting in the intention to obtain an advantage from the Community rules by creating artificially the conditions laid down for obtaining it. The existence of that subjective element can be established, inter alia, by evidence of collusion between the Community exporter receiving the refunds and the importer of the goods in the non-member country.[242]

The subjective limb is addressed through examining an objective factor, which is the existence of artificial steps. Although the court in *Emsland* examined whether the taxpayer intended to obtain a tax advantage, the existence of a tax advantage is included in the first stage of the UK GAAR.[243] Therefore, what is a determining factor of abuse in *Emsland* is merely the first stage of the GAAR, which demonstrates how wide the GAAR is. The subjective limb of the GAAR asks whether the taxpayer sought to take advantage of flaws in the tax system.[244] Ascertaining whether a taxpayer actively sought to utilise loopholes in the tax system is open to far greater interpretation than establishing the existence of a tax advantage.

The UK GAAR may have been influenced by the anti-abuse principle laid down in *Halifax Plc and others v Customs and Excise Commissioners*[245] (*Halifax*), which was heard eight years before the GAAR was introduced in the European Court of Justice.[246] The case is relevant as it focused on abuse, which is also the focus of the UK GAAR. *Halifax* involved a scheme devised by a bank which sought to avoid paying VAT. The bank sought to establish four call centres in the UK and take advantage of the VAT relief they enjoyed[247] by virtue of belonging to the financial services industry.[248] However, rather than claiming the 5% VAT relief on construction, which they were entitled to deduct, *Halifax* sought to deduct the entire amount of VAT.[249] The bank executed the scheme with the help of four of its subsidiaries.[250] Halifax lent money to one of its subsidiaries, Leeds Permanent Development Services Ltd. (Leeds), to fund the purchase and development of the land, which included the £25,000 payment for VAT.[251] Leeds then entered into an agreement with another of Halifax's subsidiaries, County

Wide Property Investments Ltd. (County), to develop the respective sites, and payment was given in advance. Leeds claimed that it was entitled to deduct the entire amount of VAT, which was equivalent to County's fees.[252] Shortly after, Halifax assigned the leases of all four sites to Leeds in return for Leeds paying a premium.[253] Leeds then reassigned the leases to another subsidiary named Halifax Property Investment Ltd. (Property). On the same day, Property had sublet the sites to Halifax in exchange for a premium.[254] The events occurred during Leeds's "partial exemption year"[255] in terms of VAT payable. County duly paid for the works carried out. Leeds then claimed VAT input repayment.

The court concluded that the scheme in *Halifax* was abusive according to a range of factors which together amounted to the *Halifax* principle.[256] These factors included examining where an arrangement "result[s] in the accrual of a tax advantage the grant of which would be contrary to the purpose of those provisions".[257] Furthermore, it is reminiscent of the UK GAAR that the court held that "it must also be apparent from a number of objective factors that the essential aim of the transactions concerned is to obtain a tax advantage".[258] Therefore, a tax advantage must be intended and gained. However, the *Halifax* principle appears narrower than the UK GAAR as the former applies to

> transactions carried out not in the context of normal commercial operations, but solely for the purpose of wrongfully obtaining advantages provided for by Community law.[259]

In contrast, the UK GAAR is far wider as gaining a tax advantage does not have to be the sole or main purpose of the arrangement which is elucidated in the main purpose test.[260] The judge in *Halifax* also held that the arrangement would not be regarded as abusive where it has "some explanation other than the mere attainment of tax advantages".[261] Nevertheless, Sinfield believes that the *Halifax* principle is generally wide as

> the terminology used by the ECJ ("abusive practice", "tax advantage", "transactions") is deliberately generic, creating flexibility that will allow the concept of abusive practice to adapt to circumstances beyond the facts in *Halifax* and beyond VAT.[262]

Therefore, it is possible to have a wide anti-abuse rule as the "ECJ formulate[d] an anti-abuse principle in much broader terms".[263] The UK GAAR used even wider terms than the *Halifax* principle, reinforcing the notion that the GAAR is wide.

Akin to the *Ramsay* approach involving ignoring artificial steps, in *Halifax*, the ECJ held that once an arrangement is found to be abusive, it "must be redefined so as to re-establish the situation that would have prevailed in the absence of the transactions constituting that abusive practice".[264] Therefore, there are many similarities between the UK and EU law approaches to tax avoidance.

Sinfield has recognised that the principles regarding abuse were viewed by the ECJ as the purposive approach to interpreting legislation.[265] This view was formed on the basis that the ECJ held "that this notion of abuse operates as a *principle governing the interpretation of Community law*".[266]

The court expressed that it was well within its jurisdiction to establish a principle in *Halifax* which "does not require express legislative recognition by the Community legislature to render it applicable to the provisions".[267] Therefore, the attitude of the court in *Halifax* is similar to that of the court in *McGuckian*, wherein the court emphasised that *Ramsay* was no more than an expression of the purposive approach.[268] However, Sinfield believes that, in the *Halifax* case, "the anti-abuse concept is formulated as a general principle of prohibiting abusive practices rather than a principle of interpretation".[269] Consequently, "the *Halifax* principle is . . . far-reaching . . . endowing the Court with new powers of redefinition to counter tax avoidance".[270]

In reinforcing the wide nature of the *Halifax* principle, it is clear that *Halifax* was based on "the ECJ's established teleological approach and its insistence on substance not form".[271] Moreover, Brittain argues that this teleological approach is usual for the ECJ as "the court frequently renders decisions which cannot be justified by reference to the language of the laws it is charged with interpreting".[272] Brittain explains that "this extra-textual aspect of the court's jurisprudence is referred to as the 'teleological' or 'purposive' method of interpretation".[273] Nevertheless, it has been argued that *Halifax* represents "a restriction of formal legal rights under EU law where the taxpayer is relying on such rights to avoid tax".[274]

The *Halifax* principle has evolved much like the *Ramsay* approach. As demonstrated in chapter 2, *Ramsay* not only had support in subsequent cases but those cases also developed the original anti-avoidance approach laid down in *Ramsay*. The *Halifax* principle underwent a similar evolution in *Cadbury Schweppes Plv v IRC*[275] (*Cadbury*). In *Cadbury*, the court held that

> in order for a restriction on the freedom of establishment to be justified on the ground of prevention of abusive practices, the specific objective of such a restriction must be to prevent conduct involving the creation of wholly artificial arrangements which do not reflect economic reality, with a view to escaping the tax normally due on the profits generated by activities carried out on national territory.[276]

Therefore, *Cadbury* specifically referred to examining artificial steps which *Halifax* did not focus on. The *Halifax* principle has also been criticised for having an "uncertain scope and inconsistent application".[277] The inclusion of what is economically real has also been regarded as an extension of *Halifax*.[278] Sinfield believes that the fact that *Cadbury* extended *Halifax* demonstrates "that the principle of prohibiting abusive practices in *Halifax* is of general application".[279]

As part of the Anti-Tax Avoidance Package, the EU Anti-Tax Avoidance Directive (ATAD) was adopted in 2016[280] as "a co-ordinated approach to tax avoidance".[281] Article 6 of this Directive contains the General Anti-Abuse Rule, which relates to corporate tax. Similar to the UK GAAR, the ATAD also incorporates a main purpose test aimed at "an arrangement or a series of arrangements which, having been put into place for the main purpose or one of the main purposes of obtaining a tax advantage".[282] Satisfying the main purpose test alone is insufficient. The ATAD appears to be more objective than the UK GAAR when establishing what would be considered abusive. The test also includes objectively examining whether the arrangement is "not put into place for valid commercial reasons which reflect economic reality".[283] The objective test avoids many of the problems of a double reasonableness test, including what amounts to reasonable or unreasonable.

Other global measures to counter tax avoidance include the G7 finance ministers recently proposing to introduce a global minimum tax of at least 15% and the removal of all digital services taxes.[284] This objective measure would have the effect of "removing any advantage that groups have enjoyed by establishing subsidiaries in low tax jurisdictions".[285] A full discussion of these proposals is beyond the scope of this book.

3.9 Conclusion

There are various problems with the provisions of the UK GAAR. The judiciary may be able to conclusively decide that an arrangement is unacceptable where a tax advantage was the main purpose of the arrangement. However, it is much more difficult to establish whether a tax advantage was one of the main purposes of embarking on the arrangement due to the existence of other purposes. The exercise of deciphering which purposes are the main purposes and which are the subordinate purposes hinders the job of the courts. Furthermore, there is no definition or helpful guidance as to what amounts to abuse in the double reasonableness test, which confers significant discretionary power in the hands of the judiciary. Moreover, the existence of the double reasonableness test unrealistically implies that a tax advantage can be the main purpose of an arrangement which HMRC deem acceptable.

One of the crucial challenges in the GAAR is the fact that where the GAAR outlines what is abusive, the term "economic purposes"[286] has not been defined. However, despite the various tests, the GAAR suggests that the main issue is whether or not Parliament can be said to have anticipated the arrangement.[287] The GAAR guidance also does not help define what amounts to an abusive arrangement. Furthermore, the GAAR's equivocal list about what is abusive is unhelpful as it cites many sources which could be utilised by HMRC and is subject to change.

Notably, the GAAR ensures that both the terms "purpose" and "intention" are included, suggesting that the GAAR seeks to examine both and that Parliament recognises that the terms are distinct. The purpose of the arrangement is mentioned in the main purpose test, and the taxpayer's intentions are sought in s207(2)(c) of the Finance Act 2013. The principle in *Halifax* established that if there is more than one purpose, the arrangement would not be considered abusive.[288] If the UK were to adopt a *Halifax*-style approach to the GAAR, it would bring tax avoidance in line with the legislation on expenditure, which requires that the expenditure must be "incurred wholly and exclusively for the purposes of the trade".[289]

The supplementary report also admitted that the taxpayer's intentions should not be considered because of their subjective connotations.[290] To reinforce that intentions are irrelevant, the GAAR guidance also echoed this.[291] Moreover, the two-stage abuse test in *Emsland* highlights that scrutinising the intentions of the taxpayer is a subjective test.[292] Including the taxpayer's intentions as a factor in determining abuse only serves to conclude the GAAR's sub-tests with yet another factor which is open to interpretation. Too much discretion can lead to judges imputing an intention on the taxpayer that they did not intend.

The GAAR guidance adds little substance to GAAR, and its recommendations arguably make the taxpayer's case more likely to fail. For example, the guidance states that the double reasonableness test can be answered by examining all the possible reasonable views.[293] However, where one of those views regards the taxpayer's arrangement as being reasonable, that view itself is then subject to scrutiny as to whether it is reasonable.[294] This approach arguably stretches the double reasonableness test further and creates a triple reasonableness test. As previously mentioned, the first reasonableness requirement derives from the double reasonableness test and assesses the reasonableness of the judge's view.[295] The second reasonableness requirement also derives from the double reasonableness test and evaluates whether the arrangement can be deemed reasonable.[296] The third reasonableness requirement derives from the GAAR guidance, which states that where there exists a view which regards the arrangement as being reasonable, this view must be assessed as to its reasonableness.[297] The excessive reliance on subjective reasonableness merely serves to weaken the taxpayer's position as the GAAR guidance does not state that a view which rejects the taxpayer's arrangement must also be tested for its reasonableness.

The scope of the GAAR appears to be wide, although it is designed to be targeted. This is undesirable as it is overly dependent on judicial discretion and subjective interpretations of key provisions. The GAAR has attempted to explain its provisions by including definitions of some of the key words, including "tax advantage", "abusive", "arrangement" and "abusive arrangement" taken as a whole. The definitions of these fundamental terms are broad. This is recognised by the GAAR guidance;[298] however, it has two important caveats which restrain judicial creativity. Firstly, even if an arrangement falls within the definition of the GAAR and the purpose or one of its main purposes is the avoidance of tax,[299] it must amount to an abusive arrangement as defined by the double reasonableness test.[300] Secondly, abuse is defined broadly, and there are many factors which constitute abuse, as laid down in the GAAR and GAAR guidance. However, even where one of these factors is satisfied, an arrangement will only be considered abusive where the result was not anticipated by Parliament.[301] As mentioned earlier, this latter safeguard is extremely broad, and the judiciary can widely interpret what Parliament intended. Disconcertingly, HMRC itself admits that wide interpretation leads to uncertainty.[302] Therefore, it would be helpful to examine the general anti-avoidance provisions in other jurisdictions to establish whether they have encountered problems with terminology in practice.

Notes

1 s206(1) Finance Act 2013.
2 s208 Finance Act 2013.
3 s207(1) Finance Act 2013.
4 *Ibid.*
5 s207(2) Finance Act 2013.
6 s211(2)(a) Finance Act 2013.
7 s206(3)(a) Finance Act 2013.
8 s206(3)(b) Finance Act 2013.
9 s206(3)(c) Finance Act 2013.
10 s206(3)(d) Finance Act 2013.
11 s206(3)(e) Finance Act 2013.
12 s206(3)(f) Finance Act 2013.
13 s206(3)(g) Finance Act 2013.
14 *'HMRC GAAR Guidance with Effect from 11 September 2020: Parts A, B and C'*, <https://assets.publishing.service.gov.uk/government/uploads/system/uploads/attachment_data/file/916667/gaar_parts_a_b_c_2020.pdf>, accessed 29.04.2021, p6.
15 *Ibid.*
16 *Ibid.*
17 *Ibid.*
18 s206 Finance Act 2013.
19 s208 Finance Act 2013.
20 s207(1) Finance Act 2013.
21 s207(2) Finance Act 2013.
22 *'HMRC GAAR Guidance with Effect from 11 September 2020: Parts A, B and C'*, <https://assets.publishing.service.gov.uk/government/uploads/system/uploads/attachment_data/file/916667/gaar_parts_a_b_c_2020.pdf>, accessed 29.04.2021, p9.
23 *Ibid*, p16.
24 *Ibid.*
25 s208 Finance Act 2013.
26 s208(c) Finance Act 2013.
27 s208(a) Finance Act 2013.
28 s208(b) Finance Act 2013.
29 s208(d) Finance Act 2013.
30 s208(e) Finance Act 2013.
31 s208(f) Finance Act 2013.
32 s207 Finance Act 2013.
33 s207(1) Finance Act 2013.
34 Krikorian, Y.H. *'The Meaning of Purpose'*, [1930], The Journal of Philosophy, Vol. 27, No. 4, p98.
35 s214 Finance Act 2013.
36 *'HMRC GAAR Guidance with Effect from 11 September 2020: Parts A, B and C'*, <https://assets.publishing.service.gov.uk/government/uploads/system/uploads/attachment_data/file/916667/gaar_parts_a_b_c_2020.pdf>, accessed 29.04.2021, p9.
37 Gammie, M. *'When Is Avoiding Tax Not Abusive? Comparative Approaches to a GAAR in Australia and the United Kingdom'*, [2013], Vol. 42, Australian Tax Review, pp279, 289.
38 Gothard, C. and Austen, J. *'"Abusive" Tax Avoidance: What Are the Implications of HMRC's Draft GAAR?'*, [2012], Vol. 18, No. 9, Trusts and Trustees, pp876–885, 878.
39 s959(1) Corporation Tax Act 2010.
40 *Ibid.*
41 *Ibid.*
42 *Ibid.*
43 *Ibid.*

44 *'HMRC GAAR Guidance with Effect from 11 September 2020: Parts A, B and C'*, <https://assets.publishing.service.gov.uk/government/uploads/system/uploads/attachment_data/file/916667/gaar_parts_a_b_c_2020.pdf>, accessed 29.04.2021, p16.
45 *Craven v White*; *IRC v Bowater*; *Property Developments Ltd. v Gregory* [1988] 3 W.L.R. 423, [1989] A.C. 398, 499 (Lord Oliver).
46 Lethaby, H. *'Analysis-Reflections on Tax and the City'*, [2014], No. 1220, Tax Journal, pp10, 11.
47 s207(1) Finance Act 2013.
48 Aaronson, G. *'A Study to Consider whether a General Anti-Avoidance Rule Should Be Introduced into the UK Tax System'*, [2012], <http://webarchive.nationalarchives.gov.uk/+/http:/www.hm-treasury.gov.uk/d/gaar_final_report_111111.pdf>, accessed 04.06.2016, p4.
49 *Ibid*, p3.
50 *Ibid*, p4.
51 *Ibid.*
52 Sullivan & Cromwell. *'UK Tax: General Anti-Abuse Rule'*, (Sullivan & Cromwell LLP, 16.07.2012), <www.sullcrom.com/siteFiles/Publications/SC_Publication_UK_Tax_General_Anti-Abuse_Rule_2.pdf>, accessed 05.06.2016, p8.
53 *IRC v McGuckian* [1997] 1 W.L.R. 991, 1006 (Lord Clyde).
54 *'HMRC GAAR Guidance with Effect from 11 September 2020: Parts A, B and C'*, <https://assets.publishing.service.gov.uk/government/uploads/system/uploads/attachment_data/file/916667/gaar_parts_a_b_c_2020.pdf>, accessed 29.04.2021, p15.
55 *Ibid.*
56 Coulson, J., et al. *'The Oxford Illustrated Dictionary'*, [1981], 2nd edn, Oxford University Press, Wiltshire, p686.
57 *'HMRC GAAR Guidance with Effect from 11 September 2020: Parts A, B and C'*, <https://assets.publishing.service.gov.uk/government/uploads/system/uploads/attachment_data/file/916667/gaar_parts_a_b_c_2020.pdf>, accessed 29.04.2021, p15.
58 *Ibid.*
59 *Ibid.*
60 *Ibid.*
61 s207(1) Finance Act 2013.
62 *Ensign Tankers (Leasing) Ltd. v Stokes* [1991] 1 W.L.R. 341, 355 (Sir Nicolas Browne-Wilkinson V.C.).
63 Krikorian, Y.H. *'The Meaning of Purpose'*, [1930], Vol. 27, No. 4, The Journal of Philosophy, p97.
64 *'HMRC GAAR Guidance with Effect from 11 September 2020: Parts A, B and C'*, <https://assets.publishing.service.gov.uk/government/uploads/system/uploads/attachment_data/file/916667/gaar_parts_a_b_c_2020.pdf>, accessed 29.04.2021, p15.
65 *Ibid*, p8.
66 *Ibid*, p20.
67 s207(2) Finance Act 2013.
68 Clifford Chance. *'The Draft GAAR: The "Double Reasonableness" Test'*, [2012], <www.cliffordchance.com/briefings/2012/09/the_draft_gaar_thedoublereasonablenesstest.html>, p3.
69 Aaronson, G. *'A Study to Consider whether a General Anti-Avoidance Rule Should Be Introduced into the UK Tax System'*, [2011], <http://webarchive.nationalarchives.gov.uk/+/http:/www.hm-treasury.gov.uk/d/gaar_final_report_111111.pdf>, accessed 25.08.2014, p40.
70 Tobin, J.J. *'Resorting to GAAR?'*, [2013], Vol. 42, No. 2, Tax Management International Journal, p102.
71 Aaronson, G. *'A Study to Consider whether a General Anti-Avoidance Rule Should Be Introduced into the UK Tax System'*, [2011], <http://webarchive.nationalarchives.gov.uk/+/http:/www.hm-treasury.gov.uk/d/gaar_final_report_111111.pdf>, accessed 25.08.2014, p64.

72 Gammie, M. *'When Is Avoiding Tax Not Abusive? Comparative Approaches to a GAAR in Australia and the United Kingdom'*, [2013], Vol. 42, Australian Tax Review, pp279, 292.
73 Rogers, W.V.H. *'Winfield & Jolowicz: Tort'*, [2006], 7th edn, Sweet and Maxwell Limited, London, p77.
74 *Ibid.*
75 *Ibid.*
76 s11(1) Unfair Contract Terms Act 1977.
77 *Ibid.*
78 *Ibid.*
79 James, M. *'Professional Negligence and the Reasonableness Test'*, [1987], Journal of Business Law, pp286, 298.
80 *Ibid.*
81 Tully, S.R. *'"Objective Reasonableness" as a Standard for International Judicial Review'*, [2015], Vol. 6, No. 3, Journal of International Dispute Settlement, pp546–567, 552.
82 *Ibid.*
83 *Ibid.*
84 *Ibid.*
85 Craig, P. *'The Nature of Reasonableness Review'*, [2013], Vol. 66, No. 1, Current Legal Problems, p131.
86 *Ibid*, p132.
87 *Ibid.*
88 s207(2) Finance Act 2013.
89 Gammie, M. *'When Is Avoiding Tax Not Abusive? Comparative Approaches to a GAAR in Australia and the United Kingdom'*, [2013], Vol. 42, Australian Tax Review, pp279, 290.
90 Craig, P. *'The Nature of Reasonableness Review'*, [2013], Vol. 66, No. 1, Current Legal Problems, pp131, 137.
91 *R (on the application of Bancoult) v Secretary of State for Foreign and Commonwealth Affairs* [2008] UKHL 61.
92 Craig, P. *'The Nature of Reasonableness Review'*, [2013], Vol. 66, No. 1, Current Legal Problems, pp131, 142.
93 *Ibid.*
94 *Ibid.*
95 *Associated Provincial Picture Houses, Limited v Wednesbury Corporation* [1948] 1 K.B. 223.
96 *Ibid*, p227 (Lord Greene M.R.).
97 *Ibid*, p226.
98 *Ibid*, p229.
99 *Ibid*, p233.
100 *Ibid*, pp233–234.
101 *Ibid*, p234.
102 Wade, H.W.R. and Forsyth, C.F. *'Administrative Law'*, [2009], 10th edn, Oxford University Press, Oxford, p293.
103 *Ibid*, p305.
104 *Ibid*, p307.
105 *Ibid*, p312.
106 *Associated Provincial Picture Houses, Limited v Wednesbury Corporation* [1948] 1 K.B. 223, 230 (Lord Greene M.R.).
107 *Ibid*, p233.
108 *'HMRC GAAR Guidance with Effect from 11 September 2020: Parts A, B and C'*, <https://assets.publishing.service.gov.uk/government/uploads/system/uploads/attachment_data/file/916667/gaar_parts_a_b_c_2020.pdf>, accessed 29.04.2021, p21.
109 *Ibid.*

110 Rogers, W.V.H. *'Winfield & Jolowicz: Tort'*, [2006], 7th edn, Sweet and Maxwell Limited, London, p76.
111 *Ibid.*
112 *Ibid.*
113 *Ibid*, p77.
114 Craig, P. *'The Nature of Reasonableness Review'*, [2013], Vol. 66, No. 1, Current Legal Problems, pp131, 149.
115 Mishcon de Reya LLP. *'A General Anti-Abuse Rule: Mishcon de Reya Response to Consultation Document – September 2012'*, <www.mishcon.com/assets/managed/docs/downloads/doc_2611/Mishcon_de_Reya_GAAR_consultation_response.pdf>, accessed 01.06.2016, p2.
116 s207(2)(a) Finance Act 2013.
117 *Ibid.*
118 *Canada Trustco Mortgage Co. v R* [2005] 2 S.C.R. 601, [41] (per curiam).
119 Gothard, C. and Austen, J. *'"Abusive" Tax Avoidance: What Are the Implications of HMRC's Draft GAAR?'*, [2012], Vol. 18, No. 9, Trusts and Trustees, pp876–885, 879.
120 *Ibid*, p880.
121 *Ibid.*
122 *Ibid.*
123 s207(2)(b) Finance Act 2013.
124 *IRC v McGuckian* [1997] 1 W.L.R. 991, 996 (Lord Browne-Wilkinson).
125 Lethaby, H. *'Aaronson's GAAR'*, [2012], British Tax Review, pp27, 28.
126 s207(2)(c) Finance Act 2013.
127 Anscombe, G.E.M. *'Intention'*, [1963], 2nd edn, Basil Blackwell, Oxford, p9.
128 *Ibid*, p28.
129 *Direct Cosmetics Ltd, and Laughtons Photographs Ltd. v Commissioners of Customs and Excise* (C-138/86) [1988], [22] (per curiam).
130 Greenberg, D. *'Dangerous Trends in Modern Legislation'*, [2015], Public Law, pp96, 101.
131 *Ibid.*
132 *Ibid.*
133 Gothard, C. and Austen, J. *'"Abusive" Tax Avoidance: What Are the Implications of HMRC's Draft GAAR?'*, [2012], Vol. 18, No. 9, Trusts and Trustees, pp876–885, 880.
134 Greenberg, D. *'Dangerous Trends in Modern Legislation'*, [2015], Public Law, pp96, 101.
135 Gammie, M. *'When Is Avoiding Tax Not Abusive? Comparative Approaches to a GAAR in Australia and the United Kingdom'*, [2013], Vol. 42, Australian Tax Review, pp279, 292.
136 *'HMRC GAAR Guidance with Effect from 11 September 2020: Parts A, B and C'*, <https://assets.publishing.service.gov.uk/government/uploads/system/uploads/attachment_data/file/916667/gaar_parts_a_b_c_2020.pdf>, accessed 29.04.2021, p10.
137 *Ibid*, p22.
138 *Ibid.*
139 s207(4)(a) Finance Act 2013.
140 Gammie, M. *'When Is Avoiding Tax Not Abusive? Comparative Approaches to a GAAR in Australia and the United Kingdom'*, [2013], Vol. 42, Australian Tax Review, pp279, 289.
141 s207(4)(b) Finance Act 2013.
142 *Ibid.*
143 s207(4)(c) Finance Act 2013.
144 *Ibid.*
145 Pagone, G.T. *'Aspects of Tax Avoidance: Trans-Tasman Observations'*, [2011], Australian Tax Review, pp40, 155.
146 Gothard, C. and Austen, J. *'"Abusive" Tax Avoidance: What Are the Implications of HMRC's Draft GAAR?'*, [2012], Vol. 18, No. 9, Trusts and Trustees, pp876–885, 879.

147 *'HMRC GAAR Guidance with Effect from 11 September 2020: Parts A, B and C'*, <https://assets.publishing.service.gov.uk/government/uploads/system/uploads/attachment_data/file/916667/gaar_parts_a_b_c_2020.pdf>, accessed 29.04.2021, p21.
148 *Ibid.*
149 *Ibid.*
150 Aaronson, G. *'A Study to Consider whether a General Anti-Avoidance Rule Should Be Introduced into the UK Tax System'*, [2011], <http://webarchive.nationalarchives.gov.uk/+/http:/www.hm-treasury.gov.uk/d/gaar_final_report_111111.pdf>, accessed 25.08.2014, p5.
151 s211(2)(b) Finance Act 2013.
152 *'HMRC GAAR Guidance with Effect from 11 September 2020: Parts A, B and C'*, <https://assets.publishing.service.gov.uk/government/uploads/system/uploads/attachment_data/file/916667/gaar_parts_a_b_c_2020.pdf>, accessed 29.04.2021, p10.
153 *Ibid*, p28.
154 s207(5) Finance Act 2013.
155 *'HMRC GAAR Guidance with Effect from 11 September 2020: Parts A, B and C'*, <https://assets.publishing.service.gov.uk/government/uploads/system/uploads/attachment_data/file/916667/gaar_parts_a_b_c_2020.pdf>, accessed 29.04.2021, p23.
156 s207(5) Finance Act 2013.
157 *'HMRC GAAR Guidance with Effect from 11 September 2020: Parts A, B and C'*, <https://assets.publishing.service.gov.uk/government/uploads/system/uploads/attachment_data/file/916667/gaar_parts_a_b_c_2020.pdf>, accessed 29.04.2021, p23.
158 *Ibid.*
159 *Ibid.*
160 DOTAS.
161 HMRC. *'Disclosure of Tax Avoidance Schemes'*, <www.gov.uk/guidance/disclosure-of-tax-avoidance-schemes-overview>, accessed 09.01.2018.
162 Aaronson, G. *'A Study to Consider whether a General Anti-Avoidance Rule Should Be Introduced into the UK Tax System'*, [2011], <http://webarchive.nationalarchives.gov.uk/+/http:/www.hm-treasury.gov.uk/d/gaar_final_report_111111.pdf>, accessed 25.08.2014, p4.
163 *Ibid*, p3.
164 Gething, H. and Silverman, A. *'What Canada's GAAR Experience Can Tell Us About New UK Rules'*, [2013], Vol. 24, International Tax Review, p56.
165 Aaronson, G. *'A Study to Consider whether a General Anti-Avoidance Rule Should Be Introduced into the UK Tax System'*, [2011], <http://webarchive.nationalarchives.gov.uk/+/http:/www.hm-treasury.gov.uk/d/gaar_final_report_111111.pdf>, accessed 25.08.2014, p3.
166 s206(1) Finance Act 2013.
167 *'HMRC GAAR Guidance with Effect from 11 September 2020: Parts A, B and C'*, <https://assets.publishing.service.gov.uk/government/uploads/system/uploads/attachment_data/file/916667/gaar_parts_a_b_c_2020.pdf>, accessed 29.04.2021, p16.
168 *Ibid*, p4.
169 Gammie, M. *'When Is Avoiding Tax Not Abusive? Comparative Approaches to a GAAR in Australia and the United Kingdom'*, [2013], Vol. 42, Australian Tax Review, pp279, 287.
170 Aaronson, G. *'A Study to Consider whether a General Anti-Avoidance Rule Should Be Introduced into the UK Tax System'*, [2011], <http://webarchive.nationalarchives.gov.uk/+/http:/www.hm-treasury.gov.uk/d/gaar_final_report_111111.pdf>, accessed 25.08.2014, p25.
171 Lethaby, H. *'Aaronson's GAAR'*, [2012], British Tax Review, pp27, 32.
172 *Ibid*, p33.
173 Lethaby, H. *'Analysis – Reflections on Tax and the City'*, [2014], No. 1220, Tax Journal, pp10, 11.
174 *Ibid.*

175 Lethaby, H. *'Aaronson's GAAR'*, [2012], British Tax Review, pp27, 28.
176 Aaronson, G. *'A Study to Consider whether a General Anti-Avoidance Rule Should Be Introduced into the UK Tax System'*, [2011], <http://webarchive.nationalarchives.gov.uk/+/http:/www.hm-treasury.gov.uk/d/gaar_final_report_111111.pdf>, accessed 25.08.2014, p28.
177 Freedman, J. *'GAAR as a Process and the Process of Discussing the GAAR'*, [2012], British Tax Review, pp22, 24.
178 *'HMRC GAAR Guidance with Effect from 11 September 2020: Parts A, B and C'*, <https://assets.publishing.service.gov.uk/government/uploads/system/uploads/attachment_data/file/916667/gaar_parts_a_b_c_2020.pdf>, accessed 29.04.2021, p28.
179 *Ibid.*
180 s212(1) Finance Act 2013.
181 Lord Reed, R. *'Anti-Avoidance Principles under Domestic and EU Law'*, [2016], British Tax Review, pp288, 289.
182 Gammie, M. *'When Is Avoiding Tax Not Abusive? Comparative Approaches to a GAAR in Australia and the United Kingdom'*, [2013], Vol. 42, Australian Tax Review, pp279, 283.
183 Lethaby, H. *'Aaronson's GAAR'*, [2012], British Tax Review, pp27, 35.
184 Freedman, J. *'GAAR as a Process and the Process of Discussing the GAAR'*, [2012], British Tax Review, pp22, 24.
185 Aaronson, G. *'A Study to Consider whether a General Anti-Avoidance Rule Should Be Introduced into the UK Tax System'*, [2011], <http://webarchive.nationalarchives.gov.uk/+/http:/www.hm-treasury.gov.uk/d/gaar_final_report_111111.pdf>, accessed 25.08.2014, p3.
186 *Ibid*, p5.
187 *Ibid.*
188 *Ibid*, p20.
189 *Ibid*, p7.
190 s206(3)(e) Finance Act 2013.
191 s206(3)(f) Finance Act 2013.
192 s206(3)(g) Finance Act 2013.
193 Aaronson, G. *'A Study to Consider whether a General Anti-Avoidance Rule Should Be Introduced into the UK Tax System'*, [2011], <http://webarchive.nationalarchives.gov.uk/+/http:/www.hm-treasury.gov.uk/d/gaar_final_report_111111.pdf>, accessed 25.08.2014, p7.
194 *Ibid*, p28.
195 *Fleming v Associated Newspapers* [1971] 3 W.L.R. 551, [1972] Ch. 170.
196 *Ibid*, p192 (Salmon J.).
197 *'HMRC GAAR Guidance with Effect from 11 September 2020: Parts A, B and C'*, <https://assets.publishing.service.gov.uk/government/uploads/system/uploads/attachment_data/file/916667/gaar_parts_a_b_c_2020.pdf>, accessed 29.04.2021, p21.
198 Aaronson, G. *'A Study to Consider whether a General Anti-Avoidance Rule Should Be Introduced into the UK Tax System'*, [2011], <http://webarchive.nationalarchives.gov.uk/+/http:/www.hm-treasury.gov.uk/d/gaar_final_report_111111.pdf>, accessed 25.08.2014, p31.
199 *Ibid.*
200 *Ibid*, p33.
201 *Ibid*, p45.
202 s207(2)(c) Finance Act 2013.
203 Aaronson, G. *'A Study to Consider whether a General Anti-Avoidance Rule Should Be Introduced into the UK Tax System'*, [2011], <http://webarchive.nationalarchives.gov.uk/+/http:/www.hm-treasury.gov.uk/d/gaar_final_report_111111.pdf>, accessed 25.08.2014, p44.
204 *Ibid*, p35.

205 *Five Oaks Properties Ltd. v HMRC* [2006] STC (SCD) 769.
206 *Ibid*, [3.2] (John F. Avery Jones).
207 *Ibid*, [3.6].
208 *Ibid*, [4.1].
209 Aaronson, G. *'A Study to Consider whether a General Anti-Avoidance Rule Should Be Introduced into the UK Tax System'*, [2011], <http://webarchive.nationalarchives.gov.uk/+/http:/www.hm-treasury.gov.uk/d/gaar_final_report_111111.pdf>, accessed 25.08.2014, p61.
210 *Ibid*, p64.
211 s207(4)(a) and s207(4)(b) Finance Act 2013.
212 Aaronson, G. *'A Study to Consider whether a General Anti-Avoidance Rule Should Be Introduced into the UK Tax System'*, [2011], <http://webarchive.nationalarchives.gov.uk/+/http:/www.hm-treasury.gov.uk/d/gaar_final_report_111111.pdf>, accessed 25.08.2014, p47.
213 *Ibid*.
214 *Ibid*.
215 *Ibid*.
216 *Ibid*.
217 *Ibid*.
218 *Ibid*.
219 *Ibid*, p50.
220 s207(5) Finance Act 2013.
221 HMRC. *'Strengthening Sanctions for Tax Avoidance'*, <www.gov.uk/government/uploads/system/uploads/attachment_data/file/399823/Strengthening_sanctions_for_tax_avoidance_-_consultation_document.pdf>, accessed 30.12.2015, p7.
222 s159 Finance Act 2016.
223 HMRC. *'Strengthening Sanctions for Tax Avoidance'*, <www.gov.uk/government/uploads/system/uploads/attachment_data/file/399823/Strengthening_sanctions_for_tax_avoidance_-_consultation_document.pdf>, accessed 30.12.2015, p7.
224 *Ibid*.
225 *Ibid*.
226 *Ibid*.
227 *Ibid*, p8.
228 *Ibid*.
229 *Ibid*, p9.
230 *Ibid*.
231 *Ibid*.
232 s209(2) Finance Act 2013.
233 *'HMRC GAAR Guidance with Effect from 11 September 2020: Parts A, B and C'*, <https://assets.publishing.service.gov.uk/government/uploads/system/uploads/attachment_data/file/916667/gaar_parts_a_b_c_2020.pdf>, accessed 29.04.2021, p24.
234 *IRC v McGuckian* [1997] 1 W.L.R. 991, 996 (Lord Browne-Wilkinson).
235 *'HMRC GAAR Guidance with Effect from 11 September 2020: Parts A, B and C'*, <https://assets.publishing.service.gov.uk/government/uploads/system/uploads/attachment_data/file/916667/gaar_parts_a_b_c_2020.pdf>, accessed 29.04.2021, p24.
236 *IRC v McGuckian* [1997] 1 W.L.R. 991, 996 (Lord Browne-Wilkinson).
237 *'HMRC GAAR Guidance with Effect from 11 September 2020: Parts A, B and C'*, <https://assets.publishing.service.gov.uk/government/uploads/system/uploads/attachment_data/file/916667/gaar_parts_a_b_c_2020.pdf>, accessed 29.04.2021, p25.
238 s209AA Finance Act 2020.
239 S212A(2) Finance Act 2016.
240 *Emsland-Stärke GmbH v Hauptzollamt Hamburg-Jonas* (C-110/99) [2000] ECR I-11569.
241 *Ibid*, [52] (per curiam).

242 *Ibid*, [53].
243 s208 Finance Act 2013.
244 s207(2)(c) Finance Act 2013.
245 *Halifax Plc and others v Customs and Excise Commissioners* (C-255/02) [2006] Ch. 387.
246 (ECJ).
247 *Halifax Plc and others v Customs and Excise Commissioners* (C-255/02) [2006] Ch. 387, 394 (Advocate General Poiares Maduro).
248 Art 13(b)(d) Sixth Council Directive 77/388/EEC of 17 May 1977.
249 *Halifax Plc and others v Customs and Excise Commissioners* (C-255/02) [2006] Ch. 387, 394 (Advocate General Poiares Maduro).
250 *Ibid.*
251 *Ibid.*
252 *Ibid.*
253 *Ibid*, p395.
254 *Ibid.*
255 *Ibid.*
256 *Ibid*, p436.
257 *Ibid.*
258 *Ibid.*
259 *Ibid*, p435.
260 s207(1) Finance Act 2013.
261 *Halifax Plc and others v Customs and Excise Commissioners* (C-255/02) [2006] Ch. 387, 436 (Advocate General Poiares Maduro).
262 Sinfield, G. *'The Halifax Principle as a Universal GAAR for Tax in the EU'*, [2011], British Tax Review, pp235, 237.
263 *Ibid*, p239.
264 *Halifax Plc and others v Customs and Excise Commissioners* (C-255/02) [2006] Ch. 387, 439 (Advocate General Poiares Maduro).
265 Sinfield, G. *'The Halifax Principle as a Universal GAAR for Tax in the EU'*, [2011], British Tax Review, pp235, 237.
266 *Halifax Plc and others v Customs and Excise Commissioners* (C-255/02) [2006] Ch. 387, 412 (Advocate General Poiares Maduro).
267 *Ibid*, p416.
268 *IRC v McGuckian* [1997] 1 W.L.R. 991, 1000 (Lord Steyn).
269 Sinfield, G. *'The Halifax Principle as a Universal GAAR for Tax in the EU'*, [2011], British Tax Review, pp235, 238.
270 *Ibid.*
271 *Ibid*, p241.
272 Brittain, S. *'Justifying the Teleological Methodology of the European Court of Justice: A Rebuttal'*, [2016], Irish Jurist, p134.
273 *Ibid.*
274 Sinfield, G. *'The Halifax Principle as a Universal GAAR for Tax in the EU'*, [2011], British Tax Review, pp235, 241.
275 *Cadbury Schweppes Plc v IRC* (C-196/04) [2006] ECR I-07995.
276 *Ibid*, [55] (per curiam).
277 Sinfield, G. *'The Halifax Principle as a Universal GAAR for Tax in the EU'*, [2011], British Tax Review, pp235, 243.
278 *Ibid.*
279 *Ibid*, p242.
280 Council Directive (EU) 2016/1164 of 12 July 2016.
281 Cédelle, A. *'The EU Anti-Tax Avoidance Directive: A UK Perspective'*, [2016], Vol. 4, British Tax Review, pp490–507, 493.

282 Article 6(1) Council Directive (EU) 2016/1164 of 12 July 2016.
283 *Ibid.*
284 Urwin, L. and Were, R.K. *'The G7 Tax Deal'*, [2021], <www.taxjournal.com/articles/-the-g7-tax-deal>, No. 1535, accessed 22.08.2021.
285 *Ibid.*
286 s207(4)(a) and s207(4)(b) Finance Act 2013.
287 s207(4)(c) Finance Act 2013.
288 *Halifax Plc and others v Customs and Excise Commissioners* (C-255/02) [2006] Ch. 387, 436 (Advocate General Poiares Maduro).
289 s34(1)(a) ITTOIA 2005.
290 Aaronson, G. *'A Study to Consider whether a General Anti-Avoidance Rule Should Be Introduced into the UK Tax System'*, [2012], <http://webarchive.nationalarchives.gov.uk/+/http:/www.hm-treasury.gov.uk/d/gaar_final_report_111111.pdf>, accessed 04.06.2016, p4.
291 *'HMRC GAAR Guidance with Effect from 11 September 2020: Parts A, B and C'*, <https://assets.publishing.service.gov.uk/government/uploads/system/uploads/attachment_data/file/916667/gaar_parts_a_b_c_2020.pdf>, accessed 29.04.2021, p15.
292 *Emsland-Stärke GmbH v Hauptzollamt Hamburg-Jonas* (C-110/99) [2000] ECR I-11569, per curiam, [53].
293 *'HMRC GAAR Guidance with Effect from 11 September 2020: Parts A, B and C'*, <https://assets.publishing.service.gov.uk/government/uploads/system/uploads/attachment_data/file/916667/gaar_parts_a_b_c_2020.pdf>, accessed 29.04.2021, p21.
294 *Ibid.*
295 s207(2) Finance Act 2013.
296 *Ibid.*
297 *'HMRC GAAR Guidance with Effect from 11 September 2020: Parts A, B and C'*, <https://assets.publishing.service.gov.uk/government/uploads/system/uploads/attachment_data/file/916667/gaar_parts_a_b_c_2020.pdf>, accessed 29.04.2021, p21.
298 *Ibid*, p9.
299 s207(1) Finance Act 2013.
300 s207(2) Finance Act 2013.
301 s207(4)(c) Finance Act 2013.
302 Aaronson, G. *'A Study to Consider whether a General Anti-Avoidance Rule Should Be Introduced into the UK Tax System'*, [2011], <http://webarchive.nationalarchives.gov.uk/+/http:/www.hm-treasury.gov.uk/d/gaar_final_report_111111.pdf>, accessed 25.08.2014, p5.

4 General anti-avoidance legislation in other jurisdictions

Introduction

It has been argued earlier that the UK GAAR includes vague provisions and examines the arrangement's purpose and the taxpayer's intentions. This chapter will examine whether such an approach is peculiar to the UK. The Economic Substance Doctrine[1] in US federal law and the general anti-avoidance rules of Australia, New Zealand, South Africa and Canada will be examined briefly. These jurisdictions have been selected because they have all have general anti-avoidance rules which were in existence prior to the UK GAAR. Furthermore, the anti-avoidance rules of New Zealand, South Africa and Canada all include "abuse" provisions, examination of which can usefully inform the debate on the equivalent UK GAAR provisions. Furthermore, these jurisdictions have an established line of case law which can provide an indication of how the UK's targeted GAAR may be applied and whether there have been any problems in the terminology used. This chapter argues that, although the UK GAAR was proposed to be targeted, it is in fact wider than the anti-avoidance rules discussed by allowing greater scope for wide judicial discretion.

4.1 The United States' Economic Substance Doctrine ("ESD")

4.1 (a) Common law background

The ESD arises from US federal case law which considers whether a business purpose exists in determining if a transaction is genuine and the economic reality of the arrangement. Therefore, it is useful to examine how the common law evolved and brought about the ESD. US tax law favours the substance over form approach, which demonstrates a commitment to identifying the reason for executing the arrangements and what the arrangement achieved and refuses to be confined to the parties' agreements.

The business purpose test was invoked in *Gregory v Helvering*[2] (*Gregory*), in which the US Supreme Court proclaimed the irrelevance of motive several times in concluding that the taxpayer engaged in unacceptable tax avoidance.[3] The taxpayer transferred shares in her company to a new corporation which she created.

DOI: 10.4324/9781003080473-5

She dissolved the new corporation shortly after its creation and transferred the shares from it to herself and subsequently sold them. However, the arrangement did not fall within §112 of the Revenue Act of 1928 as a reorganisation of the taxpayer's corporation. The court held that the scheme was carried out to ensure that the resulting tax burden would be less than if the shares were acquired by way of dividends. The absence of a "business or corporate purpose"[4] resulted in the conclusion of unacceptable tax avoidance. The judges examined the taxpayer's intentions and established that the transaction "performed as it was intended from the beginning",[5] based on a "preconceived plan".[6] Therefore, this view resembles Anscombe's argument that "a man's intention is *what* he aims at or chooses".[7] Interestingly, it was held that there exists a "rule which excludes from consideration the motive of tax avoidance".[8] Sutherland J added that to consider motive would "deprive the statutory provision in question of all serious purpose".[9]

The tendency to objectively consider the economic substance of arrangements was introduced in *Knetsch v US*.[10] The taxpayer acquired deferred annuity saving bonds from a life insurance company and borrowed in excess of his debt. He repaid the company the interest in large sums for the year on the same day to offset the indebtedness, indicating to the courts that indebtedness was never intended.[11] Only a tax advantage could be realised when examining the substance of the arrangement.[12] The taxpayer sought to deduct the interest from his income. However, the court claimed that the taxpayer and insurance company created a sham arrangement as the only benefit was a tax advantage.[13]

In the dissenting judgement, it was recognised that "tax avoidance is a dominating motive behind scores of transactions. It is plainly present here".[14] Therefore, this accords with Anscombe's definition of a motive being the "desire of [the] gain".[15] Nevertheless, the dissenting judge favoured the form over substance approach by recognising that the "transactions were real and legitimate in the insurance world and were consummated within the limits allowed by insurance policies".[16]

The consideration of motive is not always the decisive factor, as demonstrated by *Frank Lyon Co. v US*[17] (*Frank Lyon*), in which the economic substance of a sale and lease-back agreement could not be ignored despite the apparent tax avoidance purpose.[18] The transaction was "not shaped solely by tax-avoidance features that have meaningless labels attached".[19] Therefore, the existence of economic substance could not be ignored, even though tax avoidance was one of the main purposes of the arrangements.

The reasoning in *Frank Lyon* was followed in *Rice's Toyota World Inc. v CIR*[20] (*Rice*), in which the court subjectively interpreted the business purpose test. The taxpayer purchased a computer using recourse and non-recourse notes. He subsequently leased the computer back to the seller for eight years. The taxpayer claimed depreciation deductions for the computer and interest deductions paid on the non-recourse notes. The original seller then subleased the computer, which generated an income. The arrangement was found to be a sham in applying the business purpose test which "concerns the motives of the taxpayer in entering the transaction".[21] Therefore the business purpose test was applied subjectively, although economic substance was held to be an objective test.[22] The court, however, allowed only the interest deductions as "a sham transaction may contain elements whose form reflects economic substance".[23] The case illustrates the flexibility of the business purpose test as it can be applied to part of an arrangement in the same way as the UK GAAR intends to operate. However, the GAAR can be applied to reject part of an arrangement, whereas the US economic substance approach can uphold part of an arrangement.

4.1 (b) The ESD provisions

The Economic Substance Doctrine is far simpler than the UK GAAR, as will be demonstrated. The Health Care and Education Reconciliation Act 2010[24] amended the Internal Revenue Code in order to codify the ESD[25] in 2010. The ESD lays down statutory GAAR-like provisions to counter avoidance. Examining the requirements of a genuine transaction, as defined in the ESD, may help decipher whether US legislation could also allow for an examination into the taxpayer's purposes or intentions. Moreover, as the ESD was codified before the implementation of the UK GAAR, recent US tax avoidance cases may provide pointers as to how the UK GAAR may operate in relation to the taxpayer's motives, intentions or purposes.

The determination of whether cases are genuine is processed through a "deceptively rule-based"[26] two-stage test wherein both parts must be satisfied to escape tax liability. The first stage of the test is objective and dictates that a transaction is genuine and has economic substance where it "changes in a meaningful way (apart from the Federal income tax effects) the taxpayer's economic position".[27] This is fact based. This stage of the test excludes pure tax benefits,[28] which means that there must be genuine profits and losses. However, the ESD guidance states that the taxpayer's position would not change in a meaningful way where the transaction does not involve a business purpose.[29] Therefore, the business purpose test may be the more important test to satisfy. The guidance also indicates that the first and second stages of the test are intertwined.

The second stage of the ESD is akin to, although wider than, the business purpose test exemplified in *Gregory* and analyses the taxpayer's purpose through considering whether "the taxpayer has a substantial purpose (apart from the Federal income tax effects) for entering into such transaction".[30] This stage also excludes purposes purely involving tax benefits.[31] To examine whether the taxpayer had a purpose which was not tax related involves assessing evidence beyond the face of the documents and inevitably looks into the taxpayer's intentions. This half of the test has also been referred to as "the 'subjective' leg of the doctrine"[32] as it "focus[es] on motives underlying a transaction, rather than the effects of the transaction".[33] However, the subjectivity is buried by "tying consideration[s] of motives (the subjective leg of the doctrine) to effect (the objective leg of the doctrine)".[34] To reinforce the subjectivity of the second stage of the ESD, the Joint Committee on Taxation has also published guidance on the ESD, stating that anti-avoidance doctrines should inhibit any "tax-motivated transaction".[35] Therefore, considering motive is overtly encouraged by US federal law.

In determining whether a transaction satisfies both stages of the test within the ESD, there is a general rule that courts are permitted to consider the "potential for profit of a transaction".[36] Potential profit is evaluated by comparing how much profit would be made before tax to the tax allowances if the transaction were to be upheld.[37] If the pre-tax profit substantially outweighs the potential tax benefits, the ESD guidance states that the taxpayer's profit motive will be explored.[38] Potential profit is explored as the absence of a profit, and the existence of large tax reliefs enables tax avoidance motives to be inferred. However, a transaction may have a business purpose but fail to secure a potential profit. It is also difficult to predict whether a transaction may generate a profit. Therefore, the test may consider whether profit is a motive.[39] Furthermore, this provision can lead to judges frustrating an attempt to utilise tax laws which were enacted to provide tax benefits, such as an investment.[40]

It is evident that the second stage of the ESD is more important to satisfy than the first stage as the latter is dependent on the second stage in order to be satisfied.[41] By placing greater weight on the subjective element of the ESD, Congress effectively allows for greater judicial discretion. In addition to this, the ESD has been criticised for doing "little more than restate the judicial formulations leaving much the same scope for interpretation".[42]

The UK version of the business purpose doctrine examines whether there is a commercial purpose, as developed in *Furniss*. However, as demonstrated, the business purpose test has been applied in a subjective manner to examine taxpayers' motive. Therefore, judges in the UK have the commercial purpose test at their disposal, as well as the GAAR. US courts have held that although an arrangement may be motivated by tax avoidance, the economic substance of the arrangement cannot be ignored.[43] Therefore, the ESD attempts to be more objective than the UK GAAR.

4.1 (c) Case law post the American ESD

Tax avoidance cases decided after the ESD was codified in 2010 may reveal whether the ESD, as construed by the courts, takes an objective or subjective approach and whether motive is considered. The ESD was applied in *Bank of New York Mellon Corporation v CIR*.[44] The taxpayer bank engaged in "an elaborate series of pre-arranged steps"[45] under a structured trust advantaged repackaged securities (STARS) arrangement to circulate income with a UK bank to which it loaned money. The arrangement was designed to generate foreign tax credits, although it was held to lack economic substance due to the existence of tax "benefits . . . unrelated to the transaction".[46] Furthermore, the court referred to the taxpayer's "subjective business purpose",[47] illustrating that US courts treat the business purpose test as a subjective assessment. However, the court interpreted a subjective business purpose as meaning a "non-tax business purpose",[48] which, in fact, involves an objective assessment of the facts.

The taxpayer's arrangement failed in *Ricardo Garcia, Tax Matters Partner et al. v CIR*[49] (*Ricardo*). The taxpayers executed a series of transactions which lacked economic substance and a profit motive. The taxpayers invested in foreign currencies and purposely generated losses in order to offset their losses against other income. The court reiterated the preference for examining the substance over the form of the transaction by elucidating that they "don't respect the form"[50] of the transactions. The judge examined the taxpayer's intentions and concluded that the taxpayer "never intended to run businesses".[51] This use of intention coincides with Scheer's definition of intentions as "goals and courses of action".[52] Consequently, it appears that examining the taxpayer's intentions is becoming an increasingly important factor in US adjudication.

The UK GAAR can be seen as more aggressive than the ESD. The ESD analyses whether a business purpose exists. Therefore, the ESD attempts to explore how the taxpayer's arrangement can be upheld rather than seeking to disallow it. However, the UK GAAR begins the inquiry into the validity of an arrangement by immediately challenging its legitimacy. The UK GAAR analyses what amounts to an abusive arrangement and whether a tax advantage was a main purpose. Consequently, taxpayers are disadvantaged at the onset as judges are empowered to examine flaws in the arrangement. Had a business purpose test been enforced, judges may have chosen to end the inquiry into the legitimacy of arrangements upon evidence of a business purpose and not examine whether a tax advantage was a main purpose. If there is no business purpose, the provisions outlining what amounts to abuse could then be applied. The section of the GAAR which discusses the amount for economic purposes[53] is the closest UK equivalent to examining economic substance. However, as demonstrated in chapter 3, it is unclear what "economic" purposes really means. The objective considerations are laid down in the GAAR guidance which is extra-statutory and, therefore, only has "quasi-judicial authority".[54]

The ESD differs from the GAAR in that the ESD requires a business purpose.[55] Assessing the existence of a business purpose is an objective investigation rather than examining whether an arrangement is abusive under the GAAR, which initially explores the taxpayer's purpose. The GAAR could have been clearer by considering what constitutes a genuine transaction rather than stating the requirements of an abusive transaction, which encourages judges to begin by examining the taxpayer's purposes and intentions. However, the ESD and GAAR are similar in that they both consider the taxpayer's purpose. The similarities of the anti-avoidance legislation of the UK and US cannot be overstretched, and it has been advised that

> United Kingdom judges should be extremely wary of importing United States doctrines, since both the intellectual structure of the United States tax system and the administrative structure that underpins it are very different.[56]

4.2 The Australian general anti-avoidance rule

The current Australian general anti-avoidance rule is contained in Part IVA of the Income Tax Assessment Act 1936, which applies to schemes carried out after 1981. It is important to note that Australia opted for a general anti-avoidance rule rather than a general anti-abuse rule and that the former is meant to be wider than the supposedly targeted UK GAAR. However, O'Connell has recognised that the UK GAAR is "similar in many respects to Australia's general anti-avoidance rule in Pt IVA".[57]

The Australian general anti-avoidance rule was formerly contained in section 206 of the Income Tax Assessment Act 1936. The problem with the former general anti-avoidance rule was that it was "drawn in very broad and comprehensive terms"[58] and "had the potential to annihilate any transaction which had any tax consequences".[59] The discussion that follows will examine the provisions of Australia's current general anti-avoidance rule.

4.2 (a) Scheme

The Australian general anti-avoidance rule uses the term "scheme"[60] instead of the UK counterpart of an "arrangement". A scheme is defined broadly as including

> any agreement, arrangement, understanding, promise or undertaking, whether express or implied and whether or not enforceable, or intended to be enforceable, by legal proceedings[61]

and "any scheme, plan, proposal, action, course of action or course of conduct".[62] However, a scheme alone cannot be regarded as unacceptable tax avoidance, and "it must be related to the tax benefit obtained".[63] The meaning of a "scheme" is similar to the UK approach of an "arrangement" as both encompass an agreement or understanding.

4.2 (b) Tax benefit

A tax benefit has been defined as including

> an amount not being included in the assessable income of the taxpayer . . . where that amount would have been included, or might reasonably be expected to have been included, in the assessable income of the taxpayer of that year of income if the scheme had not been entered into".[64]

This provision likely refers to profit which has utilised a legitimate allowance and has ultimately not been included in the taxpayer's tax return. In addition to this, another type of tax benefit is defined as

> a deduction being allowable to the taxpayer in relation to a year of income where the whole or a part of that deduction would not have been allowable, or might reasonably be expected not to have been allowable . . . if the scheme had not been entered into.[65]

Therefore, allowable deductions which have been obtained as part of a scheme would be deemed as a tax benefit under the general anti-avoidance rule. The

UK GAAR's equivalent of a tax advantage provides a more specific list of what constitutes a tax advantage.[66] The UK GAAR encompasses more than tax reliefs and deductions, as discussed in chapter 3.

4.2 (c) Purpose

As with the UK GAAR, in the Australian general anti-avoidance rule, the taxpayer's purpose plays a central role in determining whether the taxpayer engaged in unacceptable tax avoidance.[67] The Australian general anti-avoidance rule applies where a person, who is not necessarily the "relevant taxpayer",[68] "carried out the scheme or any part of the scheme . . . for the purpose of enabling a taxpayer to obtain a tax benefit in connection with the scheme".[69] Consequently, there is a strong focus on obtaining a tax benefit rather than avoiding tax, although the former is much wider. Similarly, the general anti-avoidance rule also applies to situations in which the person "enabl[es] the relevant taxpayer and another taxpayer . . . each to obtain a tax benefit in connection with the scheme",[70] even though they are not the "relevant taxpayer".[71]

Unlike the UK GAAR, which seeks to avoid overtly examining the taxpayer's purpose and instead scrutinises the arrangement's purpose, the Australian general anti-avoidance rule flagrantly allows judges to examine not only the taxpayer's purpose but also the purpose of anyone involved in the scheme. The distinction has also been raised in case law subsequent to the Australian general anti-avoidance rule, which reaffirmed that the legislation is concerned with the taxpayer's purpose and not that of the arrangement.[72] Concerns have been raised about the decision to allow the scrutiny of the taxpayer's purpose rather than the arrangement's purpose.[73] Furthermore, "the requisite purpose is that of someone connected with the scheme, who need not be the taxpayer [and] not the purpose of the scheme itself".[74] Therefore, the danger is that "the purpose of the relevant taxpayer may be imputed".[75]

In order to ascertain whether a person had the required purpose to aid one or more taxpayers to gain a tax benefit, judges must consider eight objective criteria.[76] These criteria include "the manner in which the scheme was entered into or carried out",[77] "the form and substance of the scheme",[78] "the time at which the scheme was entered into and the length of the period during which the scheme was carried out",[79] "the result . . . that, but for this Part, would be achieved by the scheme",[80] "any change in the financial position . . . that has resulted . . . from the scheme",[81] "any change in the financial position of any person who has, or has had, any connection . . . with the relevant taxpayer",[82] including "the nature of any connection"[83] and, lastly, "any other consequence for the relevant taxpayer".[84] The criteria differ from the UK GAAR and US ESD in a number of ways. Firstly, the Australian general anti-avoidance rule respects both form and substance.[85] Secondly, their general anti-avoidance rule surveys the financial position of others connected to the taxpayer,[86] which undoubtedly broadens the scope of the legislation. Finally, the timing and length of the arrangement, which are occasionally considered in UK tax law, as in *Burmah Oil* and *Ensign Tankers*, are investigated.

The objective criteria in the Australian general anti-avoidance rule have received praise for being beneficial to both revenue officials and taxpayers.[87] Slater has argued that

> what sets Pt IVA apart from most other anti-avoidance legislation, however, is not its effectiveness from a revenue perspective: it is that is sets sufficiently identifiable and objective criteria for its operation that taxpayers may plan their affairs with some degree of assurance that their arrangements (if they are not overly ambitious) will not fall within its scope.[88]

Moreover, Gammie has stated that, compared to the UK GAAR, "Pt IVA appears the better construct".[89] This is because "its virtue lies in its refusal to articulate a concept of 'abuse' and found itself on the idea that one can conclude by reference to the specified *objective* factors".[90] However,

> Pt IVA operates when it identifies an arrangement that confers a tax benefit while the UK GAAR treats almost anything as a tax arrangement but then aims to strike down any tax arrangement for which there is no reasonable explanation.[91]

The Australian general anti-avoidance rule stipulates that the Commissioner can cancel the tax benefit gained.[92] Counteraction can occur in a number of ways, according to the facts of the case: for example, the tax benefit claimed can be computed in the assessable income.[93] Alternatively, the deduction will not be allowable,[94] or an artificial capital loss will not be sustained.[95]

4.3 Australian case law post the Australian general anti-avoidance rule

Commentators have argued that "the cases on Part IVA generally demonstrate its breadth and power to strike down tax avoidance transactions".[96] The Australian general anti-avoidance rule was applied in *Federal Commissioner of Taxation v Spotless*[97] (*Spotless*). The case concerned the taxpayer company, Spotless Services Ltd., which sought to use $40 million for short-term investment in the Cook Islands.[98] The taxpayers claimed that the interest gained on the investment was deductible as they were not required to pay tax on an investment, and they had duly paid withholding tax.[99] The transaction attracted suspicion given that the amount of interest earned in the Cook Islands was lower than in Australia, although the scheme was advantageous from a tax perspective if the investment did not attract Australian income tax.[100] The court concluded that "without the scheme there would have been no investment".[101] In order to reach the conclusion that the arrangement did come under the general anti-avoidance rule, the court considered the "dominant purpose"[102] of the arrangement, which was described as "the ruling, prevailing or most influential purpose".[103]

The judgement in *Spotless* was reminiscent of *Mallalieu*[104] in relation to the possibility of a dual purpose when the court stated that "a particular course of action may be both 'tax driven' and bear the character of a rational commercial decision".[105] The judges added that simply because a commercial purpose exists does not negate the possibility that an arrangement was embarked upon to gain a tax benefit.[106] Moreover, the court stressed that the decisive factor was that the arrangement "was not merely tax driven but that its dominant purpose was to enable the taxpayer to obtain a tax benefit",[107] which should be judged by the standards of "a reasonable person".[108] However, this approach has been criticised as "the Court appear[ed] to have simply substituted what it felt a reasonable person would conclude for the Full Federal Court's view".[109] Therefore, the double reasonableness test may be applied in a similar way with the UK GAAR. It was also made clear that the purpose sought related to the taxpayer and not the arrangement.[110] The court in *Spotless* openly rejected the *Westminster* approach,[111] the principles of which were viewed as "muffled echoes of old arguments",[112] although the court insisted that "both form and substance"[113] were relevant. Therefore, the substance of the arrangement may encompass the taxpayer's purpose.

The Australian general anti-avoidance rule was also triggered in *Commissioner of Taxation v Hart and Another*[114] (*Hart*). The taxpayers in *Hart* took out two loans: one to fund the cost of the taxpayers' private home and another for an investment property.[115] Only the interest on the investment property's loan was deductible as the taxpayer used a "wealth optimiser structure"[116] to execute the loan. The interest on the investment property was higher than the interest on the taxpayers' private residence. The taxpayers ensured that the loan for their private home was repaid first and allowed the interest on the investment property to accrue.[117] The court found the interest to be a material peculiarity as the taxpayers "willingly agreed to pay a higher rate of interest than was available",[118] which consequently raised suspicion because the interest was deductible.[119] However, the court held that the chosen structure

> depended entirely for its efficacy upon tax benefits generated by arrangements between the respondents and the lender that had no explanation other than their fiscal consequences.[120]

Due to the deductibility of the interest, the court concluded that "obtaining of the additional tax deduction was the dominant purpose of the scheme".[121] This accords with Millet's definition of a purpose as "the aim, or object, or end in view".[122] Literature given to the taxpayers prior to embarking on the scheme also boasted about the tax benefits which would be obtained through using the particular structure.[123] Therefore, the form and substance of the arrangement pointed to the taxpayers seeking a tax advantage.[124] The decision has been criticised due to the fact that a tax benefit includes "an amount not being included in the assessable income of the taxpayer of a year of income where that amount would have been included".[125] However, "it is not too difficult to envisage a scenario in which a taxpayer will either enter into a scheme which produces tax benefits or no scheme at all".[126]

The court in *Hart* stressed that the relevant purpose was that of the taxpayers and not of the arrangement.[127] In addition to this, the court also stated that the general anti-avoidance rule "does not require, or even permit, any inquiry into the subjective motives of the relevant taxpayers".[128] However, in *Hart*, the court ensured that every aspect of the general anti-avoidance rule was equally satisfied in concluding that there was a scheme which led to a tax benefit and was the dominant purpose of the taxpayers.[129]

4.4 The New Zealand general anti-avoidance rule

New Zealand's general anti-avoidance rule is contained in sBG1 and GA1 of the Income Tax Act 2007. Unlike the UK GAAR, the Australian general anti-avoidance rule and America's ESD, the New Zealand general anti-avoidance rule does not provide any systematic tests to work through the stages of the legislation. Many of the key terms of the general anti-avoidance rule are only explained in the general definitions section of the Income Tax Act 2007, which creates a complex general anti-avoidance rule, as not all of the relevant terms are contained within sBG1 and GA1. It is also important to note that the purposive approach has been placed on statutory footing in New Zealand under the Interpretation Act 1999, which states that "the meaning of an enactment must be ascertained from its text and in the light of its purpose".[130]

The meaning of the phrase "tax avoidance arrangement"[131] is provided under the Act. The phrase is equally as broad as the Australian general anti-avoidance rule in stating that it encompasses "an arrangement, whether entered into by the person affected by the arrangement or by another person".[132] The meaning of a tax arrangement is further broadened where the Act states that the general anti-avoidance rule applies where the person "directly or indirectly has tax avoidance as its purpose or effect".[133] The purpose mentioned in the New Zealand general anti-avoidance rule is that of the taxpayer rather than the arrangement. However, the addition of examining the effect as well as the main purpose of the arrangement suggests that the arrangement may be held to be unacceptable tax avoidance even though it was not the purpose of the scheme. Therefore, the New Zealand general anti-avoidance rule has a double-edged sword in considering both purpose and effect. A similar distinction was also recognised by Anscombe, who elucidated that "the inseparability of the effect is not a ground for regarding it as intended".[134] Furthermore, the inclusion of both terms ensures that the judiciary can tackle not only those arrangements which had a tax avoidance effect by which the taxpayer received a tax advantage but also those arrangements which merely had the purpose of doing so, irrespective of whether the arrangement was successful.

In defining a tax arrangement, the Income Tax Act 2007 also states that it includes the situation where an arrangement

> has tax avoidance as 1 of its purposes or effects, whether or not any other purpose or effect is referable to ordinary business or family dealings, if the tax avoidance purpose or effect is not merely incidental.[135]

Therefore, whether the arrangement involves tax avoidance as its main purpose or one of its main purposes, it is covered by the general anti-avoidance rule. The term "merely incidental"[136] acts as a safeguard to ensure that a tax benefit arising out of family or business transactions is not caught within the general anti-avoidance rule.

As with the UK's GAAR, the Tax Administration Act 1994 also refers to "an abusive tax position",[137] which has been defined as including

> taxpayers who, having taken an unacceptable tax position, have entered into or acted in respect of arrangements or interpreted or applied tax laws with a dominant purpose of taking, or of supporting the taking of, tax positions that reduce or remove tax liabilities or give tax benefits.[138]

In the aforementioned provision, the dominant purpose discussed is that of the taxpayer. Therefore, if the judiciary in the UK look to New Zealand for guidance on what amounts to abuse, the taxpayer's purpose may be sought.

An "unacceptable tax position"[139] is defined as one which "if, viewed objectively . . . fails to meet the standard of being about as likely as not to be correct".[140] The provision is quite vague, and the standard of correctness will be decided by the judiciary, who will invariably use their discretion as to the arrangement's correctness. The Tax Administration Act 1994 also serves to catch those seeking to escape their tax liabilities under both the "general tax law"[141] and "a specific or general anti-avoidance tax law".[142] Moreover, unlike with the UK GAAR, the onus is on taxpayers to show that they did not engage in tax avoidance.[143]

4.4 (a) Counteraction

The New Zealand general anti-avoidance rule states that "the Commissioner may counteract a tax advantage that a person has obtained from or under a tax avoidance arrangement".[144] In deciding whether an arrangement will be counteracted, the Commissioner will examine

> such amounts of assessable income, deductions, and available net losses as, in the Commissioner's opinion, that person would have, or might be expected to have, or would in all likelihood have, had if that arrangement had not been made or entered into.[145]

Therefore, the Commissioner has considerable discretion as to whether a taxpayer would, might or is likely to have had a profit, deduction or loss had the arrangement not been carried out.

4.4 (b) Case law post the New Zealand general anti-avoidance rule

The breadth of the New Zealand general anti-avoidance rule was illustrated in the case of *Ben Nevis Forestry Ventures Ltd. v Commissioner of Inland Revenue*[146] (*Ben Nevis*) as the appellants in the case were not party to the agreement caught by the general anti-avoidance rule.[147] The facts of the case are complex and involved an elaborate structure which encompassed various companies and agreements. The appellants were investors in a forestry development project. The dispute was based on allowances which the taxpayers claimed they were entitled to after paying back both a licence fee for land used for forestry activities[148] and insurance premiums to safeguard against the forest not making the expected return.

The likelihood of profit was also analysed in order to assess whether the scheme involved elements of artificiality. The arrangement raised suspicion when the court found evidence to suggest that "it was possible but unlikely that the net proceeds of harvesting the trees would exceed the cost of the premium".[149] The unlikelihood of profit consequently led to questions as to "whether the appellants had a true business purpose".[150] Therefore, profitability and the existence of a business purpose are intertwined in New Zealand's tax law. Thereafter, it was concluded that "it was never intended that the forest would make a profit".[151] To reinforce the lack of an intention to make a profit, the issue of timing was discussed. The premium was due to be paid in 2048, and the judiciary commented that the investors were "unlikely to be alive in 2048".[152]

Interestingly, the court in *Ben Nevis* also differentiated between "legal substance"[153] and "business substance".[154] The distinction was not made clear, although the judges later commented on the fact that "taxpayers must show that the economic purpose of the entire expense incurred, rather than simply the legal benefit relates to the income-earning process".[155] The judges in *Ben Nevis* commented on the distinction between intention and motive.[156] Whilst acknowledging that the general anti-avoidance rule is concerned "with arrangements having the 'intended effect' or object of altering the incidence of tax",[157] the judges were careful not to confuse intention or purpose with motive.[158] Rather than exile the concept of motive altogether, the court stated that "it is well established that motive is not determinative, although it may be evidence which sheds light on a purpose of tax avoidance and so is not wholly irrelevant".[159] Therefore, the taxpayer's motive is a consideration when examining their purpose, although not a significant consideration. However, as exemplified by Millet, a person can have many motives,[160] which is why motive is an unreliable consideration.

As previously mentioned, the Tax Administration Act 1994 seems to be referring to the purpose of the taxpayer rather than the arrangement.[161] However, this issue was debated in *Ben Nevis*, and the judges concluded that the relevant purpose was that of the arrangement.[162] The appellants wanted the judiciary to examine their purpose.[163] Nevertheless, the court elucidated the distinction between the appellant's purpose and the arrangement's purpose. The judges held that the purpose of the arrangement "directs attention to features of the arrangement rather than intentions of a taxpayer in taking a tax position linked to the arrangement".[164] Therefore, the court examined "the means employed"[165] rather than the appellant's purposes, which it equated with their intention.[166] As demonstrated in chapter 1, "purpose" can also denote "object [or] thing intended".[167]

There was also distinct disapproval of equating tax avoidance arrangements with sham arrangements when elucidating that the facts of *Ben Nevis* revealed no signs of a sham.[168] According to the judges, "a sham exists when documents do not reflect the true nature of what the parties have agreed".[169] In contrast, in a tax avoidance arrangement,

> even though the documents may accurately reflect the transaction which the parties intend to implement . . . the arrangement entered into gives a tax advantage which Parliament regards as unacceptable.[170]

Therefore, a tax avoidance arrangement does not automatically also give rise to a sham arrangement, even if tax avoidance was the main purpose or effect of the transactions.[171]

Examining how the New Zealand general anti-avoidance rule operates is useful as it has heeded warnings in *Ben Nevis* regarding how the legislation and precedent on tax avoidance can conflict. The judges expounded how

> there is little explicit guidance in the legislation and the current case law has become complex, through being encumbered by considerations and tests that the legislation does not specify.[172]

Therefore, judges also like having clear guidance which would inhibit their discretion. Whilst judges invariably look to established precedent in deciding cases, the New Zealand experience has revealed that case law can generate even more tests. The resulting dilemma is the possibility of having an array of tests to consider. Therefore, the judiciary in the UK should be mindful to define the limits of the GAAR and the existing tests without establishing many additional tests.

The case of *Alesco New Zealand Ltd. v Commissioner of Inland Revenue*[173] (*Alesco*) upheld the approach taken in *Ben Nevis. Alesco* demonstrates that even where taxpayers obtain the advice of leading accountants (KPMG) and where reasons as to why the general anti-avoidance rule does not apply are provided during the formation of the scheme,[174] the arrangement may nevertheless fall under the general anti-avoidance rule. The case concerned the company Alesco Corporation and its wholly owned subsidiary, Alesco New Zealand. The subsidiary company sought the acquisition of two businesses, Biolab and Robinson, with the financial support of its parent company using an inter-company arrangement and optional convertible notes.[175] The notes were issued from Alesco New Zealand to Alesco Corporation for the purchase of Biolab in exchange for the funding and the agreement that interest would be payable on the loan. However, Alesco New Zealand's claim for interest deductions and plans to offset group losses were rejected by the Commissioner.

Although "it was always intended that real money would flow from Alesco Corporation to Alesco NZ",[176] suspicion was raised regarding the "intermediate arrangements".[177] The judge held that the financing structure was artificial as irrespective of the optional convertible notes, Alesco New Zealand would not (and did not) "incur any actual expense on an annual basis".[178] Due to the financing structure utilised in *Alesco*, the court held that "its sole motivation was to find and employ the most tax effective structure".[179] Despite the fact that Heath J. echoed the approach in *Westminster* that "any taxpayer is entitled to structure its affairs to minimise its tax obligations by 'permissible' means",[180] he qualified the approach by including that an arrangement cannot be permissible where it was "not contemplated by Parliament".[181]

Finally, on the issue of counteraction, the court interestingly held that "as a matter of logic, it is not possible to counteract a tax advantage by allowing the taxpayer to obtain greater tax benefits than were actually achieved".[182] Therefore, counteraction serves as a deterrence and a form of retribution, as well as a means to recalculate tax owed or the deductions to be disallowed.

4.5 The South African general anti-avoidance rule

The South African general anti-avoidance rule is contained in the Income Tax Act 1962, as implemented in 2006, under Part IIA. It was amended by the Revenue Laws Amendment Act 20 of 2006,[183] which means that it is one of the more recent general anti-avoidance rules in the world.

South Africa's general anti-avoidance rule deals with "impermissible tax avoidance arrangements".[184] Irrespective of the context of the arrangement, the general anti-avoidance rule states that the arrangement will be deemed "an impermissible avoidance arrangement if its sole or main purpose was to obtain a tax benefit".[185] Therefore, the arrangement's purpose is a central factor in the South African general anti-avoidance rule.

The Act then goes on to state how the general anti-avoidance rule applies in business,[186] in "context[s] other than business"[187] and "in any context".[188] In relation to businesses, the South African general anti-avoidance rule seems to align broadly with the aforementioned general anti-avoidance rules. Besides having tax avoidance as a main purpose, the Act states that it will be caught by the general anti-avoidance rule if "it was entered into or carried out by means or in a manner which would not normally be employed for bona fide business purposes, other than obtaining a tax benefit".[189] This provision is wide and could encompass an impermissible financial structure, as in the New Zealand case of *Alesco*, and a range of abnormal or artificial steps in an arrangement. It has been argued that in order

> to determine whether a transaction had bona fide business purposes, the hypothetical question must be asked whether businessmen generally, not motivated by tax considerations but rather by a bona fide business purpose, would have structured the arrangement in that manner.[190]

The use of motive in this sense coincides with Anscombe's definition of motive as the "desire of [the] gain".[191] Furthermore, in a business context, an arrangement would be impermissible if "it lacks commercial substance, in whole or in part".[192] The ability to tackle part of an arrangement means that "the issue of identifying the actual scheme is largely nugatory".[193] The Act has defined a "lack of commercial substance"[194] as where

> it would result in a significant tax benefit for a party . . . but does not have a significant effect upon either the business risks or net cash flows . . . apart from any effect attributable to the tax benefit that would be obtained.[195]

Therefore, commercial substance focuses more on what is quantifiable in addition to the level of risk involved. Consequently, if the transaction does not affect the company's funds in a proportionate manner to the tax benefit obtained, suspicion will be raised. The Act has also provided additional guidance for the judiciary in deciphering whether an arrangement lacks commercial substance. As well as the commercial substance, judges may also take into account a situation in which the "legal substance or effect of the avoidance arrangement as a whole is inconsistent with, or differs significantly from, the legal form of its individual steps".[196] "Legal substance" has not been defined but may be analogous to commercial substance, wherein the arrangement must have tangible legal consequences for the business. The aforementioned provision demonstrates that South Africa has no preference for substance over form. Instead, the form and substance of the arrangement must correspond with each other.

The general anti-avoidance rule has also highlighted typical avoidance arrangements which are deemed unacceptable. Firstly, "round-trip financing",[197] which involves moving around money[198] and includes a tax benefit[199] that is designed to "significantly reduce, offset or eliminate any business risk incurred by any party in connection with the avoidance arrangement".[200]

Secondly, the existence of "an accommodating or tax indifferent party"[201] is indicative of unacceptable tax avoidance. The term is defined in the Act as including an amount not subject to tax[202] or where funds are significantly "offset either by any expenditure or loss incurred by the party in connection with that avoidance arrangement",[203] which would otherwise have been subject to tax.[204] Lastly, the general anti-avoidance rule states that arrangements which have "elements that have the effect of offsetting or cancelling each other" would lack commercial substance. The examples are useful as they indicate what would be deemed as unacceptable tax avoidance, which promotes uniformity.

After the legislation outlines how it would operate in a business context, it then states that an arrangement would be caught by the general anti-avoidance rule if

> in a context other than business, it was entered into or carried out by means or in a manner which would not normally be employed for a bona fide purpose, other than obtaining a tax benefit.[205]

The aforementioned provision is very broad, which suggests that the Parliament of South Africa is less accepting of avoidance where a business is not involved.

Finally, the general anti-avoidance rule outlines what would amount to unacceptable tax avoidance "in any context",[206] which presumably would encompass business arrangements too. The general anti-avoidance rule states that an arrangement would not be permissible where it "has created rights or obligations that would not normally be created between persons dealing at arm's length".[207] Therefore, the provision suggests that the courts must scrutinise arrangements for the existence of abnormalities.

The South African general anti-avoidance rule then echoes the words of the UK GAAR by concluding that an arrangement would not be permissible where it "would result directly or indirectly in the misuse or abuse of the provisions of this Act".[208] It is significant that a general anti-avoidance rule which is not designed to be targeted has adopted similar wording to that of a targeted GAAR. It would be expected that the type of language in the two forms of anti-avoidance legislation would differ significantly. Nevertheless, South Africa specifies abuse as one example of what is unacceptable, and the UK GAAR specifies abuse as the only instance of what is unacceptable. However, the other instance of unacceptability in the South African general anti-avoidance rule also makes reference to abnormal arrangements, as previously mentioned, which is similar to the wording in the UK GAAR.[209] Nevertheless, the abuse provision has been criticised on the basis that "it leaves room for subjectivity in that abuse can potentially mean anything to anyone".[210]

The South African general anti-avoidance rule interestingly has a section regarding the "presumption of purpose".[211] The provision primarily makes it clear that the burden of proof is on the taxpayer to show that "obtaining a tax benefit was not the sole or main purpose of the avoidance arrangement".[212] As the legislation refers to the purpose of the arrangement,[213] the taxpayer "must establish the arrangement's purpose, not his or her purpose".[214] However, as "the arrangement itself is not a thinking entity",[215] it is difficult to establish its "intending purpose".[216] Cassidy argues that the purpose of the arrangement is deliberately the object of scrutiny "to shift the focus of inquiry away from the subjective intent of the taxpayer".[217] She has blurred intentions and purposes here, although it may be done consciously to suggest that examining the taxpayer's purpose can also lead to examining the taxpayer's intentions. Cassidy, however, asserts that "a blend of objective and subjective considerations is necessary".[218] Nonetheless, the competing subjective and objective deliberations are difficult to balance, and it is uncertain how much weight will be given to each consideration. The particular difficulty lies in the fact that subjective considerations cannot be quantified. Therefore, a mixture of both subjective and objective facts inevitably favours one approach over the other. Consequently, it is undesirable to examine subjective considerations in tax law as it leaves scope for judicial discretion.

If the taxpayer is unable to prove satisfactorily that the tax benefit was not a main purpose, the legislation states that "the arrangement is presumed to have been entered into or carried out for the sole or main purpose of obtaining a tax benefit".[219] This provision suggests that one's purpose may not actually be to obtain a tax benefit, but it is deemed to be such by default, in absence of evidence to the contrary. Therefore, the provision works in a retrospective manner. Furthermore, the section on purpose confuses matters by adding that "the purpose of a step in or part of an avoidance arrangement may be different from a purpose attributable to the avoidance arrangement as a whole".[220] However, even though the South African general anti-avoidance rule acknowledges that part of the arrangement may be genuine, the arrangement will still be caught by the legislation where a tax benefit was at least one of the main purposes of the arrangement.

4.5 (a) Case law post the South African general anti-avoidance rule

The importance of commercial substance as detailed in the South African general anti-avoidance rule[221] was also reinforced in *Commissioner for the South African*

Revenue Service v NWK Limited[222] (*NWK Ltd.*). NWK Limited evaded rather than avoided tax. However, the case is important as the South African courts had difficulty distinguishing the two concepts. The case concerned a loan taken out by NWK Limited (NWK) from a subsidiary of First National Bank (FNB) named Slab Trading Company (Pty) Ltd. (Slab). The loan was taken for five years, and NWK sought to claim interest deductions on the loan. However, the court claimed that the interest deductions claimed far outweighed the actual value of the loan.

NWK issued promissory notes to Slab, which were later sold to FNB. In exchange for Slab issuing the loan to NWK, NWK agreed to provide Slab tonnes of maize. However, the judge contended that the maize used to discharge the loan was provided by FNB to NWK.[223] Slab promptly sold its right to receive the maize to FNB, and the court concluded that Slab's role in the scheme was unnecessary.[224] NWK effectively took the loan out and delivered the maize in order to repurchase it from FNB later.[225] The court held that the interest on the loan was calculated erroneously as this figure was deduced by the taxpayers deducting the value of the maize from the loan. However, the maize was undervalued, which meant that the interest amount was incorrect.[226]

The *NWK Ltd.* case provided an example of what would be classified as "round-trip financing"[227] as "the money went out of FNB's account (pursuant to the loan) and straight back into FNB's account".[228] Furthermore, the judge repeatedly commented on the idea that NWK only needed a loan of R50 million rather than over R96 million worth of promissory notes which were issued by NWK.[229] Therefore, it was held that the loan sum was artificially engineered "by taking the interest payable and calculating what capital sum was needed to generate that interest at the rate agreed".[230] However, the Tax Court held that this rationale, provided by a professor from a financial perspective, was inadmissible because it "did not deal with the intention of the parties",[231] which is necessary with tax evasion.

The judgement in *NWK Ltd.* also displayed a preference for the substance over form doctrine and gave reasons for doing so.[232] The judge stated that "the test . . . cannot simply be whether there is an intention to give effect to a contract in accordance with its terms".[233] The judge claimed that the form of an arrangement is unreliable as

> invariably where parties structure a transaction to achieve an objective other than the one ostensibly achieved they will intend to give effect to the transaction on the terms agreed.[234]

Therefore, the judge advocated examining the existence of "commercial substance".[235]

The findings of the court in the *NWK Ltd.* case is that the rationale given by the judiciary leaned more towards proving tax evasion than tax avoidance.[236] Surprisingly, the court seemed to suggest that the case could qualify as both tax evasion and tax avoidance as the judge claimed that there is "no reason why an invalid transaction cannot also be abnormal and concluded for the purposes of avoiding tax".[237] It is also interesting that the judge referred to impermissible tax avoidance arrangements as "simulated transactions",[238] which is analogous to artificial transactions. It can be said that the South African courts distinguished tax avoidance from tax evasion by stating that the latter involves simulation.[239] However, simulation is akin to artificiality, which was a term used in UK tax avoidance cases such as *Ramsay*[240] and *McGuckian*.[241] The case illustrates that the creation of the South African general anti-avoidance rule has not helped in clarifying the distinction between tax avoidance and tax evasion.

The case of *Bosch and McClelland v Commissioner of South African Revenue Services*[242] (*Bosch*) did not fall within the remit of the South African general anti-avoidance rule in regards to an employee share scheme run by the Foschini Group. The scheme was altered in 1997 in order to gain tax benefits advantageous to the employer and employees. The main difference was that the amended scheme had a time limit of 21 days from the date of notice in which the employees could exercise the option to acquire the shares.[243] However, the employees lacked many proprietary rights and liabilities over the shares until they were delivered, in three portions, on "the second, fourth and sixth anniversaries of the relevant notice date".[244] The first appellant requested that the shares be sold on their behalf, and the second appellant wanted the shares transferred to him.[245]

The central question in *Bosch* was whether the scheme granted the employees an "unconditional entitlement to acquire shares upon the exercise of the option"[246] or whether the entitlement was only triggered on the anniversary dates.[247] However, as the scheme unfolded in court, it was revealed that the Foschini Group was obliged to repurchase the shares at the original purchase price if their market value fell. Therefore, "no participant would elect to implement a deferred purchase if the price exceeded the current market value".[248] The ability to resell the shares to the Foschini Group meant that the employee could then repurchase shares at their lower market value.[249] Therefore, the deferred purchase was uncertain, which meant that the employees did not have an unconditional right to acquire the shares.[250]

The court discussed the fact that if the employees opted to sell their shares but their market value was less than the consideration, the Foschini Group was obligated to give the employee the value of the consideration.[251] However, these terms were initially viewed as "uncommercial for no regard was had to the current value of the shares".[252] Nevertheless, the judges admitted that the scheme did have a commercial purpose.[253]

The court discussed whether the arrangement came within s8A of the Income Tax Act 1962, which states that an amount is taxable where there exists

> any right to acquire any marketable security . . . if such right was obtained by the taxpayer . . . in respect of services rendered or to be rendered by him as an employee to an employer.[254]

However, it was held "that delivery of the scheme shares to the appellant did not constitute the exercise by him or her of a right to acquire the shares for the purpose of s 8 A".[255] Ultimately, the general anti-avoidance rule did not apply as the court acknowledged that, according to the arrangement, "the object was to give employees an incentive to promote the continued growth of the company by giving them the opportunity to acquire share in the company".[256]

4.6 The Canadian general anti-avoidance rule

The Canadian general anti-avoidance rule is contained in Part XVI, s245 of the Income Tax Act 1985. Parts of the Canadian general anti-avoidance rule are reminiscent of the UK GAAR in terms of the language used, as will be demonstrated. The Canadian general anti-avoidance rule is aimed at "deny[ing] a tax benefit that . . . would result, directly or indirectly, from that transaction or from a series of transactions".[257] A tax benefit has been defined broadly by the general anti-avoidance rule, which states that it "means a reduction, avoidance or deferral of tax or other amount payable under this Act or an increase in a refund of tax or other amount under this Act".[258] A transaction has been defined as including "an arrangement or event".[259]

The Act applies to where a transaction would "result directly or indirectly in a misuse of the provisions"[260] of any of the Canadian taxing statutes,[261] rules,[262] regulations[263] or treaties.[264] The general anti-avoidance rule also applies to a transaction which "would result directly or indirectly in an abuse".[265] The inclusion of the term "abuse" is similar to the UK's targeted GAAR, which is aimed at abusive transactions. The concern is that the UK's GAAR is targeted because of the inclusion of the term "abusive". However, the Canadian anti-avoidance legislation is not meant to be targeted but still uses the term "abusive". Therefore, one possible inference that may be drawn, if one is focusing on this term, is that either the UK's GAAR is as wide as a general anti-avoidance rule, or the Canadian general anti-avoidance rule is narrow and targeted.

The meaning of an "avoidance transaction"[266] confers much discretion on the judiciary due to the breadth of the definition ascribed to it. An "avoidance transaction"[267] is defined as a transaction that

> would result, directly or indirectly, in a tax benefit, unless the transaction may reasonably be considered to have been undertaken or arranged primarily for *bona fide* purposes other than to obtain the tax benefit.[268]

The inclusion of the term "directly or indirectly"[269] has led to courts surmising that it "indicates that Parliament intended the GAAR to apply even where abuse is an indirect result of a transaction",[270] allowing an excavation into the entire series of transactions.[271]

Therefore, unlike the UK GAAR, the Canadian general anti-avoidance rule has adopted a single reasonableness test in analysing the transaction's purpose.[272] Moreover, the test does not require there to be a commercial or business purpose as the aforementioned jurisdictions do. The Canadian general anti-avoidance rule simply requires there to be a "*bona fide*"[273] purpose, although this purpose must be the primary purpose of the transaction. This omission relieves the taxpayer of the burden of examining the laws in relation to businesses in comparison with other transactions, unlike the South African general anti-avoidance rule. The Act makes it clear that the purpose requirement also applies where there is a "series of transactions".[274]

The Canadian general anti-avoidance rule also outlines the various ways in which judges can approach a tax avoidance transaction.[275] Judges have the flexibility to allow or disallow "any deduction, exemption or exclusion in computing income".[276] The Act also explicitly allows the judiciary to ignore the tax effects of the transaction before them.[277]

4.6 (a) Case law post the Canadian general anti-avoidance rule

The Canadian general anti-avoidance rule is concise. Therefore, subsequent case law regarding tax avoidance has sought to elucidate the workings of the legislation. In *Canada Trustco Mortgage Co. v R*[278] (*Canada Trustco*), the Canadian Supreme Court helpfully discussed the provisions of the general anti-avoidance rule at length. The case concerned a mortgage company which participated in a sale and lease-back agreement involving trailers. The taxpayer company purchased the trailers from the sellers and leased them to another company, which then subleased the trailers back to the original sellers.[279] Canada Trustco Mortgage Company sought to offset income from its business of leasing assets by claiming capital allowances on the purchase of the trailers. The court discussed that the way the taxpayer "structured and financed the purchase, lease and sublease of the trailers contravened the object, spirit or purpose"[280] of the legislation on capital allowances. The lack of financial risk in the arrangement also weakened the taxpayer's argument.[281]

Canada Trustco adopted the main purpose test. As the Canadian general anti-avoidance rule requires arrangements to have a "*bona fide*"[282] purpose, the judges held that "if there are both tax and non-tax purposes to a transaction, it must be determined whether it was reasonable to conclude that the non-tax purpose was primary"[283] in order to avoid triggering the general anti-avoidance rule. In addition to the main purpose test, *Canada Trustco* also outlined the circumstances in which an arrangement could be considered abusive.[284] Firstly, it would be abusive if "a taxpayer relies on specific provisions of the *Income Tax Act* in order to achieve an outcome that those provisions seek to prevent".[285]

Secondly, an abusive transaction occurs "when a transaction defeats the underlying rationale of the provisions that are relied upon".[286] This provision relates to the need to apply a purposive interpretation to make sure that the legislative purpose is not defeated. Lastly,

> an arrangement that circumvents the application of certain provisions, such as specific anti-avoidance rules, in a manner that frustrates or defeats the object, spirit or purpose of those provisions[287]

would be considered abusive. The terms "object, spirit or purpose"[288] were particularly emphasised throughout the judgement. Similarly, an arrangement would not be abusive where it "was within the object, spirit or purpose of the provisions that confer the tax benefit".[289] The "object, spirit or purpose"[290] of the provisions is likely to be ascertained in relation to what the judges believe Parliament's intention is. Therefore, it does not provide revolutionary guidance.

In relation to the taxpayer's motive, the court held that "whether the transactions were motivated by any economic, commercial, family or other non-tax purpose may form part of the factual context".[291] However, the judges did not dwell on the issue of motive; therefore, it was not considered to be a central issue in practice.

Although a tax benefit is required by the general anti-avoidance rule, the court warned that when a case is heard by a Tax Court, "the magnitude of the tax benefit is not relevant at this stage of the analysis".[292] However, this suggests that the amount of the tax benefit is relevant at some stage after the case is heard by the Tax Court. The amount of the tax benefit should not be a factor as it suggests that arrangements with higher tax benefits are more at risk of being caught by the general anti-avoidance rule, which is discriminatory.

It is interesting that the judges in *Canada Trustco* displayed an aversion to the business purpose test. Examining whether the transaction was "arranged primarily for *bona fide* purposes other than to obtain the tax benefit"[293] was viewed as having "a broader scope than the expression 'business purpose'".[294] The court disliked the business purpose test for narrowing the range of permissible arrangements to those with a business purpose only.[295] The court held that the view of what is permissible is too narrow as "Parliament wanted many schemes that do not have any business purpose to endure",[296] which included investments.[297] Significantly, the court also stated that the most difficult part of the general anti-avoidance rule to apply was the abuse requirement,[298] which suggests that the UK may undergo similar difficulties. The term "abuse" has not been defined,[299] and additional problems have been encountered as the single reasonableness test allows for "judicial leeway in determining abuse".[300]

The judgement in *Canada Trustco* also acknowledged that legislation is "interpreted in a textual, contextual and purposive way".[301] To reinforce the importance of the purposive approach, it was held that the role of the general anti-avoidance rule is to "negate arrangements that would be permissible under a literal interpretation".[302] The judges also stated that the Income Tax Act 1985 "must be interpreted in order to achieve consistency, predictability and fairness so that taxpayers may manage their affairs intelligently".[303] Despite the guidance on how to approach tax avoidance cases, the court in *Canada Trustco* held that the distinction between acceptable and unacceptable tax avoidance "is far from bright".[304] The court ultimately held that the general anti-avoidance rule did not apply despite the rationale which seemed critical of the arrangement.

Canada's general anti-avoidance rule was triggered, however, in *Lipson v R*[305] (*Lipson*). The case concerned a married couple who sought to deduct the interest from a bank loan on their mortgage loan. The wife borrowed money in order to buy shares in their family company, which the husband agreed to repay to the bank. The husband then transferred the shares to his wife and used the share proceeds to purchase their house. The couple acquired a mortgage for the house that they wished to purchase but used it to repay the loan for the company shares on the same day.[306] The husband then sought to deduct the interest on the mortgage loan from his taxable dividend income.

The appellants sought to rely on the spousal attribution rules, which state that

> if an individual has transferred or lent property . . . to or for the benefit of a person who is the individual's spouse or common-law partner . . . any income or loss . . . of that person for a taxation year from the property . . . is deemed to be income or a loss . . . of the individual for the year and not of that person.[307]

The court was careful when discussing the purpose of the arrangement and stated that "adopting an 'overall purpose' test under s. 245(4) would be to cause uncertainty and inconsistency for taxpayers".[308] Instead, the court advocated examining "the 'overall result', which more accurately reflects the wording of s. 245(4)".[309] Moreover, the judge presiding over the *Lipson* case did not rule out the importance of the taxpayer's motive by holding that

> motivation, purpose and economic substance are relevant under s. 245(4) only to the extent that they establish whether the transaction frustrates the purpose of the relevant provisions.[310]

However, later the judge stated that the issue of motive was irrelevant.[311] The taxpayers' motive or purpose was largely immaterial as the appellants had readily admitted that the arrangement was conducted to avoid tax.[312] Therefore, the judges had to examine whether the arrangement could be seen as abusive. The court held that it was an abusive arrangement as utilising s74.1 of the Income Tax Act 1985 enabled the husband to claim interest deductions "which he would not have been able to do were Mrs. Lipson dealing with him at arm's length".[313]

The dissenting judges had various qualms regarding the final decision of the Supreme Court. A surprisingly contentious issue was that the general anti-avoidance rule was invoked when there existed a specific anti-avoidance provision which would have been applicable.[314] Section 74.5(11) of the Income Tax Act 1985 is a specific anti-avoidance provision aimed at tackling "artificial transactions",[315] which would otherwise prevent the spousal attribution rules under s74.1(1) of the Income Tax Act 1985 from applying where "one of the main reasons for the transfer or loan was to reduce the amount of tax that would . . . be payable . . . on the income and gains derived from the property".[316] When discussing the concept of abuse under s74.1(1), a dissenting judge stated that the meaning of abuse is

> so broad that it would include interspousal transfers of assets at fair market value for *bona fide* economic reasons. It offers, I think, too large a field of operation for the GAAR.[317]

There were concerns that the general anti-avoidance rule was being relied upon too heavily without first applying the relevant specific anti-avoidance provision.[318] Rothstein J. forewarned that

> the GAAR is a supplementary rule. It is not a catch-all provision that the Minister can choose to deploy any or every time that he suspects a taxpayer of abusive tax avoidance.[319]

There was also observable frustration due to the fact that the *Westminster* approach was not shown the expected acknowledgement.[320] Binnie J. expressed that due to the outcome of *Lipson*, he believed that the court was merely "paying lip service to the *Duke of Westminster* principle without taking seriously its role in promoting consistency, predictability and fairness in the tax system".[321]

The limits of the general anti-avoidance rule were called into question when a dissenting judge warned that "the GAAR is a weapon that, unless contained by the jurisprudence, could have a widespread, serious and unpredictable effect on legitimate tax planning".[322] As the Canadian general anti-avoidance rule is similar to the UK GAAR in terms of requiring abuse, *Lipson* provides an insight into how an abusive arrangement will be determined. However, the *Lipson* judgement also offers a useful reminder that "the GAAR is only intended to operate as a provision of last resort".[323]

4.7 Conclusion

The analysis of the general anti-avoidance rules of other jurisdictions, including the United States of America's ESD, demonstrates that there are various similarities and differences in their approach to tax avoidance. Table 4.1 illustrates an overview of the main attributes of the UK GAAR and how the jurisdictions analysed compare to the UK GAAR with regard to these attributes.

Although the anti-avoidance legislations of the jurisdictions analysed are designed to be broad, the wordings of the legislations are similar to that of the UK GAAR. The US ESD objectively focuses on mathematical differences in the taxpayer's economic position. However, this is qualified by the business purpose test. Nevertheless, the ESD begins by asking whether the transaction is genuine rather than whether it is abusive, which requires the judiciary to pursue the authenticity of the transaction rather than seek to disprove it. The ESD examines whether there exists a profit motive. Therefore, there is scope for subjective considerations to be scrutinised.

Australia's general anti-avoidance rule starts by examining whether the taxpayer sought a tax benefit. The general purpose assessed is whether a tax benefit was sought, which is similar to the UK GAAR's main purpose test. However, to determine the taxpayer's purpose, the legislation also contains eight objective criteria that the judiciary should consider, which minimises discretion. Moreover, unlike the Parliamentary contemplation test in the UK GAAR,

> Pt IVA does not require the court to hypothesise what may have been 'within Parliamentary contemplation' or to divine the 'object, spirit or purpose' of other provisions in order to find the rationale that underlies the words that may not be captured by the bare meaning of the words themselves.[324]

New Zealand's general anti-avoidance rule is similar to the UK GAAR. New Zealand also assesses whether the arrangement is abusive, although this is done in relation to the arrangement's purpose. The legislation also examines whether

Table 4.1 Comparison of general anti-avoidance rules

	United Kingdom	*United States of America*	*Australia*	*New Zealand*	*South Africa*	*Canada*
Purpose	Yes. Arrangement's purpose. Main purpose test.	Yes. Business or substantial purpose.	Yes. Taxpayer's purpose judged by eight objective criteria.	Yes. Taxpayer's purpose and effect of scheme.	Yes. Sole or main purpose test. Arrangement's purpose	Yes. Taxpayer's purpose.
Abuse	Yes.	No.	No.	Yes.	Yes. Misuse or abuse.	Yes. Misuse or abuse.
Reasonableness	Yes. Double reasonableness test.	No.	No.	No.	No.	Yes. Single reasonableness test.
Intentions	Yes.	No.	No.	No.	No.	No.

tax avoidance is the arrangement's purpose or merely the effect of the arrangement. *Ben Nevis* and *Alesco* also highlighted that the taxpayer's motive is relevant. Furthermore, the judges in *Ben Nevis* differentiated between tax avoidance and shams. *Ben Nevis* was also significant as it heeded strong warnings about the need for detailed legislation to prevent a flurry of complex tests developing from case law.[325] Therefore, judges themselves recognise the problems of having too much judicial discretion. As the taxpayer's motives were discussed in *Alesco*,[326] it illustrates how, although the anti-avoidance rule discusses the purpose of the arrangement, the taxpayer's motives can be examined in practice.

South Africa's case law demonstrates the confusion that can occur in deciding tax cases, despite having a general anti-avoidance rule which should minimise this problem. Furthermore, the issue of simulation blurred tax avoidance and tax evasion. Their anti-avoidance legislation also examines abuse and the arrangement's purpose. If the UK continues to examine the taxpayer's intentions as well as whether the arrangement contained elements of artificiality, the UK may also struggle to distinguish between tax avoidance and tax evasion.

Canada's general anti-avoidance rule also analyses whether there is abuse of the taxing statute. *Canada Trustco* warned that the abuse requirement is difficult to apply in practice; therefore, the UK may face similar difficulties. As observed in *Canada Trustco*, Canada dislikes the business purpose test and instead assesses whether there is a bona fide purpose.[327] The purpose sought after works to prove the taxpayer's case rather than disprove it, like the UK GAAR's approach. Moreover, *Canada Trustco* established that where there is more than one purpose for embarking on an arrangement, the purpose which is unrelated to tax must be the main purpose for an arrangement to be successful.[328] Therefore, *Canada Trustco* maintains that the arrangement must be examined from the point of view of supporting the taxpayer's arrangement.

New Zealand, South Africa and Canada all mention abuse in their general anti-avoidance legislation. However, examining abuse cannot be what makes the UK GAAR targeted when it is the approach adopted in general anti-avoidance rules. Purpose is a strong theme emanating from all the anti-avoidance legislation examined. However, none of the jurisdictions analysed put the ability to examine the taxpayer's intentions on statutory footing.

Although Australia's general anti-avoidance rule appears to be the widest, it also provides the greatest guidance in determining the taxpayer's purpose. The New Zealand, South African and Canadian general anti-avoidance rules all mention "abuse", which is seemingly narrow. However, there is less guidance. This chapter demonstrates that all the general anti-avoidance legislation, including the United States' ESD, examines either the arrangement's purpose or the taxpayer's purpose. Therefore, it is unsurprising that the UK adopted the main purpose test. Nevertheless, while the taxpayer's intentions and even motives were raised in the case law of the various jurisdictions, none of the general anti-avoidance legislation, nor the United States' ESD, included the term "intention". Therefore, the UK GAAR is unique in this respect as the GAAR relies on the discretion of the judiciary to uncover the taxpayer's subjective intentions. In contrast to other jurisdictions, in the most crucial part of the UK GAAR, which determines whether an arrangement is abusive, judges are permitted to examine whether the taxpayer intended to utilise the loopholes in the tax system.[329] The discretion so given may, if unconstrained or too wide, be problematic. Therefore, it is helpful to examine how much discretion the judiciary may actually have and why a wide discretion may be undesirable.

Notes

1 ESD.
2 *Gregory v Helvering* 293 U.S. 465 (1935).
3 *Ibid*, pp468–469 (Sutherland J.).
4 *Ibid*, p469.
5 *Ibid.*
6 *Ibid.*
7 Anscombe, G.E.M. *'Intention'*, [1963], 2nd edn, Basil Blackwell, Oxford, p18.
8 *Gregory v Helvering* 293 U.S. 465 (1935), 470 (Sutherland J.).
9 *Ibid.*
10 *Knetsch v US* 364 U.S. 361 (1960).
11 *Ibid*, p364 (Brennan J.).
12 *Ibid*, p366.
13 *Ibid*, p365.
14 *Ibid*, p371 (Douglas J.).
15 Anscombe, G.E.M. *'Intention'*, [1963], 2nd edn, Basil Blackwell, Oxford, p18.
16 *Knetsch v US* 364 U.S. 361 (1960) 371 (Douglas J.).
17 *Frank Lyon Co. v US* 435 U.S. 561 (1978).
18 *Ibid*, p583 (Blackmun J.).
19 *Ibid*, p584.
20 *Rice's Toyota World Inc. v CIR* 752 F.2.d 89 (4th Cir. 1985).
21 *Ibid*, p92 (Judge Phillips).
22 *Ibid*, p95.
23 *Ibid*, p96.
24 s1409 Health Care and Education Reconciliation Act 2010.
25 Internal Revenue Code 1986 s7701(o).
26 Madison, A.D. *'Rationalising Tax Law by Breaking the Addiction to Economic Substance'*, [2011], Vol. 47, Idaho Law Review, p444.
27 Internal Revenue Code 1986 s7701(o)(1)(a).
28 *Ibid.*
29 IRS. *'Internal Revenue Bulletin: 2010–40'*, <www.irs.gov/irb/2010-40_IRB/ar09.html#d0e2360>, accessed 04.07.2016.
30 Internal Revenue Code 1986 s7701(o)(1)(b).
31 *Ibid.*
32 Bankman, J. *'The Economic Substance Doctrine'*, [2000], Vol. 74, No. 5, Southern California Law Review, p12.
33 *Ibid.*
34 *Ibid.*
35 Joint Committee on Taxation. *'Technical Explanation of the Revenue Provisions of the "Reconciliation Act of 2010" as Amended, in Combination with the "Patient Protection and Affordable Care Act"'*, [2010], <www.jct.gov/publications.html?func=startdown&id=3673>, accessed 05.07.2016, p149.

36 Internal Revenue Code 1986 s7701(o)(2)(a).
37 IRS. '*Internal Revenue Bulletin: 2010–40*', <www.irs.gov/irb/2010-40_IRB/ar09.html #d0e2360>, accessed 04.07.2016.
38 *Ibid.*
39 *Rice's Toyota World Inc. v CIR* 752 F.2.d 89 (4th Cir. 1985), 92 (Judge Phillips).
40 Bankman, J. *'The Economic Substance Doctrine'*, [2000], Vol. 74, No. 5, Southern California Law Review, p13.
41 IRS. *'Internal Revenue Bulletin: 2010–40'*, <www.irs.gov/irb/2010-40_IRB/ar09.html #d0e2360>, accessed 04.07.2016.
42 Slater, A.H. *'Part IVA: An International Perspective'*, [2013], Vol. 42, No. 3, Australian Tax Review, pp149, 150.
43 *Frank Lyon Co. v US* 435 U.S. 561 (1978), 584 (Blackmun J.).
44 *Bank of New York Mellon Corporation v CIR* 140 T.C. No. 2 (2013).
45 *Ibid*, p25 (Judge Kroupa).
46 *Ibid*, p35.
47 *Ibid*, p28.
48 *Ibid*, p29.
49 *Ricardo Garcia, Tax Matters Partner et al. v CIR* T.C. Memo 2013–49 (2013).
50 *Ibid*, p61 (Judge Holmes).
51 *Ibid.*
52 Scheer, R.K. *'Intentions, Motives and Causation'*, [2001], Vol. 76, No. 297, Philosophy, p399.
53 s207(4)(a) Finance Act 2013.
54 ICAEW. *'General Anti-Abuse Rule'*, <www.ion.icaew.com/TaxFaculty/26685>, accessed 05.07.2016.
55 Internal Revenue Code 1986 s7701(o)(5)(a).
56 Tiley, J. *'Judicial Anti-Avoidance Doctrines: The US Alternatives- Part 1'*, [1987], British Tax Review, pp180.
57 O'Connell, A. *'The GAAR Panels in Australia and the UK: Identical Twins or Distant Cousins?'*, [2013], 42 Australian Tax Review p269.
58 Cashmere, M. *'A GAAR for the United Kingdom? The Australian Experience'*, [2008], British Tax Review, pp125, 129.
59 *Ibid.*
60 s177A(1)(b) Income Tax Assessment Act 1936.
61 s177A(1)(a) Income Tax Assessment Act 1936.
62 s177A(1)(b) Income Tax Assessment Act 1936.
63 *Federal Commissioner of Taxation v Hart* (2004) 217 CLR 216, [9] (Gleeson CJ and McHugh J.).
64 s177C(1)(a) Income Tax Assessment Act 1936.
65 s177C(1)(b) Income Tax Assessment Act 1936.
66 s208 Finance Act 2013.
67 s177D Income Tax Assessment Act 1936.
68 s177D(1)(a) Income Tax Assessment Act 1936.
69 *Ibid.*
70 s177D(1)(b) Income Tax Assessment Act 1936.
71 s177D(1)(a) Income Tax Assessment Act 1936.
72 *Commissioner of Taxation v Hart and Another* (2004) 206 ALR 207, [63] (Gummow and Hayne JJ.).
73 Cashmere, M. *'A GAAR for the United Kingdom? The Australian Experience'*, [2008], British Tax Review, pp125, 136.
74 *Ibid.*
75 *Ibid.*
76 s177D(2) Income Tax Assessment Act 1936.
77 s177D(2)(a) Income Tax Assessment Act 1936.

78 s177D(2)(b) Income Tax Assessment Act 1936.
79 s177D(2)(c) Income Tax Assessment Act 1936.
80 s177D(2)(d) Income Tax Assessment Act 1936.
81 s177D(2)(e) Income Tax Assessment Act 1936.
82 s177D(2)(f) Income Tax Assessment Act 1936.
83 s177D(2)(h) Income Tax Assessment Act 1936.
84 s177D(2)(g) Income Tax Assessment Act 1936.
85 s177D(2)(b) Income Tax Assessment Act 1936.
86 s177D(2)(f) Income Tax Assessment Act 1936.
87 Slater, A.H. *'Part IVA: An International Perspective'*, [2013], Vol. 42, No. 3, Australian Tax Review, pp149, 149.
88 *Ibid.*
89 Gammie, M. *'When Is Avoiding Tax Not Abusive? Comparative Approaches to a GAAR in Australia and the United Kingdom'*, [2013], Vol. 42, Australian Tax Review, pp279, 291.
90 *Ibid.*
91 *Ibid.*
92 s177F Income Tax Assessment Act 1936.
93 s177F(1)(a) Income Tax Assessment Act 1936.
94 s177F(1)(b) Income Tax Assessment Act 1936.
95 s177F(1)(c) Income Tax Assessment Act 1936.
96 Kobetsky, M., Brown, C., Fisher, R., Villios, S. and Gillies, P. *'Income Tax: Text, Materials and Essential Cases'*, 9th edn, [2016], The Federation Press, Sydney, p620.
97 *Federal Commissioner of Taxation v Spotless* (1996) 141 ALR 92.
98 *Ibid*, p94 (per curiam).
99 *Ibid*, p95.
100 *Ibid.*
101 *Ibid*, p103.
102 *Ibid*, p96.
103 *Ibid*, p98.
104 *Mallalieu v Drummond* [1983] 3 W.L.R. 409, [1983] 2 A.C. 861, 872 (Lord Brightman).
105 *Federal Commissioner of Taxation v Spotless* [1996] 141 ALR 92, 93 (per curiam).
106 *Ibid.*
107 *Ibid*, p105 (McHugh J.).
108 *Ibid*, p102 (per curiam).
109 Harris, P.A. *'Australia's General Anti-Avoidance Rule: Part IVA Has Teeth but Are Some Missing?'*, [1998], British Tax Review, pp124, 134.
110 *Federal Commissioner of Taxation v Spotless* [1996] 141 ALR 92, 99 (per curiam).
111 *Ibid*, p96.
112 *Ibid.*
113 *Ibid.*
114 *Commissioner of Taxation v Hart and Another* [2004] 206 ALR 207.
115 *Ibid*, [3] (Gleeson CJ and McHugh J.).
116 *Ibid*, [6].
117 *Ibid*, [48] (Gummow and Hayne JJ.).
118 *Ibid*, [60].
119 *Ibid.*
120 *Ibid*, [18] (Gleeson CJ and McHugh J.).
121 *Ibid*, [61] (Gummow and Hayne JJ.).
122 Millet, P. *'Artificial Tax Avoidance: The English and American Approach'*, [1986], British Tax Review, pp327, 330.
123 *Commissioner of Taxation v Hart and Another* [2004] 206 ALR 207, [67] (Gummow and Hayne JJ.).
124 *Ibid*, [71].

125 s177C(1)(a) Income Tax Assessment Act 1936.
126 Harris, P.A. *'Australia's General Anti-Avoidance Rule: Part IVA Has Teeth but Are Some Missing?'*, [1998], British Tax Review, pp124, 135.
127 *Commissioner of Taxation v Hart and Another* [2004] 206 ALR 207, [63] (Gummow and Hayne JJ.).
128 *Ibid*, [65].
129 *Ibid*, [91]-[92] (Callinan J.).
130 s5(1) Interpretation Act 1999.
131 sYA1 Income Tax Act 2007.
132 *Ibid.*
133 *Ibid.*
134 Gormally, L. *'Intention and Side Effects: John Finnis and Elizabeth Anscombe'*, cited in Keown, J. and George, R. '*Reason, Morality and Law: The Philosophy of John Finnis'*, [2013], Oxford University Press, Oxford, p106.
135 sYA1 Income Tax Act 2007.
136 *Ibid.*
137 s141D(2) Tax Administration Act 1994.
138 s141D(1) Tax Administration Act 1994.
139 *Ibid.*
140 *Ibid.*
141 s141D(6)(a) Tax Administration Act 1994.
142 s141D(6)(b) Tax Administration Act 1994.
143 s149A(2)(b) Tax Administration Act 1994.
144 sBG1(2) Income Tax Act 2007.
145 sGB1(1)(a) Income Tax Act 2007.
146 *Ben Nevis Forestry Ventures Ltd. v Commissioner of Inland Revenue* (2009) 2 NZLR 289.
147 *Ibid*, p304 (Elias CJ and Anderson J.).
148 *Ibid*, p306.
149 *Ibid*, p334 (Tipping and McGrath JJ.).
150 *Ibid*, p335.
151 *Ibid.*
152 *Ibid*, p336.
153 *Ibid*, p306 (Elias CJ and Anderson J.).
154 *Ibid.*
155 *Ibid*, p353 (Tipping and McGrath JJ.).
156 *Ibid*, p308 (Elias CJ and Anderson J.).
157 *Ibid.*
158 *Ibid.*
159 *Ibid.*
160 Millet, P. *'Artificial Tax Avoidance: The English and American Approach'*, [1986], British Tax Review, pp327, 330.
161 s141D(1) Tax Administration Act 1994.
162 *Ben Nevis Forestry Ventures Ltd. v Commissioner of Inland Revenue* [2009] 2 NZLR 289, 354 (Tipping and McGrath JJ.).
163 *Ibid.*
164 *Ibid.*
165 *Ibid.*
166 *Ibid.*
167 Coulson, J., et al. *'The Oxford Illustrated Dictionary'*, [1981], 2nd edn, Oxford University Press, Wiltshire, p686.
168 *Ben Nevis Forestry Ventures Ltd. v Commissioner of Inland Revenue* [2009] 2 NZLR 289, 313 (Tipping and McGrath JJ.).

169 *Ibid.*
170 *Ibid.*
171 *Ibid*, p314.
172 *Ibid*, pp309–310.
173 *Alesco New Zealand Ltd. v Commissioner of Inland Revenue* (2012) 2 NZLR 252.
174 *Ibid*, p261 (Heath J.).
175 *Ibid*, p257.
176 *Ibid*, p284.
177 *Ibid*, p257.
178 *Ibid*, p289.
179 *Ibid*, p278.
180 *Ibid*, p292.
181 *Ibid.*
182 *Ibid*, p296.
183 Under Part ZZA.
184 s80A Income Tax Act 1962.
185 *Ibid.*
186 s80A(a) Income Tax Act 1962.
187 s80A(b) Income Tax Act 1962.
188 s80A(c) Income Tax Act 1962.
189 s80A(a)(i) Income Tax Act 1962.
190 Olivier, L. and Haniball, M. '*International Tax: A South African Perspective*', 5th edn, [2011], Siber Ink CC, Cape Town, South Africa, p530.
191 Anscombe, G.E.M. '*Intention*', [1963], 2nd edn, Basil Blackwell, Oxford, p18.
192 s80A(a)(ii) Income Tax Act 1962.
193 Cassidy, J. '*The Holy Grail: The Search for the Optimal GAAR*', [2009], The South African Law Journal, pp740, 752.
194 s80C Income Tax Act 1962.
195 s80C(1) Income Tax Act 1962.
196 s80C(2)(a) Income Tax Act 1962.
197 s80C(2)(b)(i) Income Tax Act 1962.
198 s80D(1)(a) Income Tax Act 1962.
199 s80D Income Tax Act 1962.
200 s80D(1)(b)(ii) Income Tax Act 1962.
201 s80C(2)(b)(ii) Income Tax Act 1962.
202 s80E(1)(a)(i) Income Tax Act 1962.
203 s80E(1)(a)(ii) Income Tax Act 1962.
204 s80E(b) Income Tax Act 1962.
205 s80A(b) Income Tax Act 1962.
206 s80A(c) Income Tax Act 1962.
207 s80A(c)(i) Income Tax Act 1962.
208 s80A(c)(ii) Income Tax Act 1962.
209 s207(2)(b) Finance Act 2013.
210 Kujinga, B.T. '*Analysis of Misuse and Abuse in Terms of the South African General Anti-Avoidance Rule: Lessons from Canada*', [2012], The Comparative and International Law Journal of Southern Africa, pp42, 50.
211 s80G Income Tax Act 1962.
212 s80G(1) Income Tax Act 1962.
213 s80A Income Tax Act 1962.
214 Cassidy, J. '*The Holy Grail: The Search for the Optimal GAAR*', [2009], The South African Law Journal, pp740, 766.
215 *Ibid.*
216 *Ibid.*

217 *Ibid.*
218 *Ibid*, p767.
219 s80G(1) Income Tax Act 1962.
220 s80G(2) Income Tax Act 1962.
221 s80C Income Tax Act 1962.
222 *Commissioner for the South African Revenue Service v NWK Limited* (27/10) [2010] ZASCA 168.
223 *Ibid*, [26] (Lewis JA).
224 *Ibid*, [72].
225 *Ibid*, [85].
226 *Ibid*, [27].
227 s80D(1)(b)(ii) Income Tax Act 1962.
228 *Commissioner for the South African Revenue Service v NWK Limited* (27/10) [2010] ZASCA 168, [61] (per Lewis JA).
229 *Ibid*, [65].
230 *Ibid.*
231 *Ibid.*
232 *Ibid*, [55].
233 *Ibid.*
234 *Ibid.*
235 *Ibid*, [57].
236 *Ibid*, [39].
237 *Ibid*, [93].
238 *Ibid*, [38].
239 *Ibid*, [93].
240 *WT Ramsay Ltd. v IRC*; *Eilbeck v Rawling* [1981] 2 W.L.R 449, [1982] A.C. 300, 321 (Lord Wilberforce).
241 *IRC v McGuckian* [1997] 1 W.L.R. 991, 996 (Lord Browne-Wilkinson).
242 *Bosch and McClelland v Commissioner of South African Revenue Services* (A 94/2012) [2012] ZAWCHC 188.
243 *Ibid*, [12] (Davis J.).
244 *Ibid.*
245 *Ibid*, [17].
246 *Ibid*, [43].
247 *Ibid.*
248 *Ibid*, [76].
249 *Ibid.*
250 *Ibid*, [77].
251 *Ibid*, [45].
252 *Ibid*, [75].
253 *Ibid*, [90].
254 s8A(1)(a) Income Tax Act 1962.
255 *Bosch and McClelland v Commissioner of South African Revenue Services* (A 94/2012) [2012] ZAWCHC 188, [93] (Davis J.).
256 *Ibid*, [12].
257 s245(2) Income Tax Act 1985.
258 s245(1) Income Tax Act 1985.
259 *Ibid.*
260 s245(4)(a) Income Tax Act 1985.
261 s245(4)(a)(v) Income Tax Act 1985.
262 s245(4)(a)(iii) Income Tax Act 1985.
263 s245(4)(a)(ii) Income Tax Act 1985.
264 s245(4)(a)(iv) Income Tax Act 1985.
265 s245(4)(b) Income Tax Act 1985.

266 s245(3) Income Tax Act 1985.
267 *Ibid.*
268 s245(3)(a) Income Tax Act 1985.
269 *Ibid.*
270 *Lipson v R* [2009] 1 S.C.R. 3, [37] (LeBel J.).
271 *Ibid.*
272 s245(3)(a) Income Tax Act 1985.
273 *Ibid.*
274 s245(3)(b) Income Tax Act 1985.
275 s245(5) Income Tax Act 1985.
276 s245(5)(a) Income Tax Act 1985.
277 s245(5)(d) Income Tax Act 1985.
278 *Canada Trustco Mortgage Co. v R* [2005] 2 S.C.R. 601.
279 *Ibid*, [3] (per curiam).
280 *Ibid*, [68].
281 *Ibid*, [70].
282 s245(3)(a) Income Tax Act 1985.
283 *Canada Trustco Mortgage Co. v R* [2005] 2 S.C.R. 601, [27] (per curiam).
284 *Ibid*, [45].
285 *Ibid.*
286 *Ibid.*
287 *Ibid.*
288 *Ibid.*
289 *Ibid.*
290 *Ibid.*
291 *Ibid*, [58].
292 *Ibid*, [19].
293 s245(3)(a) Income Tax Act 1985.
294 *Canada Trustco Mortgage Co. v R* [2005] 2 S.C.R. 601, [33] (per curiam).
295 *Ibid.*
296 *Ibid.*
297 *Ibid.*
298 *Ibid*, [37].
299 *Ibid.*
300 *Ibid.*
301 *Ibid*, [11].
302 *Ibid*, [13].
303 *Ibid*, [12].
304 *Ibid*, [16].
305 *Lipson v R* [2009] 1 S.C.R. 3.
306 *Ibid*, [5] (LeBel J.).
307 s74.1(1) Income Tax Act 1985.
308 *Lipson v R* [2009] 1 S.C.R. 3, [16] (LeBel J.).
309 *Ibid*, [34].
310 *Ibid*, [38].
311 *Ibid*, [42].
312 *Ibid*, [11].
313 *Ibid*, [42].
314 *Ibid*, [117] (Rothstein J.).
315 s74.5(11) Income Tax Act 1985.
316 *Ibid.*
317 *Lipson v R* [2009] 1 S.C.R. 3, [76] (Binnie J.).
318 *Ibid*, [116] (Rothstein J.).
319 *Ibid.*

320 *Ibid*, [98] (Binnie J.).
321 *Ibid*.
322 *Ibid*, [55].
323 *Ibid*, [119] (Rothstein J.).
324 Slater, A.H. *'Part IVA: An International Perspective*, [2013], Vol. 42, No. 3, Australian Tax Review, pp149, 159.
325 *Ben Nevis Forestry Ventures Ltd. v Commissioner of Inland Revenue* [2009] 2 NZLR 289, pp309–310 (Tipping and McGrath JJ.).
326 *Alesco New Zealand Ltd. v Commissioner of Inland Revenue* [2012] 2 NZLR 252, 278 (Heath J.).
327 s245(3)(a) Income Tax Act 1985.
328 *Canada Trustco Mortgage Co. v R* [2005] 2 S.C.R. 601, [27] (per curiam).
329 s207(2)(c) Finance Act 2013.

5 Discretion under the UK GAAR

Introduction

This chapter will examine the scope of discretion that may be available to judges in applying the provisions of the GAAR. Although Parliament may have intended for the GAAR to be examined by the judiciary in a general manner, this approach is undesirable as a wide discretion can cause uncertainty for taxpayers and inconsistencies in applying the GAAR. An analysis of the concept of judicial law-making will serve to address the circumstances in which judges make law, especially when considering that the vagueness of the GAAR would permit judges to fill in any gaps therein. The analysis will help clarify whether *Ramsay* can be seen as an anti-avoidance doctrine, which, in turn, will address the view that principles like *Ramsay* are undesirable. The way in which judges interpret statutes generally will be outlined in order to provide an understanding of what factors judges may consider, such as their conceptions of what is just. HMRC's role will also be discussed in order to establish how much involvement and discretion it has in the application of the GAAR, particularly when determining what is not abusive. Lastly, the relationship between tax law and morality will be assessed in order to support the proposition that the two concepts should remain separate.

5.1 The ambiguous GAAR

The wide nature of the GAAR unavoidably leaves room for judicial discretion. The implications of this will be examined. The width of the GAAR is largely due to the fact that the core provision which lays down what an abusive arrangement means is then divided and subdivided to provide a multitude of definitions for each of the key terms. Furthermore, most of the core terms which are defined either in the GAAR or GAAR guidance take the form of a test. Therefore, the judiciary are left with various definitions and tests, and it is unclear how they all operate together contemporaneously. The inclusion of those tests also fuels judicial discretion as the nature of the tests requires judicial opinion.

The GAAR is said to be targeted at tax arrangements, and this term is defined within the GAAR. Within this definition is the requirement of a tax advantage,[1] which has its own definition in the GAAR.[2] The examples outlining what amounts to a tax advantage are broad and would capture many arrangements.

DOI: 10.4324/9781003080473-6

The problematic breadth of the GAAR stems from the fact that the terms "abusive" and "arrangement" have been separated and defined again in the GAAR. As mentioned in chapter 3, an "arrangement" has been defined broadly in the GAAR,[3] and the guidance reaffirms that this term has been constructed widely.[4] Although the abuse requirement is designed to narrow the scope of the GAAR, the initial stage of the GAAR, which applies to an "arrangement", has been widely defined. Therefore, the initial stage of the GAAR applies to a variety of arrangements.

The double reasonableness test provides a definition of what is abusive. However, the GAAR subsequently subdivided and defined the test to produce three more provisions which the judiciary are to be mindful of when applying the GAAR. These further considerations are also capable of additional wide interpretation. The first consideration is essentially examining the end result.[5] The second point seeks to uncover any artificial steps,[6] although it is not clear to what end these will be assessed. However, it can be presumed that artificial steps will be ignored. Lastly and significantly, the GAAR allows an inquiry into the intentions of the arrangement.[7] Although the GAAR makes reference to the arrangement's intentions, this enquiry can become entangled with examining the taxpayer's intentions because the arrangement itself cannot have an intention.

The double reasonableness test, therefore, has many tiers which the judiciary must work their way through, and it is unclear how the various stages of the test piece together. Inevitably, with the wide nature of the tests, judges are bound to interpret these in their own individualised ways, and this approach could potentially generate widespread inconsistency. There is likely to be inconsistency until there is an established line of case law under the GAAR. Thereafter, the doctrine of *stare decisis* will provide greater certainty in the outcome of tax cases. The terms of the GAAR may lead to judges "interven[ing] to stop avoidance where they think that the avoidance is stopping the tax system from working properly or sensibly".[8] Although Tiley was referring to avoidance rather than abuse, the same argument could apply to abusive arrangements.

5.2 HMRC's role

The conditions under which an arrangement would not be considered abusive are also clouded with ambiguity. As mentioned earlier, an arrangement would not be regarded as abusive if it corresponds with "established practice",[9] which is wide and can raise questions as to the point at which a practice can be said to be established. However, the permissibility of this defence is largely curtailed by the requirement that, as well as being established, HMRC must also agree with the practice.[10] The latter requirement may be viewed as perverse, seeing as HMRC's main role is to collect taxes. Therefore, the GAAR provides apparent safeguards to the taxpayer, although, when observed closely, these safeguards are not entirely reliable.

HMRC is involved in deciding whether an arrangement is abusive in two important ways. Firstly, the HMRC GAAR guidance provides key information which is not contained in the GAAR legislation. Therefore, if the judiciary want to seek further direction on the legislation, they will turn to the HMRC GAAR guidance.

Secondly, HMRC has considerable power as the legislation specifically states that acceptable schemes must be indicated by HMRC in their guidance.[11] As this point is contained in the GAAR legislation, it demonstrates Parliament's willingness to grant this power to HMRC. HMRC can therefore outline the boundaries of abusive and unabusive tax avoidance more precisely than the GAAR has done. Consequently, Parliament granted both HMRC and the judiciary significant discretion.

There has been controversy over the fact that HMRC has published the GAAR guidance. The problem with HMRC being involved in writing the guidance is that "the fact that it . . . [is] drafted by HMRC is a significant divergence from the Report, which presented independent guidance as an important safeguard for taxpayers".[12] Therefore, the fact that HMRC has drawn up guidance departs from the original plan of having guidance drafted by an independent panel. Furthermore, the GAAR guidance does not provide much clarity in understanding the GAAR, which unfortunately reinforces the need for judicial discretion and reliance on the GAAR guidance.

5.3 Judicial discretion

Due to the many branches of the GAAR, the judiciary can interpret the legislative provisions broadly using their discretion. Although judges typically use their discretion when adjudicating, deciphering a taxpayer's motive, intention or purpose is undesirable due to the inherent subjectivity involved. The dilemma which discretion can potentially cause is the resulting inconsistency in deciding cases, which, in turn, may lead to uncertainty for taxpayers. Nevertheless, the doctrine of *stare decisis* and the purposive construction may curb discretion in practice.

Judges are able to infer the purpose of the transactions from what they can subjectively ascertain from the parties' conduct by "look[ing] . . . broadly at the facts even if there is no tax avoidance motive around".[13] Moreover, as has been suggested, while the GAAR would allow for judicial discretion due to the various statutory tests, it would also encourage such discretion through explicitly allowing the taxpayer's intentions to be examined. Therefore, the GAAR needs to be more objective and precise as

> the objectivity of the principles removes all notion of discretion from the hands of the judge. He need not decide issues on the cloudy basis of social, political, or economic philosophy, because he has before him the clear principles of the law.[14]

Rather than examining the taxpayer's intentions and the arrangement's purpose, "tax law could be made more certain by the more extensive use of objective tests and quantitative criteria in its administration".[15]

The UK's current tax system is largely made up of rules. Dworkin has asserted that loopholes in the law are "filled by judicial discretion",[16] which reinforces the notion that discretion is likely to be used when applying the GAAR. Discretion can involve applying subjective reasoning to decide the outcome of a case and can give wider choice in deciding cases, compared to situations wherein the statute is clear.

There are varying levels of discretion. At the very least, it must be acknowledged that judges will employ their discretion "in a weak sense"[17] when applying the GAAR. Dworkin explains that this soft sense of discretion can be used where "the standards an official must apply cannot be applied mechanically but demand the use of judgement".[18] The GAAR has been designed to require the judiciary to use their discretion when applying the legislation in order to determine whether an arrangement can be considered abusive. The requirement to consult the GAAR guidance, without Parliament explicitly stating the extent to which it should be relied on, further reinforces the necessity for judges to use their discretion. Dworkin's other form of weak discretion may not be applicable to common law rules as it relates to situations wherein an "official has final authority to make a decision and cannot be reviewed and reversed by any other official".[19]

Judges are entrusted with the task of ascertaining whether an arrangement is abusive by determining whether "such a result was not the anticipated result when the relevant tax provisions were enacted"[20] by Parliament. Therefore, ascertaining the intention of Parliament is explicitly required by the GAAR and can also be seen as favouring the purposive approach which "is a relatively recent development".[21] However, in interpreting legislation,

> the author and the author's intention are beyond our reach. The text has been severed from its author and is now in our (the reader's) time and space. We cannot ask the author what the meaning is (in law it would be improper to do so in any event).[22]

Therefore, it is difficult to expect "judges . . . [to] try to do what the legislature would have done".[23] Moreover, Gammie argues that "the only intention that can be accorded to Parliament is in the legislative words that it uses, properly construed in accordance with its evident policy and purpose".[24]

Some commentators contend that "it is for the courts to control the interpretation of the vague rules".[25] Whilst it is true that many, including Parliament, are relying on the judiciary to interpret the GAAR and form a sturdy line of case law, it is preferable for Parliament to make the provisions clear in the first instance in order to provide taxpayers with certainty before case law has been established. Others suggest that the level of judicial discretion may be too great and question whether "our tax law [is] still about rules or is it really about what is acceptable to the court".[26] The uncertainty of the line between acceptable and abusive tax avoidance has led commentators to query whether "it [has] become the case that something which mitigates tax will only succeed if it passes some judicial smell test". "Must a tax scheme be fragrant to succeed?"[27] Therefore, it is evident that "Mr Aaronson has not solved the problem of distinguishing unacceptable from acceptable tax planning".[28] The GAAR simply "gives a discretionary power to the courts to do so".[29]

Too much judicial discretion is undesirable as

> discretion is . . . associated with a lower amenability to legal challenge as compared with rule-based decision-making, on the basis that a failure to adhere to a rule may be more easily questioned than the exercise of discretion.[30]

Moreover, "although it is an undisputed fact that judges act independently, it does not follow that their own views will not be reflected in their judgements".[31] The tax system is already complex. Therefore, it is essential to reduce "the contribution of discretion to complexity".[32]

Due to the discretion which the GAAR grants to the judiciary, it is essential that judges strike a balance between upholding the intention of Parliament and providing justice as "when people dispute, they take refuge in the judge and to go to the judge is to go to justice".[33] Ensuring that Parliament's will, as expressed in legislation, is upheld and taxpayers are not penalised for relying on Parliament's will will ensure justice. Justice is expected as "the nature of the judge is to be a sort of animate justice".[34] Moreover, "compliance will follow as long as taxpayers know what they are supposed to do [and] are treated in a procedurally just manner".[35] The concept of justice will be discussed further later in this chapter.

The various definitions and tests within the GAAR seem like they are restricting judicial discretion. However, due to the wide nature of the various definitions, the explanation of the various terms does little to limit discretion. Admittedly, judges are faced with a difficult task in applying the GAAR due to the layered nature of the legislation and have a large role in interpreting the legislation due to the wide provisions. Moreover, it has been argued that

> uncertainty may itself lead to arbitrary exercises of power by unelected judges. Thus, to reduce the exercises of such arbitrary power, the Parliament has to extirpate as much vagueness from the law as is possible. It is true that this is likely to augment rather than to diminish the length of legislation but this is a price which has to be paid for certainty and to save us from the blandishments of judicial law making.[36]

5.3 (a) Judicial law-making

Judges have themselves elucidated that

> the constitutional duty of the tribunals and the courts is plain: to construe the language of the legislation in accordance with the principles of statutory interpretation, to analyse the transactions in question in accordance with the applicable general law and to apply the correct construction of the legislation to them.[37]

As a function of the judiciary is to interpret the law, there will invariably be some degree of discretion. Interpretation of legislation is central as "no draftsman, however fertile his imagination, can think of everything".[38] Establishing whether the judiciary can exercise a legislative-like function in adjudicating will reinforce

Ramsay as forming a legal principle. This suggests that the formation of such principle can recur with the existence of an ambiguous GAAR. Furthermore, as the GAAR is ambiguous, the eventual direction which the GAAR will take will be moulded by the judiciary. Although this is the case with all pieces of legislation, it will take many years for stability in case law to occur, and this could cause uncertainty to taxpayers in the meantime.

As illustrated, the GAAR, being wide, places much decision-making power in the hands of the judiciary. Consequently, it can be argued that "whoever has power to determine what those rules of conduct shall be and what shall be the remedy for their breach is potentially a legislator".[39] This legislative potential was worryingly recognised by a judge, Diplock L.J. as he then was, who recognised that judges can be "compelled to act as legislators".[40] The compulsion to act as a legislator is expected with the wide UK GAAR. However, Lord Diplock suggested that the legislative role of the courts is more habitual as he claims that judges "pretend to be no more than codifiers. But this is legal fiction".[41] Therefore, the tendency to legislate through adjudication can span further than the field of tax law.

The underlying message in Lord Diplock's speech is not to accuse judges of intentionally overstepping their constitutional boundaries but to emphasise how their legislative role is an unavoidable result of adjudication due to the legal principle of *stare decisis*.[42] The creation of principles, which are followed by future courts, are formed unconsciously as judges are "rarely . . . explicitly concerned with future conduct".[43] Lord Diplock expressed his views in the 1960s, before *Ramsay* was established in the early 1980s. Consequently, he may not have envisaged that judicial activism would flourish.[44] Accordingly,

> over a period of . . . 30 years, courts have moved from regarding tax as purely a statutory thing, liability to which is to be determined only by reading the statute, to regarding it as something which is as susceptible to the common law method as anything else.[45]

To reinforce the indirect legislative role, Lord Diplock also strongly asserted that "never are the courts explicitly concerned with what is general".[46] However, it can be argued that judges are concerned with general policy considerations, particularly in tax cases, in which tax avoidance is a topical issue. Furthermore, it can also be said that judges seek general legal principles deriving from existing case law in order to apply the same legal standard to achieve uniformity. Therefore, the legislative role of judges can be a positive function of the judiciary. Curiously, Lord Diplock asserts that the legislative role is exercised by the judiciary where the consequences for particular actions are decided and expected to be followed in the future.[47] However, contrary to his earlier contention, this suggests that judges are concerned with future decision-making. Furthermore, their expectations may not transform into reality, particularly with a wide GAAR in which judges can disagree as to the meanings of particular provisions. Although this may be the case with all legislation, there needs to be certainty with the GAAR as it overrides all other tax statutes.

Pertinently, Lord Diplock discusses tax law specifically and explains how judges legislate in relation to this topic without necessarily intending to do so.[48]

He explains how tax cases are generally concerned with "dispute[s] as to whether a particular kind of gain is taxable"[49] and that "whenever the court decides that kind of dispute it legislates about taxation".[50] The court effectively "makes a law taxing all gains of the same kind",[51] although levying taxes is Parliament's role. However, a counter-argument is that the court is simply determining whether the transaction is one which Parliament has said shall be taxable.

The uniqueness of tax cases as compared to other areas of law is elucidated perceptively by Lord Diplock who enunciated that

> anyone who has decided tax appeals knows that most of them concern transactions which Members of Parliament and the draftsman of the Act had not anticipated, about which they had never thought at all.[52]

The elaborate schemes which are utilised in tax avoidance cases cause existing Parliamentary legislation to be ill-equipped to deal with the inventive variations of tax schemes which may be why the provisions of the GAAR are purposely wide and vaguely drafted. However, the GAAR should not be promoted as being targeted if the application is intended to be wide. The judiciary have much power by merely being the body which ultimately applies the law as

> whoever has final authority to explain what Parliament meant by the words that it used makes law as much as if the explanation it has given were contained in a new Act of Parliament. It will need a new Act of Parliament to reverse it.[53]

Therefore, it is evident that judges enjoy some power, and this is recognised by judges themselves. For example, in *Ramsay*, Lord Wilberforce commented on the purpose of the scheme and sought to unravel it,[54] prior to the GAAR being enacted. However, the purposive approach only applies to statutes, not the facts of cases.

It could be said that examining the purpose of tax schemes in *Ramsay* inspired Parliament to subsequently include this requirement in the GAAR,[55] particularly as other cases such as *Craven* discussed the lack of a business purpose at length.[56] These landmark decisions "laid down sub-rules which determined what classes of transactions attracted liability to tax".[57]

The creation of Parliamentary rules as compared to judge-made law differs due to the perspectives adopted when legislating. Lord Diplock, writing extra-judicially, suggests that the differences lie in the fact that Parliament attempts

> to foresee how human beings will react in the future to a new rule of conduct in circumstances which of necessity will be different from those which existed before the law was passed.[58]

Unlike with judge-made law, once legislation has been passed, "Parliament has no opportunity to explain its meaning – short of passing an amending Act",[59] which is why legislation must be drafted clearly in the first instance. In contrast, Lord Diplock believes that judges make law less creatively and according to "actual experience of what human beings have in fact done and what were in fact the consequences of their doing so".[60] However, although judges are limited to the facts of the case before them, they can nevertheless form a principle which will apply to the interpretation of a particular provision or a specific gain. Some may argue that the development of the common law is necessary and desirable due to the flexibility with which judges can create rules.[61] However, it can also be argued that principles created by the judiciary lack Parliamentary endorsement and are improper as judges are unelected.[62] In *The Commissioners for HMRC v Mayes*[63] (*Mayes*), the judges displayed much deference to Parliament.[64] The court clearly did not like the conclusion they formed, although the judges acknowledged that

> even if the courts do not like the result, they have no means at their disposal to amend a law enacted by Parliament. Their sole function is to decide the case on their best understanding of the relevant transactions and the applicable law, whatever that may be. Whether or not the courts approve of the outcome is beside the point. It is not for judges to shoulder the law-making responsibilities of Parliament.[65]

Common law rules can be viewed as less desirable than statute law due to the lack of scrutiny from a democratically elected body.[66] However, the value of common law has been acknowledged as Laws L.J. explained how, as a result of the decision in *Schmidt v Secretary of State*, "the doctrine of legitimate expectation has of course been much deployed in the administrative law cases".[67] Furthermore, the doctrine

> has become a major instrument in the common law's insistence on fair dealing by public bodies, and the protection against abuse of power which the common law provides.[68]

Nevertheless, there is the additional concern that judicial precedents are habitually

> pieced together from the statements by individual members of the Courts of the reasons why in particular circumstances a particular decision was reached, [and] there is no exclusive linguistic formula in which the rule is expressed.[69]

The *Ramsay* approach is even more fragmented as it is pieced together from principles deriving from *Ramsay* and its supporting cases. Furthermore, with judicial legislation, there is always the underlying concern as to whether the judge-made law reflects Parliament's will. Similarly, there is the additional concern that "Parliamentary law is the slave of the precise words which the professional draftsman chooses to express its will".[70]

Other problems with common law rules include the fact that "judge-made law is law made in arrear: it is known only after it is broken",[71] which is the main problem with the GAAR. In addition to this, Lord Diplock also acknowledges that criticisms may derive from the view that "judge-made law is difficult to ascertain and often complicated".[72] In elucidating the perceived problems with the creation of common law rules, Lord Diplock's final and arguably weakest claim is "that judges by training, temperament and age are too averse to change to be entrusted with the development of rules of conduct for a brave new world".[73] If this last point were true, the *Ramsay* approach would not have been created. Therefore, judges do encourage change where they feel change is needed. Due to the problems with common law rules, Lord Diplock explains that judges should only legislate in private law as opposed to public law.[74] As tax law is a branch of public law, it falls outside of the sphere of judicial rule-making, if Lord Diplock's theory is applied.

Consequently, Lord Diplock elucidates how judges can create legislation primarily through interpretation[75] but also by means of the creation of rules derived from deciding cases.[76] However, he does not suggest that judges are wandering into forbidden territory by legislating in this manner. Lord Diplock justifies the judiciary's actions by stating that it all legitimately forms part of the common law.[77] Furthermore, Dworkin indicates that discretion is necessary for the development of law as "doctrines of legislative supremacy and precedent incline toward the *status quo*".[78] Although evolution of legal rules is necessary, it must also be balanced with the need for legal certainty. The creation of principles deriving from the common law should only be encouraged in the absence of statutory rules.

Having a tax system which promotes certainty is essential. Cases like *Ramsay* and *Furniss* were brought to court due to the uncertainty in computing the taxpayers' liabilities. Expensive and lengthy hearings can be minimised with legislation which stimulates certainty for both the revenue and taxpayer.[79] The vague GAAR encourages considerable judicial discretion. This fuels uncertainty. However, "people should be able to arrange their affairs with knowledge of what their resulting liability to tax will be".[80] The level of certainty is diminished where there exists the ability to use significant discretion. In cases which form new legal principles, the judge "has legislated new legal rights, and then applied them retrospectively to the case at hand".[81]

It can be argued that the *Ramsay* approach was the result of judicial discretion which thereafter rejected the *Westminster* approach. Dworkin's explanation of rules and principles helps support the argument that the *Ramsay* approach is robust. Principles "incline a decision one way . . . and they survive intact when they do not prevail",[82] which is why *Ramsay* survived an attack on its constitutional legitimacy in *Westmoreland*. However, rules differ from principles as "when a contrary result has been reached, the rule has been abandoned or changed".[83] Therefore, *Ramsay* did form a new approach. However, Poscher argued that "the way in which adjudication proceeds does not depend on the norm to be implemented; rather, it depends on the case to be judged according to the norm".[84]

Understandably, there exists an invariable "conflict inherent in the judicial process between the need for certainty and the need for change".[85] However, it can be said that Parliament has sacrificed legal certainty to accommodate change by enacting the GAAR.

5.3 (b) Interpretation

The argument that "statutes and common law rules are often vague and must be interpreted"[86] is convincing, particularly with the ambiguous UK GAAR. The way in which judges interpret the law generally is important to comprehend as it can help provide a meaningful understanding of how the GAAR will be interpreted in practice. Moreover, it is important to understand how the taxpayer's acts are interpreted by the judiciary. Conceptions of what is just can also colour one's interpretation. Therefore, it is necessary to decipher what conceptions of justice are applied in judicial interpretation of statutes.

Interpretation has been defined as "a rational activity that gives meaning to a legal text".[87] Moreover, it has been acknowledged that "the application of the GAAR is a complex matter of statutory interpretation",[88] although it has also been recognised that "an interpreter sometimes reaches his or her interpretive conclusion by intuition".[89] It is important that judicial interpretation remains within its constitutional boundaries as levying taxes is Parliament's role. A clearer explanation can be expounded in regards to criminal law as, although judges can interpret the law,[90] "they are not authorised to fill gaps in ways that define new crimes".[91] However, as discussed earlier, judges presiding over cases which have attracted the GAAR will have to fill in the gaps of the wide legislation. Therefore, the doctrine of the separation of powers is also an underlying issue in adjudication. Although the purposive interpretation has been viewed as the norm by many of the cases supporting the *Ramsay* approach, it has been recognised that

> the excessive literalism that previously prevailed in construing tax legislation was at least partially attributable to a judicial acceptance that the imposition of tax is a matter for Parliament not the judiciary.[92]

Therefore, the literal approach to construing tax legislation can, at the very least, be praised for upholding the doctrine of the separation of powers and generating "legal certainty and predictability for citizens".[93] Similarly, it has been recognised that the purposive approach to interpretation is not always the most objective approach as "after all, the purpose of taxing statutes is to collect tax and to approach tax cases on that understanding of their purpose may lead to a bias against the taxpayer".[94] Consequently, the purposive approach may lead the judge to find that the scheme comes under the remit of the GAAR and is a form of unacceptable tax avoidance in order to collect more taxes. Even where the purpose of a provision is to provide tax relief, "the GAAR will apply to deny a tax advantage where the purpose of the legislation is to give that advantage"[95] where an arrangement is deemed abusive. Therefore, the GAAR overlays all tax legislation and can deny the very tax benefits which Parliament explicitly permits.

The purposive approach has also been criticised as the

> purposive construction inevitably involves attributing a meaning to a statute different from that which an ordinary reading of the words gives: unless

> that is so, there is no need to construe purposively; it is only necessary to construe.[96]

Aaronson also admitted that

> in some cases, the Courts, under the guise of purposive interpretation, have been prepared to stretch the interpretation of tax legislation in order to thwart tax avoidance schemes which they regard as abusive.[97]

Moreover, Aaronson recognised that

> the degree of willingness to do so varied from judge to judge, and also reflected the degree of disapproval with which the judge regarded the particular transaction. This produced considerable uncertainty.[98]

The purposive approach plays a key role in tax law. Freedman states that the "GAAR . . . [is] simply . . . another piece of legislation to apply purposively".[99] However, if all aspects of tax avoidance transactions are purposively interpreted, it can be said that the quest for examining purpose can cause the judiciary to stray too far from Parliament's intentions.

The concept of justice is central to interpretation according to Dworkin as "justice is an institution we interpret".[100] Justice is a key factor in taxation as the government reinforces the idea that "all taxpayers should pay their fair share".[101] However, what amounts to fair raises questions as to what standards of justice are being applied.[102] For example, "a libertarian thinks that income taxes are unjust because they take property from its owner without his consent".[103] The libertarian perspective was clearly not the standpoint of the previous coalition government which sought to tackle tax avoidance. Dworkin states that the libertarian view is in direct contrast with the egalitarian perspective, which places emphasis on redistributive justice.[104] The disparity in views on justice demonstrates that, in order to interpret the law in a uniform manner, there must be a general agreement as to what is considered just, whereby the "judge restores equality".[105] However, Aristotle claims that "the just . . . is the lawful and the fair, the unjust the unlawful and the unfair".[106]

The GAAR guidance provides an outline of what should no longer be viewed as just. It dismisses "old cases to the effect that taxpayers are free to use their ingenuity to reduce their tax bills by any lawful means".[107] Therefore, in interpreting legislation or cases being heard before them, judges are predisposed to reject cases which display marks of inventive tax planning. Consequently, *Westminster*'s influence has been undermined following the GAAR. Judges presiding over tax avoidance cases are more concerned with what is not permitted than with what is permitted; therefore, the hallmarks of tax avoidance will be discussed in chapter 7 to facilitate a way in which there is consensus as to what is not generally just.

Dworkin gave an account of interpretation by rationalising what he termed "constructive interpretation".[108] This form of interpretation accords closely with the conventional purposive interpretation as the former involves "imposing purpose on an object or practice".[109] Dworkin had anticipated possible abuse of interpretation through discretion but curtailed the practice of "constructive interpretation"[110] by stating that "it does not follow . . . that an interpreter can make of a practice . . . anything he would have wanted it to be".[111] Dworkin believed that a restriction on interpretation stems from the idea that "the history or shape of a practice or object constrains the available interpretations of it".[112] However, as illustrated by *Barclays* and *Westmoreland*, which departed from *Ramsay*, judges do not allow themselves to be constrained by established precedents.

As demonstrated, judges tend to examine not only the arrangement itself but also what the taxpayer was seeking to achieve in executing the arrangement. An analogy can be drawn between the propensity to examine the taxpayer and the arrangement with how Dworkin states practices can be interpreted.[113] In relation to practices, he argues that it is important to analyse the practice rather than those performing it[114] by asserting that it is central to decipher "what *it* means, not what *they* mean".[115] Therefore, it is better to examine the taxpayer's arrangement than what they hoped to gain by executing the arrangement.

Interpretation becomes an even greater issue when it is considered that few cases have been brought under the GAAR, signifying the lack of an established line of case law to provide an indication as to how the GAAR should be interpreted. Therefore, it is possible to characterise new cases yet to be heard under the GAAR as "hard case[s]",[116] which exist "when no settled rule dictates a decision either way".[117] Dworkin asserts that these cases are resolvable by reference to "either policy or principle".[118] He describes a policy as "justify[ing] a political decision by showing that the decision advances or protects some collective goal of the community".[119] However, a principle has a narrower scope as Dworkin elucidates that a "principle justif[ies] a political decision by showing that the decision respects or secures some individual or group right".[120] It is therefore evident that it is the wider policy factors which the judiciary will consider when interpreting the GAAR. However, any attempt at predictability is curtailed by the fact that there are differing views as to what is considered just and, therefore, what is regarded as unjust or abusive.

Greenberg recognises that there is considerable fluidity in the wording of the GAAR.[121] He explains that the flexibility is due to the fact "that the Government is no longer prepared to put up with the inconvenience of being constrained by the actual meaning of the legislation".[122] Therefore, by drafting in imprecise terms, "the Government [is] . . . taking continual control of what the legislation is to be taken to mean".[123] However, it is the judiciary who invariably enjoy control over the meaning of legislation and HMRC over the content of the guidance.

Despite the fact that the judiciary have wide powers in interpreting the GAAR, it is for HMRC to decide whether to invoke the GAAR in the first instance. Therefore,

> the powers of judges to interpret statutes is, no doubt, significant. But unlike the power of legislators and the Executive, it cannot be exercised on a whim and it awaits parties with a court case to give it the breath of life.[124]

5.4 Morality

There has been an overlap between law and morality when discussing tax avoidance due to the widespread view that all taxpayers have to contribute their fair share of taxes. Although the purposive approach to the interpretation of tax law is the general view, some warn that

> in adopting a purposive approach to taxing statutes judges must avoid the temptation to import their own perceptions of the morality of the taxpayer's conduct into the interpretational exercise.[125]

There is much scope for judges to impart their views on morality due to the wide GAAR provisions, which demand interpretation. If the GAAR is found to be too ambiguous, the judiciary may settle the dispute using their perceptions of what is morally correct.

There is a threat of moral considerations being at the fore of adjudication due to the widespread controversy

> about taxpayers, especially large corporations, not paying as much tax as they ought. But that is a debate that should take place in the court of public opinion, not the courts of law.[126]

Issues of what is moral should remain separate from tax law as "intellectual biography is not a legal argument".[127] However, Dworkin claimed that it can be argued that "morality is a matter of objective fact".[128] He rationalised this argument by giving the crime of genocide as an example.[129] Dworkin asserted that

> our opinions are not just subjective reactions to the idea of genocide, but opinions about its actual moral character. We think, in other words, that it is an objective matter- a matter of how things really are- that genocide is wrong.[130]

This argument rests on the belief that these opinions "are universal and . . . absolute. They are part of the fabric of the universe, resting, as they do, on timeless, universal truths about what is sacred and fundamentally right or wrong".[131]

There are arguments condemning the fact that the GAAR was formulated to satisfy concerns that tax avoidance is an immoral practice. The ACCA addressed the issue of morality in tax law,[132] which became a topical issue, before the introduction of the UK GAAR, when the tax avoidance practices of Google, Starbucks and Amazon came to light with corresponding claims that tax avoidance is immoral.[133] However, the ACCA rejects this notion and believes that it is "wrong to try to ascribe a moral value system to the calculation of a tax base"[134] as "morality cannot be measured in this context".[135]

A flurry of multinational companies have engaged in tax avoidance, which has attracted disapproval for being immoral. Generally, more people are concerned about tax avoiders as commentators have remarked that "10 years ago news of a company minimising its corporation tax would have been more likely to be inside the business pages than on the front page".[136] Apple had apparently been avoiding corporation tax from 2009 to 2012 in the US and Ireland.[137] The company had avoided paying US$44 billion in tax.[138] Apple's Irish subsidiaries were incorporated in Ireland but were centrally managed and controlled in America.[139] Tax avoidance was achieved through a surprisingly uncomplicated plan of ensuring that the subsidiaries were not classified as resident in either America or Ireland for tax purposes.[140] Ireland determines tax residency according to where the company is centrally managed and controlled. However, America determines tax residency based on where the company was incorporated.[141] Therefore, rather than working directly with the foreign distributors,

> Apple . . . created a trilateral scenario in which the Irish subsidiaries were inserted between the two companies and booked a substantial portion of the profits arising from the transaction.[142]

Commentators recognised that "the huge noise – on the internet especially – generated by the congressional and parliamentary investigations of tax avoiders is probably not good for brand Ireland".[143] Starbucks also attracted palpable condemnation when it became known to the public in 2013 that it had not paid corporation tax since 2009.[144] The public became more passionate about tackling tax avoiders during this time and took to the streets in protest of Starbucks' tax avoidance schemes.[145] Starbucks crumbled under public pressure, rather than a legal obligation to pay tax, and admitted that "it would pay more corporation tax after a public outcry and an investigation by MPs".[146] Consequently, in 2013, Starbucks paid £5 million in taxes.[147]

The tactic of damaging a company's integrity in order to reverse the effects of a tax avoidance scheme seems to have worked with Starbucks. Starbucks were particularly vulnerable to the effects of public condemnation as their consumers "are 'mobile' in the sense that it is relatively easy for such customers to switch from buying coffee from Starbucks to buying from another coffee shop down the street".[148] There have also been concerns over the fact that Starbucks' payment of tax was "voluntary".[149] Ting argues that "taxation should not be discretionary. It is an insult to the tax system when taxpayers can decide if they want to pay some tax, and if so, when and how much to pay".[150] Therefore, although Starbucks eventually decided to pay tax, the decision demonstrates that the UK's tax system does not operate effectively. Moreover,

> labelling a tax preference as "tax avoidance" signals to the popular press and to the world at large that a section of the community is benefitting inappropriately in some way even though the reason why they are benefitting is not their inappropriate behaviour but the failure of government and revenue authority to take more timely action.[151]

Despite the threat of reputational damage seeming to work as a method to reverse tax avoidance, others argue that this approach to taxation is undesirable. Devereux believes that whilst damaging the integrity of Starbucks has worked in the past, "the only long-term solution is fundamental reform, not arbitrary naming and shaming".[152] Whilst these multinational corporations have engaged in tax avoidance and people are entitled to protest, "we have a legal system to ensure that companies pay the right amount of tax".[153] The problem with media frenzies surrounding tax avoidance is that

> claims that particular companies are exploiting loopholes are typically based on scant information, and sometimes appear to be based on a misunderstanding of the tax system. Starbucks is a case in point. Part of the argument is that Starbucks has paid little UK tax despite having high UK sales, regardless of the location of sales being irrelevant for determining existing taxes on profit.[154]

The reason Starbucks was able to pay little tax was due to issues regarding the residency of the business for tax purposes. Therefore, Devereux recommends that "perhaps, a good case could also be made for a reform that allocates taxes on profit according to where sales are generated".[155] Consequently, the real solution should be aimed at reforming the tax system rather than causing reputational damage to big corporations which the UK's economy heavily depends on. Shaming businesses into paying tax also sends out a misleading message to the public that tax is based on morality rather than the law.

The ACCA argues that "whether or not businesses in the UK are paying enough tax is not something that should be subject to moral pressures but should be determined by the law".[156] Consequently, tax law and morality should remain separate as "morality simply clouds the issue".[157] However, Lethaby argues that

> I also continue to believe that there is a distinction – a moral distinction, if we are going to have to bring morality into it – between personal tax avoidance and corporate tax avoidance.[158]

The introduction of the GAAR could therefore be a response to a desire to uphold moral values about tax avoidance and an attempt by the "legislators [to] make citizens good by forming habits in them . . . [as] this is the wish of every legislator".[159] Critics of the GAAR claim that tax avoiders are perceived as troublemakers and

> what our GAAR is intended to do is to deny, under the guise of law, the benefit of the words in the statute to some chosen class of alleged miscreants whose only misdemeanour is to ask that the law be applied to them honestly.[160]

5.5 Conclusion

The GAAR has attempted to avoid vagueness by providing definitions of some of the key terms within the legislation. However, the definitions of the targeted GAAR are wide and do little to promote certainty. The vague drafting consequently means that judicial interpretation and discretion are not only expected but also needed. However, wide discretion can lead to inconsistency because judges will have their own interpretations of what the provisions mean and, therefore, what they encompass. HMRC also retains wide continuous power in deciding what should be classified as abusive. Consequently, deciding whether the GAAR applies relies heavily on the discretion of HMRC and of the judiciary. It is desirable to strive towards the "ideal that adjudication should be as unoriginal as possible".[161] However, Parliament seems to have granted judges considerable discretion in applying the GAAR. Such wide discretion is unfortunate. Cases should be judged on their own merit without the use of judicial anti-avoidance approaches such as the *Ramsay* approach. The UK now has both a targeted GAAR and a wide common law anti-avoidance doctrine. The *Ramsay* approach demonstrates "that the judicial urge to search for a unifying principle is hard to resist".[162]

Although judge-made law can be useful in guiding legislation for future cases, it cannot cure the problem of the ambiguous GAAR in the first instance. There is bound to be uncertainty for the taxpayers who are expected to test the boundaries of abusive tax avoidance before a consistent line of case law is formed. Furthermore, it is Parliament's role to make legislation. Therefore, it is unreasonable to expect the judiciary to fill in the wide gaps left by Parliament. Despite the fact that there are some restrictions on how a judge will decide a case, the breadth of the legislation allows scope for judicial creativity, which may generate inconsistency. The issue of morality also needs to be excluded from tax law as the GAAR is not about paying one's fair share of taxes but about not engaging in abusive tax avoidance. Issues of morality tend to undermine the legality of tax avoidance altogether. Lethaby argues that introducing the GAAR had "one potential benefit [which] was freeing the courts from the need to 'strangle' the words of the legislation to reach an equitable result".[163] However, the GAAR has also attracted a range of other criticisms, which will be the focus of the next chapter.

Notes

1 s206 Finance Act 2013.
2 s208 Finance Act 2013.
3 s214 Finance Act 2013.
4 *'HMRC GAAR Guidance with Effect from 11 September 2020: Parts A, B and C'*, <https://assets.publishing.service.gov.uk/government/uploads/system/uploads/attachment_data/file/916667/gaar_parts_a_b_c_2020.pdf>, accessed 29.04.2021, p9.
5 s207(2)(a) Finance Act 2013.
6 s207(2)(b) Finance Act 2013.
7 s207(2)(c) Finance Act 2013.
8 Tiley, J. *'Tax Avoidance Jurisprudence as Normal Law'*, [2004], British Tax Review, pp304, 308.
9 s207(5) Finance Act 2013.
10 *Ibid.*
11 *Ibid.*
12 Bhogal, S. and Fryer, B. *'The UK GAAR: What Needs Answering'*, [2012], International Tax Review, [no pagination].

13 Ault, H.J. and Arnold, B.J. '*Comparative Income Taxation: A Structural Analysis'*, [2004], 2nd edn, Aspen Publishers, America, p133.
14 Stroup, D.G. *'Law and Language: Cardozo's Jurisprudence and Wittgenstein's Philosophy'*, [1984], Vol. 18, No. 2, Valparaiso University Law Review, p334.
15 Van Horn, L.G. *'The Need for More Objective Tax Laws'*, [1973], Vol. 51, The Tax Magazine, Taxes, pp589, 590.
16 Freeman, M.D.A. '*Lloyd's Introduction to Jurisprudence'*, [2008], 8th edn, Sweet and Maxwell Limited, London, p717.
17 Dworkin, R. *'Taking Rights Seriously'*, [1996], Duckworth, Biddles Ltd., Great Britain, p31.
18 *Ibid.*
19 *Ibid.*
20 s207(4) Finance Act 2013.
21 Aaronson, G. *'A Study to Consider whether a General Anti-Avoidance Rule Should Be Introduced into the UK Tax System'*, [2011], <http://webarchive.nationalarchives.gov.uk/+/http:/www.hm-treasury.gov.uk/d/gaar_final_report_111111.pdf>, accessed 25.08.2014, p16.
22 Walshaw, C. *'Where Are We with Statutory Interpretation'*, [2014], New Zealand Law Journal, p254, [no pagination].
23 Dworkin, R. *'Justice in Robes'*, [2006], The Belknap Press of Harvard University Press, London, p251.
24 Gammie, M. *'When Is Avoiding Tax Not Abusive? Comparative Approaches to a GAAR in Australia and the United Kingdom'*, [2013], Vol. 42, Australian Tax Review, pp279, 292.
25 Evans, C., Freedman, J. and Krever, R. *'The Delicate Balance: Tax, Discretion and the Rule of Law'*, [2011], IBFD, Amsterdam, p35.
26 Goldberg, D. '*Acceptability, Morality and Balance in Taxation'*, [2000], British Tax Review, pp106, 107.
27 *Ibid.*
28 McKie, S. *'The Philosopher's Stone or the Emperor's New Clothes – an Old Conundrum'*, [2012], Private Client Business, pp124, 132.
29 *Ibid.*
30 Harris, N. *'Law in a Complex State: Complexity in the Law and Structure of Welfare'*, [2013], Hart Publishing, Oxford, p6.
31 Olivier, L. and Haniball, M. *'International Tax: A South African Perspective'*, 5th edn, [2011], Siber Ink CC, Cape Town, South Africa, p513.
32 Harris, N. *'Law in a Complex State: Complexity in the Law and Structure of Welfare'*, [2013], Hart Publishing, Oxford, p6.
33 Aristotle. *'The Nicomachean Ethics of Aristotle: Translated with an Introduction by Sir David Ross'*, [1954], Oxford University Press, Great Britain, p115.
34 *Ibid.*
35 Braithwaite, V. *'Taxing Democracy'*, [2016], Routledge, London, p3.
36 The Hon Justice Perram, N. *'The Perils of Complexity: Why More Law Is Bad Law'*, [2010], Vol. 39, Australian Tax Review, pp179, 184.
37 *The Commissioners for HMRC v Mayes* [2011] EWCA Civ 407, [17] (Mummery L.J.).
38 Zander, M. *'The Law-Making Process'*, [2015], 7th edn, Hart Publishing Ltd., Oxford and Portland, p125.
39 Diplock, K. *'The Court as Legislators'*, [1965], The Holdsworth Club of the University of Birmingham, <http://kessler.co.uk/wp-content/uploads/2012/05/CourtsAsLegistlators.pdf>, accessed 13.02.2016, p2.
40 *Ibid.*
41 *Ibid.*
42 *Ibid*, p3.

43 *Ibid*, p2.
44 Garnett, M. and Lynch, P. *'Exploring British Politics'*, [2016], 4th edn, Routledge, Great Britain, p203.
45 Goldberg, D. *'How Clear, Transparent, Accessible and Foreseeable Is Tax Law and Practice?'*, [2013], Private Client Business, pp238, 241.
46 Diplock, K. *'The Court as Legislators'*, [1965], The Holdsworth Club of the University of Birmingham, <http://kessler.co.uk/wp-content/uploads/2012/05/CourtsAsLegistlators.pdf>, accessed 13.02.2016, p3.
47 *Ibid.*
48 *Ibid*, p6.
49 *Ibid.*
50 *Ibid.*
51 *Ibid.*
52 *Ibid.*
53 *Ibid.*
54 *WT Ramsay Ltd. v IRC* [1982] AC 300, per Lord Wilberforce, p232.
55 s207(1) Finance Act 2013.
56 *Craven v White*; *IRC v Bowater*; *Property Developments Ltd. v Gregory* [1989] A.C. 398, per Lord Templeman, p483.
57 Diplock, K. *'The Court as Legislators'*, [1965], The Holdsworth Club of the University of Birmingham, <http://kessler.co.uk/wp-content/uploads/2012/05/CourtsAsLegistlators.pdf>, accessed 13.02.2016, p8.
58 *Ibid*, p13.
59 *Ibid*, p14.
60 *Ibid*, p13.
61 *Ibid.*
62 Dworkin, R. *'Taking Rights Seriously'*, [1996], Duckworth, Biddles Ltd., Great Britain, p84.
63 *The Commissioners for HMRC v Mayes* [2011] EWCA Civ 407.
64 *Ibid*, [20] (Mummery L.J.).
65 *Ibid.*
66 Diplock, K. *'The Court as Legislators'*, [1965], The Holdsworth Club of the University of Birmingham, <http://kessler.co.uk/wp-content/uploads/2012/05/CourtsAsLegistlators.pdf>, accessed 13.02.2016, p15.
67 Laws, L.J. *'Lecture III: The Common Law and Europe: Hamlyn Lectures 2013'*, [2013], <www.judiciary.gov.uk/wp-content/uploads/JCO/Documents/Speeches/laws-lj-speech-hamlyn-lecture-2013.pdf>, p2.
68 *Ibid.*
69 Diplock, K. *'The Court as Legislators'*, [1965], The Holdsworth Club of the University of Birmingham, <http://kessler.co.uk/wp-content/uploads/2012/05/CourtsAsLegistlators.pdf>, accessed 13.02.2016, p14.
70 *Ibid*, p14.
71 *Ibid*, p16.
72 *Ibid.*
73 *Ibid.*
74 *Ibid*, p15.
75 *Ibid*, p6.
76 *Ibid*, p8.
77 *Ibid*, p11.
78 Dworkin, R. *'Taking Rights Seriously'*, [1996], Duckworth, Biddles Ltd., Great Britain, pp37–38.
79 Van Horn, L.G. *'The Need for More Objective Tax Laws'*, [1973], Vol. 51, The Tax Magazine, Taxes, p589.

80 Diplock, K. *'The Court as Legislators'*, [1965], The Holdsworth Club of the University of Birmingham, <http://kessler.co.uk/wp-content/uploads/2012/05/CourtsAsLegistlators.pdf>, accessed 13.02.2016, p7.
81 Dworkin, R. *'Taking Rights Seriously'*, [1996], Duckworth, Biddles Ltd., Great Britain, p81.
82 *Ibid*, p35.
83 *Ibid.*
84 Poscher, R. *'Insights, Errors and Self Misconceptions of the Theory of Principles'*, [2009], Vol. 22, No. 4, Ratio Juris, pp425–454, 439.
85 Diplock, K. *'The Court as Legislators'*, [1965], The Holdsworth Club of the University of Birmingham, <http://kessler.co.uk/wp-content/uploads/2012/05/CourtsAsLegistlators.pdf>, accessed 13.02.2016, p16.
86 Dworkin, R. *'Taking Rights Seriously'*, [1996], Duckworth, Biddles Ltd., Great Britain, p82.
87 Barak, A. *'Purposive Interpretation in Law'*, Princeton University Press, Princeton and Oxford, NJ, p3.
88 *Canada Trustco Mortgage Co. v R* [2005] 2 S.C.R. 601, per curiam, p76.
89 Barak, A. *'Purposive Interpretation in Law'*, Princeton University Press, NJ, p39.
90 *Ibid*, p17.
91 *Ibid.*
92 *Ibid.*
93 Bell, J. and Engle, G. *'Cross Statutory Interpretation'*, [1995], 3rd edn, Butterworths, London, p32.
94 Barak, A. *'Purposive Interpretation in Law'*, Princeton University Press, Princeton and Oxford, NJ, p17.
95 Goldberg, D. *'How Clear, Transparent, Accessible and Foreseeable Is Tax Law and Practice?'*, [2013], Private Client Business, pp238, 241.
96 *Ibid.*
97 Aaronson, G. *'A Study to Consider whether a General Anti-Avoidance Rule Should Be Introduced into the UK Tax System'*, [2011], <http://webarchive.nationalarchives.gov.uk/+/http:/www.hm-treasury.gov.uk/d/gaar_final_report_111111.pdf>, accessed 25.08.2014, p18.
98 *Ibid*, p24.
99 Freedman, J. *'Analysis-GAAR: Challenging Assumptions'*, [2010], No. 1046, Tax Journal, pp12, 13.
100 Dworkin, R. '*Law's Empire*', [1998], Hart Publishing, Oxford, p73.
101 *'HMRC GAAR Guidance with Effect from 11 September 2020: Parts A, B and C'*, <https://assets.publishing.service.gov.uk/government/uploads/system/uploads/attachment_data/file/916667/gaar_parts_a_b_c_2020.pdf>, accessed 29.04.2021, p5.
102 Dworkin, R. *'Law's Empire'*, [1998], Hart Publishing, Oxford, p73.
103 *Ibid.*
104 *Ibid*, p76.
105 Aristotle. *'The Nicomachean Ethics of Aristotle: Translated with an Introduction by Sir David Ross'*, [1954], Oxford University Press, Great Britain, p115.
106 *Ibid*, p107.
107 *'HMRC GAAR Guidance with Effect from 11 September 2020: Parts A, B and C'*, <https://assets.publishing.service.gov.uk/government/uploads/system/uploads/attachment_data/file/916667/gaar_parts_a_b_c_2020.pdf>, accessed 29.04.2021, p5.
108 Dworkin, R. *'Law's Empire'*, [1998], Hart Publishing, Oxford, p52.
109 *Ibid.*
110 *Ibid.*
111 *Ibid.*
112 *Ibid.*

113 *Ibid*, p63.
114 *Ibid.*
115 *Ibid.*
116 Dworkin, R. *'Taking Rights Seriously'*, [1996], Duckworth, Biddles Ltd., Great Britain, p83.
117 *Ibid.*
118 *Ibid.*
119 *Ibid*, p82.
120 *Ibid.*
121 Greenberg, D. *'Dangerous Trends in Modern Legislation'*, [2015], Vol. 96, Public Law, p5.
122 *Ibid.*
123 *Ibid.*
124 Pagone, G.T. *'Aspects of Tax Avoidance: Trans-Tasman Observations'*, [2011], Vol. 40, Australian Tax Review, p186.
125 The Honourable Mr Justice Malcolm Wallis. *'Is Tax Really Different?'*, [2016] British Tax Review pp299, 301.
126 *Ibid.*
127 Dworkin, R. *'Justice in Robes'*, [2006], The Belknap Press of Harvard University Press, London, p254.
128 Dworkin, R. *'Objectivity and Truth: You'd Better Believe It'*, [1996], Vol. 25, No. 2, Philosophy and Public Affairs, pp87–139, 96.
129 *Ibid*, p92.
130 *Ibid.*
131 *Ibid*, p97.
132 ACCA. *'The UK General Anti-Abuse Rule'*, <www.accaglobal.com/content/dam/acca/global/PDF-technical/tax-publications/tech-tp-ukgaar.pdf>, accessed 02.06.2016, p3.
133 Richard Murphy. *'Amazon, Google and Starbucks Are Struggling to Defend Their Tax Avoidance'*, (The Guardian, 13.11.2012), <www.theguardian.com/commentisfree/2012/nov/13/amazon-google-starbucks-tax-avoidance>, accessed 03.06.2016.
134 ACCA. *'The UK General Anti-Abuse Rule'*, <www.accaglobal.com/content/dam/acca/global/PDF-technical/tax-publications/tech-tp-ukgaar.pdf>, accessed 02.06.2016, p3.
135 *Ibid.*
136 Barford, V. and Holt, G. *'Google, Amazon, Starbucks: The Rise of "Tax Shaming"'*, (BBC, 21.05.2013), <www.bbc.co.uk/news/magazine-20560359>, accessed 06.02.2017.
137 Robert Peston. *'Is Apple's Tax Avoidance Rational?'*, (BBC News, 21.05.2013), <www.bbc.co.uk/news/business-22607349>, accessed 06.02.2017.
138 Ting, A. *'iTax-Apple's International Tax Structure and the Double Non-Taxation Issue'*, [2014] British Tax Review, p40.
139 *Ibid*, p44.
140 *Ibid.*
141 *Ibid.*
142 *Ibid*, p61.
143 Robert Peston. *'Is Apple's Tax Avoidance Rational?'*, (BBC News, 21.05.2013), <www.bbc.co.uk/news/business-22607349>, accessed 06.02.2017.
144 BBC. *'Starbucks Pays UK Corporation Tax for First Time since 2009'*, <www.bbc.co.uk/news/uk-politics-23019514>, accessed 06.02.2017.
145 *Ibid.*
146 *Ibid.*
147 *Ibid.*
148 Ting, A. *'iTax-Apple's International Tax Structure and the Double Non-Taxation Issue'*, [2014] British Tax Review, pp40, 68.
149 *Ibid.*
150 *Ibid.*

151 Gammie, M. *'When Is Avoiding Tax Not Abusive? Comparative Approaches to a GAAR in Australia and the United Kingdom'*, [2013], Vol. 42, Australian Tax Review, pp279, 281.
152 Michael Devereux. *'Name and Shame Is No Way to Close Tax Loopholes'*, (Financial Times 22.10.2012), <www.ft.com/content/c70afb8e-194c-11e2-af4e-00144feabdc0>, accessed 06.02.2017.
153 *Ibid.*
154 *Ibid.*
155 *Ibid.*
156 ACCA. *'The UK General Anti-Abuse Rule'*, <www.accaglobal.com/content/dam/acca/global/PDF-technical/tax-publications/tech-tp-ukgaar.pdf>, accessed 02.06.2016, p3.
157 *Ibid.*
158 Lethaby, H. *'Analysis-Reflections on Tax and the City'*, [2014], No. 1220, Tax Journal, pp10, 11.
159 Aristotle. *'The Nicomachean Ethics of Aristotle: Translated with an Introduction by Sir David Ross'*, [1954], Oxford University Press, Great Britain, p29.
160 Goldberg, D. *'How Clear, Transparent, Accessible and Foreseeable Is Tax Law and Practice?'*, [2013], Private Client Business, pp238, 242.
161 Dworkin, R. *'Taking Rights Seriously'*, [1996], Duckworth, Biddles Ltd., Great Britain, p84.
162 Tiley, J. *'Tax Avoidance Jurisprudence as Normal Law'*, [2004], British Tax Review, pp304, 308.
163 Lethaby, H. *'Analysis-Reflections on Tax and the City'*, [2014], No. 1220, Tax Journal, pp10, 11.

6 Criticisms of the GAAR

Introduction

This chapter explores the various criticisms which the GAAR has attracted. The majority of the criticisms that will be referred to in this chapter are from practitioners. Since they are entrusted with providing tax advice to their clients, they are most affected by the GAAR in practice. The purpose of this chapter is to examine the potential problems with the GAAR when it is "applied in the real world".[1] Criticisms of the main tests within the GAAR will be examined, including the main purpose test and the double reasonableness test. Views on the scope of the GAAR will also be analysed in order to determine whether the legislation is perceived as having clearly identifiable boundaries. Moreover, there have been criticisms regarding the extent to which the GAAR guidance can be relied on by taxpayers and tax advisors. Therefore, this issue will be explored.

There have also been widespread concerns about the UK's international competitiveness following the GAAR. Accordingly, the question of whether the GAAR could damage the UK's competitive reputation will be examined. Furthermore, the issue of complexity will be addressed to analyse the extent to which the GAAR contributes to a complex tax system. In addition to this, the issue of uncertainty in the tax system will be examined in order to assess whether the GAAR will contribute towards making tax liability uncertain. Certainty is also particularly important to corporate taxpayers which need to keep precise accounts of their outgoings. Lastly, there are various constitutional issues which have been raised due to the nature of the GAAR which will be explored. Practitioners had expressed concern about the GAAR before its inception when discussing the draft GAAR. Therefore, practitioner views on the draft GAAR will also be included.

6.1 The main purpose test

The main purpose test has been strongly criticised, and doubts have been cast as to how it will operate in practice.[2] Due to the numerous tax avoidance cases which the test will apply to, Grant Thornton states that it "cannot be considered a useful filter".[3] Therefore, it can be said that the test does little to aid in uncovering whether an arrangement is abusive. Fundamentally, as a tax arrangement is

DOI: 10.4324/9781003080473-7

defined in terms of the main purpose test, the definition of a tax arrangement has been criticised for being "effectively a general anti-avoidance rule".[4] The main purpose test is wide, although the breadth of the GAAR is reined in by virtue of the abuse requirement.

Mishcon de Reya has also identified problems with the elusive term "purpose" in the main purpose test in the GAAR, which seeks to uncover whether the "obtaining of a tax advantage was the main purpose, or one of the main purposes, of the arrangements".[5] The firm argues that the purpose requirement of the test is unfeasible because

> discussions as to the precise intention behind the arrangements may not have been put into writing at the outset or the tax benefits may only have been discovered or pursued after the arrangements were agreed.[6]

Therefore, there are concerns that the purpose of an arrangement may not always be evident and that purposes are changeable. This argument is persuasive. The argument coincides with Krikorian's view that there can be a "growing purpose of which we become aware at a comparatively advanced stage of our action".[7] If an arrangement does not contain an express purpose, this may be constructively imposed on taxpayers. Mishcon de Reya has also recognised not only that there can be a link in the terms "intention" and "purpose" in the main purpose test but also that the courts should only examine the taxpayer's intentions as evidenced in writing.

After acknowledging that the purpose of the arrangement may not always be made explicit, Mishcon de Reya also identified problems with how it will be decided whether the "tax advantage was the main purpose, or one of the main purposes, of the arrangements"[8] in practice. Interestingly, the firm appropriately speculated that perhaps

> after an individual or company enjoys a significant tax saving, HMRC will seek to demonstrate that the obtaining of a tax advantage was the main purpose and that it is caught by the GAAR.[9]

This argument has merit. If this retrospective method is employed, it would be unfair and would illustrate that the test does little to differentiate between acceptable and abusive tax avoidance. Therefore, the main purpose test appears to serve as a tool for HMRC to argue that a taxpayer did have a tax avoidance purpose. Although courts do not have to accept retrospective arguments, this may nevertheless influence the outcome of the case. Furthermore, there is the additional concern that, if this is how the main purpose test will be used, it may be employed "several years after the arrangements were entered into and the taxpayer may by that point have no evidence to refute HMRC's allegations".[10] If this should happen, it would violate the rule of natural justice which encompasses that "a man's defence must always be fairly heard".[11]

The main purpose test has also been criticised for being unnecessarily wide by Sullivan & Cromwell as it encompasses "more than just egregious and contrived schemes".[12] Therefore, the firm acknowledges that the GAAR does little to rectify the question of what amounts to abusive tax planning. This argument accords with the discussion in chapter 3 regarding the width of the GAAR. Moreover, the requirement of gaining a tax advantage as one of the central reasons for embarking on the transaction is also unhelpful as

> any attempt . . . to define the dividing line between acceptable and unacceptable tax planning by reference to a fiscal purpose risks the GAAR applying to the very categories of transactions which the Government wishes to promote.[13]

Consequently, practitioners argue that the main purpose test is wide and does not serve as a meaningful filter. These arguments are in line with what has already been argued herein. Therefore, much rests on the double reasonableness test to clarify the dividing line between abusive and acceptable tax avoidance.

6.2 The double reasonableness test

The double reasonableness test is what the judiciary will use to determine whether an arrangement is abusive or not. Subsequent to the main purpose test, the double reasonableness test has been condemned for being unhelpful, because

> it will be very difficult to persuade the Advisory Panel or the tribunal on an appeal that an arrangement which is designed to defeat the will of Parliament is nevertheless a reasonable course of action.[14]

Therefore, the double reasonableness test unrealistically implies that an arrangement will still be seen as reasonable even though its main purpose or one of its main purposes was to gain a tax advantage. Consequently, the concern is that the main purpose test operates as more than a mere filter since satisfying the main purpose test leaves little hope of arrangements then being considered reasonable. Accordingly, "the reasonableness test does not add anything, unless it is reasonable to design arrangements to defeat the will of Parliament".[15]

The double reasonableness test could be better targeted, as suggested by Macfarlanes. The firm recommended that it is essential to include "an express requirement that the arrangement must comprise elements which are artificial or contrived".[16] If these key terms were included in this stage of the GAAR, it would "make the second filter a genuine safe harbour for responsible tax planning and confine the GAAR to artificial and abusive schemes".[17] The inclusion of an artificiality test would move the UK GAAR in line with the general anti-avoidance rules of South Africa, Canada and Australia. These countries specifically refer to artificiality in their anti-avoidance legislation. Therefore, critics have argued that instead "of an 'abuse' test we have been given a 'reasonableness' test".[18]

Concerns about the GAAR from when the foundations of the legislation were being laid in the draft GAAR were expressed by Mishcon de Reya. The firm was especially concerned about the nature of double reasonableness test, which it predicted would generate uncertainty.[19] Mishcon de Reya argued that even a "single reasonableness test"[20] "sets a range which is difficult to delineate in practice".[21] Therefore, the double reasonableness test fuels uncertainty in the tax system due to the ambiguous nature of the test. Furthermore, in regards to reasonableness, it has not been made clear as to "whose tolerance level matters for the purposes of judging what is tolerable or intolerable".[22] Lethaby also argued that the double reasonableness test would be construed subjectively as

> whilst "reasonable" is ostensibly a term which implies objective judgement, and indeed it is a term which lawyers are supposed to be able to construe given its frequent use in statute and contractual documents, "reasonableness" is in real life invariably in the eyes of the beholder.[23]

Similar concerns about subjectivity have been raised by McKie:

> [B]ecause no standard of reasonableness and no principles by which reasonable choices may be distinguished from unreasonable ones are provided, we are left to guess how the courts will make an unguided judgement of reasonableness which, in practice, must be highly subjective.[24]

Consequently, the reasonableness of an arrangement is for the judiciary to decide in a subjective manner.

The double reasonableness test has been criticised by Sullivan & Cromwell[25] for similar reasons, as mentioned earlier.[26] However, Sullivan & Cromwell recognise a palpable concern, which is that "applying the GAAR would involve what are necessarily subjective judgments as to whether a set of facts meets the double reasonableness test".[27] Although the firm does not delve deeply into the issue of subjectivity, it is valuable to recognise that it has acknowledged that there is scope and genuine concern about the likelihood of subjective decisions when the GAAR is applied in practice. Furthermore, although the GAAR has provided vague guidelines as to what amounts to abuse,[28] Grant Thornton believes that there are still "potential problems arising as a result of the subjective interpretation of the term 'abusive'".[29] Moreover, it has been argued that "the concept of abuse is inherently nebulous".[30]

The difficulty in remaining objective has also been raised as "it would be hard to sustain an objective distinction between what is 'reasonable tax planning' and what is not".[31] Grant Thornton also found various problems with the GAAR, and many, interestingly, related to the subjective nature of the legislation. For example, the double reasonableness test has been criticised due to the "subjective nature of what may be deemed reasonable".[32] Grant Thornton also rightly points out that "there is no attempt to define reasonableness and so the test is highly subjective".[33] Due to the lack of meaningful guidance as to how to measure reasonableness, unsurprisingly, "there will be a wide variety of views as to what is reasonable tax planning and what is unreasonable".[34] Until a common definition of "reasonableness" is constructed through case law, there is likely to be considerable uncertainty for taxpayers and advisors alike due to the invariable lack of uniformity.[35] Furthermore, the double reasonableness test has also been condemned for being subjective, due to the fact that

> as recent newspaper articles have shown, what is reasonable in the view of tax advisors, and indeed HMRC, will not be the same as what is reasonable in the view of the general public.[36]

The scope for subjectivity in the GAAR has also been linked to realisations that the legislation is wide.[37] Moreover, the Aaronson Report states that "what can in any particular case reasonably be regarded as a reasonable response will, of course, depend on the precise circumstances".[38] Therefore, the Aaronson Report elucidates that reasonableness will be decided on a case-by-case basis.

6.3 The scope of the GAAR

The breadth of the GAAR has attracted criticism. Some take the view that "what is in truth a general anti-avoidance rule is being missold as a general anti-abuse rule".[39] The GAAR is designed to be targeted. However, HMRC states that "because the GAAR will only apply to abusive avoidance arrangements this applies equally to any arrangements which might be caught by the GAAR".[40] As the GAAR can apply to those arrangements which might trigger the GAAR, it suggests that arrangements other than those which are abusive or are borderline cases can fall within the web of the GAAR. Nevertheless, Aaronson warned that the GAAR "is not to be wielded as a weapon to intimidate taxpayers in relation to arrangements to which it could not apply".[41]

The scope of the GAAR has also been criticised for not being "entirely clear".[42] The ACCA remarked on the ambiguous scope of the GAAR.[43] It criticised the guidance for "not being entirely clear whether 'less-than abusive' planning may be caught".[44] The more tangible threat is that the GAAR may "creep into other areas of what are currently perfectly legitimate tax planning initiatives".[45] Therefore, the GAAR and GAAR guidance do little to make clear the distinction between acceptable and abusive tax avoidance. Sullivan & Cromwell has also echoed these concerns by stating that "it is far from clear that the revised 'double reasonableness' test does accept that there is a sphere of legitimate tax minimisation".[46] Therefore, the vague nature of the double reasonableness test may lead to legitimate tax avoidance cases falling under the GAAR. Furthermore, Whitehouse remarks that the term "tax advantage"[47] is "given a familiarly wide meaning to encompass (broadly) all forms of tax mitigation".[48]

The significance attributed to the double reasonableness test has also attracted criticisms that "the actual GAAR is capable of being read as a wider general anti-avoidance rule because its crucial filter is based on reasonableness, not artificiality".[49] The bar determining abusive tax avoidance is therefore lowered as claiming that an arrangement is not reasonable sets a lower threshold than examining artificiality. Consequently, an arrangement may not be artificial but still deemed unreasonable. Although the GAAR attempted to be targeted with the inclusion of the term "abusive",

> neither the revised GAAR legislation nor the Guidance provide any comfort that the GAAR will not operate as a general anti-avoidance rule or that it will reduce the uncertainty surrounding the scope and application of any such rule.[50]

Some claim that HMRC welcomes the uncertainty inherent in the UK GAAR.[51] Due to the central role HMRC plays in the operation of the GAAR,

> HMRC find a GAAR tempting as a significant new weapon in maximising tax revenues because the uncertainty of its application would confer on them a de facto power of discretionary taxation.[52]

Although HMRC may relish the blurred boundaries of the GAAR, "that very uncertainty, however, is the reason why business and the professions have opposed it".[53]

The GAAR has also been criticised as the scope of the GAAR is wider than the Aaronson Report described.[54] For example, the Aaronson Report did not include inheritance tax within the GAAR's scope,[55] but nevertheless, inheritance tax is included in the GAAR.[56] However, Whitehouse rightly points out that the inclusion of inheritance tax is unnecessary due to "the plethora of anti-avoidance provisions that already apply in the IHT legislation".[57] Therefore, widening the final GAAR has been criticised as containing "an element of overkill".[58]

6.4 HMRC GAAR guidance

The guidance is important as the "HMRC guidance and explanation on the scope and meaning of the legislation pervades all areas of the tax code".[59] HMRC has been entrusted with the drafting of the GAAR guidance; therefore, "representations that the Guidance should be totally independent went unheeded".[60] However, the legal nature of the HMRC GAAR guidance has been criticised. The GAAR states that courts "must take into account . . . HMRC's guidance".[61] However, Grant Thornton questions whether this "mean[s] that the judge must review the opinion, but can fully disregard it if he believes the opinion is incorrect, as a matter of law".[62] In addition to this, Mishcon de Reya condemned the use of the supplementary HMRC GAAR guidance as, although a scheme may satisfy the GAAR guidance, it is not the GAAR itself nor is it binding.[63] Although some have described the guidance as having "quasi statutory status",[64] advisors can "never be completely sure that the guidance can be followed with confidence".[65] Therefore, there remains much uncertainty about the extent to which the guidance should be relied on in practice.

Sullivan & Cromwell has raised serious and substantiated reservations about the HMRC GAAR guidance in relation to the discretion it gives HMRC.[66] The firm characterises HMRC as being "the third player"[67] in tax avoidance cases as "HMRC will draft the guidance [therefore,] have more discretion to ignore it".[68] Similarly, Lethaby also believes that

> the inclusion of HMRC materials is potentially controversial because of the perceived risk of HMRC making self-serving pronouncements about what they consider falls or does not fall within the scope of certain statutory provisions.[69]

Sullivan & Cromwell provides an example of other HMRC guidance being interpreted in favour of HMRC in relation to tax residency,[70] providing an indication as to how the HMRC guidance may be applied to cases falling under the GAAR. The firm stated that the tax residency "decision underscores the risks in relying on HMRC guidance and – even more so – any supposed general HMRC practice".[71] The cases in question were heard prior to the implementation of the statutory residency test, although they do highlight the ability of HMRC to depart from the guidance and the difficulty in "hold[ing] HMRC to its word".[72] Consequently, the firm has warned that "it will be an uphill struggle for taxpayers to convince the courts that HMRC has bound itself to take any particular approach".[73] Therefore, as Sullivan & Cromwell pointed out, there are widespread reservations as to the extent to which taxpayers can rely on the HMRC GAAR guidance in practice. The reservations are justified given that HMRC was active in amending and updating the HMRC GAAR guidance in 2013 and 2015. Therefore, taxpayers must ensure that they keep up-to-date with the changes.

The general involvement by HMRC has raised concerns as

> if they reasonably consider the taxpayer's conduct to be an abuse of the system, [they can] change the law for him alone to deny the tax advantage provided for by the purposively construed legislation.[74]

Consequently, the unfairness does not derive from the denial itself but from the fact that "the basis for the denial of the intended advantage is the disapproval of the administrator".[75]

Due to the difficulty in understanding the meaning of key terms in the GAAR, such as "reasonable", the guidance may be viewed as a helpful supplement. Some have acknowledged that "the guidance is a valiant attempt to reduce that uncertainty but, because avoidance is treated by HMRC as inherently unreasonable, it ultimately fails in that objective".[76] However, others suggest that the guidance widens the GAAR and "confirms our worst fears that the GAAR will be a general anti-avoidance rule in all but name".[77]

The HMRC GAAR guidance superficially addresses the issue of what does not fall under the GAAR's remit.[78] The guidance broadly states that "any reasonable choice of a course of action is kept outside the target area of the GAAR".[79] However, the guidance provides examples of arrangements which would not be caught by the GAAR. The first example is simple and discusses that a taxpayer who owns their own company can choose to extract their profits by way of a salary or dividend accumulated over time.[80] This example is well known and reveals little about the remits of the GAAR. The second example explains that taxpayers will not be condemned for making use of individual savings accounts wherein taxpayers benefit from tax relief.[81] Again, this simple example does not clarify the limits of GAAR in terms of more complex arrangements. Lastly, the guidance adds that there would be no abuse of inheritance tax laws where parents gifts their child an asset without the parents having a benefit in that asset. The GAAR guidance inadvertently admits that these examples are unhelpful and do little to educate taxpayers as to the remits of the GAAR as they "clearly fall outside the target area of the GAAR".[82] These elementary examples have unsurprisingly been attacked due to the fact that

> none of the examples in Part B to which the GAAR is said not to apply would pass through the first filter, because they are innocuous transactions which do not involve avoidance, as properly defined.[83]

The examples given are arrangements which involve tax avoidance in the technical sense, although they do not even come close to the line between acceptable and abusive tax avoidance. Therefore, the guidance does not attempt to advise businesses and tax advisors who usually carry out more complex arrangements. However, in past tax avoidance cases, judges have warned that hypothetical scenarios may not always be helpful as

> the facts of examples are not always adequate for the purpose of giving informed answers. The examples selected are sometimes slanted to vindicate the advocate's viewpoint.[84]

The examples of acceptable tax avoidance outlined have been rebuked for being immaterial.[85] The examples do not serve a useful purpose as "they do not pass through the first filter [therefore,] their reasonableness is never tested".[86] Moreover,

> these examples tell us nothing about what forms of tax planning pass through the first filter but nevertheless fall outside the scope of the GAAR because they are reasonable.[87]

Therefore, the guidance would benefit from providing an example in which the main purpose test applies, but the double reasonableness test does not apply. This illustration would serve to clarify the distinction between abusive and acceptable tax avoidance. The Aaronson Report also recommended including

> an authoritative source of guidance as to the sort of cases to which the GAAR should apply. This could be achieved by having guidance notes included as a schedule to the Finance Act which enacts the GAAR itself, so that it gains the authority attaching to legislation.[88]

However, the types of schemes which the GAAR guidance refers to appear to be less helpful than the guidance envisaged by the Aaronson Report.

The GAAR guidance also states that making use of the reliefs in the tax legislation will not trigger the GAAR.[89] The guidance provides examples of such reliefs, including "business property relief, Enterprise Investment Scheme (EIS), capital allowances [and] Patent Box)".[90] However, the use of reliefs is a contentious issue as the guidance acknowledges that "experience has shown that incentives and reliefs can be abused".[91] Nevertheless, it can be argued that "such forms of behaviour are normally ones which taxpayers would not undertake if the relief were not given. If it were otherwise, the incentive would be unnecessary".[92]

The guidance outlines what arrangements would attract the GAAR and advises that

> where taxpayers set out to exploit some loophole in the tax laws, for example, by entering into contrived arrangements to obtain a relief but incurring no equivalent economic risk, they will fall into the target area of the GAAR.[93]

Therefore, engaging in real economic risk is essential to avoiding the application of GAAR. However, the example of acceptable tax avoidance given in the guidance can be criticised. This is because acquiring an individual savings account does not carry economic risk but, is a form of permissible tax avoidance. The key term in the guidance is therefore "contrived". In spite of the fact that the term "contrived" is significant, as it sets a higher level of unacceptability than the test of reasonableness, no examples are given of what would amount to a contrived arrangement. The broad example nevertheless "tells us about what forms of responsible tax planning are excluded from the GAAR".[94]

Part D of the GAAR guidance provides examples of when the GAAR might apply. However, these are limited in their usefulness as its contents "are not . . . to be taken as indicating HMRC's blanket acceptance of approval of all transactions . . . of a similar type".[95] Moreover, no "single factor or consideration [is] conclusive as to the application of the GAAR".[96] Interestingly, the GAAR guidance highlights the fact that the taxpayer's motives are irrelevant by stating "tax motivated transactions will not necessarily fall to be treated as part of an abusive arrangement".[97]

Earlier in this book, a recommendation was made for the GAAR to include the term "artificial" to bring the rule in line with the anti-avoidance legislation of South Africa, Canada and Australia. Part D of the GAAR guidance recognises the value of this inclusion as it indicates that abusive tax planning would include an element of artificiality.[98]

6.5 The lack of a clearance system

There has been cynicism as to why there is no prior clearance system in place. HMRC has confirmed that they "will not give either formal or informal clearances that the GAAR doesn't apply".[99] However, there will be "open discussions with taxpayers about commercial transactions".[100] The lack of a clearance procedure means that "no assurances about the tax treatment of a transaction will be given in any situation where, in HMRC's view, the arrangements constitute tax avoidance".[101]

Grant Thornton has also expressed deep concerns about the lack of a clearance procedure as it may increase uncertainty for taxpayers.[102] Warnings about the uncertainty which the lack of a clearance system will cause have also been echoed by Lethaby.[103] However, Freedman explained there were also fears "that a clearance system might degenerate into a de facto requirement to apply for clearance for every transaction and so increase costs".[104] Nevertheless, Freedman acknowledged that a clearance system would be useful.[105]

The lack of a clearance system has sparked concerns about creating confusion regarding the tax system as Sullivan & Cromwell expressed that "there is a real concern that an informal system of semi-transparent confirmations is developing, without taxpayers having any reassurance".[106] However, it is vital that the UK's tax system is seen to be transparent in order to promote certainty for taxpayers in their economic affairs.

Aaronson's report provided convincing reasons as to why a clearance system should not be implemented. Aaronson advised that "an effective clearance system would impose very substantial resource burdens on taxpayers and HMRC alike".[107] Understandably, a clearance system would be costly. Disconcertingly, Aaronson also cautioned against a clearance system as it "inevitably in practice give[s] discretionary power to HMRC who would effectively become the arbiter of the limits of responsible tax planning".[108] Therefore, the GAAR study group acknowledges that too much discretionary power by HMRC is "wrong as a matter of constitutional principle".[109] However, HMRC was assigned the role of drafting the GAAR guidance, which plays a central role in interpreting the GAAR. Furthermore, claims that a clearance system is not necessary as the GAAR is targeted are less convincing.[110] The scope of the GAAR is uncertain; therefore, assertions that the GAAR's scope is identifiable are unpersuasive.

The fact that the Aaronson Report states that existing clearance systems could also apply to the GAAR where available[111] suggests that the GAAR Study Group does not condemn the concept of a clearance system but sought to avoid it due to the costs involved. However, the report stated that the extension of the clearance system would be provided for in the GAAR itself,[112] although no such provision is included in the GAAR.

6.6 The UK's international competitiveness

One of the pertinent issues is the threat which the GAAR could pose to commercial investment in the UK.[113] The Aaronson Report also acknowledged "the fragility of the UK economy"[114] and that a GAAR with a wide scope could "carry a real risk of undermining the ability of business and individuals to carry out sensible and responsible tax planning".[115]

As previously mentioned, the lack of a clearance procedure fuels uncertainty,[116] and "international businesses and entrepreneurs could be less likely to base themselves in the UK"[117] because of this and in order to avoid having to deal with an ambiguous GAAR. Discouraging foreign investors could have a disastrous impact on the UK's economy. However, Aaronson argued that a GAAR would create "a more level playing field for business enterprises which conduct responsible tax planning".[118] These businesses "would no longer have their competitiveness undermined by others which seek to reduce their tax burden by contrived and artificial schemes".[119]

The ACCA has observed that the GAAR could harm the UK's international competitiveness.[120] With such vague and strict rules in place, the UK could be seen as "not business friendly",[121] which could have widespread detrimental effects on the economy. The GAAR could also act as a deterrent in more ways than primarily envisaged as the ACCA warns that

> the GAAR runs the risk . . . of deterring investment by businesses that look to reinvest any savings they have made from financial planning initiatives back into their businesses, in research and development or job creation.[122]

Therefore, the ACCA suggests that money saved through tax avoidance schemes is ultimately fed back into the UK's economy in a positive way. Furthermore, in an attempt to collect more taxes, the government may have to deal with the long-term, unintentional side effects of gradually losing future investment, which may lose the UK more taxes than it can recover under the GAAR. The ACCA also cautioned that "deterring abusive tax planning is one thing, deterrence of reinvestment by small and growing businesses is another".[123]

The ACCA respects the government's decision to tackle tax avoidance,[124] although it has interestingly pointed out that the creation of the GAAR was unnecessary.[125] The ACCA logically argues that "if government and Parliament want UK businesses to pay more tax than they currently pay, the tax system needs wholesale change on a global basis".[126] The ACCA believes that tax avoidance stems from "transfer pricing and profit shifting".[127] However, these issues will not be explored any further so as to focus the issues on the GAAR. Furthermore, the corporation tax rate in the UK is fairly low at 19%, which is lower than the global average tax rate of 23.64%.[128] Therefore, if the goal of the GAAR is to raise taxes, the government could simply raise corporation tax.

Some argue that a GAAR would not be damaging to the UK's international competitiveness. Freedman claims that, in reality,

> most taxpayers are very familiar with GAARs in other countries and with anti-abuse laws in domestic law as well as in treaties and many would probably be surprised to hear that the UK had no statutory rule.[129]

Although the concept of a GAAR may not be alien to foreign investors, the ambiguity of the UK's GAAR may prove to be discouraging. For example, Goldberg asserted that "there are many examples of GAARs in the world, but our proposed draft is the most objectionable I have seen".[130] Furthermore, due to the fact that taxpayers are not permitted to utilise the shortcomings in the law, “it is the uncertainty generated by ‘what Parliament would have done’ that in the past has caused business such fear of a general anti-avoidance rule”.[131] Although the UK’s focus is on abuse rather than avoidance, there is greater uncertainty with the GAAR as the line between abuse and acceptable tax avoidance is not made clear. In contrast, although wider, a general anti-avoidance rule is far clearer in terms of what it seeks to tackle.

As the concerns of the GAAR on the UK’s international competitiveness are predictions, KPMG sought to provide quantifiable evidence to suggest that the impact of the GAAR is minimal. KMPG gathered their evidence by surveying companies and comparing their views on the expected impact of the GAAR versus the actual impact that the GAAR has had on the workings of their company after the its implementation.[132] KPMG focused on large companies, with 62% of those surveyed having turnovers of more than £1 billion;[133] 102 companies were surveyed before the introduction of the GAAR in 2013, and 104 companies were surveyed after the implementation of the GAAR in 2014.[134] Assessing company responses during this period is helpful as it can show how attitudes may have changed during the pivotal phase in which the GAAR was merely a proposal and after it was introduced.

The companies were asked various questions. Firstly, the companies were asked whether they believed that the GAAR could potentially “catch legitimate tax mitigation”.[135] In 2013, significantly, 71% of the companies believed that the GAAR could apply to legitimate schemes; 23% of the companies thought that the targeted GAAR would remain within its mandated remit; and 6% of companies were unsure. These figures show that the majority of the companies surveyed largely expected the GAAR to operate more widely than it was designed to. KPMG then surveyed the companies in 2014 and asked them whether “as a result of the GAAR, [they] have . . . decided not to pursue what [they] . . . would believe to be legitimate tax mitigation”.[136] In response to this, 93% of companies claimed that the GAAR had not prevented them from engaging in tax mitigation. However, 4% of companies did believe that the GAAR impeded their tax mitigation activities, and 3% of companies were undecided. The 2014 statistics, surprisingly, show that the companies drastically changed their views about the GAAR. However, the question asked in 2014 was narrower than the question asked in 2013, which may have affected the results.

KPMG widened the second question posed to the companies by enquiring whether the companies believed that the GAAR would catch genuine commercial transactions.[137] In 2013, 56% of the companies surveyed believed that the GAAR could catch genuine commercial transactions;[138] 37% of companies believed that genuine commercial transactions would not be affected;[139] and 7% did not know whether genuine transactions could be caught by the GAAR.[140] In 2014, KPMG asked the companies whether the GAAR had dissuaded them from carrying out genuine transactions.[141] An overwhelming 97% of companies claimed that the GAAR did not dissuade them from engaging in genuine commercial transactions.[142] Only 3% of companies stated that they did not know whether the GAAR has deterred them, and none of the companies claimed that the GAAR discouraged them from embarking on genuine transactions.[143]

The statistics on the GAAR's corporate impact appear to suggest that there were grave concerns before the implementation of the GAAR but that the introduction of the GAAR seemed to put these concerns rapidly to rest. The survey results portray the idea of a GAAR as initially worrying, but the final GAAR was well drafted. However, the reliability of the results can be criticised on the basis that the "interviews were conducted with 104 senior tax decision makers".[144] Therefore, the interviews were carried out with one person from each company and do not reflect the views of the entire company. Furthermore, the job status of 11% of the people who took the survey was merely described as "other",[145] which makes it difficult to ascertain how or whether the GAAR affected their daily decision-making. The survey does not help significantly with understanding how overseas investors feel about the impact of the GAAR as only 24% of the companies surveyed were foreign-owned subsidiaries.[146] Therefore, the results of the survey should be treated with caution.

In addition to the encumbrance the GAAR can cause corporations, "the GAAR risks becoming an administrative burden on non-corporate taxpayers"[147] when completing their self-assessed tax return.[148] Sullivan & Cromwell also shares the same concern as the ACCA in regards to those who may not consider the GAAR when completing their self-assessed tax return and be liable to penalties.[149] The necessity to self-assess based on the GAAR "introduces considerable uncertainty in self-assessing accurately".[150] However, some candidly believe that "no taxpayer will self-assess the operation of the GAAR".[151]

Due to the serious concerns surrounding the GAAR, some are understandably of the opinion that it should not have been implemented at all.[152] However, it can also be argued, to a limited extent, that "the risk is that any GAAR, however carefully crafted, will undermine the UK's attractiveness".[153] Therefore, with some concerns, like the potential threat to the UK's competitiveness in the global market, the very existence of the GAAR can cause problems. Lethaby also warns that "the UK will need to tread carefully to avoid undermining over a decade's worth of inching towards a more competitive tax regime".[154]

6.7 Complexity

Ideally, an efficient tax system must "be easy for taxpayers to understand and for Government to administer".[155] The UK currently struggles with having the "longest tax code in the world".[156] This is due to the fact that new provisions have been continuously introduced by the annual Finance Acts for approximately 130 years,[157] which indicates that the UK does not have a clear and concise tax system. The length of the UK's tax legislation is problematic as "length makes it hard to grasp; the language and the structure make it difficult to understand".[158] Consequently, "complexity is the midwife of taxpayer error, leading to incorrect returns".[159] Complexity matters as it makes the tax system inefficient.[160] It is also expensive and burdensome for taxpayers to obtain professional advice on how to arrange their affairs effectively, even for mere compliance.[161] In order to establish whether the tax system has been made more complex by the GAAR, it is important to analyse what factors contribute to making a tax system complex. Thereafter, it is helpful to examine views as to whether the GAAR has contributed towards complexity.

The simplicity of a tax system is measured by considering two main factors: "the ease in which a taxpayer may comply"[162] with their tax obligations and "the authorities' ability to administer the Act and collect the tax due".[163] As previously mentioned, there are numerous reasons taxpayers may find it challenging to fulfil their tax obligations, including the extent to which one should rely on the GAAR guidance[164] and the problems taxpayers may encounter if they complete a self-assessed tax return.[165] Therefore, it can be said that the GAAR fails to meet the first criterion as the legislation has made it more burdensome for taxpayers to satisfy their tax obligations. Moreover, "even the basic tax return, let alone the various supplementary pages, is now a formidable document".[166] Secondly, it is not yet certain how the GAAR will be managed by HMRC or the courts, although there was widespread doubt as to how the guidance would operate alongside the GAAR in practice[167] and the extent to which the judiciary should pay heed to it.[168] Consequently, the GAAR has made the tax system more complex than it was.

The GAAR is a significant piece of legislation which has introduced substantial changes in the tax system. It has increased the burden of taxpayers to comply with the GAAR, courts to interpret the various provisions and HMRC to oversee the guidance. The Office of Tax Simplification has warned that "change in itself causes complexity".[169]

As discussed, the GAAR does seem to worsen the existing problem of complexity. However, it can be argued that making the tax system simpler was not one of the objects of creating the GAAR.[170] Mishcon de Reya has recognised this fact by stating that "it seems unfortunate that the GAAR is not intended to assist with simplifying the existing complex tax legislation and regime".[171] However, a complex tax system also heightens the inconvenience to taxpayers as the "GAAR . . . appears more likely to catch tax planning designed simply to avoid the many traps in the UK's very complex tax code".[172]

Even proponents of the GAAR claim that it does little to solve the problem of the UK's complex tax system as "a GAAR needs to be backed up by improved legislation and possibly further moves towards principles-based legislation".[173] Parliament's intention in relation to specific provisions may no longer be clear in light of the GAAR as

> when an Act attempts . . . to deal specifically with every class of transaction which the draftsman can foresee, it becomes difficult indeed to extract from the mass of detail any principle which the Courts can say with confidence Parliament intended to be applicable to any class of transaction which the draftsman did not foresee.[174]

Therefore, judges cannot unreservedly claim that Parliament intended specific cases to fall within the GAAR. Moreover, it can be argued that "the pursuit of the intention of Parliament is logically incoherent because it makes assumptions about the mental states of members of Parliament which do not bear any relation to reality".[175] Gammie also argues that

> it is frequently said of particular tax avoidance arrangements that they do not or ought not achieve the tax benefit claimed because they are plainly incompatible with the legislative intention of Parliament or the spirit of the law that Parliament has enacted. A simple response is that, if it was so plain, why did Parliament not say so?[176]

Furthermore, "if Parliament knows what it wants to tax, how is it that Parliament makes such a consistent mess of the matter by not plainly saying what it intends?"[177] Therefore, Gammie asserts that it is fundamental to tackle complexity as "the first-best must always be for governments to articulate clearly in legislation what they want to tax rather than make it up after the event".[178]

In order to tackle complexity, the problems in the tax system must be acknowledged as "the domestic and cultural features which contribute to a lack of clarity are, first, an unwillingness to be honest about the true effects of our tax system".[179] Complexity is a big problem in the UK tax system, and it is evident that the government did not seek to simplify the tax system when proposing the GAAR. Moreover, "length alone accordingly contributes considerably to a lack of clarity, transparency, accessibility and foreseeability in our system".[180] The GAAR inevitably adds to the existing lengthy tax system. Therefore, "we cannot blame business[es] for using the rules that policy-makers themselves have put in place".[181]

6.8 Uncertainty

The GAAR has also been criticised for increasing the uncertainty in the tax system.[182] The main problem stems from the fact that some of the main provisions are vague and subjective, which provides uncertainty as to how the legislation will be applied in practice. Although it is "unrealistic to expect that tax laws might not evolve under the common law process",[183] even common law rules depart from previous established rules, as demonstrated by the *Ramsay* approach departing from the *Westminster* approach. Therefore, it would be better to have clear legislation that promotes certainty than a line of case law which can be overruled at any time. Although established case law can help provide an indication of how legislation will operate in practice, "case law will take some years to develop".[184] Therefore, there is the risk of uncertainty for years to come. The length of time needed to develop a reliable line of case law is due to various factors, including the fact that the GAAR applies to an array of taxes. Therefore, a variety of taxes each need to have a clear line of case law established.

Others argue that the promise of the formation of a body of case law later on is insufficient to defend vague legislation in the present. Stroup elucidates that a duration of uncertainty is wholly unacceptable as "to know what is the law in a particular case only after it has been adjudicated by a court is to know law too late for it to serve as a guide for conduct in that situation".[185] Therefore, the ambiguous tests within the GAAR do little to direct taxpayers as to what is considered permissible tax avoidance. The extent to which taxpayers should rely on the GAAR guidance adds to the uncertainty of it all. Stroup indicates that equivocal legislation can also undermine the law more generally, due to the fact that

> it is questionable what social role, if any, law can play when citizens are forced to go about their business capable only of "guessing" whether the judiciary will find their actions to be within the law.[186]

Furthermore, due to the rejection of the proposed GAAR in 1998, taxpayers may now be more sceptical about having a GAAR of any kind. Worryingly, the GAAR proposed in 1998 was rejected for failing to generate a fair "balance of interests between tax gatherers and taxpayers".[187] Therefore, there may be inequality in applying the double reasonableness test, which involves balancing the competing interests. Significantly, the GAAR was also rejected on the grounds that the proposed test involved HMRC substantiating taxpayers' motives to avoid tax, which was problematic to prove.[188] The GAAR, therefore, appears to be making tax compliance more difficult and uncertain for taxpayers, which adds to the pre-existing problems of the complexity and length of the tax system.

Supporters of the GAAR believe that uncertainty helps reduce tax avoidance because "if bright lines are drawn they will be manipulated by those devising schemes".[189] Therefore, "the creation of *some* uncertainty will be regarded by GAAR supporters as a good thing – achieving the goal of deterrence in part relies on it".[190] Similarly, Pagone believes that "uncertainty plays a key part of commerce and social decision-making, and its adoption through taxation by discretionary powers is in part a means of combating tax avoidance".[191] However, "all taxation must have a proper legislative basis".[192] Moreover, the problems found with the double reasonableness test alone "will leave matters in an unacceptably uncertain state".[193] Consequently, some believe that the double reasonableness test is unreasonable as "it is certainly not 'reasonable' (singly or doubly) to leave taxpayers and their advisers in the middle of nowhere without a map and a compass".[194] Others argue that certainty is not the correct test, and the focus should be on fairness and practicality.[195] Nevertheless, it is difficult to defend the proposition that a complex GAAR is fair when it is borne in mind that tax avoidance is a legal activity. Moreover,

> a problem for taxpayers is that tax is a cost. It is a personal cost and a cost of doing business and predictability of that cost is often an important ingredient in personal and business decision-making. Tax uncertainty may be a net gain to the community but not for individual taxpayers.[196]

It is important that the GAAR is clear as "voluntary compliance, so critical to the tax law's integrity, depends upon its intelligibility".[197] It has been suggested that certainty could be promoted by making "fewer changes in tax so that the people could consider their economic choices and make long-term financial plans and decisions".[198] However, the ideal of making fewer changes in the tax system seems like an unattainable goal, given that changes to the Finance Acts are embedded into the system every year.

Although certainty is desirable, some theorised that a GAAR which provides certainty cannot be achieved as

> if one of our leading revenue law QCs, assisted by a distinguished committee, cannot, after a year's work, draft a GAAR which provides reasonable certainty of application, it cannot be done.[199]

Lethaby has found "it imperative that the architects of the GAAR make it clear where on the aggression spectrum previously decided cases would, in their view, fall".[200] This approach would provide an indication of how abuse would be measured in future cases as the cases are unlikely to be drastically different from those heard in the past.

As previously mentioned, the subjective nature of the GAAR can yield varying opinions, which can encourage uncertainty. Therefore, the GAAR has not "remove[d] the uncertainty which has debilitated our tax law since the *Ramsay* decision".[201] Certainty is imperative as "agreement is a necessary feature of the normativity of our practices".[202] There "must be harmony in application, over time"[203] in order to create certainty as "it is the basis of our legal judgements".[204]

6.9 Constitutional issues

The GAAR has also been criticised for potentially violating fundamental constitutional law principles, in particular, the Rule of Law. The lack of certainty in the GAAR is unfortunate as taxpayers should be fully aware of the demarcations of acceptable and unacceptable tax avoidance. Examining the rationale behind the Polish GAAR being struck down as unconstitutional may help decipher where the shortcomings in the UK GAAR lie.

This discussion will use Lord Bingham's conception of the Rule of Law because it accords most closely with the issues thrown up by the Polish constitutional court which will be discussed. Lord Bingham formulated a detailed analysis of eight tenets which encompass the Rule of Law. The first and most applicable tenet is that "the law must be accessible and so far as possible intelligible, clear and predictable".[205] This tenet is important as

> the individual citizen needs to know what the law is – both criminal and civil – in order to plan and undertake his or her actions within the legal framework. In terms of commercial transactions also, the economy depends on there being a clear system of rules to which all can comply and thereby be sure that their dealings are lawful.[206]

Lord Bingham's second tenet is also relevant to the discussion in chapter 5 regarding discretion. Lord Bingham stated that "questions of legal right and liability should ordinarily be resolved by application of the law and not the exercise of discretion".[207] In contrast to

> Dicey's opposition to unfettered discretion, Lord Bingham accepts that officials and judges need some leeway in decision-making and the application of rules, but insists that the discretion granted must be limited so that its exercise does not become arbitrary. Discretion must not be unconstrained.[208]

The third tenet advocated by Bingham is that "the laws of the land should apply equally to all, save to the extent that objective differences justify differentiation".[209] This rule exemplifies "equality before the law".[210] The fourth tenet relates to ministers and states that

> ministers and public officers at all levels must exercise the powers conferred on them in good faith, fairly and for the purpose for which the powers were conferred, without exceeding the limits of such powers.[211]

Moreover, "public officials must also respect the rules of fairness and natural justice and powers must be exercised reasonably and rationally".[212] Public officials can be held to account through judicial review if they exceed their powers. Therefore, HMRC can be held to account if they exceed their powers as conferred by Parliament under the GAAR.

The fifth tenet refers to human rights and states that "the law must afford adequate protection of fundamental human rights".[213] Lord Bingham's sixth tenet is that "means must be provided for resolving, without prohibitive cost or inordinate delay, bona fide civil disputes which the parties themselves are unable to resolve".[214] In addition to this, the seventh tenet is that "adjudicative procedures provided by the state should be fair".[215] This encompasses "the need for an independent and politically impartial judiciary",[216] which is particularly relevant as tax avoidance is a topical issue. Lastly,

> the rule of law requires compliance by the state with its obligations in international law, the law which whether deriving from treaty or international custom and practice governs the conduct of nations.[217]

It has been argued that the GAAR is "evidence that tax laws are so vague as to be considered in violation of the Rule of Law".[218] The lack of certainty has also led to the conclusion that "GAARs breach the Rule of Law by failing to identify the standard of tax law in advance".[219] However, an unpersuasive counter-argument is that the wide GAAR can actually serve to uphold the Rule of Law. It has been rationalised that

> only those persons with the sophistication to create a novel transaction (to implicate the GAAR) would therefore hold the *special rights*, and be effectively a *ruling*-class from a tax perspective. The wide-penumbra of a GAAR

> may therefore be necessary to *maintain* the Rule of Tax Law, and not to breach it.[220]

Other objections to the GAAR include the fact that it places undue burden on taxpayers. Greenberg tackles the GAAR from a constitutional standpoint and remarks that

> what is even more inconceivable, however, is that it is unlawful to "exploit" the legislature's failure to enact what it might have wished to enact [and this provision] was itself enacted by the legislature without any serious controversy of a constitutional nature.[221]

The legislation requires the courts to block Parliament's shortcomings from being utilised and examine the spirit of the law where the legislation has not expressly laid this out. However, the guesswork involved in this exercise is wholly inappropriate as it reduces certainty and conflicts with Smith's maxim of certainty in the tax system.[222] Moreover, using the judiciary to levy tax where the gaps in the legislation permit avoidance goes beyond the purposive approach.

There are also palpable concerns over the combination of vague tests within the GAAR, coupled with compulsory guidance formulated by HMRC.[223] The guidance has been criticised on the basis that

> by demanding judicial deference to HMRC's guidance, the GAAR offends against established principles, and essentially allows public bodies to put a particular gloss or spin on legislation after its enactment.[224]

Although the GAAR does not make clear the extent to which the courts should use the guidance, Greenberg speculates that "the duty would be nugatory if it did not imply at least some degree of deference". The resulting problem is that "taxpayers' tax liability will in part be decided by HMRC and the other members of the advisory panel rather than parliament".[225] Greenberg also asserts that the GAAR allows for the erosion of the separation of powers doctrine by overlapping the roles of the executive and judiciary.[226] The problem stems from the idea that "the purpose of the GAAR is to give the Executive continual control over the meaning of legislation".[227] However, the executive interpretation of legislation overlaps with the judiciary's role to interpret legislation in the courts.[228] Furthermore, this is inconsistent with the fact that Parliament has explicitly recognised the need for judicial independence.[229] Moreover,

> the task of determining what the legislation means will be performed, on a continual basis, by a combination of the Executive and an unelected body of professionals appointed by the Executive.[230]

Therefore, there will be ongoing oversight by the executive, which undermines the separation of powers doctrine. It is Parliament's role to legislate, although the GAAR has been constructed in a fragmented way due to the inclusion of the guidance, which means that "the scope of the GAAR could, therefore, easily be expanded by HMRC without scrutiny by parliament".[231]

Consequently, it can be said that there are potential infringements of constitutional law principles in the workings of the GAAR. An effective example of how tax legislation may breach constitutional law doctrines can be demonstrated by the former Polish GAAR. In 2004, Poland's constitutional court declared that the Polish GAAR was unconstitutional.[232] The court stated that the legislation breached Article 2 of the constitution, which explicitly upholds the Rule of Law.[233] It was made clear that the Rule of Law encompasses "the principles of legal certainty, legal security and protection of trust in the State and its laws".[234]

The ambiguous nature of the legislation was also criticised for being unconstitutional as

> the constitutional requirements of correct legislation are infringed, in particular, when the wording of a legal provision is so vague and imprecise that it creates uncertainty amongst its addressees as regards their rights and duties, by creating an exceedingly broad framework within which authorities charged with applying the provision are required, *de facto*, to assume the role of law-maker in respect of these vaguely and imprecisely regulated issues.[235]

Judges had a difficult task in applying the GAAR due to the various tests and the breadth of the legislation, which the Polish constitutional court found unacceptable. Furthermore, as established, the GAAR can cause uncertainty, which the Polish courts found to be unacceptably problematic. The court also acknowledged that "where legal provisions exceed a certain degree of ambiguity this may in itself constitute grounds for declaring such provisions to be unconstitutional"[236] as it conflicts with the Rule of Law.[237] Furthermore, there was doubt as to whether the interpretation of vague phrases in the legislation could be "uniform and rigorous"[238] when used in practice. Therefore, concerns about resulting uncertainty and lack of uniformity were also at the heart of the debate.

There was also a problem with the fact that the Minister of Finance had the power to "issue interpretations of tax law"[239] which were binding.[240] The court acknowledged that

> in the event of conflict between the administrative court's legal assessment of a concrete case and the Minister's abstract interpretation, the court's legal assessment would have absolute priority.[241]

However, the argument was that the Minister's interpretations would nonetheless remain binding,[242] which would exacerbate the problem of blurring the distinctions "between law-making and law-interpretation".[243] The binding interpretations allowed the Minister to "exert an influence in the sphere of taxpayers' rights and freedoms, a sphere whose regulation is permissible solely by legal instruments".[244] Therefore, it was apparent that the Minister was charged with a power which he should not have been granted. The Minister's problematic involvement in adjudication also reinforces the fact that the judiciary and executive should remain separate, particularly where taxation is at issue.

The Polish example highlights the requirements for legislation to adhere to the Rule of Law. However, the UK's legal system does not adhere to the practice of constitutional review; therefore, the UK GAAR cannot be struck down for being unconstitutional as the doctrine of Parliamentary Sovereignty has remained intact.

6.10 Conclusion

Since the GAAR is relatively new, some argue that "it is, of course, easy to criticise a GAAR and especially one that has no track record".[245] However, the criticisms of the GAAR discussed in this chapter are substantial and highlight the inadequacies of the GAAR and GAAR guidance. The main purpose test in the GAAR would encompass many tax avoidance cases. The judiciary are also able to infer that a taxpayer did have a tax avoidance purpose, and they may do so in practice. The fact that the GAAR has been condemned for being laced with subjectivity is also central as the main purpose test, for example, can be interpreted so as to require an examination of the taxpayer's subjective motives. Ascribing a motive to the taxpayer is simpler than examining whether the taxpayer has escaped the GAAR according to the statutory provisions, which is why judges may opt for the motive approach.

Understandably, the main purpose test has been criticised for being so wide that its usefulness has diminished. The main purpose test is also difficult to reconcile with the double reasonableness test as only very innocuous arrangements can have tax avoidance as a main purpose but nevertheless be reasonable. Therefore, the requirement of abuse does little to target the scope of the GAAR. Consequently, the scope of the GAAR is unclear as to whether unabusive cases can be caught within the GAAR's remit. Moreover, as demonstrated, the GAAR's scope is wider than the original Aaronson Report, which did not include inheritance tax as one of the GAAR's targeted taxes. The general scope of the GAAR is unclear as it seeks to examine the reasonableness of arrangements rather than a truly targeted consideration such as artificiality, which is a better factor to examine.

The extent to which taxpayers can rely on the HMRC GAAR guidance and whether it is, in fact, binding on courts is uncertain. As mentioned previously, the guidance introduces rules including that the arrangement must be "contrived"[246] to attract the GAAR, and it is uncertain as to whether this requirement works alongside the abuse requirement in the GAAR or as a supplementary factor where cases are ambiguous. However, the addition of the term "contrived" does help narrow the scope of the GAAR and guide the judiciary to apply the GAAR to a specific group of cases. Furthermore, the guidance is generally unhelpful and does not accurately highlight what arrangements would not be regarded as abusive, as well as the particular circumstances in which the main purpose test would apply but the double reasonableness test would not. The lack of a clearance system is an understandable criticism due to the assurance and certainty a clearance system would provide to taxpayers. However, the costs involved in providing a clearance system do adequately justify why it was not set up.

Although the results from the KMPG survey do show that the UK has not lost its competitive edge, the survey is not entirely reliable due to the small sample size in each company. Moreover, although countries are familiar with general anti-avoidance rules, a targeted GAAR is different from the more familiar general anti-avoidance rules, as discussed in chapter 4. Many criticisms of the GAAR which have been cited derive from views of law firms which have offices in other countries. Therefore, it is unrealistic to presume that firms are content with the drafting of the GAAR and view the UK as still internationally competitive.

Complexity in the UK tax system remains an issue for both the government and taxpayers alike. However, it is evident that simplifying the tax system is lower than tax avoidance on the political agenda. The GAAR simply adds to the already lengthy tax system, due to the addition of rules rather than a set of clear principles. Although supporters of the GAAR claim that a degree of uncertainty is a positive deterrence, a helpful line of case law will take many years to develop. Therefore, the GAAR does promote uncertainty because before case law is established, taxpayers will largely be guinea pigs, subjected to an experiment to test how the GAAR will affect those with similar arrangements. The law must be clear beforehand, and the current GAAR merely shows that the concerns from the GAAR proposed in 1998 have not been heeded. It is a truism that "in all areas of law, but especially in the sphere of tax, the law must be certain and foreseeable".[247]

Examining constitutional law issues demonstrates that the GAAR can be seen to be undermining fundamental doctrines, such as the separation of powers where judicial independence is imperative. Judges are charged with the power of filling in the gaps of the legislation. The ambiguous nature of some of the provisions in the GAAR also serve to belittle the Rule of Law. This was found to be unacceptable with the former Polish GAAR. Prior to the introduction of the GAAR, Goldberg lamented that "as a matter of politics, not as a matter of necessity or economic good sense or sensible taxation, we are now to have a GAAR".[248] The various criticisms of and concerns about the GAAR inevitably raise the question of whether the UK GAAR was needed.

Notes

1 ACCA. *'The UK General Anti-Abuse Rule'*, <www.accaglobal.com/content/dam/acca/global/PDF-technical/tax-publications/tech-tp-ukgaar.pdf>, accessed 02.06.2016, p4.
2 Grant Thornton LLP. *'A General Anti-Abuse Rule: Comments on the Consultation Document Released on 12 June 2012'*, <www.grant-thornton.co.uk/Global/GAAR%20consultation%20response.pdf>, accessed 06.06.2016, p3.
3 *Ibid.*
4 Macfarlanes. *'The GAAR: An Anti-Avoidance Rule in All but Name'*, [2012], <www.macfarlanes.com/media/382363/the-gaar-an-anti-avoidance-rule-in-all-but-name.pdf>, p2.
5 s207(1) Finance Act 2013.
6 Mishcon de Reya LLP. *'A General Anti-Abuse Rule: Mishcon de Reya Response to Consultation Document – September 2012'*, <www.mishcon.com/assets/managed/

docs/downloads/doc_2611/Mishcon_de_Reya_GAAR_consultation_response.pdf>, accessed 01.06.2016, p2.

7 Krikorian, Y.H. *'The Meaning of Purpose'*, [1930], Vol. 27, No. 4, The Journal of Philosophy, p97.

8 s207(1) Finance Act 2013.

9 Mishcon de Reya LLP. *'A General Anti-Abuse Rule: Mishcon de Reya Response to Consultation Document – September 2012'*, <www.mishcon.com/assets/managed/docs/downloads/doc_2611/Mishcon_de_Reya_GAAR_consultation_response.pdf>, accessed 01.06.2016, p2.

10 *Ibid.*

11 Wade, H.W.R. and Forsyth, C.F. *'Administrative Law'*, [2009], 10th edn, Oxford University Press, Oxford, p372.

12 Sullivan & Cromwell. *'UK Tax: General Anti-Abuse Rule'*, (Sullivan & Cromwell LLP, 16.07.2012), <www.sullcrom.com/siteFiles/Publications/SC_Publication_UK_Tax_General_Anti-Abuse_Rule_2.pdf>, accessed 05.06.2016, p8.

13 McKie, S. *'The Philosopher's Stone or the Emperor's New Clothes – an Old Conundrum'*, [2012], Private Client Business, p124.

14 Macfarlanes. *'The GAAR: An Anti-Avoidance Rule in All but Name'*, [2012], <www.macfarlanes.com/media/382363/the-gaar-an-anti-avoidance-rule-in-all-but-name.pdf>, p3.

15 *Ibid.*

16 *Ibid.*

17 *Ibid.*

18 Whitehouse, C. *'A Cause for Concern II: Sleepwalking into a GAAR'*, [2012], Private Client Business, pp211, 212.

19 Mishcon de Reya LLP. *'A General Anti-Abuse Rule: Mishcon de Reya Response to Consultation Document – September 2012'*, <www.mishcon.com/assets/managed/docs/downloads/doc_2611/Mishcon_de_Reya_GAAR_consultation_response.pdf>, accessed 01.06.2016, p2.

20 *Ibid.*

21 *Ibid.*

22 Lethaby, H. *'Aaronson's GAAR'*, [2012], British Tax Review, pp27, 34.

23 *Ibid*, p38.

24 McKie, S. *'The Philosopher's Stone or the Emperor's New Clothes – an Old Conundrum'*, [2012], Private Client Business, pp124, 132.

25 Sullivan & Cromwell. *'UK Tax: General Anti-Abuse Rule'*, (Sullivan & Cromwell LLP, 16.07.2012), <www.sullcrom.com/siteFiles/Publications/SC_Publication_UK_Tax_General_Anti-Abuse_Rule_2.pdf>, accessed 05.06.2016, p6.

26 Mishcon de Reya LLP. *'A General Anti-Abuse Rule: Mishcon de Reya Response to Consultation Document – September 2012'*, <www.mishcon.com/assets/managed/docs/downloads/doc_2611/Mishcon_de_Reya_GAAR_consultation_response.pdf>, accessed 01.06.2016, p2.

27 Sullivan & Cromwell. *'UK Tax: General Anti-Abuse Rule'*, (Sullivan & Cromwell LLP, 16.07.2012), <www.sullcrom.com/siteFiles/Publications/SC_Publication_UK_Tax_General_Anti-Abuse_Rule_2.pdf>, accessed 05.06.2016, p6.

28 s207(2)(c) Finance Act 2013.

29 Grant Thornton. *'A General Anti-Abuse Rule: Comments on the Consultation Document Released on 12 June 2012'*, <www.grant-thornton.co.uk/Global/GAAR%20consultation%20response.pdf>, accessed 06.06.2016, p5.

30 Gething, H. and Silverman, A. *'What Canada's GAAR Experience Can Tell Us about New UK Rules'*, [2013], Vol. 24, International Tax Review, pp56, 57.

31 Sullivan & Cromwell. *'UK Tax: General Anti-Abuse Rule'*, (Sullivan & Cromwell LLP, 16.07.2012), <www.sullcrom.com/siteFiles/Publications/SC_Publication_UK_Tax_General_Anti-Abuse_Rule_2.pdf>, accessed 05.06.2016, p10.

32 Grant Thornton. *'A General Anti-Abuse Rule: Comments on the Consultation Document Released on 12 June 2012'*, <www.grant-thornton.co.uk/Global/GAAR%20consultation%20response.pdf>, accessed 06.06.2016, p3.
33 *Ibid*, p4.
34 *Ibid.*
35 *Ibid.*
36 *Ibid.*
37 *Ibid.*
38 Aaronson, G. *'A Study to Consider whether a General Anti-Avoidance Rule Should Be Introduced into the UK Tax System'*, [2011], <http://webarchive.nationalarchives.gov.uk/+/http:/www.hm-treasury.gov.uk/d/gaar_final_report_111111.pdf>, accessed 25.08.2014, p63.
39 Macfarlanes. *'The GAAR: An Anti-Avoidance Rule in All but Name'*, [2012], <www.macfarlanes.com/media/382363/the-gaar-an-anti-avoidance-rule-in-all-but-name.pdf>, p5.
40 HMRC. *'Dealing with HMRC Guidance: Seeking Clearance or Approval for a Transaction'*, (HMRC, 17.11.2015), <www.gov.uk/guidance/seeking-clearance-or-approval-for-a-transaction>, accessed 05.06.2016.
41 Aaronson, G. *'A Study to Consider whether a General Anti-Avoidance Rule Should Be Introduced into the UK Tax System'*, [2011], <http://webarchive.nationalarchives.gov.uk/+/http:/www.hm-treasury.gov.uk/d/gaar_final_report_111111.pdf>, accessed 25.08.2014, p29.
42 ACCA. *'The UK General Anti-Abuse Rule'*, <www.accaglobal.com/content/dam/acca/global/PDF-technical/tax-publications/tech-tp-ukgaar.pdf>, accessed 02.06.2016, p4.
43 *Ibid.*
44 *Ibid.*
45 *Ibid.*
46 Sullivan & Cromwell. *'UK Tax: General Anti-Abuse Rule'*, (Sullivan & Cromwell LLP, 16.07.2012), <www.sullcrom.com/siteFiles/Publications/SC_Publication_UK_Tax_General_Anti-Abuse_Rule_2.pdf>, accessed 05.06.2016, p10.
47 s208 Finance Act 2013.
48 Whitehouse, C. *'A Cause for Concern II: Sleepwalking into a GAAR'*, [2012], Private Client Business, p211.
49 Macfarlanes. *'The GAAR: An Anti-Avoidance Rule in All but Name'*, [2012], <www.macfarlanes.com/media/382363/the-gaar-an-anti-avoidance-rule-in-all-but-name.pdf>, p2.
50 *Ibid*, p5.
51 McKie, S. *'The Philosopher's Stone or the Emperor's New Clothes – an Old Conundrum'*, [2012], Private Client Business, p124.
52 *Ibid.*
53 *Ibid.*
54 Whitehouse, C. *'A Cause for Concern II: Sleepwalking into a GAAR'*, [2012], Private Client Business, pp211, 212.
55 Aaronson, G. *'A Study to Consider whether a General Anti-Avoidance Rule Should Be Introduced into the UK Tax System'*, [2012], <http://webarchive.nationalarchives.gov.uk/+/http:/www.hm-treasury.gov.uk/d/gaar_final_report_111111.pdf>, accessed 04.06.2016, p44.
56 s206(3)(e) Finance Act 2013.
57 Whitehouse, C. *'A Cause for Concern II: Sleepwalking into a GAAR'*, [2012], Private Client Business, pp211, 212.
58 *Ibid.*
59 Gammie, M. *'When Is Avoiding Tax Not Abusive? Comparative Approaches to a GAAR in Australia and the United Kingdom'*, [2013], Vol. 42, Australian Tax Review pp279, 289.

60 Macfarlanes. *'The GAAR: An Anti-Avoidance Rule in All but Name'*, [2012], <www.macfarlanes.com/media/382363/the-gaar-an-anti-avoidance-rule-in-all-but-name.pdf>, p4.
61 s211(2)(a) Finance Act 2013.
62 Grant Thornton. *'A General Anti-Abuse Rule: Comments on the Consultation Document Released on 12 June 2012'*, <www.grant-thornton.co.uk/Global/GAAR%20consultation%20response.pdf>, accessed 06.06.2016, p5.
63 Mishcon de Reya LLP. *'A General Anti-Abuse Rule: Mishcon de Reya Response to Consultation Document – September 2012'*, <www.mishcon.com/assets/managed/docs/downloads/doc_2611/Mishcon_de_Reya_GAAR_consultation_response.pdf>, accessed 01.06.2016, p3.
64 Grant Thornton. *'Briefing on a General Anti-Abuse Rule – What Does It Mean for You?'*, <www.grant-thornton.co.uk/PageFiles/30789/General-Anti-Abuse-rule-v4.pdf>, accessed 03.06.2016, p1.
65 Mishcon de Reya LLP. *'A General Anti-Abuse Rule: Mishcon de Reya Response to Consultation Document – September 2012'*, <www.mishcon.com/assets/managed/docs/downloads/doc_2611/Mishcon_de_Reya_GAAR_consultation_response.pdf>, accessed 01.06.2016, p3.
66 Sullivan & Cromwell. *'UK Tax: General Anti-Abuse Rule'*, (Sullivan & Cromwell LLP, 16.07.2012), <www.sullcrom.com/siteFiles/Publications/SC_Publication_UK_Tax_General_Anti-Abuse_Rule_2.pdf>, accessed 05.06.2016, p10.
67 *Ibid.*
68 *Ibid.*
69 Lethaby, H. *'Aaronson's GAAR'*, [2012], British Tax Review, pp27, 39.
70 Sullivan & Cromwell. *'UK Tax Residence: Supreme Court Decision in Davies and Gaines-Cooper'*, (Sullivan & Cromwell 31.10.2011), <www.sullcrom.com/UK-Tax-Residence-10-31-2011/>, accessed 06.06.2016.
71 *Ibid.*
72 *Ibid.*
73 *Ibid.*
74 Goldberg, D. *'How Clear, Transparent, Accessible and Foreseeable Is Tax Law and Practice?'*, [2013], Private Client Business, pp238, 241.
75 *Ibid.*
76 Macfarlanes. *'The GAAR: An Anti-Avoidance Rule in All but Name'*, [2012], <www.macfarlanes.com/media/382363/the-gaar-an-anti-avoidance-rule-in-all-but-name.pdf>, p2.
77 *Ibid*, p4.
78 *'HMRC GAAR Guidance with Effect from 11 September 2020: Parts A, B and C'*, <https://assets.publishing.service.gov.uk/government/uploads/system/uploads/attachment_data/file/916667/gaar_parts_a_b_c_2020.pdf>, accessed 29.04.2021, p6.
79 *Ibid.*
80 *Ibid.*
81 *Ibid.*
82 *Ibid*, p7.
83 Macfarlanes. *'The GAAR: An Anti-Avoidance Rule in All but Name'*, [2012], <www.macfarlanes.com/media/382363/the-gaar-an-anti-avoidance-rule-in-all-but-name.pdf>, p4.
84 *The Commissioners for HMRC v Mayes* [2011] EWCA Civ 407, [40] (Mummery L.J.).
85 Macfarlanes. *'The GAAR: An Anti-Avoidance Rule in All but Name'*, [2012], <www.macfarlanes.com/media/382363/the-gaar-an-anti-avoidance-rule-in-all-but-name.pdf>, p4.
86 *Ibid.*

87 *Ibid.*
88 Aaronson, G. *'A Study to Consider whether a General Anti-Avoidance Rule Should Be Introduced into the UK Tax System'*, [2011], <http://webarchive.nationalarchives.gov.uk/+/http:/www.hm-treasury.gov.uk/d/gaar_final_report_111111.pdf>, accessed 25.08.2014, p29.
89 *'HMRC GAAR Guidance with Effect from 11 September 2020: Parts A, B and C'*, <https://assets.publishing.service.gov.uk/government/uploads/system/uploads/attachment_data/file/916667/gaar_parts_a_b_c_2020.pdf>, accessed 29.04.2021, p7.
90 *Ibid.*
91 *Ibid.*
92 McKie, S. *'The Philosopher's Stone or the Emperor's New Clothes – an Old Conundrum'*, [2012], Private Client Business, p124.
93 *'HMRC GAAR Guidance with Effect from 11 September 2020: Parts A, B and C'*, <https://assets.publishing.service.gov.uk/government/uploads/system/uploads/attachment_data/file/916667/gaar_parts_a_b_c_2020.pdf>, accessed 29.04.2021, p6.
94 Macfarlanes. *'The GAAR: An Anti-Avoidance Rule in All but Name'*, [2012], <www.macfarlanes.com/media/382363/the-gaar-an-anti-avoidance-rule-in-all-but-name.pdf>, p4.
95 *'HMRC GAAR Guidance with Effect from 11 September 2020: Part D – Examples'*, <https://assets.publishing.service.gov.uk/government/uploads/system/uploads/attachment_data/file/916666/gaar-part-d-2020.pdf>, accessed 09.05.2021, p D1.7.
96 *Ibid*, p D4.2.
97 *Ibid*, p D1.3.
98 *Ibid*, p D2.5.
99 HMRC. *'Dealing with HMRC Guidance: Seeking Clearance or Approval for a Transaction'*, (HMRC, 17.11.2015), <www.gov.uk/guidance/seeking-clearance-or-approval-for-a-transaction>, accessed 05.06.2016.
100 *Ibid.*
101 *Ibid.*
102 Grant Thornton LLP. *'A General Anti-Abuse Rule: Comments on the Consultation Document Released on 12 June 2012'*, <www.grant-thornton.co.uk/Global/GAAR%20consultation%20response.pdf>, accessed 06.06.2016, p1.
103 Lethaby, H. *'Aaronson's GAAR'*, [2012], British Tax Review, pp27, 38.
104 Freedman, J. *'Analysis- GAAR: Challenging Assumptions'*, [2010], No. 1046, Tax Journal, pp12, 14.
105 *Ibid.*
106 Sullivan & Cromwell. *'UK Tax: General Anti-Abuse Rule'*, (Sullivan & Cromwell LLP, 16.07.2012), <www.sullcrom.com/siteFiles/Publications/SC_Publication_UK_Tax_General_Anti-Abuse_Rule_2.pdf>, accessed 05.06.2016, p4.
107 Aaronson, G. *'A Study to Consider whether a General Anti-Avoidance Rule Should Be Introduced into the UK Tax System'*, [2012], <http://webarchive.nationalarchives.gov.uk/+/http:/www.hm-treasury.gov.uk/d/gaar_final_report_111111.pdf>, accessed 04.06.2016, p4.
108 *Ibid.*
109 *Ibid*, p34.
110 *Ibid*, p6.
111 *Ibid*, p34.
112 *Ibid.*
113 Grant Thornton LLP. *'A General Anti-Abuse Rule: Comments on the Consultation Document Released on 12 June 2012'*, <www.grant-thornton.co.uk/Global/GAAR%20consultation%20response.pdf>, accessed 06.06.2016, p1.
114 Aaronson, G. *'A Study to Consider whether a General Anti-Avoidance Rule Should Be Introduced into the UK Tax System'*, [2011], <http://webarchive.nationalarchives.

gov.uk/+/http:/www.hm-treasury.gov.uk/d/gaar_final_report_111111.pdf>, accessed 25.08.2014, p3.

115 *Ibid.*

116 Grant Thornton LLP. *'A General Anti-Abuse Rule: Comments on the Consultation Document Released on 12 June 2012'*, <www.grant-thornton.co.uk/Global/GAAR%20consultation%20response.pdf>, accessed 06.06.2016, p1.

117 *Ibid.*

118 Aaronson, G. *'A Study to Consider whether a General Anti-Avoidance Rule Should Be Introduced into the UK Tax System'*, [2011], <http://webarchive.nationalarchives.gov.uk/+/http:/www.hm-treasury.gov.uk/d/gaar_final_report_111111.pdf>, accessed 25.08.2014, p4.

119 *Ibid.*

120 ACCA. *'The UK General Anti-Abuse Rule'*, <www.accaglobal.com/content/dam/acca/global/PDF-technical/tax-publications/tech-tp-ukgaar.pdf>, accessed 02.06.2016, p3.

121 *Ibid.*

122 *Ibid.*

123 *Ibid.*

124 ACCA. *'The UK General Anti-Abuse Rule'*, <www.accaglobal.com/content/dam/acca/global/PDF-technical/tax-publications/tech-tp-ukgaar.pdf>, accessed 02.06.2016, p3.

125 *Ibid.*

126 *Ibid*, p3.

127 *Ibid.*

128 KMPG. *'Corporate Tax Rates Table'*, <https://home.kpmg/xx/en/home/services/tax/tax-tools-and-resources/tax-rates-online/corporate-tax-rates-table.html>, accessed 04.11.2021.

129 Freedman, J. *'Analysis – GAAR: Challenging Assumptions'*, [2010], No. 1046, Tax Journal, pp12, 13.

130 Goldberg, D. *'How Clear, Transparent, Accessible and Foreseeable Is Tax Law and Practice?'*, [2013], Private Client Business, pp238, 241.

131 Macfarlanes. *'The GAAR: An Anti-Avoidance Rule in All but Name'*, [2012], <www.macfarlanes.com/media/382363/the-gaar-an-anti-avoidance-rule-in-all-but-name.pdf>, p2.

132 KPMG, *'KPMG Annual Survey of Tax Competitiveness 2014'*, (12.2014), <www.kpmg.com/UK/en/IssuesAndInsights/ArticlesPublications/Documents/PDF/Tax/annual-tax-competitiveness-survey-2014.pdf>, accessed 01.10.2016, p5.

133 *Ibid*, p18.

134 *Ibid*, p5.

135 *Ibid.*

136 *Ibid.*

137 *Ibid.*

138 *Ibid.*

139 *Ibid.*

140 *Ibid.*

141 *Ibid.*

142 *Ibid.*

143 *Ibid.*

144 *Ibid*, p18.

145 *Ibid.*

146 *Ibid.*

147 ACCA. *'The UK General Anti-Abuse Rule'*, <www.accaglobal.com/content/dam/acca/global/PDF-technical/tax-publications/tech-tp-ukgaar.pdf>, accessed 02.06.2016, p3.

148 *Ibid.*
149 Sullivan & Cromwell. *'UK Tax: General Anti-Abuse Rule'*, (Sullivan & Cromwell LLP, 16.07.2012), <www.sullcrom.com/siteFiles/Publications/SC_Publication_UK_Tax_General_Anti-Abuse_Rule_2.pdf>, accessed 05.06.2016, p4.
150 *Ibid.*
151 Macfarlanes. *'The GAAR: An Anti-Avoidance Rule in All but Name'*, [2012], <www.macfarlanes.com/media/382363/the-gaar-an-anti-avoidance-rule-in-all-but-name.pdf>, p3.
152 ACCA. *'The UK General Anti-Abuse Rule'*, <www.accaglobal.com/content/dam/acca/global/PDF-technical/tax-publications/tech-tp-ukgaar.pdf>, accessed 02.06.2016, p4.
153 Clifford Chance. *'What Will the Proposed New General Anti-Avoidance Rule Mean for British Business?'*, (21.11.2011), <www.cliffordchance.com/content/dam/cliffordchance/PDF_2/Client_Briefing1_21_November_2011.pdf>, accessed 06.06.2016, p1.
154 Lethaby, H. *'Analysis – Reflections on Tax and the City'*, [2014], No. 1220, Tax Journal, pp10, 11.
155 Sampath, K.R. *'Tax Avoidance under Direct Tax Laws'*, [2007], Company Law Institute Press, Chennai, p5.
156 David Gauke MP. *'The Office of Tax Simplification'*, <www.davidgauke.com/content/office-tax-simplification>, accessed 06.06.2016.
157 Morse, G. and Williams, D. *'Davies: Principles of Tax Law'*, [2008], 6th edn, Sweet & Maxwell, London, p35.
158 Goldberg, D. *'How Clear, Transparent, Accessible and Foreseeable Is Tax Law and Practice?'*, [2013], Private Client Business, pp238, 239.
159 Williams, D.E. *'Self-Assessment: A Practitioner's View'*, [1999], British Tax Review, pp229, 231.
160 Broke, A. *'Simplification of Tax or I Wouldn't Start from Here'*, [2000], British Tax Review, pp18, 20.
161 *Ibid.*
162 Cassidy, J. *'Concise Income Tax'*, [2004], 3rd edn, The Federation Press, Sydney, p6.
163 *Ibid.*
164 Sullivan & Cromwell. *'UK Tax Residence: Supreme Court Decision in Davies and Gaines-Cooper'*, (Sullivan & Cromwell, 31.10.2011), <www.sullcrom.com/UK-Tax-Residence-10-31-2011/>, accessed 06.06.2016.
165 Sullivan & Cromwell. *'UK Tax: General Anti-Abuse Rule'*, (Sullivan & Cromwell LLP, 16.07.2012), <www.sullcrom.com/siteFiles/Publications/SC_Publication_UK_Tax_General_Anti-Abuse_Rule_2.pdf>, accessed 05.06.2016, p4.
166 Williams, D.E. *'Self-Assessment: A Practitioner's View'*, [1999], British Tax Review, pp229, 230.
167 Sullivan & Cromwell. *'UK Tax Residence: Supreme Court Decision in Davies and Gaines-Cooper'*, (Sullivan & Cromwell, 31.10.2011), <www.sullcrom.com/UK-Tax-Residence-10-31-2011/>, accessed 06.06.2016.
168 Grant Thornton LLP. *'A General Anti-Abuse Rule: Comments on the Consultation Document Released on 12 June 2012'*, <www.grant-thornton.co.uk/Global/GAAR%20consultation%20response.pdf>, accessed 06.06.2016, p5.
169 Office of Tax Simplification. *'Review of Tax Reliefs: Final Report'*, [2011], www.hm-treasury.gov.uk/d/ots_review_tax_reliefs_final_report.pdf, accessed 06.06.2016, p19.
170 Mishcon de Reya LLP. *'A General Anti-Abuse Rule: Mishcon de Reya Response to Consultation Document – September 2012'*, <www.mishcon.com/assets/managed/docs/downloads/doc_2611/Mishcon_de_Reya_GAAR_consultation_response.pdf>, accessed 01.06.2016, p2.
171 *Ibid.*

172 Sullivan & Cromwell. *'UK Tax: General Anti-Abuse Rule'*, (Sullivan & Cromwell LLP, 16.07.2012), <www.sullcrom.com/siteFiles/Publications/SC_Publication_UK_Tax_General_Anti-Abuse_Rule_2.pdf>, accessed 05.06.2016, p10.
173 Freedman, J. *'Analysis – GAAR: Challenging Assumptions'*, [2010], No. 1046, Tax Journal, pp12, 14.
174 Lord Justice Diplock. *'The Court as Legislators'*, [1965], The Holdsworth Club of the University of Birmingham, <http://kessler.co.uk/wp-content/uploads/2012/05/CourtsAsLegistlators.pdf>, accessed 13.02.2016, p9.
175 The Hon Justice Perram, N. *'The Perils of Complexity: Why More Law Is Bad Law'*, [2010], Vol. 39, Australian Tax Review, pp179, 181.
176 Gammie, M. *'When Is Avoiding Tax Not Abusive? Comparative Approaches to a GAAR in Australia and the United Kingdom'*, [2013], Vol. 42, Australian Tax Review, pp279, 283.
177 *Ibid.*
178 *Ibid.*
179 Goldberg, D. *'How Clear, Transparent, Accessible and Foreseeable Is Tax Law and Practice?'*, [2013], Private Client Business, pp238, 240.
180 *Ibid.*
181 OECD. *'2nd Global Forum on Transfer Pricing: Addressing Base Erosion and Profit Shifting'*, <www.oecd.org/about/secretary-general/2nd-global-forum-on-transfer-pricing-addressing-base-erosion-and-profit-shifting.htm>, accessed 08.06.2016.
182 Sullivan & Cromwell. *'UK Tax: General Anti-Abuse Rule'*, (Sullivan & Cromwell LLP, 16.07.2012), <www.sullcrom.com/siteFiles/Publications/SC_Publication_UK_Tax_General_Anti-Abuse_Rule_2.pdf>, accessed 05.06.2016, p10.
183 Bogenschneider, B.N. *'Wittgenstein on Why Tax Law Is Comprehensible'*, [2015], British Tax Review, pp252, 256–257.
184 Sullivan & Cromwell. *'UK Tax: General Anti-Abuse Rule'*, (Sullivan & Cromwell LLP, 16.07.2012), <www.sullcrom.com/siteFiles/Publications/SC_Publication_UK_Tax_General_Anti-Abuse_Rule_2.pdf>, accessed 05.06.2016, p10.
185 Stroup, D.G. *'Law and Language: Cardozo's Jurisprudence and Wittgenstein's Philosophy'*, [1984], Vol. 18, No. 2, Valparaiso University Law Review, p339.
186 *Ibid.*
187 Tax Law Review Committee. *'A General Anti-Avoidance Rule for Direct Taxes: A Consultative Document'*, [1999], <www.ifs.org.uk/comms/comm77.pdf>, accessed 08.06.2016, pii.
188 Tiley, J. and Loutzenhiser, G. *'Revenue Law: Introduction to UK Tax Law; Income Tax; Capital Gains Tax; Inheritance Tax'*, [2012], 7th edn, Hart Publishing, Oxford, p105.
189 Freedman, J. *'Analysis – GAAR: Challenging Assumptions'*, [2010], No. 1046, Tax Journal, pp12, 14.
190 Lethaby, H. *'Aaronson's GAAR'*, [2012], British Tax Review, pp27, 38.
191 Pagone, G.T. *'Aspects of Tax Avoidance: Trans-Tasman Observations'*, [2011], Australian Tax Review, pp40, 149.
192 Gammie, M. *'When Is Avoiding Tax Not Abusive? Comparative Approaches to a GAAR in Australia and the United Kingdom'*, [2013], Vol. 42, Australian Tax Review, pp279, 283.
193 Lethaby, H. *'Aaronson's GAAR'*, [2012], British Tax Review, pp27, 38.
194 *Ibid*, p40.
195 Freedman, J. *'Defining Taxpayer Responsibility: In Support of a General Anti-Avoidance Principle'*, [2004], British Tax Review, pp332, 335.
196 Pagone, G.T. *'Aspects of Tax Avoidance: Trans-Tasman Observations'*, [2011], Australian Tax Review, pp40, 163.
197 Schuck, P.H. *'Legal Complexity: Some Causes, Consequences and Cures'*, [1992], Vol. 42, No. 1, Duke Law Journal, p24.

198 Sampath, K.R. *'Tax Avoidance under Direct Tax Laws'*, [2007], Company Law Institute Press, Chennai, p5.
199 McKie, S. *'The Philosopher's Stone or the Emperor's New Clothes – an Old Conundrum'*, [2012], Private Client Business, pp124, 125.
200 Lethaby, H. *'Aaronson's GAAR'*, [2012], British Tax Review, pp27, 38.
201 Stockton, F. and Bretten, G.R. '*The Ramsay Doctrine: An Interim Review*', [1987], British Tax Review, pp280, 281.
202 Patterson, D. *'Wittgenstein on Understanding and Interpretation (Comments on the Work of Thomas Morawetz)'*, [2006], Vol. 29, No. 2, Philosophical Investigations, p131.
203 *Ibid.*
204 *Ibid.*
205 Lord Bingham. *'The Rule of Law'*, [2007], Cambridge Law Journal, pp67, 69.
206 Barnett, H. *'Constitutional and Administrative Law'*, [2016], 11th edn, Routledge, Oxon, p67.
207 Lord Bingham. *'The Rule of Law'*, [2007], Cambridge Law Journal, Vol. 67, 72.
208 Barnett, H. *'Constitutional and Administrative Law'*, [2016], 11th edn, Routledge, Oxon, p67.
209 Lord Bingham. *'The Rule of Law'*, [2007], Cambridge Law Journal, Vol. 67, 73.
210 Barnett, H. *'Constitutional and Administrative Law'*, [2016], 11th edn, Routledge, Oxon, p67.
211 Lord Bingham. *'The Rule of Law'*, [2007], Cambridge Law Journal, pp67, 78.
212 Barnett, H. *'Constitutional and Administrative Law'*, [2016], 11th edn, Routledge, Oxon, p67.
213 Lord Bingham. *'The Rule of Law'*, [2007], Cambridge Law Journal, pp67, 75.
214 *Ibid*, p77.
215 *Ibid*, p80.
216 Barnett, H. *'Constitutional and Administrative Law'*, [2016], 11th edn, Routledge, Oxon, p67.
217 Lord Bingham. *'The Rule of Law'*, [2007], Cambridge Law Journal, pp67, 81–82.
218 Bogenschneider, B.N. *'Wittgenstein on Why Tax Law Is Comprehensible'*, [2015], British Tax Review, pp252, 254.
219 *Ibid*, p261.
220 *Ibid*, p259.
221 Greenberg, D. *'Dangerous Trends in Modern Legislation'*, [2015], Public Law, pp96, 102.
222 Smith, A. *'An Inquiry into the Nature and Causes of the Wealth of Nations'*, "An Electronic Classics Series Publication" <https://eet.pixel-online.org/files/etranslation/original/The%20Wealth%20of%20Nations.pdf>, accessed 01.02.2022, p676.
223 Greenberg, D. *'GAAR Proposals Could Be Unconstitutional'*, (AccountancyAge, 23.10.2012), <www.accountancyage.com/aa/feature/2219190/gaar-proposals-could-be-unconstitutional>, accessed 08.06.2016.
224 *Ibid.*
225 *Ibid.*
226 Greenberg, D. *'Dangerous Trends in Modern Legislation'*, [2015], Public Law, pp96, 102.
227 *Ibid.*
228 *Ibid.*
229 s3 Constitutional Reform Act 2005.
230 Greenberg, D. *'Dangerous Trends in Modern Legislation'*, [2015], Public Law, pp96, 102–103.
231 Greenberg, D. *'GAAR Proposals Could Be Unconstitutional'*, (AccountancyAge, 23.10.2012), <www.accountancyage.com/aa/feature/2219190/gaar-proposals-could-be-unconstitutional>, accessed 08.06.2016.

232 KPMG. *'New General Anti-Avoidance Rule in Polish Tax Law'*, (KPMG, July 2014), <www.kpmg.com/PL/en/IssuesAndInsights/ArticlesPublications/Documents/2014/Tax-Alert-New-General-Anti-Avoidance-Rule-in-Polish-Tax-Law.pdf>, accessed 09.06.2016, p1.
233 Judgement of the Polish Constitutional Court of 11.05.2004, Case No. K 4/03, p4.
234 *Ibid.*
235 *Ibid.*
236 *Ibid.*
237 *Ibid.*
238 *Ibid*, p5.
239 *Ibid*, p1.
240 *Ibid.*
241 *Ibid*, p8.
242 *Ibid.*
243 *Ibid*, p7.
244 *Ibid.*
245 Gammie, M. *'When Is Avoiding Tax Not Abusive? Comparative Approaches to a GAAR in Australia and the United Kingdom'*, [2013], Vol. 42, Australian Tax Review pp279, 291.
246 *'HMRC GAAR Guidance with Effect from 11 September 2020: Parts A, B and C'*, <https://assets.publishing.service.gov.uk/government/uploads/system/uploads/attachment_data/file/916667/gaar_parts_a_b_c_2020.pdf>, accessed 29.04.2021, p7.
247 Sinfield, G. *'The Halifax Principle as a Universal GAAR for Tax in the EU'*, [2011], British Tax Review, pp235, 243.
248 Goldberg, D. *'How Clear, Transparent, Accessible and Foreseeable Is Tax Law and Practice?'*, [2013], Private Client Business, pp238, 241.

7 Was the GAAR needed?

Introduction

Clearly, the government believed that the GAAR's implementation was desirable. The GAAR study group also made it clear in the Aaronson Report that the UK needed a GAAR.[1] The purpose of this chapter is to examine whether the GAAR was really needed in terms of whether the legislation has added a new dimension to the pre-existing *Ramsay* approach. A comprehensive analysis of what constitutes the *Ramsay* approach and an outline of the key components of the GAAR will be given. Understanding the central components of both the *Ramsay* approach and the GAAR will facilitate a comparison of the two anti-avoidance measures, which will reveal whether the GAAR's provisions help tackle arrangements which *Ramsay* could not be applied to. Although the GAAR may be important in terms of supplementing the *Ramsay* approach, it is also essential to examine case law on tax avoidance before and after the GAAR was introduced. Examining case law before the GAAR will reveal whether the judges needed more than the *Ramsay* approach to tackle tax avoidance. Assessing case law after the GAAR will uncover whether, despite the existence of the GAAR, *Ramsay* is still being developed. This is because the Aaronson Report stated that the GAAR was implemented in order to mitigate the possibility of judges

> seek[ing] to extend the application of the *Ramsay* principle beyond the stage already reached in the decided cases. This was, again, to reduce uncertainty affecting the centre ground of tax planning.[2]

If it is found that *Ramsay* is still being developed, it will strengthen the argument that the addition of the GAAR was not needed. Lastly, whether the GAAR is merely a deterrence to ensure that people do not engage in abusive tax avoidance will be analysed. An analysis of whether the GAAR is needed is important as "anecdotal evidence prior to the introduction of the GAAR suggested that HMRC were succeeding in approximately 85% of tax appeals regarding tax avoidance schemes".[3]

DOI: 10.4324/9781003080473-8

7.1 *Ramsay* versus the GAAR

7.1 (a) The overall Ramsay *approach*

The *Ramsay* approach is an accumulation of the landmark cases which supported *Ramsay*. These cases refined the *Ramsay* approach and built on it. From the earlier analysis, it is possible to provide a comprehensive explanation of what the *Ramsay* approach entails in order to compare it to the GAAR.

The *Ramsay* approach applies to arrangements with a series of transactions. There is a preference for substance over form, giving preference to the substance of the documents, rather than the legitimacy of the individual transactions. There is also a preference for the purposive approach rather than the literal approach to construing legislation. The transactions are constructed so as to be fiscally "self-cancelling",[4] which, in turn, introduces the concept of artificiality. The individual transactions are examined holistically as one "composite transaction".[5] Discussions of artificiality then lead to asking whether the arrangement was executed solely to gain a tax benefit. *Ramsay* also sought to uncover what the taxpayers' intentions were and whether these intentions were fulfilled or not. There is also an objective dimension which places emphasis on the aim and effect of the transactions. The level of risk involved is also material. Lastly, judges may examine how remote the end result is at the time of the intermediate transactions.

Burmah Oil placed greater emphasis on the taxpayer's intentions in building on the *Ramsay* approach. Lord Diplock added that there should be a "preordained series of transactions".[6] In addition to this, the taxpayer should be acting in accordance with a prearranged timetable. *Burmah Oil* also took the artificiality requirement further by introducing the necessity of a commercial purpose.[7] The judges overtly stated that steps which are deemed artificial can be ignored.[8] Furthermore, the judges are entitled to examine whether there is any real loss or hardship suffered.[9] Finally, *Burmah Oil* echoed *Ramsay* by reinforcing the necessity of examining the effect of the arrangement.

Furniss echoed the preordained requirement in *Burmah Oil*, but there was an emphasis that the arrangement should be inflexible for *Ramsay* to apply. Importance was also given to the taxpayer's intentions, the notion of artificiality and the effect of the arrangement. *Furniss* indicated that *Ramsay* applied to cases in which arrangements are executed "solely for fiscal purposes".[10] The connection between the individual steps was further emphasised by adding that they should be "clearly interconnected and mutually dependent on one another"[11] to fall under the *Ramsay* approach.

Ensign Tankers reiterated the applicability of *Ramsay* to composite transactions. The case also reinforced the main principles in the aforementioned cases by focusing on the taxpayer's object and the overall effect of the arrangement.

McGuckian stressed that *Ramsay* was simply about the purposive approach to statutory construction prevailing over the traditional literalist approach. However, there was also an emphasis on the purpose of the transactions in uncovering whether they were artificial. In stressing the purposive approach, *McGuckian* also placed importance on the intention of Parliament.

Tower MCashback reinforced the importance of purpose in terms of what was acquired at the end of the scheme. The court also focused on how much money was actually expended.

7.1 (b) The main features of the GAAR

As previously mentioned, the provisions of the GAAR are arduous and complex, given the fact that the HMRC GAAR guidance forms part of it. Therefore, only the main provisions of the GAAR legislation itself will be analysed and compared to the *Ramsay* approach.

In order for the GAAR to be triggered, first there must be a tax advantage.[12] Secondly, there must be a tax arrangement,[13] which is the point at which the main purpose test is considered. The main purpose test essentially delves into why the taxpayer embarked on the arrangement and whether there were other reasons they carried out the transactions which are unrelated to tax benefits.[14] Deciphering whether an arrangement is abusive or not uses the double reasonableness test.[15] In determining abuse, judges are permitted to examine policy considerations,[16] the existence of artificial or abnormal steps[17] and the intention of the taxpayer.[18]

The inclusion of "abuse" is supposedly what gives the GAAR its targeted dimension, although, given the various factors which the courts can analyse when determining "abuse", the term is given a wide meaning.

7.1 (c) The Ramsay *approach versus the GAAR*

The first comparison of the *Ramsay* approach and the GAAR relates to scope. The *Ramsay* approach is a creation of the common law; therefore, there are no limits on the extent to which the approach can be developed. For example, in *Ensign Tankers*, the judges narrowed the meaning of "purpose" from the original *Ramsay* formulation. However, there are limits to the application of the approach, which are provided for by its prerequisites. In contrast, the GAAR is a piece of carefully drafted legislation which is aimed at tackling only those arrangements which are abusive. Therefore, the scope of the GAAR was designed to be narrow.

The *Ramsay* approach and the GAAR have many features in common. For example, the *Ramsay* approach seeks to view the individual transactions holistically. Similarly, the GAAR guidance states that a tax arrangement, as provided for under the GAAR, can encompass the entire series of transactions.[19] Secondly, the *Ramsay* approach examines the intention of the taxpayers[20] in determining both what the aim of the taxpayer was[21] and whether that intention was fulfilled when the arrangement was complete. The court made it clear that it was determined to prevent the taxpayers' crooked intentions from materialising.[22] Furthermore, in *Ramsay*, Lord Wilberforce also made explicit reference to the purpose of the scheme in concluding that the taxpayer's purpose was to avoid tax.[23] Correspondingly, the GAAR has the main purpose test, which specifically examines whether a tax advantage was one of the main purposes of the arrangement.[24] Moreover, the GAAR examines "whether the arrangements are intended to exploit any shortcomings in those provisions".[25] Therefore, the *Ramsay* approach is equally wide in examining the intentions of the taxpayers. This is due to the fact that the *Ramsay* approach examines the taxpayers' intention to gain a tax advantage whereas the GAAR analyses the existence of an intention to avoid tax.

The GAAR and *Ramsay* approach differ at the stage at which the GAAR becomes targeted. The GAAR is targeted at abusive arrangements, which are determined by the double reasonableness test.[26] In contrast, the judges in *Ramsay* did not seek to limit the scope of the approach by stating that it is targeted at those arrangements which are abusive. Nevertheless, the court expressed the limitations of the approach and mentioned the possibility of a general anti-avoidance rule being introduced, although acknowledging that "if so general an attack upon schemes for tax avoidance as the revenue suggest is to be validated, that is a matter for Parliament".[27] However, later decisions highlighted "the general scope of the Ramsay principle",[28] which indicates that the principle is not limited to certain taxes like the GAAR. Consequently, despite the similarities, the *Ramsay* approach is broader than the GAAR. Nevertheless, there are situations that will escape *Ramsay* but will be caught by the GAAR.

Despite the fact that the GAAR appears to be narrower than the *Ramsay* approach, this is not the case when determining what amounts to abuse. The GAAR mirrors the *Ramsay* approach where it allows the intentions of the taxpayer to be examined[29] and scruitinises the existence of artificial steps.[30] Artificial steps may be ascertained by examining one of the *Ramsay* requirements of whether the transactions are "self-cancelling".[31] If what makes the GAAR unique is the inclusion of abuse, it largely fails in its attempt to be targeted if determining an abusive transaction mirrors the *Ramsay* approach. However, it can be argued that the GAAR is wider than the *Ramsay* approach due to a provision which is a determinative factor of abuse where the "result was not the anticipated result when the relevant tax provisions were enacted".[32] This provision is very wide and can be interpreted in HMRC's favour where the taxpayer has utilised an unexpected loophole in the tax system.

The similarities between the GAAR and *Ramsay* approaches are numerous. The main feature that the GAAR has, which the *Ramsay* approach does not make reference to, is the double reasonableness test. As previously mentioned, this test has been criticised for not contributing much to the application of the GAAR.

If the crux of the GAAR is the inclusion of the undefined term "abuse", it should contain elements which are unique when compared to *Ramsay*. Determining abuse by reference to the taxpayer's intentions and the existence of artificiality does not help in making the GAAR distinct from *Ramsay*. Nevertheless, "at least the GAAR is *law*".[33]

7.2 Contemporary tax avoidance before the GAAR

Aaronson's report clearly highlighted that the GAAR was needed as *Ramsay* could not prevent some abusive schemes from being successful.[34] Therefore, the cases cited in Aaronson's report as being immune to a purposive construction will be discussed in order to ascertain whether the GAAR was needed.

The notorious *Mayes*[35] case was undoubtedly a catalyst for the creation of the GAAR. Aaronson cited *Mayes* in his report and stated that the judge "was unable to find a purposive interpretation sufficient to defeat it".[36] *Ramsay* could not be applied to the case, despite the judge stating that there were "pre-ordained, composite, artificial and tax-motivated events".[37] The scheme targeted high-net-worth individuals in the UK.[38] Therefore, the court did not want the scheme to succeed as "if it did, about £24m would be lost in tax".[39]

Mayes involved a tax scheme called SHIPS 2. The aim of the scheme was to "use the corresponding deficiency relief as loss, pay less income tax and claim capital gains tax (CGT) loss relief".[40] The scheme involved non-resident companies purchasing life insurance policies in which the companies eventually made a loss. The main question was whether the taxpayer was entitled to "corresponding deficiency relief",[41] which was generated by the inclusion of steps 3 and 4 of the scheme. Therefore, the court discussed at length whether these two steps could be disregarded as "commercially pointless".[42]

The scheme in *Mayes* involved seven individual steps. Firstly, a man from Jersey used money he had borrowed to purchase two premiums and two bonds, which included 20 life insurance policies, from the American Insurance Group (AIG). He then allocated the bonds to a company in Luxembourg, referred to as JSI, for £256,085. In step 3 of the scheme, for each policy in one of the bonds, JSI then paid a top-up premium of £375,000 to AIG. JSI also subsequently paid £50,000 to AIG for each policy in the second bond, which totalled £150 million for both bonds. However, a few weeks later, in step 4 of the scheme, JSI withdrew the money paid to AIG, which was viewed as a partial surrender of the policies, leaving £5,000 in each bond.[43] JSI then assigned the bonds to a company in England, and they were then assigned to Mr Mayes for £125,949 for the first bond and £7,155 for the second bond. In the final step, the taxpayer surrendered both bonds to AIG and took the £1780.94 proceeds. He then claimed he was entitled to both ""“corresponding deficiency relief" (i.e. a loss"[44] of almost £2 million) and an allowable loss of over £100,000 for capital gains tax purposes.[45] The court held that he was entitled to these tax reliefs.[46]

Despite the *Ramsay* approach being considered, it could not be applied. *Ramsay's* holistic approach made the court speculate that the steps involving JSI paying the top-up premium and withdrawing them a few weeks later should be ignored due to their self-cancelling nature.[47] However, *Ramsay* could not be applied as

> the tax avoidance purpose and self-cancelling nature of the steps did not by themselves entitle the court to disregard the steps, when there was nothing in the ICTA provisions indicating or contemplating that, as a matter of construction, such steps were not to count.[48]

Steps 3 and 4 could not be disregarded as "they were genuine legal events with real legal effects",[49] despite the fact that they were "commercially unreal".[50] To do so would be an error of law.[51] Furthermore, the court claimed that the legislation could not be purposively interpreted to deny the tax relief as the Income and Corporation Taxes Act 1988 (ICTA) "provisions . . . [did] not readily lend themselves to a purposive commercial construction".[52] For example, s549 of the ICTA, which the taxpayer's relied on, states that

> a corresponding deficiency occurring at the end of the final year shall be allowable as a deduction from his total income for that year of assessment, so far as it does not exceed the total amount treated as a gain.[53]

Therefore, the literal approach was applicable.

Ramsay began to falter in *Mayes* as a case to which all judges must refer. Mummery L.J. indicated that *Ramsay* was not an anti-avoidance principle to be applied in all cases as he "doubt[ed] whether, since Mawson, it really is necessary to return each time to the base camp in *Ramsay* and trek through all the authorities from then on".[54] He also explicitly stated that "*Ramsay* did not lay down a special doctrine of revenue law"[55] and that "the *Ramsay* principle is the general principle of purposive and contextual construction of all legislation". Thomas L.J. reluctantly concurred with Mummery L.J.'s decision,[56] although he seemed to disagree with the decision because the taxpayer was wealthy. He stated that the result of the *Mayes* case was that

> the higher rate taxpayers with large earnings or significant investment income who have taken advantage of the scheme have received benefits that cannot possibly have been intended and which must be paid for by other taxpayers.[57]

Toulson L.J. also reluctantly agreed with Mummery L.J.'s decision, which he felt concluded "in a result which instinctively seems wrong, because it bears no relation to commercial reality and results in a windfall which Parliament cannot have foreseen or intended".[58] The words of Toulson L.J. are reminiscent of s207(4)(c) of the Finance Act 2013, which states that an arrangement is indicative of abuse where the "result was not the anticipated result when the relevant tax provisions were enacted".[59] The similarity could suggest that the words of Toulson L.J. were taken into account when drafting the GAAR.

Mummery L.J. signalled that Parliament should take action if the result of the case was viewed as objectionable.[60] The judge warned that "if the taxpayer succeeds and HMRC and Parliament do not like the result, the law can be re-adjusted for the future in a Finance Act".[61] It is clear from the implementation of the GAAR and the specific dislike of the *Mayes* case, as described in the Aaronson Report,[62] that Parliament paid heed to the words of Mummery L.J. Thomas L.J. echoed the words of Mummery L.J., stating that "it must be for Parliament to consider the wider implications of the decision as it relates to the way in which revenue legislation is structured and drafted".[63]

Aaronson stated that "SHIPS 2 shows the inadequacy of the existing means of combating highly artificial tax avoidance schemes"[64] in concluding that the UK did need a GAAR. The fact that Aaronson specifically mentioned *Mayes* in his report suggests that the type of scheme involved in this case would be caught by the GAAR for being abusive. Nevertheless, the GAAR seems like an extreme response, given that *Mayes* was "a rare taxpayer victory in a pure avoidance case".[65] The *Mayes* case also seems to suggest that the judiciary is powerless without the GAAR and that the *Ramsay* approach can only be applied in certain circumstances. Therefore, it is helpful to examine cases after the implementation of the GAAR to determine the extent to which the judiciary is relying on the *Ramsay* approach and whether the GAAR could have been applied by HMRC.

7.3 Tax avoidance since the GAAR

Ramsay was relied on in the joint appeals of *UBS AG v Commissioners for HMRC*[66] (*UBS*) and *DB Group Services (UK) Ltd. v Commissioners for HMRC* (*DB Group Services*). The *UBS* case involved the bank, UBS, seeking to provide bonuses to their employees in a manner which avoided liability to tax on the bonuses. In order to accomplish their objective, the bank established an offshore company based in Jersey, ESIP Ltd., with the aim of providing their employees shares. The money injected into ESIP Ltd. by UBS was equal to the amount of the employee bonuses. UBS instructed ESIP Ltd. to place the money given to them into an account which would generate interest. UBS sought to give the shares the character of restricted securities within the meaning of s423(1) of the Income Tax (Earnings and Pensions) Act 2003 (ITEPA). The shares were regarded as restricted securities as the rights of the employees as shareholders stated that there would be an automatic sale of the shares when the value of the FTSE 100 Index exceeded 6.5% above its original value. If this improbable event occurred within the stipulated three-week period, the shares would then be sold for 90% of their market value.

Under s425(2) of the ITEPA 2003, restricted securities are exempt from tax if they are related to employment. However, s426 of the ITEPA 2003 states that the securities will be taxable where there is a chargeable event, such as the cessation of the securities being considered restricted securities. Nevertheless, UBS sought to rely on s429 of the ITEPA 2003, which states that no tax will arise where the restriction affects an entire class of shares in the same manner, and the company is controlled by the employees.

The scheme was further reinforced by ensuring that ESIP purchased call options from UBS. This purchase had the effect of safeguarding against the unlikely possibility that the value of the FTSE 100 Index exceeded 6.5% above its original value, and the shares would be automatically sold for 90% of their market value. If this eventuality took place, the shares' market value would then be worth 110% of their original value, and the employees would be entitled to 99.2% of the share value.[67] However, this eventuality did not take place. ESIP also bought shares in UBS so that ESIP shares would be judged in accordance with the success of the UBS shares. ESIP ceased operating and closed when all the employees redeemed their shares. Chapter 3 of the ITEPA 2003, which imposes a tax on securities where their market value has been artificially reduced by 10% or more, was also discussed.

In the *DB Group Services* case, Deutsche Bank AG employed a similar scheme to the one in the *UBS* case. Deutsche Bank also wanted its employees to benefit from bonuses in the form of shares in an offshore company they created. In order to give them the appearance of restricted securities, the shares could be forfeited when the employee who held the share ceased to be employed by Deutsche Bank AG "for any reason other than redundancy, death or disability, or without cause".[68] The court found it unlikely that any employee would voluntarily resign or be dismissed by reason of misconduct because their shares were at stake.[69] However, in order to qualify for the tax exemption under s429 of the ITEPA 2003, the offshore company had to be unrelated to Deutsche Bank AG. However, the court found that the bank did control the offshore company.[70]

In forming its opinion, the court sought to unravel the unexpressed purpose of Chapter 2 of the ITEPA 2003.[71] Following the case of *Abbott v Philbin*,[72] Parliament amended Chapter 2 of the ITEPA 2003 to ensure that the tax was levied when employees acquired their shares and not when restrictions on the shares were lifted.[73] Therefore, the court surmised that

> Chapter 2 was introduced partly for the purpose of forestalling tax avoidance schemes [which] makes it difficult to attribute to Parliament an intention that it should apply to schemes which were carefully crafted to fall within its scope, purely for the purpose of tax avoidance.[74]

The court also found it

> difficult to accept that Parliament can have intended to encourage by exemption from taxation the award of shares to employees, where the award of the shares has no purpose whatsoever other than the obtaining of the exemption itself.[75]

Therefore, much of the court's rationale lay in determining the purposes for which Chapter 2 was amended and why the shares were awarded. The discussion as to what Parliament did not intend also corresponds with what amounts to abuse in the GAAR.[76] Therefore, if HMRC sought to invoke the GAAR, it is possible that the arrangement would be deemed abusive.

The general permissibility of such share schemes was also questioned. The court condemned

> the encouragement of such schemes, unlike the encouragement of employee share ownership generally . . . [as they] would have no rational purpose, and would indeed be positively contrary to rationality, bearing in mind the general aims of income tax statutes.[77]

The wide argument regarding share schemes in general is reminiscent of Barak's argument mentioned in chapter 5. He argued that "the purpose of taxing statutes is to collect tax and to approach tax cases on that understanding of their purpose may lead to a bias against the taxpayer".[78] Nevertheless, in determining that the purpose of amending Chapter 2 of the ITEPA 2003 was to prevent tax avoidance schemes,[79] the court applied this rationale to the relevant provisions. Under s423 of the ITEPA 2003, qualifying as restricted securities requires the existence of "any contract, agreement, arrangement or condition which makes provision to which any of subsections (2) to (4) applies".[80] However, in light of the purpose of the Act, the court interpreted this provision

> as being limited to provision having a business or commercial purpose, and not to commercially irrelevant conditions whose only purpose is the obtaining of the exemption.[81]

Thereafter, the court sought to determine whether the restrictions placed on the securities had a business or commercial purpose as advocated by the *Ramsay* approach. In regards to the *UBS* case, the court concluded that the automatic sale provision where the value of the FTSE 100 Index exceeded 6.5% above its original value within the given three-week period "had no business or commercial rationale beyond tax avoidance".[82] Furthermore, "the benefit to the employee was not truly dependent on the contingency set out in the condition".[83] Consequently, the court decided to ignore the conditions attached to the shares, which had the effect of preventing the shares from being regarded as restricted securities. However, had HMRC invoked the GAAR at an earlier stage, the arrangement in this case would have been likely to satisfy the main purpose test. Therefore, the *UBS* and *DB Group Services* cases would have been sufficient to trigger the GAAR had HMRC sought to apply it.

In relation to the *DB Group Services* case, the court believed that the restrictions which were placed on the shares were artificial.[84] The court reasoned that

> the forfeiture provision operated for only a very short period, during which the possibility that it might be triggered lay largely within the control of the employee who would be adversely affected. It had no business or commercial purpose, and existed solely to bring the securities.[85]

The cases supporting the *Ramsay* approach were followed as Lord Reed stated that "the appeals thus belong to the line of cases mentioned in *Barclays Mercantile*".[86] This line of cases included *Furniss* and *Burmah Oil*.[87] Chapter 2 of the ITEPA 2003 was purposively applied in order to conclude that the conditions attached to the employees' securities did not have a business or commercial purpose and took into account the practical effect of the conditions.[88]

The intentions of the taxpayers were examined, and the court concluded that due to the "minor risk"[89] involved, "the scheme should therefore be considered as it was intended to operate, without regard to the possibility that it might not work as planned".[90] Therefore, the scale of risk is a factor which the judiciary considers when deciding whether an arrangement will be considered unacceptable tax avoidance. Moreover, the case demonstrates that the intentions of the taxpayer are still being sought after the implementation of the GAAR. As the GAAR specifically refers to the taxpayer's intentions,[91] it would have been permissible to scrutinise the taxpayer's intentions under the GAAR. Finally, the court decided that "income tax is payable on the value of the shares as at the date of their acquisition".[92] The court was able to hinder the "sophisticated attempts of the Houdini taxpayer . . . [from] escap[ing] from the manacles of tax".[93]

The court also applied the *Ramsay* approach in *Chappell v The Commissioners for HMRC*[94] (*Chappell*). In *Chappell*, the taxpayer sought to make a tax deduction totalling £303,123. He acquired two manufactured overseas dividends which together amounted to the sum of the deduction sought. The scheme involved various steps. Firstly, the taxpayer and Barsbury Limited entered into an agreement called a Global Masters Securities Lending Agreement.[95] Barsbury lent securities to the taxpayer under the agreement that the taxpayer would pay an amount equal to the interest and dividends to Barsbury. Thereafter, by using borrowed funds, Barsbury was, in turn, issued loan notes worth over £6 million by Santi Crescent Limited (SCL), which were then temporarily borrowed by the taxpayer. By virtue of another agreement, SCL was then obliged to pay interest on the loan notes. The taxpayer then disposed of the loan notes by transferring them to Berry Lane Limited (BLL), which paid over £6 million for the notes. When the interest subsequently became due, the taxpayer gave the money to Barsbury. The amount of interest paid was also the sum which the taxpayer sought to deduct. The taxpayer then acquired additional loan notes from Qintar Limited (QL), which were worth over £6 million. He then transferred these notes to Barsbury to repay what he had borrowed earlier.

The main issue concerned the source of the various sums being transferred in the scheme which derived from loans, predominantly from the Société Générale Bank and Trust (SGBT), based in Luxembourg. The monies were transferred using a company named Brecknock using SG Hambros Bank & Trust (Jersey) Limited (SGH). SGH also held the loan notes on behalf of the taxpayer. The companies SCL, Brecknock and Barsbury all had accounts at SGBT. Brecknock transferred over £6 million to Barsbury to subscribe for the loan notes.[96] On behalf of Barsbury, SCL then paid in the subscription funds into Brecknock's account. The taxpayer then used the loan notes to repay Barsbury the loan of the notes. Therefore, the monies in the scheme flowed from the same SGBT account which the court found circularly involved: the taxpayer selling the notes to BLL, the sum which the taxpayer sought to deduct being transferred to Barsbury and the taxpayer acquiring loan notes from QL.[97] The court held that the "amounts . . . cancelled each other out".[98] The fact that SCL "did not carry on a trade and its only purpose was to service this and other similar tax schemes"[99] was not fatal to the taxpayer's case.

Despite the fact that Mummery L.J. in *Mayes* found it unnecessary to assess *Ramsay* and the subsequent supporting cases,[100] Patten L.J. assessed the *Ramsay* approach and the subsequent supporting cases in a patchwork of lengthy quotes cited from these cases. The taxpayer lost his case as "the scheme was not *Ramsay*-proof".[101]

Rather than focus on whether the arrangement was abusive, the question the court focused on was whether the scheme should

> fall to be construed and treated like those in *MacNiven* so as to confer tax relief even though the transaction in question forms part of a scheme which was designed solely for the purpose of obtaining that relief and has no wider or other commercial justification.[102]

The taxpayer relied on regulation 2B of the Income Tax (Manufactured Overseas Dividends) Regulations 1993, which relates to the lending of securities. The court considered whether Parliament intended for the type of transaction in *Chappell* under these Regulations. The taxpayer's argument was that the payments made in the scheme were annual payments, and he was therefore entitled to deduct this sum from his taxable earnings under s349(1) Income and Corporation Tax Act 1988. However, the Revenue argued that the scheme "had no commercial or other purpose apart from the avoidance of tax".[103] This conclusion indicates that the arrangement would have failed the GAAR's main purpose test, had it been invoked by HMRC. Moreover, the court was not persuaded by arguments made on behalf of the taxpayer that the literal approach should be applied.[104] The judges acknowledged that applying a literal construction to the legislation would

> confer tax relief even though the transaction in question forms part of a scheme which was designed solely for the purpose of obtaining that relief and has no wider or other commercial justification.[105]

UBS and *DB Group Services* both demonstrate that *Ramsay* is still being invoked since the GAAR's implementation, despite the fact that the GAAR could also have been applied. The reluctance to evoke the GAAR early on is in line with "the Australian GAAR [which] remained untested in the courts for eight years before . . . an avalanche of cases commenced".[106]

Given the timespan since the GAAR was first enacted, there now exists a body of GAAR advisory panel opinion notices to better explain how the GAAR operates.[107]

An example of a case which attracted a GAAR notice involved the funding of an employee benefit trust which was deemed to be abusive under the GAAR.[108] The taxpayer was the only shareholder and director of the company. The company purchased £5 million of gold which was immediately re-sold to the original seller. As a result, the taxpayer enjoyed a director's loan of £5 million and triggered an obligation on the taxpayer to fund the employee benefit trust. There are various features of the transaction which were found to be abnormal by the advisory panel. These include the use of gold as an employee reward and the timing of the transaction.[109] Consideration of the timing of the transactions is consistent with the approach taken in both *Burmah Oil* and *Ensign Tankers*. This demonstrates that timing ought to have been included in the GAAR test.

7.4 The GAAR as a deterrent

As the *Ramsay* approach and the GAAR have similar components, the dormant GAAR may have been introduced to serve as a mere deterrent. Moreover, as mentioned earlier, tax avoidance is the lowest contributing factor to the tax gap, which began to decline before the GAAR was even introduced.[110] Gammie argues that "the *Ramsay* principle has ensured that HMRC have prevailed in most cases without the need for a statutory GAAR".[111]

Bloom remarked that "the United Kingdom GAAR is sleeping".[112] Even if the GAAR is a mere deterrent, Lethaby argues that "evidence suggests that it is having some deterrent effect, at least around the margins".[113] However, she also contends that the GAAR has not lessened the volume of legislation being implemented as "HMRC's kneejerk reactions to newly disclosed schemes have not abated, with the corporate profits transfer TAAR . . . just being the latest example".[114] Moreover, Lethaby suggests that the GAAR is not being implemented, even where

> apparently, HMRC had received disclosures of schemes designed to circumvent an only just announced new rule aimed at stopping profit stripping using total return swaps with tax havens, and so it responded with another hastily drafted bit of legislation which wildly overreaches.[115]

Therefore, Lethaby questioned "what on earth is the GAAR for if not to counteract contrived attempts to get around some new anti-avoidance rules? Why couldn't HMRC just be bold enough to rely on it?"[116] Consequently, there appears to be a reluctance to invoke the GAAR, and the tendency to add to the volume of pre-existing tax legislation remains.

7.5 Conclusion

The GAAR overtly shows that Parliament sought hard to win in the "the contest between the state and the citizen".[117] The *Ramsay* approach will continue to be invoked as long as a purposive interpretation of the legislation can be used to defeat an unacceptable scheme. Where the *Ramsay* approach cannot be applied, HMRC may seek to invoke the GAAR in order to argue that Parliament did not intend the result. The GAAR will be used where a scheme may be technically compliant, but Parliament did not intend for the provisions to be used in the manner in which they were. However, at the stage of applying the GAAR, the court may still examine elements of the *Ramsay* approach. Nevertheless, as previously mentioned, one of the main reasons the GAAR was implemented was to prevent the extension of the *Ramsay* approach.[118] The cases discussed which were heard after the implementation of the GAAR did not extend the *Ramsay* approach. Nonetheless, the reliance on *Ramsay* can lead to the *Ramsay* approach being further developed in the future.

The GAAR and the *Ramsay* approach have many limbs in common. Both seek to examine arrangements holistically, including the purpose of the arrangement, the intentions of the taxpayer and the existence of artificial steps. The double reasonableness test is the main element which genuinely distinguishes the GAAR from the *Ramsay* approach. However, as discussed in chapter 3, as the GAAR fails to define what is "reasonable", this test is largely open to subjective interpretation. Therefore, the double reasonableness test could contribute to widening the scope of the GAAR, which does not, in reality, sufficiently distinguish *Ramsay* and the GAAR in terms of scope.

Mayes illustrated the need for a GAAR which could apply to cases in which Parliament had not envisaged that the provisions of the relevant Act could be used to avoid tax. The court was unable to ignore the steps they found to be artificial because the relevant Act did not permit them to do so, even though the arrangement was regarded as "commercially unreal".[119] The GAAR should therefore make reference to the need for a commercial purpose and to examine the existence of artificial steps. The scope of *Ramsay* was restricted in *Mayes*. It was in *Mayes* that all the elements which make up the *Ramsay* approach were pushed to the side, and the court focused on *Ramsay* in terms of the purposive approach. The court's final decision was unwillingly in the taxpayer's favour as discussions of whether it was right for the wealthy taxpayer to lose his case overshadowed the case. *Mayes* is significant because the judges suggested that *Ramsay* alone was insufficient to tackle all tax avoidance. The government may have also introduced the GAAR to placate the public into believing that lost tax revenue from cases like *Mayes* is unlikely to recur.

Ramsay was successfully relied on in the *UBS* and *DB Group Services* cases. These conjoined cases did not allow the lack of a GAAR to permit the tax avoidance schemes. Although the court was more readily able to confirm Parliament's intentions by reference to the amended Chapter 2 of the ITEPA 2003, it also believed that the outcome of the schemes would not have been what Parliament intended.[120] The rationale of what Parliament would not have intended could have also been applied in *Mayes*. However, *Mayes* represented a point at which the judiciary were unwilling to fill the gaps in legislation left by Parliament, holding that "it is not for judges to shoulder the law-making responsibilities of Parliament".[121] In *UBS* and *DB Group Services*, importance was also placed on the purpose of the schemes, and unlike in *Mayes*, this factor contributed to deciding that the schemes should not succeed. The court also added that the arrangement should have "a business or commercial purpose",[122] which was an extra-statutory requirement used to frustrate the scheme. The "commercial purpose"[123] requirement echoes the words of Lord Diplock in *Burmah Oil*. Therefore, *Ramsay* was followed, unlike in *Mayes*, wherein the judges appeared hindered by having to "return each time to the base camp in *Ramsay* and trek through all the authorities from then on".[124]

In *UBS* and *DB Group Services*, the court focused on traditional elements of the *Ramsay* approach, such as the fact that the scheme was self-cancelling and examining the purpose of the scheme. The cases also demonstrate that the taxpayer's intentions are being sought by virtue of invoking the *Ramsay* approach, despite the fact that Parliament legitimises examining the taxpayer's intentions under the

GAAR. This reliance on *Ramsay* is likely to continue, and it had been predicted that the GAAR will not be utilised until well after the year 2020.[125] Consequently, the *Ramsay* approach has survived the enactment of GAAR. Aaronson stated that the GAAR was not designed to make the *Ramsay* approach redundant but to ensure that the approach would not need to be further extended by the judiciary in future cases.[126]

The GAAR's most lethal provision to tackle abusive tax avoidance schemes seems to be where it defines abuse as being where the "result was not the anticipated result when the relevant tax provisions were enacted".[127] Under *Ramsay*, the courts could consider Parliament's intentions. However, examining whether Parliament anticipated a tax avoidance scheme is wider as it examines what Parliament omitted rather than what it intended as evidenced in the legislation. Determining what Parliament would have anticipated is largely for the judiciary to decide by using their discretion. However, the discretion of the judges would not be arbitrary. It is likely that the courts will examine the end result of a scheme to ascertain whether it would have been rejected had Parliament considered it. However, the anticipation provision in the GAAR can eradicate those schemes which do not fall under *Ramsay* as it goes further than purposively construing the legislation.

It can be argued that the GAAR is serving as an effective deterrent against the more egregious and abusive schemes. Therefore, it can be said that a GAAR was needed or, at least, that having one seems to be proving helpful. However, with the uncertain remit of the GAAR and the ability to decide what Parliament anticipated, some argue that "at least with *Ramsay* one could hazard a guess as to which page one was on, even if not the precise coordinates".[128] While Lethaby may be correct, the discussions in this chapter have shown that *Ramsay* does require a helping hand in cases where judges find themselves unable to intervene in view of their proper constitutional role. That helping hand, it seems, could very well be the GAAR.

Notes

1 Aaronson, G. *'A Study to Consider whether a General Anti-Avoidance Rule Should Be Introduced into the UK Tax System'*, [2011], <http://webarchive.nationalarchives.gov.uk/+/http:/www.hm-treasury.gov.uk/d/gaar_final_report_111111.pdf>, accessed 25.08.2014, p21.

2 Aaronson, G. *'A Study to Consider whether a General Anti-Avoidance Rule Should Be Introduced into the UK Tax System'*, [2012], <http://webarchive.nationalarchives.gov.uk/+/http:/www.hm-treasury.gov.uk/d/gaar_final_report_111111.pdf>, accessed 04.06.2016, p27.

3 Cannon, P. *'GAAR: A Practical Approach'*, [2018], 3rd edn, Key Haven Publications Ltd., Oxford, p3.

4 *WT Ramsay Ltd. v IRC; Eilbeck v Rawling* [1981] 2 W.L.R 449, [1982] A.C. 300, 328 (Lord Wilberforce).

5 *Ibid*, p324.

6 *IRC v Burmah Oil Co Ltd.* [1982] S.C. (H.L.) 114, 124 (Lord Diplock).

7 *Ibid.*

8 *Ibid*, p126 (Lord Fraser of Tullybelton).
9 *Ibid*, p131.
10 *Furniss v Dawson* [1983] 3 W.L.R. 635, 651 (Oliver L.J.).
11 *Ibid.*
12 s208 Finance Act 2013.
13 s207(1) Finance Act 2013.
14 *Ibid.*
15 s207(2) Finance Act 2013.
16 s207(2)(a) Finance Act 2013.
17 s207(2)(b) Finance Act 2013.
18 s207(2)(c) Finance Act 2013.
19 *'HMRC GAAR Guidance with Effect from 11 September 2020: Parts A, B and C'*, <https://assets.publishing.service.gov.uk/government/uploads/system/uploads/attachment_data/file/916667/gaar_parts_a_b_c_2020.pdf>, accessed 29.04.2021, p16.
20 *WT Ramsay Ltd. v IRC*; *Eilbeck v Rawling* [1981] 2 W.L.R 449, [1982] A.C. 300, 333 (Lord Fraser of Tullybelton).
21 *Ibid*, p324.
22 *Ibid*, p326 (Lord Wilberforce).
23 *Ibid*, p323.
24 s207(1) Finance Act 2013.
25 s207(2)(c) Finance Act 2013.
26 s207(2) Finance Act 2013.
27 *WT Ramsay Ltd. v IRC*; *Eilbeck v Rawling* [1981] 2 W.L.R 449, [1982] A.C. 300, 325 (Lord Wilberforce).
28 *The Commissioners for HMRC v Mayes* [2011] EWCA Civ 407, [21] (Mummery L.J.).
29 s207(2)(c) Finance Act 2013.
30 s207(2)(b) Finance Act 2013.
31 *WT Ramsay Ltd. v IRC*; *Eilbeck v Rawling* [1981] 2 W.L.R 449, [1982] A.C. 300, 328 (Lord Wilberforce).
32 S207(4)(c) Finance Act 2013.
33 Lethaby, H. *'Analysis – Reflections on Tax and the City'*, [2014], No. 1220, Tax Journal, pp10, 11.
34 Aaronson, G. *'A Study to Consider whether a General Anti-Avoidance Rule Should Be Introduced into the UK Tax System'*, [2012], <http://webarchive.nationalarchives.gov.uk/+/http:/www.hm-treasury.gov.uk/d/gaar_final_report_111111.pdf>, accessed 04.06.2016, p20.
35 *The Commissioners for HMRC v Mayes* [2011] EWCA Civ 407.
36 Aaronson, G. *'A Study to Consider whether a General Anti-Avoidance Rule Should Be Introduced into the UK Tax System'*, [2012], <http://webarchive.nationalarchives.gov.uk/+/http:/www.hm-treasury.gov.uk/d/gaar_final_report_111111.pdf>, accessed 04.06.2016, p20.
37 *The Commissioners for HMRC v Mayes* [2011] EWCA Civ 407, [1] (Mummery L.J.).
38 *Ibid*, [2].
39 *Ibid*, [14].
40 *Ibid*, [2].
41 *Ibid.*
42 *Ibid*, [30].
43 *Ibid.*
44 *Ibid*, [2].
45 *Ibid*, [30].
46 *Ibid*, [85].
47 *Ibid*, [32].

48 *Ibid*, [56].
49 *Ibid*, [78].
50 *Ibid.*
51 *Ibid.*
52 *Ibid.*
53 s549 Income and Corporation Taxes Act 1988.
54 *The Commissioners for HMRC v Mayes* [2011] EWCA Civ 407, [71] (Mummery L.J.).
55 *Ibid*, [74].
56 *Ibid*, [100] (Thomas L.J.).
57 *Ibid.*
58 *Ibid*, [101] (Toulson L.J.).
59 S207(4)(c) Finance Act 2013.
60 *The Commissioners for HMRC v Mayes* [2011] EWCA Civ 407, [20] (Mummery L.J.).
61 *Ibid.*
62 Aaronson, G. *'A Study to Consider whether a General Anti-Avoidance Rule Should Be Introduced into the UK Tax System'*, [2012], <http://webarchive.nationalarchives.gov.uk/+/http:/www.hm-treasury.gov.uk/d/gaar_final_report_111111.pdf>, accessed 04.06.2016, p20.
63 *The Commissioners for HMRC v Mayes* [2011] EWCA Civ 407, [100] (Thomas L.J.).
64 Aaronson, G. *'A Study to Consider whether a General Anti-Avoidance Rule Should Be Introduced into the UK Tax System'*, [2012], <http://webarchive.nationalarchives.gov.uk/+/http:/www.hm-treasury.gov.uk/d/gaar_final_report_111111.pdf>, accessed 04.06.2016, p21.
65 Self, H. *'Do We Still Need a GAAR'*, [2016], No. 1321, Tax Journal, p15, [no pagination].
66 *UBS AG v Commissioners for HMRC*; *DB Group Services (UK) Ltd. v Commissioners for HMRC* [2016] UKSC 13.
67 *Ibid*, [32] (Lord Reed).
68 *Ibid*, [52].
69 *Ibid.*
70 *Ibid*, [59].
71 *Ibid*, [74].
72 *Abbott v Philbin* [1961] A.C. 352.
73 *UBS AG v Commissioners for HMRC*; *DB Group Services (UK) Ltd. v Commissioners for HMRC* [2016] UKSC 13, [75] (Lord Reed).
74 *Ibid*, [77].
75 *Ibid.*
76 S207(4)(c) Finance Act 2013.
77 *Ibid.*
78 Barak, A. *'Purposive Interpretation in Law'*, Princeton University Press, Princeton and Oxford, NJ, p17.
79 *UBS AG v Commissioners for HMRC; DB Group Services (UK) Ltd. v Commissioners for HMRC* [2016] UKSC 13, [77] (Lord Reed).
80 s423(1) Income Tax (Earnings and Pensions) Act 2003.
81 *UBS AG v Commissioners for HMRC*; *DB Group Services (UK) Ltd. v Commissioners for HMRC* [2016] UKSC 13, [85] (Lord Reed).
82 *Ibid*, [86].
83 *Ibid*, [87].
84 *Ibid*, [88].
85 *Ibid.*
86 *Ibid*, [89].
87 *Ibid.*

88 *Ibid*, [98].
89 *Ibid*, [88].
90 *Ibid.*
91 s207(2)(c).
92 *UBS AG v Commissioners for HMRC; DB Group Services (UK) Ltd. v Commissioners for HMRC* [2016] UKSC 13, [98] (Lord Reed).
93 *Ibid*, [1].
94 *Chappell v The Commissioners for HMRC* [2016] EWCA Civ 809.
95 *Ibid*, [15] (Patten L.J.).
96 *Ibid*, [17].
97 *Ibid*, [19].
98 *Ibid.*
99 *Ibid*, [20].
100 *The Commissioners for HMRC v Mayes* [2011] EWCA Civ 407, [71] (Mummery L.J.).
101 Thomas, R. *'Chappell v HMRC: The Swan Really Has Sung Its Last: The Court of Appeal Considers the Deductibility of Annual Payments'*, [2017], British Tax Review, pp27, 28.
102 *Chappell v The Commissioners for HMRC* [2016] EWCA Civ 809, [34] (Patten L.J.).
103 *Ibid*, [3].
104 *Ibid*, [39–40].
105 *Ibid*, [34].
106 Calvert, T. and Dabner, J. *'GAARs in Australia and South Africa: Mutual Lessons'*, [2012], Vol. 7, No. 1, Journal of Journal of the Australian Tax Teachers Association, pp53, 54.
107 HMRC. *'GAAR Advisory Panel Opinions'*, <www.gov.uk/government/collections/tax-avoidance-general-anti-abuse-rule-gaar>, accessed 25.05.2021.
108 HMRC. *'Redacted and Sub-Panel Approved Version of Opinion Notice Originally Issued on 9 November 2017'*, <https://assets.publishing.service.gov.uk/government/uploads/system/uploads/attachment_data/file/665661/GAAR_Panel_Opinion_employee_reward_gold_bullion___comp_2.pdf>, accessed 19.06.2021.
109 *Ibid*, p5.
110 HMRC. *'UK Tax Gap at a Glance in 2014–2015'*, <www.gov.uk/government/uploads/system/uploads/attachment_data/file/561312/HMRC-measuring-tax-gaps-2016.pdf>, accessed 28.01.2017, p19.
111 Gammie, M. *'When Is Avoiding Tax Not Abusive? Comparative Approaches to a GAAR in Australia and the United Kingdom'*, [2013], Vol. 42, Australian Tax Review, pp279, 292.
112 Bloom, D. *'Tax Avoidance – a View from the Dark Side'*, [2016], Vol. 39, Melbourne University Review, pp950, 980.
113 Lethaby, H. *'Analysis-Reflections on Tax and the City'*, [2014], No. 1220, Tax Journal, pp10, 11.
114 *Ibid.*
115 *Ibid.*
116 *Ibid.*
117 *The Commissioners for HMRC v Mayes* [2011] EWCA Civ 407, [18] (Mummery L.J.).
118 Aaronson, G. *'A Study to Consider whether a General Anti-Avoidance Rule Should Be Introduced into the UK Tax System'*, [2012], <http://webarchive.nationalarchives.gov.uk/+/http:/www.hm-treasury.gov.uk/d/gaar_final_report_111111.pdf>, accessed 04.06.2016, p27.
119 *The Commissioners for HMRC v Mayes* [2011] EWCA Civ 407, [78] (Mummery L.J.).

120 *UBS AG v Commissioners for HMRC; DB Group Services (UK) Ltd. v Commissioners for HMRC* [2016] UKSC 13, [77] (Lord Reed).
121 *The Commissioners for HMRC v Mayes* [2011] EWCA Civ 407, [20] (Mummery L.J.).
122 *UBS AG v Commissioners for HMRC; DB Group Services (UK) Ltd. v Commissioners for HMRC* [2016] UKSC 13, [85] (Lord Reed).
123 *IRC v Burmah Oil Co Ltd.* [1982] S.C. (H.L.) 114, 124 (Lord Diplock).
124 *The Commissioners for HMRC v Mayes* [2011] EWCA Civ 407, [71] (Mummery L.J.).
125 Self, H. *'Do We Still Need a GAAR'*, [2016], No. 1321, Tax Journal, p15, [no pagination].
126 Aaronson, G. *'A Study to Consider whether a General Anti-Avoidance Rule Should Be Introduced into the UK Tax System'*, [2012], <http://webarchive.nationalarchives.gov.uk/+/http:/www.hm-treasury.gov.uk/d/gaar_final_report_111111.pdf>, accessed 04.06.2016, p27.
127 s207(4)(c) Finance Act 2013.
128 Lethaby, H. *'Aaronson's GAAR'*, [2012], British Tax Review, pp27, 40.

8 Conclusion and recommendations for reform

It has been established that the terms "motive", "intention" and "purpose" are occasionally used interchangeably. This is undesirable as motives and intentions are highly subjective cognitive influences.[1] Motives are unconscious influences which are usually emotional responses to situations. Intentions are consciously made and are the interim plans one makes before fulfilling the eventual purpose. Lastly, purposes are formed consciously in relation to a predetermined goal, which is typically specific. In tax law, it is more objective to examine the purpose of an arrangement which is identifiable by the nature of the transactions executed. The majority of the dividend stripping cases examined did not give importance to the taxpayer's motives.[2] However, the cases on trading showed how, although motive is a badge of trade, the court also examined taxpayers' purposes and intentions.[3] *Taylor* illustrated how the taxpayer's intentions can change. The disparities in similar cases like *Kirkham*, *Iswera* and *Reinhold* demonstrate how examining the taxpayer's motives, intentions and purposes can generate inconsistencies.

The taxpayer's motive, intention and purpose were predominantly examined in the cases supporting *Ramsay*. Supporters of the *Westminster* approach preferred to scrutinise Parliament's intentions[4] and apply the remoteness test, which examined how remote the end result was at the time of the intermediate transactions.[5] In *Ramsay*, the court referred to the taxpayer's motive, intention and purpose. However, these were not always discussed in the correct context. *Burmah Oil* also scrutinised the taxpayer's intentions in determining whether the scheme was preplanned.[6] It is evident how motives can be ascribed as the trading cases of *Iswera* and *Wisdom* demonstrated. The ability to examine both primary and secondary motives confuses matters further. Therefore, even in trading, where there has been a long-established practice of examining taxpayer motives, there is still unpredictability and inconsistency. Expenditure permits scrutinising purpose,[7] although a purpose can also be ascribed without the taxpayer's knowledge of that purpose.[8] Familiar anti-avoidance principles facilitate motive, intention and purpose being considered, including the substance over form doctrine, the step transaction doctrine[9] and the holistic approach.

The provisions of the GAAR can be widely interpreted. The various stages of the GAAR, which uses sub-tests to explain each requirement, are layered in

DOI: 10.4324/9781003080473-9

nature. The main purpose test encapsulates many arrangements. In contrast, the approach in *Halifax* scrutinises whether the sole purpose of the arrangement was to acquire a tax advantage.[10] The standards of the double reasonableness test unrealistically imply that a tax advantage can be the main purpose of an arrangement which is also considered reasonable. The definition of "reasonable" is also open to wide interpretation. Abuse relates to whether a taxpayer "intended to exploit any shortcomings"[11] in the tax legislation. Furthermore, the Aaronson Report also states that it is necessary to examine the intentions of all those involved in the arrangement.[12] However, the GAAR guidance states that examining intentions is both unnecessary and inappropriate.[13] Moreover, the Aaronson Report states that intentions should not be considered due to their subjective connotations.[14] An intention can be imputed, or the tax advisor's intentions could be imputed on the taxpayer. Rather than examining whether the taxpayer sought to utilise loopholes,[15] *Emsland* merely asks whether a tax advantage was intended and examines the existence of artificial steps.[16] Moreover, *Emsland* confirms that examining intentions is a subjective test.[17] The purposive approach and the anticipation requirement in the GAAR[18] ensure that what Parliament did and did not intend can both be broadly examined. The GAAR guidance creates a triple reasonableness test by adding that if an arrangement can be viewed as reasonable, that view must also be tested as to its reasonableness.[19] However, a view which rejects the taxpayer's arrangement does not have to be tested for its reasonableness. HMRC's approval of certain practices is subject to change and gives the GAAR's remit a fluctuating quality.

New Zealand, South Africa and Canada all mention abuse in their general anti-avoidance legislation. However, none of the jurisdictions analysed put the ability to examine the taxpayer's intentions on statutory footing like the UK GAAR.[20] Rather than seeking to strike down an arrangement by examining whether a tax advantage was a main purpose of the scheme, the American and Canadian approaches seek to vindicate the arrangement by examining whether there was another "substantial purpose"[21] or any "*bona fide* purposes other than to obtain the tax benefit".[22] New Zealand[23] and Australia[24] scrutinise the purposes of others in the scheme. Concerns have also been raised that "the purpose of the relevant taxpayer may be imputed",[25] which is also a concern for the UK GAAR under the main purpose test. However, unlike with the UK GAAR, the Australian general anti-avoidance rule laid down objective criteria[26] to ascertain whether a person had that purpose.[27] Although New Zealand examines both purpose and effect, the legislation becomes targeted where it refers to abuse.[28] The New Zealand approach examines whether the tax advantage was the taxpayer's "dominant purpose",[29] which is narrower than the UK GAAR's main purpose test.[30] However, the abuse provision in the South African general anti-avoidance rule[31] has been criticised for being open to subjective interpretation.[32] Similarly, the Canadian cases of *Canada Trustco* and *Lipson* criticised the Canadian abuse provision for being ill-defined[33] and broad.[34] As demonstrated, the UK GAAR's main purpose test and means to ascertain abuse are both wide when compared with the anti-avoidance legislation of other jurisdictions.

The Canadian case of *Lipson* rightly criticised the term "abuse" for being too wide. Therefore, the test for abuse in the UK GAAR is subject to significant judicial discretion. Determining abuse has been stretched by the sub-tests which establish abuse. Judges can examine underlying policy considerations.[35] However, leaving tax policy considerations to the judiciary was criticised in *Canada Trustco* as the judiciary's views would ultimately override taxing statutes and is inappropriate because formulating policy is not within the courts' jurisdiction.[36] The GAAR has proven to be ambiguous due to the way in which an abusive arrangement has been defined. The various tests which are used to establish whether an arrangement is abusive examine the taxpayer's intentions and inevitably involve judicial discretion. Moreover, HMRC decides what is not abusive, and as this view is subject to change, this can prove to be burdensome for taxpayers in keeping up-to-date with the changes. Judicial discretion can lead to extra-statutory considerations, as demonstrated by the cases supporting *Ramsay*, and promote uncertainty. Ambiguity can lead to the GAAR being extended through the formation of common law principles. The purposive approach is also being over-stretched as tax avoidance now involves examining the purpose of the taxpayer, the taxpayer's arrangement, the taxing provisions and the GAAR. It is not surprising if judges get swayed by policy matters in practice; however, tax law and morality should remain separate.

The GAAR's criticisms have merit. The main purpose test is not very helpful since purposes are subject to change. Furthermore, purposes may be constructively imposed by HMRC or the judiciary if they are not evidenced in writing. The standard of reasonableness has not been made clear. Therefore, the double reasonableness test is likely to be decided on a case-by-case basis by balancing competing interests and using discretion. This would fuel uncertainty. The scope of the GAAR is broad, and it is far from clear what is abusive and what is not. Furthermore, HMRC wrote the GAAR guidance, which gives HMRC wide discretionary powers to amend it at will. Although simplification was not a goal, the GAAR contributes to the complexity of the current tax system by adding to the volume of existing tax legislation and potentially making compliance difficult. The GAAR also contributes to uncertainty due to the vague double reasonableness test, the main purpose test and the tests to ascertain abuse. There are constitutional issues raised by the GAAR, including the fact that the vagueness of legal rules is contrary to the Rule of Law. All these factors can damage the UK's international competitiveness by discouraging potential investors from doing business in the UK due to the uncertainty in the tax system caused by the GAAR.

The *Ramsay* approach and the GAAR have similarities whereby both take a holistic approach, assess the existence of artificial steps, scrutinise the taxpayer's intentions, examine the arrangement's purpose and have scope to analyse the taxpayer's purpose. However, the GAAR is designed to target abuse, whereas *Ramsay* is aimed at tax avoidance schemes in general, which makes *Ramsay* broader. *Mayes* demonstrated that *Ramsay*-style arguments, such as the purposive approach, the existence of a self-cancelling arrangement and a tax avoidance purpose were insufficient to defeat the arrangement. *Mayes* also pushed for the implementation of a GAAR. However, *UBS*, *DB Group Services* and *Chappell* illustrated that *Ramsay* is still being relied on after the implementation of the GAAR. In *UBS* and *DB Group Services*, the court went further than examining what Parliament intended by scrutinising what Parliament would not have intended. Ascertaining what Parliament intended uses the legislation as the basis of the decision. In contrast, deciphering what Parliament did not intend requires a larger degree of judicial discretion. The tax gap figures show that tax avoidance is the lowest source of lost revenue, and the study does not specify what percentage is lost to abusive arrangement or acceptable tax avoidance. The government should tackle legal interpretation issues and money lost through the hidden economy,[37] which have further-reaching benefits such as catching criminals and simplifying the tax system.

Recommendations for reform

Repealing the GAAR is unlikely to happen as

> adopting a GAAR, as the UK has done in 2013, marks the crossing of the Rubicon and one would not suppose that having done so Parliament will be tempted in the future to repeal the GAAR.[38]

However, there are ways in which the GAAR could be improved to reduce uncertainty and reliance on subjective factors. The scope of the GAAR could also be better targeted by confining the applicability to income tax, capital gains tax, corporation tax and petroleum revenue tax, as recommended by the Aaronson Report.[39]

The main purpose test should also be amended, which would change the way an arrangement is defined. The scope of the GAAR could be made better targeted by adopting the EU approach in *Halifax*. The principle in *Halifax* states that one of the factors that points to abuse is the sole purpose of the arrangement being to acquire a tax advantage.[40] Therefore, the main purpose test would be replaced by the sole purpose test. As discussed in chapter 6, the double reasonableness test, which defines what amounts to abuse, fuels subjective discretion as to how "reasonableness" should be interpreted. Therefore, the double reasonableness test should be replaced. Abuse could instead be determined by whether a taxpayer repeatedly avoids "the same type of income"[41] annually.[42] Consequently, the abuse requirement would be targeted at "serial avoiders"[43] as stated in HMRC's consultation document. Targeting the most persistent offenders is likely to narrow the scope of the current wide GAAR.

The double reasonableness test also has criteria which should be taken into account.[44] The provision pertaining to the intention of the arrangement[45] should be removed due to the problems raised throughout this book regarding the ability to scrutinise the taxpayer's motive, intention and purpose. The provision relating to the examination of policy considerations should also be removed for the reasons outlined in chapter 3. Therefore, rather than intentions and policy considerations being at the fore of determining abuse, abuse should instead be based on objective hallmarks. These hallmarks will help uncover whether an arrangement could be considered artificial rather than reasonable. The double reasonableness test would therefore be replaced with an artificiality test.

The GAAR would be made clearer if it listed the hallmarks of tax avoidance as with the Australian general anti-avoidance rule.[46] Many of the hallmarks of tax avoidance are extra-statutory considerations listed in the *Ramsay* approach. Therefore, it would also help to give legitimisation to *Ramsay*. For example, the UK GAAR could put the consideration of a commercial purpose on statutory footing,[47] rather than exploring whether gaining a tax advantage was one of the main purposes. Furthermore, the GAAR could also include objective factors considered in the Australian general anti-avoidance rule and raised in *Burmah Oil* and *Ensign Tankers*, such as the timing and length of the arrangement.[48] Courts should also be permitted to consider "any change in the financial position . . . that has resulted . . . from the scheme",[49] which adopts the Australian approach. Other considerations can include whether the scheme is self-cancelling,[50] which would further legitimise *Ramsay*. The amended GAAR could also adopt the remoteness test devised in *Craven*, which involves examining how remote the end result is at the time of the intermediate transactions.[51] Another objective requirement can be to evaluate the level of risk involved in the scheme, which was the approach adopted in *Barclays*.[52] A reformed GAAR would benefit from retaining the provision in the current GAAR regarding examining "contrived or abnormal steps".[53]

If Parliament was to be reluctant in devising a list of the hallmarks of tax avoidance, Lethaby has also pointed out that it would be useful to provide an indication as to how aggressive decided anti-avoidance case law is considered post the GAAR.[54] Placing decided cases on the "aggression spectrum"[55] would serve to provide examples of the types of schemes deemed abusive by the GAAR and clarify its scope. For example, *Westminster* may be on the lower end of the spectrum, whereas *Mayes* would be on the upper end of the aggression scale.

Abuse is currently decided in terms of the subjective double reasonableness test. However, rather than having reasonableness as a standard for abuse, the GAAR could also be better targeted by requiring schemes to have elements of artificiality.[56] This recommendation would ensure that the UK GAAR has a high standard of abuse like South Africa, Canada and Australia, which all refer to artificiality in their general anti-avoidance rules. Alternatively, the GAAR could include the term "artificial".

Some of the terms used in the GAAR should also be explicitly defined. For example, where the GAAR gives examples of abuse, the term "economic purposes"[57] has not been defined in the GAAR and does not have a generic meaning to warrant the omission of a definition. As recommended in chapter 3, the term "economic purposes"[58] could be defined as meaning a tax advantage. Therefore, the requirement would specify that the arrangement must obtain a higher profit than the tax advantage gained or that large losses or unusually generous deductions are indicative of abuse. This would also accord with the definition proposed in the Aaronson Report. Unusually large losses or deductions can also be a hallmark of abuse. Moreover, the provision allowing scrutiny into whether the result of the scheme was anticipated by Parliament should be amended for the reasons outlined in chapter 3. Instead, the requirement which qualifies the examples of abuse should relate to whether the purpose of the relevant tax provisions was to give effect to those types of arrangements. Consequently, the emphasis should be on what Parliament did intend rather than what it did not intend.

To maintain impartiality, HMRC should not have written the GAAR guidance. The Aaronson Report also stated that guidance should be drawn up independently of HMRC.[59] Working towards simplifying the tax system in general would also help decrease lost sources of revenue. For example, as chapter 7 illustrated, a high level of revenue is being lost due to legal interpretation problems and taxpayer error.[60] These recommendations would facilitate a fairer playing field between HMRC and the taxpayer in their "fiscal chess game".[61]

Notes

1 Chapter 1.
2 However, the court gave importance to motive in *Lupton*.
3 As demonstrated in *Ensign* and *Arndale*.
4 *Westmoreland Investments Ltd. v MacNiven* [2001] UKHL 6, [2003] 1 A.C. 311, [29] (Lord Hoffmann).
5 *Craven v White*; *IRC v Bowater*; *Property Developments Ltd. v Gregory* [1988] 3 W.L.R. 423, [1989] A.C. 398, 481 (Lord Keith).
6 *IRC v Burmah Oil Co Ltd.* [1982] S.C. (H.L.) 114, 130 (Lord Fraser of Tullybelton).
7 s34(1)(a) ITTOIA 2005.
8 *Mallalieu v Drummond* [1983] 3 W.L.R. 409, [1983] 2 A.C. 861, 867 (Lord Elwyn-Jones).
9 Tiley, J. *'Judicial Anti-Avoidance Doctrines: The US Alternatives – Part 2'*, [1987], British Tax Review, pp220, 236.
10 *Halifax Plc and others v Customs and Excise Commissioners* (C-255/02) [2006] Ch. 387, 435 (Advocate General Poiares Maduro).
11 s207(2)(c) Finance Act 2013.
12 Aaronson, G. *'A Study to Consider whether a General Anti-Avoidance Rule Should Be Introduced into the UK Tax System'*, [2011], <http://webarchive.nationalarchives.gov.uk/+/http:/www.hm-treasury.gov.uk/d/gaar_final_report_111111.pdf>, accessed 25.08.2014, p64.
13 *'HMRC GAAR Guidance with Effect from 11 September 2020: Parts A, B and C'*, <https://assets.publishing.service.gov.uk/government/uploads/system/uploads/attachment_data/file/916667/gaar_parts_a_b_c_2020.pdf>, accessed 29.04.2021, p15.
14 Aaronson, G. *'A Study to Consider whether a General Anti-Avoidance Rule Should Be Introduced into the UK Tax System'*, [2012], <http://webarchive.nationalarchives.gov.uk/+/http:/www.hm-treasury.gov.uk/d/gaar_final_report_111111.pdf>, accessed 04.06.2016, p4.
15 s207(2)(c) Finance Act 2013.
16 *Emsland-Stärke GmbH v Hauptzollamt Hamburg-Jonas* (C-110/99) [2000] ECR I-11569, [53] (per curiam).
17 *Ibid*, [53].
18 s207(4)(c) Finance Act 2013.
19 *'HMRC GAAR Guidance with Effect from 11 September 2020: Parts A, B and C'*, <https://assets.publishing.service.gov.uk/government/uploads/system/uploads/attachment_data/file/916667/gaar_parts_a_b_c_2020.pdf>, accessed 29.04.2021, p21.
20 s207(2)(c) Finance Act 2013.
21 Internal Revenue Code 1986 s7701(o)(1)(b).

22 s245(3)(a) Income Tax Act 1985.
23 s177C(1)(a) Income Tax Assessment Act 1936.
24 s141D(1) Tax Administration Act 1994.
25 Cashmere, M. *'A GAAR for the United Kingdom? The Australian Experience'*, [2008], British Tax Review, pp125, 136.
26 Outlined in Chapter 4.
27 s177D(2) Income Tax Assessment Act 1936.
28 s141D(2) Tax Administration Act 1994.
29 s141D(1) Tax Administration Act 1994.
30 s207(1) Finance Act 2013.
31 s80A(c)(ii) Income Tax Act 1962.
32 Kujinga, B.T. *'Analysis of Misuse and Abuse in Terms of the South African General Anti-Avoidance Rule: Lessons from Canada'*, [2012], The Comparative and International Law Journal of Southern Africa, pp42, 50.
33 *Canada Trustco Mortgage Co. v R* [2005] 2 S.C.R. 601, [37] (per curiam).
34 *Lipson v R* [2009] 1 S.C.R. 3, [76] (Binnie J.).
35 s207(2)(a) Finance Act 2013.
36 *Canada Trustco Mortgage Co. v R* [2005] 2 S.C.R. 601, [41] (per curiam).
37 HMRC. *'UK Tax Gap at a Glance in 2014–2015'*, <www.gov.uk/government/uploads/system/uploads/attachment_data/file/561312/HMRC-measuring-tax-gaps-2016.pdf>, accessed 28.01.2017, p5.
38 Gammie, M. *'When Is Avoiding Tax Not Abusive? Comparative Approaches to a GAAR in Australia and the United Kingdom'*, [2013], Vol. 42, Australian Tax Review, pp279, 282.
39 Aaronson, G. *'A Study to Consider whether a General Anti-Avoidance Rule Should Be Introduced into the UK Tax System'*, [2011], <http://webarchive.nationalarchives.gov.uk/+/http:/www.hm-treasury.gov.uk/d/gaar_final_report_111111.pdf>, accessed 25.08.2014, p7.
40 *Halifax Plc and others v Customs and Excise Commissioners* (C-255/02) [2006] Ch. 387, 435 (Advocate General Poiares Maduro).
41 HMRC. *'Strengthening Sanctions for Tax Avoidance'*, <www.gov.uk/government/uploads/system/uploads/attachment_data/file/399823/Strengthening_sanctions_for_tax_avoidance_-_consultation_document.pdf>, accessed 30.12.2015, p7.
42 *Ibid.*
43 *Ibid.*
44 s207(2) Finance Act 2013.
45 s207(2)(c) Finance Act 2013.
46 s177D(2) Income Tax Assessment Act 1936.
47 *Furniss v Dawson* [1984] 2 W.L.R. 226, [1984] A.C. 474, 492 (Oliver L.J.).
48 s177D(2)(c) Income Tax Assessment Act 1936.
49 s177D(2)(e) Income Tax Assessment Act 1936.
50 *WT Ramsay Ltd. v IRC*; *Eilbeck v Rawling* [1981] 2 W.L.R 449, [1982] A.C. 300, 328 (Lord Wilberforce).
51 *Craven v White*; *IRC v Bowater*; *Property Developments Ltd. v Gregory* [1988] 3 W.L.R. 423, [1989] A.C. 398, 481 (Lord Keith).
52 *Barclays Mercantile Business Finance v Mawson* [2002] EWCA Civ 1853, [2002] WL 31676325, [36] (Peter Gibson L.J.).
53 s207(2)(b) Finance Act 2013.
54 Lethaby, H. *'Aaronson's GAAR'*, [2012], British Tax Review, pp27, 38.
55 *Ibid.*
56 Macfarlanes. *'The GAAR: An Anti-Avoidance Rule in All But Name'*, [2012], <www.macfarlanes.com/media/382363/the-gaar-an-anti-avoidance-rule-in-all-but-name.pdf>, p3.
57 s207(4)(a) Finance Act 2013.
58 *Ibid.*

59 Aaronson, G. *'A Study to Consider whether a General Anti-Avoidance Rule Should Be Introduced into the UK Tax System'*, [2012], <http://webarchive.nationalarchives.gov.uk/+/http:/www.hm-treasury.gov.uk/d/gaar_final_report_111111.pdf>, accessed 04.06.2016, p34.

60 HMRC. '*UK Tax Gap at a Glance in 2014–2015*', <www.gov.uk/government/uploads/system/uploads/attachment_data/file/561312/HMRC-measuring-tax-gaps-2016.pdf>, accessed 28.01.2017, p5.

61 Aaronson, G. *'A Study to Consider whether a General Anti-Avoidance Rule Should Be Introduced into the UK Tax System'*, [2012], <http://webarchive.nationalarchives.gov.uk/+/http:/www.hm-treasury.gov.uk/d/gaar_final_report_111111.pdf>, accessed 04.06.2016, p15.

Index

Note: page locators in **bold** indicate a table.

Made in the USA
Las Vegas, NV
19 September 2026

70abd184-1ab9-42a4-8b06-d08d361770d2R01